WE ARE AN IMAGE FROM THE F

The Greek Revolt of December

WE ARE AN IMAGE FROM THE FUTURE
The Greek Revolt of December 2008

Edited by A.G. Schwarz, Tasos Sagris, and Void Network

AK
PRESS
EDINBURGH · OAKLAND · BALTIMORE

We are an Image from the Future: The Greek Revolt of December 2008

This edition © 2010 AK Press (Oakland, Edinburgh, Baltimore)

ISBN-13: 978-1-84935-019-8

Library of Congress Control Number: 2010921020

AK Press
674-A 23rd Street
Oakland, CA 94612
USA
www.akpress.org
akpress@akpress.org

AK Press
PO Box 12766
Edinburgh, EH8 9YE
Scotland
www.akuk.com
ak@akedin.demon.co.uk

The above addresses would be delighted to provide you with the latest AK Press distribution catalog, which features the several thousand books, pamphlets, zines, audio and video products, and stylish apparel published and/or distributed by AK Press. Alternatively, visit our web site for the complete catalog, latest news, and secure ordering.

Visit us at www.akpress.org *and* www.revolutionbythebook.akpress.org.

Follow Void Network [Theory, Utopia, Empathy, Ephemeral Arts] at:
www.voidnetwork.blogspot.com | voidinternational@gmail.com

Please contact A.G. Schwarz at: animagefromthefuture@gmail.com

Printed in Canada on acid-free paper with union labor.

Cover design by Kate Khatib
Front cover photo © by Elen Grigoriadou. Back cover photo © by Kostas Tsironis

TABLE OF CONTENTS

The Street Has Its Own History—Tasos Sagris 1
Solidarity is a Flame—A.G. Schwarz 2

1. Prologues

Map of Greece 5
Chronology: 19th–20th Century 5
Alkis: December is a result of social and political processes going
back many years, Part I 8
Panagiotis Kalamaras: There were many people who felt we had an
unfinished revolution 14
23.10: I began to get involved when I was 16 17

2. And Now One Slogan that Unites Us All: Cops, Pigs, Murderers!

Chronology: September 2000–November 2008 27
Argiris: Exarchia Square and the neighborhood assemblies.......... 29
Iulia: Do you join the Party to fuck or do you fuck to join the
Party? 31
J.: The raves and free spaces is where the collective consciousness
is coming together 34
Lefteria ston Yiannis Dimitraki 38
The Permanent Crisis in Education—TPTG 41
Nikos: The supermarket expropriations were very successful........ 52
The Prisoners' Hunger Strike... 53
N. & Mi: The prisoners gained a new ability to coordinate
their actions 55
You Talk About Material Damages, We Speak About Human Life—
Panagiotis Papadimitropoulos 56

3. These Days are for Alexis

Map of Athens.. 77
Chronology: December 6–25, 2008.. 77
The World Left Behind 94
Lito: Suddenly I heard a bang 94
23.10: I ran to the Polytechnic 98
Homo Sacer Quartet—Flesh Machine....................................... 101
Mrs. S.: I was in the heart of the catastrophe........................... 102
Little John: Okay, now we're going to fuck everything up 105

Andreas: We started with 300 people, and came back with 500..... 108
Anna: That's how big this thing was 110
Yiannis: In Patras, 1,000 people came out to the demonstrations .. 111
Vortex: That was the craziest moment of all December for me 112
Pavlos and Irina: This is the spirit of the revolt........................ 116
Their Democracy Murders—the Polytechnic University
Occupation 131
Alexander, Thodoris, Vlasis, & Kostas: All the kids felt so much
power yelling at the cops 144
A Black Immigrant's Cry of Despair 150
These Days Are Ours, Too—the Haunt of Albanian Immigrants.. 151
Invitation to the Open Popular Assembly of the Liberated City
Hall of Aghios Dimitrios 153
Katerina: I thought the revolution was coming 154
Maria: I want to eliminate everything that represents the
alienation of our lives... 154
Sofia, Vasilis, Bill, and Irini: Before the revolt, all the Greeks were
enslaved.. 156
Transgressio Legis: One day we jacked a fire engine, got on the CB
radio, and said, "tonight, you motherfuckers, we will burn you all".. 161
We Are Here, We Are Everywhere, We Are an Image from the
Future—Ego Te Provoco... 165
Ego Te Provoco: The media worked as part of the
counterinsurgency 169
Vortex: The occupation of the national TV 173
Call for a New International 176
Em: In London, the response was immediate 184
Pere: In Barcelona, we quickly organized a solidarity protest 186
Adams: Many foreigners have been killed 187
Open Letter from the Soldiers 189
Eliza: The Treaty of Varkiza is broken 191
The Logic of Not Demanding—A.G. Schwarz 192
Not this History But this Rage is Ours—Ankara
Anarchy Initiative... 194
To those who rise up in Greece—ABC Wellington 196
A Bedouin Anytime! A Citizen Never—Ego Te Provoco 197
Kostas Tsironis: I don't care if I don't take even one more
picture, I just want to be okay with myself................................ 199

Journal entry of one of the insurrectionists 205
To all those who did not speak with words 206

4. Obedience Stopped, Life is Magical

Chronology: December 28–March 4 213
Alexis Grigoropoulos Street 215
Koukouloforos 216
The Spirit of December on a Global Scale—A.G. Schwarz 219
Maya: Konstantina was the first to join the union 225
Ego Te Provoco: We need to make it obvious that it is
easy to attack 229
Andreas: We finally understood that many people supported us .. 232
Panagiotis Kalamaras: The myth of Sisyphus 234
Transgressio Legis: When there is strong social conflict, you
raise the tension of the attacks 235
Assembly of Media Workers: We want to occupy the media,
and use it for the movement 237
December's Riots as Mediated by the Image of Mass Media—
Leandros Kyriakopoulos 241
Mi: The new neighborhood assemblies 244
Kill the Sexist In Your Head—the menses flow 247
The Limitations of Anti-Sexism—Sissy Doutsiou 248
Adriani and Flora: Now there are more social centers in
Thessaloniki 261
Jana: Many people were saying that they want Bulgarian
society to be "like in Greece" 262
Little John: The next step is to create the places where all the
people can meet 265
The Rebellion, the Workplaces, and the Rank'N'File Unions—
TPTG 266
Elina: More old people and leftists are coming nearer to the
anarchist ideas 269
Lito: Now I really know what terrorism means 271

5. Breaking New Ground

Chronology: March–October 2009 277
Alexis Grigoropoulos Park 282

Daredevil: We intervene in the daily flow of things to
interrupt it 283
The House of Maria Kallas 286
The Assassination of Prisoner Katerina Goulioni 288
Conversation on a park bench in Thessaloniki 289
Sakis and Dina: Now there's no going back 291
Kostas: We decided to occupy the university rectorate 292
Alkis: December is a result of social and political processes
going back many years, Part II 294
Kazana Poli: You could see the hatred in their eyes 299
Giorgos Voutsis-Vogiatzis 300
We Are Winning—A.G. Schwarz 302
Iulia: I feel very lucky to be living in these times 303
The Political Parties After December 305
Claim of responsibility for an arson attack 306
N. & Mi: The prisoners of December 308
Letter from Anarchist A. Kiriakopoulos 310
What the Cops Told Us 311
Specialized Guerrilla, Diffuse Guerrilla 313
A Hot Summer... 317
Conversation with the Owner of a Small Hotel on the Train
from Athens to Patras 319
Yiannis: Maybe it's gotten worse 321
The Media Try to Kill Memory—A.G. Schwarz 322
Alexander, Thodoris, Vlasis, & Kostas: All the people went back
to their private lives 326
The Passage to Revolution—Transgressio Legis 327
The Unanimity of the Fearful—Conspiracy of the Cells of Fire 330
December Revisited—Void Network 333
What Greece Means (to me) for Anarchism—A.G. Schwarz 351
Nothing Changed, Everything is Different—Tasos Sagris 358

Glossary 368
Photo Credits 371

The Street Has Its Own History

Tasos Sagris from Void Network / Laboratory for
Kosmo-Politikal Consciousness

> *The street had its own History,*
> *someone wrote it on the wall with paint, …*
> *It was just a word: FREEDOM…*
> *but the passerby said it was only written by the children*

—**Fragment from "The Street," a Greek song from the struggle
against the dictatorship in the '70s.**

The street has its own history. It doesn't need historians, it doesn't need intellectuals or sociologists to speak in its name. Nobody can write the History of December 2008 and we assure you that a project like this is beyond our capabilities or intentions.

Just as we don't have any official history of the Paris Commune or the Spanish Revolution this is not the History of the Greek Insurrection. Through fragments, rumors, myths, and stories the social insurrection finds its way directly into the hearts and the minds of the common people of the future.

Many years after our time a young girl or boy will find a fifteen-second video on the Internet from Greece, December 2008, a moment captured on a cell phone, a barricade in the middle of the street, a group of fifteen-year-old friends attacking the riot police with molotovs in their hands, amidst a fog of tear gas taking revenge for the assassination of a schoolmate, someone they didn't know at all, but he was one of them, and now they avenge him.

The girls and boys of the future will hear through rumors and myths that the Greek youth revolted for more than a month because of the police assassination of a young boy, that they smashed, looted, and burned hundreds of police stations, banks, offices, government buildings, and luxury shops all across the country. They will hear that the anarchists, the autonomists, the utopians, the naïve romantics, and the leftists took part in this struggle. They will hear that the immigrants fought also, for their own reasons, against police brutality and racism.

The history of our times is written in short notes posted on Indymedia during the fight—short videos and photos taken by people who created these stories and were among the fighters. It is written by people who felt the panic of the riot, the pain in the lungs from the tear gas, people who ran in the streets, smashed the symbols of this civilization, burned away their fears and faced down the danger of participating on the front line of the battles of our times.

Hence, this book is just a fifteen-second video shot with a cell phone in the middle of the riots, it's just a story you heard on a train going from Paris to Barcelona, it's just a memory of the smile of a boy on a beach in Greece, it's just a wave

1

on the ocean of global struggle for liberation from capitalist democracy, for the end of exploitation, the end of alienation, the end of suffering.

We say this clearly to you: this is not the book of the history of the Greek insurrection of December 2008. It is just our effort to share with you the experience before it fades away, it is our walks in the empty streets of Athens one year after the revolt and our few memories that get lost in the night, it is a tear for Alexis long after his assassination, it is our hatred for any state and any police and any army of this planet, the hate that gets stronger and stronger every day, it is the rage that becomes a book or a barricade or a stone in your hand. This is not the history of the December 2008 riots, the real history is hidden inside the hearts of those who fought the battle.

But we hope this book can be a thunderclap in the silent night of social apathy, a howl of craziness in the middle of a luxury shopping mall, it can be the sound of a smashing window, the smell of gasoline on your hands. Maybe it can be an image from the future. But this is up to you.

Because you are the future of this world and the revolutions that come will be the story of your life, not a narration, not just history, but the story of our lives…

Solidarity is a Flame

A.G. Schwarz

Solidarity is a Flame that cannot be extinguished

Words from a poster urging support for the Greek insurrection

It was a miserable winter evening tied down with the razor wire of routine and obligation when I realized that, if I let myself, I was free to do whatever I wanted. Of course it's not the first time I've thought this, but it's a realization that's heavy with the responsibility that accompanies it: it sinks like a stone amidst the empty interactions that people our worlds, and we have to keep reaching for it and picking it up again.

What I wanted to do that particular evening was to go back to Greece. I was tired of nourishing myself on the smallest signs of life that our dream gives off in these inhospitable circumstances, or the more dramatic signs from somewhere else that one can find on the Internet.

But I didn't want to go to Greece just to pick myself up, as important as that was. What good would it do for me to replenish my inspiration if all my friends were slowly hardening? If people were citing the insurrection in Greece not to take hope or strategic lessons but to prove to themselves that the struggle is only possible someplace far away? Or, even worse, if people were saying that the struggle in Greece is just as doomed as anywhere else, citing the fact that the fires had died down after Christmas?

But in cryptic emails the Greek comrades were insisting that even though the fires had gone out, nothing had gone back to normal. I realized that as anarchists we focus a lot on the strange alchemy that suddenly explodes in insurrection, we drool over the insurrections themselves, but in regards to what comes after, we know almost nothing. Is it because we're trapped waiting for a riot that never ends, or do we fear the demands the revolution will make of us, *once we've burned everything?* And what does happen after the angry crowds of the insurrection disappear?

I felt a need to go to Greece, to talk to people there, find out what was happening and why, and share these stories with as much of the rest of the world as possible. So I wrote to my friends there with my proposal, they wrote back with ideas of their own, and I started to look into how the hell I could get over there without any money, being for the past months, unemployed, another victim of the crisis.

Suddenly, the winter darkness was the cloak for an em-ber that could burst again into flames. The obligations and routines that pretended to tie down my future blew away like paper.

Everything is possible again. The struggle welcomes us back ecstatically.

GREECE

Thessaloniki

Athens

Chronology: 19th–20th Century

19th century: Going back to 1860, a growing anarchist movement appears in Greece comprised of many different tendencies, including anarcho-syndicalist, anarchist-communist, individualist, and Christian anarchists, involved mostly in publishing, cultural work, forming revolutionary organizations, and taking active part in workers' and peasants' struggles.

Early 20th century: Anarchists have active groups in every city in Greece, and play a prominent role in several struggles. Popular hero and anarchist peasant Marinos Antypas is largely credited for leading the struggle to liberate Greek peasants from post-Ottoman feudalism. In 1913 anarchist Alexandros Schinas successfully assassinates Greek King George I in Thessaloniki. He was arrested and tortured though he refused to give up any names, and was subsequently murdered by police.

1920s and 1930s: Greek anarcho-syndicalists participate in many workers struggles and wildcat strikes, collaborating with the Communists, whose hit squads assassinate several influential anarchists.

1936–1944: First under the Metaxas dictatorship (1936–1940) and later under the Nazi occupation, many anarchists and other leftists are killed or imprisoned in concentration camps. A strong guerrilla movement eventually pushes out the Nazis, who are weakened by major defeats elsewhere on the Eastern Front, and the country mostly liberates itself before the British arrive. Unbeknownst to the Greek people, Stalin and Churchill had come to an agreement that Greece should be in the British sphere of influence.

December 1944–1949: Armed organizations and the rank and file of the Communist Party launch an uprising that leads to a lengthy civil war. From the beginning, Communist hit squads assassinate anarchists, Trotskyists, dissidents, and other political opponents.

1950–1967: After the right wing wins the civil war with the help of the British and the CIA, a constitutional monarchy rules Greece for nearly two decades, suppressing, persecuting, and exiling socialists, anarchists, and others. Greek anarchism remains alive principally in the activity of a few writers and poets living abroad or in penal colonies on the islands.

1967–1974: As the Greek youth begin to radicalize and fight against the government and the conservative culture, the military takes power in a coup and rules in the form of a junta for nearly a decade. Despite the repression, resistance against the regime continues to grow.

1971: Christos Konstantinidis founds *Diethnis Vivliothiki* (International Library), a publishing collective that releases translations of classical anarchist and Situationist texts as well as contemporary countercultural and anarchist works in Greek. He and his comrades help to instigate and radicalize the student uprising that starts on November 14, 1973. Their banners "Down with the State, Down with Capital, Down with Authority!" adorn the front gates of the Polytechnic for the first days of the uprising, until communists take them down.

November 17, 1973: The State responds to a university student uprising by sending tanks into the Polytechnic, killing at least twenty-two people. Several months later the Turkish state attacks and partially captures the island of Cyprus. Under the combined stress of these calamities, the dictatorship transfers power to a democratic government. The date of November 17 forever remains engraved in the popular consciousness as a symbol of struggle, and is marked by major demonstrations every year.

1976: The anarchist publisher *Eleftheros Typos* (Free Press) is founded in Athens by a politically active Greek returning from London, and begins to translate and publish influential libertarian texts. Simultaneously, rock, hippy, and freak countercultures rejected by the Left adopt anarchist characteristics and are influential in turning neighborhoods like Plaka (around the Acropolis) and then Exarchia into autonomous zones and expanding the anarchist space.

October 1977: A cell of Popular Revolutionary Struggle is involved in a shoot-out with police as they try to place a bomb outside the factory of German company AEG in response to the German state's assassination of RAF leadership. Christos Kassimis is killed.

1979: A vast student movement begins occupying the universities in all major cities, influenced largely by leftists and anarchists.

October 1981: The Socialist Party, PASOK, comes into power, leading to the institutionalization of much of the Left.

Early 80s: A new generation constituting a punk counterculture adopts violent practices, popularizing the use of molotovs and confrontations with police, and are denounced as provocateurs by the leftists.

December 1984: In what might be the first major Greek Black Bloc, thousands of anarchists attack the Hotel Caravel in Athens, forcing the cancellation of a far-right conference that had drawn such reactionaries as Le Pen of France.

May 15, 1985: Christos Tsoutsouvis, an ex-member of Popular Revolutionary Struggle, is involved in a shoot-out with police in Athens while trying to steal a car for an action. He kills three cops and is shot to death. In the following days, there are major riots in his honor in various cities throughout Greece.

November 17, 1985: After the annual November 17 demonstration, police fatally shoot fifteen-year-old Michalis Kaltezas in the back of the head during street fighting with anarchists at the Polytechnic. There are major riots in response.

1986: A national conference attempts to unite all the anarchist currents in Greece, though they do not succeed and their effort generates much controversy among other anarchists. The Greek anarchist space remains fragmented. The following year, those who still agree with the project, involving many different groups from the whole country, form the Anarchist Union.

October 1, 1987: Michalis Prekas resists a police attempt to search his house in an anti-terror investigation, and is killed.

As usual, major riots follow.

April 15, 1988: Anarchists start the squat Lelas Karagiani in Athens. It hosts many discussions, film showings, concerts, and other events, defends itself against multiple fascist attacks, and still exists in 2010.

March 2, 1990: Anarchists in Athens form the hardcore punk squat Villa Amalias, which still exists in 2010.

Winter 1991: A massive movement of high school students, occupying 1,500 schools and all the major universities, and bringing hundreds of thousands of people into the streets, succeeds in blocking the right-wing government from privatizing the universities through outsourcing contracts with private companies and changing the constitution to allow private universities. Police in Patras kill teacher and member of the far Left, Nikos Temponeras, in front of the occupied school he is defending along with his students, leading to two days of rioting in Athens.

November 1995: Anarchists and youth occupy the Polytechnic in solidarity with an ongoing prisoner hunger strike. Police invade the campus and arrest 500 people.

July 1996: Anarchist Christoforos Marinos is assassinated in mysterious circumstances in Piraeus.

None of the chronologies presented in this book represent even a tenth of the happenings and important events. They are intended only to give the reader an idea of the progression and kind of events, not their scale or frequency...

December is a result of social and political processes going back many years, Part I

Alkis: An anarchist, squatter, publisher, and worker

First, I want to say that I am not a historian. I'm an activist, a fighter on the front lines in the anarchist struggle since the end of the '70s. I don't know how precise my knowledge of anarchist history is, as it is a product of my memory and the things I heard and learned from other comrades during the years of my participation in this struggle.

As far as I know, concerning the post-war period, the first anarchists appeared early in the '70s and the last years of the dictatorship, as a result of the influence of the revolt of May '68 which mainly had an impact on the Greeks living abroad, but also on those living here. By saying the influence of May '68 I also mean what came before that, the Situationists and other radical positions. In that sense the birth of anarchy in Greece, as a movement, does not refer so much to traditional anarchism—with its most significant moment being the Spanish Revolution and its main expressions the anarchist federations and the anarcho-syndicalist organizations—but mainly to the antiauthoritarian, radical political waves of the '60s.

As I said before, in Greece anarchists appeared in the beginning of the '70s and that is when they made their first publications and analysis about the Greek reality from an antiauthoritarian point of view.

The presence and participation of anarchist comrades in the events of the revolt of November 1973 was very significant, not in terms of numbers but rather in terms of their particular, remarkable political contribution, as they did not limit themselves to slogans against the dictatorship, but instead adopted broader political characteristics, which were anticapitalist and antistate. They were also among the few who started this revolt together with militants from the extreme Left. And they were so visible that representatives of the formal Left condemned their presence in the events, claiming that the anarchists were provocateurs hired by the dictatorship, while they also condemned their slogans, characterizing them as foreign and unrelated with the popular demands. In reality, the formal Left was hostile to the revolt itself because they were supporting the so-called democratization, a peaceful transition from dictatorship to democracy. And since they could not stop the spontaneous revolt of '73 in which youth and workers participated, they came with the intent to manipulate it and then, after the fall of the dictatorship, to exploit it politically.

During the revolt of '73 there were two tendencies: those who wanted it to be controlled and manipulated, in the context of fighting against the dictatorship, in favor of democracy, and against American influence; and those, of whom anarchists formed an important part, who saw the revolt in a broader way, against authority and capitalism. These two tendencies continued to clash, also after the dictatorship, in the era we call *metapolitefsi*, which means after the colonels gave the power to the politicians. It was a conflict between those who supported civil democracy and those who were against it. The first tendency considered the events of the Polytechnic as a revolt for democracy, while those who were against the regime of civil democracy saw the events of the Polytechnic as a revolt for social liberation. The echo of this conflict lasts until today, in a way.

So, this is how anarchists appeared, and this was their contribution…

After the colonels handed over power to the politicians, two major forces appeared in Greece. From the one side, there were radical political and social forces disputing the existing political, social, and economic order, and this was expressed by parts of the youth and workers as well. And on the other side there were the political forces of domination—from the conservative right wing that was in government, to their allies on the formal Left that became incorporated in the political system after the fall of the dictatorship. The right wing government was trying to repress and terrorize the radical political and social forces we mentioned before, and so did the institutional Left, with its own means, when it couldn't control and manipulate them. Among these radical political and social forces were the anarchists, who were in conflict with even the most radical traditional concepts of the Left, such as the central role of the working class, the hierarchical organization in political parties, the idea of the vanguard, the vision of taking power, and the socialist transformation of society from above.

An important moment of the social struggle during the first years of *metapolitefsi*, at the end of the '70s, was the struggle in the universities, sparked by the efforts of the right wing government to institute educational reform. In this struggle anarchists also had a significant presence, as well as other groups and individuals with an antiauthoritarian and libertarian perspective. To a large degree, this struggle surpassed the boundaries of the university and university students as a subject, assuming wider radical characteristics and attracting the presence and participation of many more people. Not strictly students, but youth generally, like high schoolers, and workers as well. It was an important moment in which the anarchists spread their influence among wide social sectors that were fighting.

A little while after this struggle against the educational reform, anarchists, almost alone, carried out another struggle—solidarity with the prisoners' struggles. There, they demonstrated another characteristic of their radicalism: they didn't hesitate to engage in questions that were seen as taboo for society, like the question of prisons and prisoners, and they expressed their solidarity with them, fighting together with

9

them for their demands—the abolition of disciplinary penalties, denunciation of tortures, and granting prisoners with life sentences the right to have their cases examined by appeals courts—while always maintaining their vision of a society without any prisons at all.

A very important event of that period that shows the political and social dynamics of the subjects of resistance and, at the same time, the ferocity of political power, was a demonstration that took place on the 17th of November, 1980, on the seventh anniversary of the Polytechnic revolt, an event which actually defined the political developments of those times. (Every year there was and still is a demonstration on the anniversary.) That particular year the government had forbidden the demonstration from going to the US Embassy. The youth organizations, as well as the student organizations controlled by the Communist and the Socialist Parties, obeyed the prohibition; however, political organizations of the extreme Left, which were strong in that period of time, decided to attempt to continue the demonstration to the American Embassy, defying the prohibition laid down by the government and the police.

So, on the night of the 17th of November, 1980, next to the Parliament building, in the street leading to the embassy, thousands of demonstrators were confronted by a very strong force of police. The effort of the first lines of demonstrators, who were members of the extreme Left, to push forward to the American Embassy was followed by a massive attack by the police forces in order to disperse the crowd. But despite the police attacks there was a strong and lasting resistance by several thousand people, youth and workers, members of the extreme Left, anarchists and autonomists, who set up barricades in central Athens—barricades that the police used armored vehicles to dismantle. During these clashes two demonstrators were murdered by the police, Iakovos Koumis and Stamatina Kanelopoulou, both members of extreme Left organizations, and hundreds were injured, some seriously. Among the ones injured, two were wounded by live ammunition, one of them in the chest, shot by police outside the Polytechnic.

During these clashes many capitalist targets were attacked and looted, like department stores, jewelry shops, and the like. This type of attack, which was one of the first expressions of metropolitan violence not strictly limited to targeting the police, but also expressions and symbols of wealth, was condemned even by the extreme Left, whose political culture recognized only the police as a legitimate target. But a new phenomenon of metropolitan violence was emerging. Besides engaging in confrontations with the police, demonstrators were also destroying and looting capitalist targets, and that is exactly what was condemned by the Left.

Those events of November 1980 were, as we mentioned, an expression of the political and social dynamics of the first years of *metapolitefsi*, but also the culmination and the end of the hegemony of the extreme Left on these dynamics. The

Left didn't manage to explain, in their own terms, the extent and the form of the events to their followers. However, these same events were a catalyst for the fall of the right wing government, one year later.

In the beginning of the '80s, as a result of a major effort by a part of the political system to control and manipulate the social, political, and class resistances and demands, a new political change occurred and the Socialist Party, PASOK, came to power (October '81). In that period this seemed to be a huge, historical change. It created a lot of illusions, it incorporated and neutralized old militants in the institutions and marked the end of these first years of *metapolitefsi*, the end of a variety of spontaneous social and class struggles which had appeared in the first years after the fall of the dictatorship.

So, after this political change, anarchists who were hostile to any kind of mediation and incorporation into the institutions were in a sense alone against this new authority, which had many controlled and manipulated supporters, many adherents full of illusions.

PASOK came to power in order to modernize Greek society. They repealed laws that were products of the civil war era—when the Right had crushed the Left in an armed conflict—and the post-civil war era, and satisfied a series of demands coming from the Left; demands that did not at all undermine the authoritarian and class organization of society but, on the contrary, that modernized and strengthened it by making it come closer to the model of the Western European societies.

This political change meant that a large part of the Left was weakened and absorbed into the system, it also meant that the anarchists together with autonomists and antiauthoritarians in general manifested a single effort to intervene socially. Organizing amongst the youth, they organized the first squats in Greece, influenced by similar projects in Western Europe.

The first squat, in Exarchia, became the epicenter of anarchist and antiauthoritarian mobilizations, and led to other occupations in Athens and Thessaloniki. Eventually it was attacked and evicted, a victim of government repression, in the beginning of 1982. The same happened with the other squats as well.

(On that point, we could also mention that from the end of the '70s and especially in the beginning of the '80s a repressive operation by the State was conducted in order to corrupt and destroy the resistance movement by spreading heroin in the social spaces of the youth. This operation was very new then, unprecedented in Greece, and anarchists came in face-to-face conflict with that, fighting against it in the social spaces, in the places of the youth, and also inside the squats.)

The first years of government by PASOK were full of artificially cultivated aspirations for changes, ones that were of course neither essential nor subversive. They were years of a broad social consent to political power, against which

11

anarchists stood alone, to a large degree. But very soon this political authority showed its true face and its profound class character against the lower social classes, as well as its repressive ambitions with regards to those resisting—anarchists, leftists, and insubordinate youth. The turning point, the end of the illusions, was in 1985, a year scarred by the police murder of fifteen-year-old Michalis Kaltezas who was shot in the back of the head outside the Polytechnic during riots between anarchists and insubordinate youth on one side and the police on the other, after the end of the 17th of November demonstration that year.

This murder triggered a series of insurrectionary events whose major moments were the occupation of the Chemistry University and the Polytechnic. Moreover, it caused a deeper uprising of consciousness and hostile dispositions against the police and authority that gave birth to numerous events of resistance in the following years, since it was not something that was expressed and exhausted in one moment, but became a precedent of many violent and combative moments of resistance in the following years. It formed a "tradition" of similar events; these events burst forth either as reactions to state murders, or as expressions of solidarity with the struggles of oppressed people, such as the prisoners. It is also within these conditions that a new wave of squats, mainly by anarchists and antiauthoritarian groups, appeared and rooted socially, thus broadening the fronts as much as the influence of the struggle.

For example we can mention the clashes with the police and the occupation of the Polytechnic for seventeen days in 1990, after the acquittal of the cop who murdered Kaltezas.

The extensive social clashes in the streets of Athens in 1991, lasting a full two days, after the murder of the teacher and Left fighter, Nikos Temponeras, by para-state thugs in a student-occupied school in the city of Patras.

The uprising of anarchists and youth in November, 1995, during the anniversary of the '73 revolt, in which they occupied the Polytechnic in solidarity with the revolt of the prisoners which was going on at the same time. This revolt in the prisons was under fire from the whole propaganda mechanism of the State and by the media, and it was facing the immediate threat of a police invasion in the prison facilities.

In an effort to suppress the '95 Polytechnic revolt and attack the anarchists and the youth—not only for the resistance they were engaged in at that specific moment but also for all the events that they had created during the previous years, and the events which they were threatening to continue—the State made use of the major propaganda assault by the media, which had been waged to extract social consent for the plans of repression. The police invaded the occupied Polytechnic on the morning of the 17th of November, 1995 and arrested more than 500 occupants, but the entire repressive operation was a failure: they wanted to present the anarchists as very few and isolated, as small gangs of rioters—the stereotype presented by the State is of "50 known unknowns"—but they turned out to have great influence on youths. They also failed to terrorize anarchists with the arrests and the prosecutions in the courts, because the majority of defendants remained insubordinate, turning the trials that followed into another point of strong conflict with the State.

In the following years, this phenomenon of refusal and resistance by anarchists, antiauthoritarians, and insubordinate youth spread socially, leading to a variety of political initiatives, social interventions, counter-information projects, events of resistance, and the creation of new self-organized spaces. No strategy of domination was left unchallenged, neither the policies against the immigrants, nor the 2004 Olympics, the international political and economic summits, the participation of Greece in military plans and operations of the West against the countries of the East.

Based simultaneously on the political and organizational values of social solidarity, direct action, equality, anti-hierarchy, and self-organization, anarchists didn't hesitate and didn't fail to answer, at least to the extent they could, any attack by the State against society, and its most marginalized parts. They always stood side by side with the oppressed people and with those of them who fought back, refusing the dilemmas and defying the blackmails that the State utilizes in order to extract consent. And they did that clearly and regardless of the cost they would have to pay. They consistently stayed outside and against all institutions, outside and against the political system. At a time when others, no matter how radical they appeared, were adopting the mentality of the State, the anarchists stood alone against such proposals. The result was that the Left lost its influence among the most radical parts of society, while for the anarchists, the same thing that was said to be a weakness that would lead to their social isolation, was and still is exactly their strength: the fact that they stayed outside the political system and all institutions. Because when the people revolt they surpass the institutions and their restrictions, and communicate very well with the anarchists.

We hardly have any money, we work unselfishly in small, fluid affinity groups, but this is our strength...

This interview continues in Chapter 5...

There were many people who felt we had an unfinished revolution

Panagiotis Kalamaras: Publisher of Libertarian Culture editions

One thing that is certain, during the dictatorship and afterward, there were lots of people who liked rock and roll. We didn't have '68, but lots of Greeks traveled, they lived in France and Italy, they saw how it was to live with girls and take long walks in the city and listen to rock and roll.

One of the first anarchist books ever published in Greek was by George Garbis (publisher of *Eleftheros Typos*—Free Press Publications) who lived in London, and the other anarchist publication was by people who spoke other languages and could make translations. You see the cultural influence from other countries was very important.

After the collapse of the junta there were many people who had the feeling that we had an unfinished revolution. Many people felt that the Communist Party sold out and joined the authority. So we have these two elements, that we wanted another way of life and that on the political level it was clear that the people of the far Left didn't really believe in revolution.

In my opinion, the first anarchist uses of violence in demonstrations, was a way to let everyone know that the anarchists were absolutely different. They used violence so other people could see that they didn't compromise with the State like all the leftists did. And especially for that reason the Communists attacked the anarchists very severely, because the anarchists made the criticism that they were supporting the State.

The Communist Party is in a very strong position in Greece. They fought a civil war. Whole families were in the Communist Party. Thirty years ago if you said you were not with the Communists or the Maoists or the Trotskyists, you were in a difficult position. And our position from the beginning was to make no compromise with the authorities.

The occupations organized by the student movement in 1979, were our first organized battles to prove that we were something different. We mostly called ourselves autonomists then, not anarchists, because we were influenced by the Italians. But we weren't Marxist-Leninists. There were anarchists, but they didn't start calling themselves anarchists until '81, '82. And then it wasn't just to name themselves and identify themselves, but to be provocative. After the Socialists came to power in 1981, we said we were anarchists to be provocative. Because then this word didn't have a political meaning, connected to a political movement like in the United States. It meant that we do what we want. It had a bad meaning socially, it was a bad word. But we said we were anarchists to show that we had no connection with the State, with the elections. And we identified ourselves through violence.

But it was also an existentialist question, not only a political choice but a reflection that we wanted a different everyday life. So from the '80s the anarchists started squatting and communal living, things like this. Because we don't want to wait until after the revolution to live how we want to live. And for this reason we had big debates in the '90s about merchandise, do we sell beer or give it away, in the punk shows do we charge entrance or not?

The first appearance of anarchists on the streets was the May Day protest in 1976. It arose in the midst of the existing movements, and during this time there were demonstrations every day. But the anarchists came out of this and differentiated themselves from it through violence and a new kind of protest. Also at this time there were many wildcat strikes. The anarchists had a soil to grow in. If you do not have soil you cannot have flowers.

With the student movement in '79, the anarchists did not have a strong presence, there were very few of us, but we had the mentality that we organized ourselves without Parties, and that we made parties in the streets, not just a typical solemn demonstration. And after this student movement lots of left organizations completely collapsed and lots of the people became anarchists, at least in their mentality. The anarchist mentality, how we organized, was very influential in '79. There were some university occupations that were done in a lawful way but then other people self-organized the occupations with an open assembly and this was much more successful and empowering.

Legally, in the eyes of the authorities, we do not have the right of self-defense. With the Left, or with workers, they don't believe in fighting back if the police beat them, they don't believe in self-defense. The anarchists have the absolute opposite mentality. We don't wait for the police to attack us, we attack first. The Left only debate self-defense. In their view they are the ones being beaten. They have a victim mentality. They play the victim so that society will sympathize with these poor people beaten by the cops.

In Greece there was a civil war and the Left lost. They not only lost, they were tortured and murdered and wiped out, and they internalized this defeat. The anarchists are different. In Greece we have not been defeated. In fact we now have the upper hand.

The first anarchist demonstration that was completely anarchist was in 1984, with the visit of the French fascist Le Pen. It was his first visit to Greece. We had a big demo, a lot of people. What's important is not the number of people but the fact that we were very heavily armed, well equipped, and not in a spontaneous way either. We were prepared. Many people went down the street to burn down the hotel where Le Pen was staying and to fight face to face with the police. For me this was the birth of the present anarchist movement. It was a rupture.

In Greece there is no influence of traditional anarchism because with us it started in the '70s. Here many people who say they are anarchist have never read Bakunin or Kropotkin. We had a big movement in the classical sense until the First World War. But because of the big influence of the Communist Party all this disappeared. It didn't come back until the '70s.

Is there a tradition of anarchist bandits and bank robbers in Greece?

No, this is a misconception. In Greece we don't have anarchists who rob banks to fund the movement. We don't have the tradition of expropriations for buying weapons or anything else for the movement, like Brigati Rossi or Durruti. Sure there are individuals who are personally anarchists who rob banks for themselves, because they oppose work. But there are also nationalists or fascists or leftists or apolitical people who rob banks. We don't have the phenomenon of anarchist bank robbers in Greece. I don't like these stories, like this British historian, people on the outside who have this preconceived idea in their head of political expropriations. It's absolutely not true. Groups like the 17th of November never talked about how they acquired their money, and they denied making robberies. Yes a lot of people in the movement support bank robbers and they have sympathy for this activity but this is different from being an organized movement activity. If there are people in the anarchist movement involved in this, they would never say it because they would be outlawed.

It's not safe. We are not living in the '30s, we are living in the 21st century, we must be careful.

I began to get involved when I was 16

23.10: A person involved in the anarchist movement for some years

I began to get involved when I was sixteen, when I was a student. This was 1990, when we had a very big student movement in Greece. This was my first involvement in the anarchist movement. In 1995 I attended the Polytechnic, when there was an incident in which the police invaded the university and arrested over 500 anarchists. They had given a warning first, so I was not in this group of people who got arrested.

The years that followed were years of decline for the anarchist movement. There were fewer people, many of those who were arrested were very young and after they got charges they were afraid to remain involved in the movement. So the movement was very small. There were lots of conflicts in the movement. In my opinion there were three wings. One wing was the people who gathered in the Polytechnic, another wing of the movement were people involved with the anarchist newspaper *Alfa*, today these are the people of Alpha Kappa. They were a smaller wing. And a third wing were a kind of Autonomia. But Greek autonomists are very idiosyncratic. They are not dissident Marxists as in other countries. Rather,

many of them were ex-anarchists who were disappointed with the anarchist movement, especially after 1995.

In 1996 there was an incident that strongly divided the anarchist movement. The death of the anarchist Christoforos Marinos. The confusion around his death, I believe, created the division between the wing that gathered in the Polytechnic and the wing around *Alfa* newspaper. Do you want to hear the story about Christoforos Marinos? Okay.

He was killed on a boat, a ferry going to one of the islands, by the special forces of the Greek police. Officially, he committed suicide, but there are many indications that it was murder. Because in the same boat was the wife of the then prime minister. Many people in the police considered Marinos a very dangerous person. When they found out that on one side of the boat was the prime minister's wife, and then this anarchist Marinos was on the other side, they stormed the boat and shot him. But some people from *Alfa* said he was crazy and he committed suicide, some other anarchists maintained that he was murdered.

Marinos had a long story in the anarchist movement. He had been arrested in the past for involvement with an armed group, then after his arrest police found a safe house, and in this house they found the fingerprint of another person, a leftist. Some people claimed that Marinos had given the address of the safe house, but this is not true. But Marinos got the reputation of a traitor. Many people viewed him with suspicion. Maybe because of this incident Marinos tried to exaggerate his activities in order to fix his reputation. Sometime in 1995 he was involved in a robbery, the treasury of a hospital. During this robbery a clerk was killed. Some people were arrested, not anarchists, and one of them claimed that Christoforos was involved. The police arrested him, and when he went to jail he began a hunger strike, for about sixty days. At the same time, another anarchist, Kostos Kalaremas, accused of bank robbery, was also on hunger strike. One of the reasons the Polytechnic was invaded in 1995 was because there were two powerful hunger strikes at the same time. The Polytechnic had been occupied in solidarity with these hunger strikes.

You must understand, the Polytechnic is occupied every year, every 17th of November, to commemorate the student riots against the dictatorship. Since the '80s this has become a date for the anarchists, because at that time the leftists began to integrate with the political system and abandon the political violence. So they occupy the university every year, but one of their causes this year was for the two prisoners.

And after the police invasion of the Polytechnic, the two prisoners were freed. Marinos was put on house arrest. He violated his house arrest and one day there was a shooting attack against the offices of the governing party, the Socialists. After the death of Christoforos Marinos, police arrested an anarchist who confessed that he was the driver of the motorbike used for this shooting attack, and in the backseat was Marinos, the shooter. He also said that Marinos had become mentally unstable after his hunger strike. This guy justified the police action, he gave them the excuse they needed, by saying Marinos was crazy. The guy who informed on Marinos was defended by the people of the *Alfa* newspaper, and they adopted the story that he was crazy. Other people defended Marinos, said he wasn't crazy and that the police murdered him. This created a strong division.

In 1998 there were two very big movements and one significant incident, which was exclusively anarchist. A well-known anarchist was arrested, Nikos Maziotis. His arrest began a process whereby many anarchists began to gather in a permanent assembly in Polytechnic. This helped the movement to regain its power. And those who gathered represented only one wing of the anarchist movement.

In the summer, there was a strong movement of professors and teachers, and anarchists were also strongly involved. This helped us to regain our self-confidence as a movement. And then in the winter of 1998 the movement of the high school students began. Going back to 1990 there is a strong tradition of student movements. Every winter they occupied their schools. I think in January of 1999, or maybe February, there was the bombing of Yugoslavia, so there were many demonstrations, many riots. Anarchists had a violent presence in all these incidents; riots in the demonstrations, small groups that carried out arsons. And these incidents, these actions, these movements all helped the anarchist movement rise again.

Something else, an external factor: from '98 to '99, a process began in Greece to reform the universities. There was an increase in university enrollment because of the reforms. In my opinion, that helped the rise of the anarchist movement, the rise of movements in general, that all these new people were going to study. There was also a small decline of leftists in the universities. In my very personal opinion, the leftist groups inside the universities had created a model of action, of presence, based on making an occupation of their university building every year for a few weeks, to show strength in order to collect followers and voters—every April we have student elections—and they all had the same model, they tried to do the same thing every year. People got bored. So this kind of action declined.

In my opinion what happened in the last five years was a decline of some traditional anarchist groups. By traditional I mean very old groups that had belonged to the wing of the Polytechnic assembly. Some anarchist groups were marginalized or they withdrew from Exarchia, from the center of anarchist politics. Maybe these groups were marginalized because their cycle had ended, they didn't have anything else to give. In my opinion there was a political vacuum, there were not other groups to replace them. Alongside this, there were very many new young people who participated in the anarchist movement. Many young people were coming to Exarchia, and there was also an increase in direct actions. Well-organized actions, attacks on police stations. Some were quite sophisticated, quite daring. The traditional groups, in my opinion, operated on a strategy of intervention and participation with the existing social movements. The newer anarchists were characterized by illegalism and individualism, by individualism I mean struggle as a subjective process. I supported these new ideas but now I think you need a balance of the two approaches.

What allowed the movement to sustain itself and continue itself generation to generation?

I have doubts about this. It was not something in the movement, I think. Anarchism had become an underground trend for young people. One reason was the sophistication of these actions. They were not spontaneous. Many young people saw all these actions, these activities, and they were impressed, so it became an underground trend. But I'm not very sure about this. It's very subjective.

19

1. Anarchist Marinos Antipas, assassinated in 1907.

2. In 1910, inspired by the vision, passion, and martyrdom of Antipas, Greek peasants revolt to liberate the land from feudalism.

3. Anarcho-syndicalist K. Speras was active in the labor unrest of the metal mines and the Commune of 1916 on the island of Serifos.

4. T. Kouzoupis, the first anarchist killed during the strikes and Commune of Serifos in 1916.

5. Youth in arms, active in anti-Nazi resistance and the Greek Civil War.

6. Searching for dead friends and relatives.

7. Aris Velouchiotis, leader of Greek Popular Liberation Army. Velouchiotis is a hero for refusing to accept communist compromise and the "Treaty of Varkiza." He was betrayed to the nationalists in 1945, assassinated, and his head was displayed in the village of Trikala as a warning.

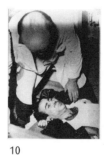

10

12

11

8

9

8. The Civil War in Greece.

9. Athens, 1944.

10. Cultural and political leader Gregory Lambrakis was killed in Thessaloniki in 1963, a time of social upheaval in Greece.

11. Gregory Lambrakis's funeral.

12. Sotiris Petroulas was killed in 1965. By this time widespread riots and instability characterized Greek society, opening the way for the CIA-backed dictatorship of 1967.

We are an Image from the Future

13

14

15

16

17

18

19

20

21

13–15. Dictatorship, 1967–1973.

16–21. Images from the revolt against the dictatorship in 1973, including the occupation of the Polytechnic School. Banner slogans included: "Power to the People," "Bring Down Authority," "General Insurrection," and "Labor Assemblies." For modern Greek anarchists, these demonstrations mark the beginning of their history.

22

23

24

25

22. Polytechnic, Athens 1973.

23. Athens riots, November 1973.

24. Banner reads: "Down with Authority! People Attack!"

25. Banner reads: "General Insurrection!"

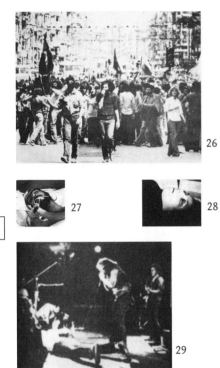

26

30

31

33

27   28

32

29

26. Strikes organized directly by factory workers and peasants, occupations of universities, student movements, hard rock and punk counter-culture, changes in social morals, riots, street fights, and wild demonstrations characterise the mid-'70s to early '80s.

27–28. In 1980 police assassinate J. Koumis and S. Kanelopoulou during the Nov. 17 anniversary riots, a new generation is politicized and shown that the struggle against authority had not been won with the transition to a democratic government.

29. Rory Gallagher's concert on September 12, 1981 brought together people from many different music scenes and united anarchist youth. For hours before and after the show, people rioted and fought with police, beginning a tradition of free public concerts that also serve as battles with authority.

30. Christos Tsoutsouvis, an armed revolutionary, killed during shootout with policemen on May 15, 1985. Three cops died from his gun that day.

31. On Nov. 17 1985, Michalis Kaltezas is killed by police during rioting. A university occupation ensues and the Exarchia neighborhood becomes the center of the social struggle that continued for months.

32. Assembly at the Chemistry school the night of Kaltezas's assassination

33. The banner reads: "Our Small Hordes Demand Utopia! Neither Fascism Nor Democracy! Long Live Anarchy!"

34–35. In the late '80s, the Anarchist / Antiauthoritarian / Autonomist / Libertarian Movement becomes stronger through demonstrations, solidarity concerts, and clashes with the police.

36. In 1987, police kill armed revolutionary Michalis Prekas.

37. Banner reads: "We Are the Blossom of the Greek Youth," January 1990.

38. In 1991, the neo-conservative government tries to reform education. More than 2000 high schools and every university in the country was under occupation for more than three months. The strongest youth movement in the Greek history appears, with very strong anarchist influences.

39. On January 8, 1991, Nikos Temponeras, a teacher at the central High School of Patras was assassinated by paramilitaries while helping his students defend the occupied school from an attack organized by police, right wing paramilitaries and town leaders. Demonstrations and riots in most Greek cities erupted, involving hundreds of thousands of people.

40. The anarchist space enters a new era, connecting the practices of anarchists with more general sectors of society. The generation that appeared during January 1991 will influence the social struggles of our times and offer new dimensions to anarchist tactics and strategies.

41–42. November 17, 1995. Two anarchist prisoners are on hunger strike. The annual riots are heavier than normal and the night ends with the breaking of the university asylum. Police enter the Polytechnic school and arrest 504 anarchists.

43. Christoforos Marinos, one of the two recent prisoners on hunger strike is assassinated by the police on July 23, 1996, one year after his liberation. The text in the poster says: Honor to the Anarchist Christoforos Marinos. Assassinated by the State on 23-7-96: "I don't have anything else to contribute except my life… I don't have anything else to claim, except my Freedom."

Chronology: September 2000–November 2008

September 2000: Greek anarchists participate in the Black Bloc during the international mobilization against the International Monetary Fund meeting in Prague, making connections and creating mutual influence with the anarchist movements of other countries. They subsequently played a major role in the protests against the G8 in Genova, Italy, in 2001.

May 2002: Anarchists in Iraklion squat a former hospital, Evangelismos, creating one of the biggest squats in all Crete. The squat plays an important role in spreading anarchist ideas throughout the island in the following years. The squat still exists in 2010.

June 2003: Greek anarchists with comrades from abroad play a major role in the mobilizations, protests, and riots against the European Union Summit in Thessaloniki. During the organization of these protests, the organization Antiauthoritarian Current (AK) is created, establishing assemblies and social centers in many major cities of Greece. They also attempt to be a nationwide organization similar to the earlier Anarchist Union.

2004: The Olympic Games come to Athens, and with them the usual accompaniment of urban renewal, ethnic cleansing, heavy policing, and technologies of social control. The first neighborhood assemblies arise to defend the areas of Akropolis and Exarchia from the results of the Games, and there are also solidarity campaigns with the hyper-exploited immigrant workers doing most of the construction. However these struggles are not so successful.

March 20, 2004: Anarchists in Thessaloniki squat a huge abandoned factory to create the social center Fabrika Yfanet.

May 1, 2005: AK organizes a demonstration of dignity and solidarity for the workers at the shipyards of Perama, an area that is hit with many economic problems.

August 22–28, 2005: Anarchists in Bulgaria and Greece organize a No Border Camp on both sides of the border, including an attack on a detention facility that is later closed down. Some immigrants held there are liberated during the attack.

2006–2007: Students across Greece occupy their universities and create a major movement against the restructuring of higher education under the European Union's Plan Bolonya. Despite the strong resistance, the restructuring was passed into law in March 2007, though the politicians had to do it with the smell of tear gas in the air and the sound of fireworks exploding outside the front door of Parliament. However, the students did not give up their struggle and this pressure has prevented the university administrations from implementing the legal changes.

23 April 2007: After imprisoned anarchist bank robber Yiannis Dimitrakis is beaten by prison guards, other prisoners riot in solidarity in Malandrinos prison and subsequently in all major prisons in the country. Outside the prisons there are several solidarity actions, including anarchist groups on motorcycles attacking police stations with molotov cocktails.

August 2007: Major forest fires break out across Greece in a coordinated way, burning huge swaths of forest and killing dozens of people. Many Greeks realize that these fires are set by developers who want to clear land for construction, as Greek law prohibits construction in forested areas. More than 5,000 people from a diversity of economic classes and cultural backgrounds gather outside Parliament to shout at all the political parties, "kick them all out!"

August 18, 2007: In Thessaloniki, Nigerian immigrant Tony Onoya dies after a run-in with police who had previously beat him up. Officially, he died falling off a balcony while trying to escape, but immigrant eyewitnesses say he was pushed. Subsequently, hundreds of Nigerians and other immigrants, joined by local anarchists and antiauthoritarians, gather and riot.

January 30, 2008: Immigrants along with AK Patras and the Network for the Defense of Immigrants organize a protest that brings together over 1,500 immigrants, mostly Afghans, calling for asylum and respect for their human rights.

February 2, 2008: About sixty members of the Greek neo-nazi group Golden Dawn attempt to march in Athens. They are attacked by 400 anarchists and extreme leftists, but the police move in to protect the fascists and attack the anarchists. During the resulting riot, fascists and riot police work together on the streets to fight against anarchists. The collaboration is caught on video and aired widely, proving to Greek society the link between the police and the fascists. The same day, about ten anarchists on motorbike attack an Athens police station with molotovs, and the next day about twenty hooded anarchists on foot throw molotovs at a group of riot police guarding the Socialist Party offices in Athens.

June 2008: Wealthy Greek industrialist Giorgos Mylonas is kidnapped after he made a comment that Greek workers would simply have to tighten their belts to survive new austerity measures. His wife pays twelve million euros for his release. In their communique the kidnappers say that workers are kidnapped and ransomed every day of their lives. It is later learned that the four kidnappers include anarchists Polikarpos Georgiadis and Vaggelis Hrisohoides, along with legendary outlaw Vassilis Palaiokostas, who with his brother Nikos has been carrying out robberies and prison breaks for decades.

August 29–31, 2008: Antiauthoritarians and people from the far Left hold a No Border Camp in Patras, demonstrating in solidarity with the immigrants in the port city, which is a common entry point to Italy and the rest of Europe.

November 2008: Eight thousand prisoners all across Greece participate in a hunger strike, pressing sixteen demands. Antiauthoritarians inside and outside the prison strongly support the struggle. The prisoners win the majority of their demands.

December 5, 2008: Normalcy reigns. No one predicts anything out of the ordinary. Horoscopes call for more of the same.

Exarchia Square and the neighborhood assemblies

Argiris: A longtime anarchist activist from Athens

So it was like this. We were sitting in a house, something like four hundred meters away from Exarchia Square. This was around June, 2003. It was like 2:30 in the afternoon, we were drinking coffee and smoking the first joint of the day. And suddenly they called us on the telephone. Our friend was in the square, she said to us that there were some workers on the square, and some machines, construction machines, and it was looking like they wanted to begin construction on the square, in the general spirit of construction for the Olympic Games. At that period there was gentrification in all the city for the Olympics. So immediately we understood that our turn had come to face this problem in the square. The funniest thing I remember is that immediately from the moment we hung up the telephone, though we were just four people in the middle of a big city, we had a natural, powerful feeling that we could stop all the Mayor's construction projects by ourselves. That afternoon I felt this passionate enthusiasm that had no rationality, just this feeling of power and commitment. Because we decided that would never happen, it would never happen for sure. We were sure. There were four of us walking to the square and I felt like I belonged to an army.

It was like we were carrying a monster with us, and this monster was the reputation, the mythology of the anarchist movement in general. We carried with us all the power of all the actions that had come before us. We were not just four people, we were 2,000 people.

And so when we arrived there, we went directly to the workers and we asked, *What are you doing here? Who is responsible for this work?*

They say, *We don't know, we don't know*, but they pointed out this fat guy in the café drinking a frappe and overseeing the work. He was in charge. And as we went to speak to this man, we saw that they had already made a big hole, 1.5 meters deep, 2 meters wide. So we go to this man and we ask him, *Why are you here? What do you want to do?*

They've made a plan for big changes to the square, he said. The planning is already decided. He's not responsible for these decisions but he's responsible for finishing the construction. And we asked him very politely, *What is the plan, what will the square look like?*

He said they would throw away the statue, the classical statue in the middle of the square with the ancient god Eros. The statue was symbolic for the punks and it was something like a guardian angel for the junkies who hung out there. They write graffiti on it, sticking up posters or announcements. It is the symbolic center of the square.

29

We're surprised, so we ask if he's sure they were going to remove the statue.

He says, *Yes, all the middle of the square will be taken up by a pool, with a fountain.*

The benches of the square were old, falling apart, so we asked about the benches, will they put in new benches?

No, we're going to rip it all out and put in new things.

What kind of new things?

We will put in a cement platform for the people to sit on.

How is it possible for old people to sit on this cement thing? No one will come to sit.

It doesn't matter, normal people don't hang out here. I don't care what you say, it's already planned.

So we said to him, *You stay here and wait, just see what happens.*

All that afternoon, there were many people like us calling each other and talking about this. And through this, an assembly for Exarchia Square was called. So next afternoon, spreading the word by phone or word of mouth, about 400 people gathered. Half of them were inhabitants of the area, and half were anarchists who hung out on the square. And then we went and we threw all the construction machines in this hole, destroyed them, we told the workers that the people of the square would not allow them to work here, we would not allow them to build a metal barrier around the square to hide the construction from the public view. And we said that whatever construction will happen in the future, the locals will decide the design, and any construction will happen in the public view. Out of this struggle the assembly of the "Initiative of Exarchia Residents" was born, and this assembly continues today, playing an important role in resisting the police presence in the neighborhood.

Because of this organized struggle, the construction stopped for many months, and in the period that followed, the representatives from the assembly of Exarchia went to the construction company and asked about the planning. In the beginning, the company said that because they were a private company they didn't have any obligation to show us the plans. So the assembly decided they didn't have to allow any construction, and that only if the construction company accepts the architectural ideas of the assembly would any construction be allowed to happen. So the assembly prepared plans, which included an expansion of the green area of the square, to add more trees and bushes, keep the statue, not put in the fountain, and they would install new high-quality benches.

In the first months, the mayor of the city sent riot police to guard the construction site. But because of the inhabitants' negation of the plan, the riot police could not save the construction project. They couldn't enforce it themselves. And after one month the riot police left, because every time they went away for a moment, we destroyed the machines and the metal construction barriers. Three times this happened. So the works stopped. And they stopped for almost one year. And it was very funny because during that period, there was no cement, the construction workers had taken away all the paving stones to prepare the construction. Suddenly Exarchia Square was bare earth. So in the meantime we enjoyed this, we put up a volleyball net and announced that now we had a beach in the square.

To defend the square, the anarcho-punks stayed there. All around the square all different sorts of people regularly gathered, but in the middle of the square it was the anarcho-punks. This lasted for almost one year, the period of the beach in the park.

Due to all these factors, the construction company realized they had to accept the planning of the inhabitants' assembly, and they announced their concession. As this was the period of the reconstruction around the Acropolis, for the Olympics, this was when the first two neighborhood assemblies started. Philopapou, around the Acropolis, was the first one, and then the assembly of the inhabitants of Exarchia. Both of these assemblies were successful in stopping construction projects and stopping gentrification. The spirit of these two assemblies produced many other neighborhood assemblies in other parts of Athens and other cities throughout Greece.

This was the beginning of a new period in the anarchist movement, the meeting of the powerful direct action of the anarchists with the interests and the hopes of the inhabit-ants, their dreams for their own neighborhood. The inhabit-ants felt this confluence between their dreams and the power of the direct actions of the insurrectionist anarchists, that it was good.

31

Do you join the Party to fuck or do you fuck to join the Party?

Iulia: A participant in the queer and anarchist movements

There's a saying that sums up the gender dynamics on the Left: Do you join the party to fuck or do you fuck to join the party? It's better with the anarchists but there are still problems. I flirt with the anarchists, I feel much closer to them, but I don't want to label myself. Mostly I participate in local things, projects that are happening in my immediate area. I do a lot of art.

Generally you could say that in Greece there is quite a conservative logic. The feminist movement in Greece in the '80s had visibility, they had some successes, but then they disappeared or became part of the mainstream political scene, merging with the Socialist Party or others. So I don't think there is a tradition for gender politics. I think in revolutionary terms it was always quite closed, never open to other issues. The anarchist idea of freedom is very big, very open, and it doesn't have room for tendencies within it that have a limited focus.

I prefer to say that I'm an anarchist than to say that I'm a feminist. The problem is very philosophical, between the partial and the total. If I protest for my partial freedom, as a woman, I would focus on being able to get a good job, receiving welfare from the State when I have a baby. That would be my partial freedom, and it would be completely compatible with capitalism. But I'm against identity politics because it carries a greater danger of entering into mainstream politics. I don't think that you should rely on the State for partial freedom. This is vain, at the end of the day, because you don't change the social relations. You just say you want a better position within the existing framework.

But when you strive for total freedom, you need to have the whole picture in your head, and then you can't rely on the State or coexist with capitalism in order to win just a part of that freedom, because by doing so you would negate your total freedom. However, you also have to leave room for all the individual parts within your conception of freedom. Otherwise you become apathetic to women, to workers, you just say *I'm an anarchist* and that's that. You have to synthesize and analyze how it would work, understand all the different kinds of oppression so you can understand the totality of freedom. You have to understand how it works. You can't just have a god of freedom, you can't believe in freedom generally or abstractly.

I don't want to generalize and say that the leftists or the anarchists are misogynistic, but I want to say there is a tendency that overshadows the politics of gays and lesbians and their struggles don't become visible. That's why I think it's quite closed. You have this ideology of revolution and freedom, you go out and smash things out of anger, but you don't actually look for ways to get there.

Lots of anarchists don't question what is considered to be normal. We have romantic couples that control each other with jealousy, or maybe I take on the role of the girlfriend and have very mainstream ideas of how I should behave. Together we fight for revolution but within each of us we sustain norms that are bourgeois. If I go out to participate in the struggle but then I come back and on my couch I'm doing the same things as everyone else, there is no revolution. People carry these norms with them subconsciously, and if they don't work on changing themselves internally, they'll sabotage whatever revolution they make. But if we work on our relationships then we can go beyond simple opposition to the State.

The anarchist movement in Greece is a revolutionary subject group. But this umbrella of the anarchist movement, which is a powerful thing, creates the trap of making people suspicious of anyone who doesn't wear the label of anarchist. So it's not easy to get access, and also not easy to introduce new lines of politics. So the subject group can become a bit sexist. And the anarchist movement here excludes aesthetic matters, cultural matters, spiritual matters. There is a very straightforward political identity they want to carry, and okay, theoretically it's very libertarian, but practically their personal relations are the same, they're mainstream and bourgeois. In terms of gender dynamics, in my experience it's common to create relationships that don't go beyond normality. You don't risk making it revolutionary, you don't create any openness. But when you risk it you find out you had been living in a relationship with the same old jealousies and forms of control, without a spirit of friendship or solidarity. I'm not saying the anarchists should be blamed, they just sustain an unconscious function. It's normality.

But it's difficult if we don't have anything concrete to propose. It starts on a very small scale, dealing with the relations between us. That's why I advocate having an inward focus.

I had a friend who wanted to do a belly dance performance at Villa Amalias [an anarcho-punk squat], and they rejected the idea as misogynist. But for her it was an art form, it was spiritual, and it's strange how they can turn it around and tell you that you can't do certain things with your body. Taking things out of context, that's queer to me. But the belly dancing wasn't allowed to be put in a new context.

You can see that the flows are a bit blocked. At the assemblies they'll talk for three hours about the ideas and the theory, and then when it comes to the organization, everybody splits in groups, and this makes me really angry, because the important thing is the organization. If everybody is in small groups specializing in what we are going to organize, then what are we doing at the general assemblies, just discussing the idea of freedom? And to me that's where you see some of these macho dynamics, macho in the sense of having leaders.

33

If we talk about desire—I'm reading Deleuze now—with desire what's necessary is that it functions not that it is analyzed. So if you go to an assembly and don't discuss how it's going to function, that's problematic for me. For three hours everybody says the same thing. In Greece we don't have a pragmatic culture and for me that reflects the gender relations. You have the same structure, the abstract specialists, after a while it's like a revolutionary bureaucracy. And yet everything still happened in December so I don't want to dismiss it, but there's also a problem because everything is being carried out by groups that are quite closed.

The other thing that becomes obvious, because they are not open to spiritual, cultural, or aesthetic matters, the idea of violence is a holy thing for the anarchists. You have to be violent in a way, and that excludes a lot of things. I think that's very uncultivated, sometimes it's not very strategic and leads to people doing stupid things without taking precautions just to prove that they can do it.

If we suppose that the anarchists in Greece are sexist I would say that it has to do with their relationship to violence in a way that excludes other activities that are more *feminine* in quotation marks. They have to be heroic and if they're not they're not important in the movement. It's this structure of small factions each with their own leader or face, a persona, and I don't like that. It's a patriarchal structure. Greek society is quite patriarchal and we carry these structures into our own groups as well.

As for valuing masculine labor over feminine labor, we lack the organization in which the importance of feminine labor becomes obvious. The heroic acts are more important; that's the only narrative we have, and so the feminine labor is not valued. I think that's why we don't have many squats in Greece, because it requires organization. But we're getting more and more squats.

The heroic aspect is consumed in the solidarity as well. I don't like to say this because you have to support the people when they go to prison, but everything else seems to stop after a while. In the years before December, all the focus was going to supporting the heroes and not to the other aspects of the struggle.

The raves and free spaces is where the collective consciousness is coming together

J.: A libertarian freethinker and organizer of underground happenings since the late '80s

Let's say we have three different phases in the anarchist movement. The first phase was in the '80s, and it was characterized by Eastern philosophies, Western philosophies, psychedelic views, all combined and non-puritan. It was not differentiated. But this all changed in the mid-90s when the movement Italianized, so to speak. It began to copy the Italian model, to differentiate itself and distance itself from its cultural aspects, saying the only way to be effective was to be militant. It adopted a more objective and materialistic view. The major influences during the '90s were the Italian autonomia, to a lesser extent things like Green Anarchy from the American movement, and very much so the Situationist International and the new formulation of metropolis, the capitalistic centers as metropolis, the places where the spectacle is more actively formulated. The German underground and punk rock also had an influence, and these were not so tolerant of other approaches. In the '80s it was easier to speak together about Proudhon or the Doors or the psychedelic communes. In the '90s there were two currents. The prominent one was very materialistic and rational, based on Western anarchist thinkers. The second one, very much a minority, had to do with spirituality and seeking utopias. However this second current has larger reflections in the rest of society. There are lots of people moving in this alternative way but they move in small groups, they are not creating big congregations or assemblies like the first current.

The third phase—that led to December—is that there are so many people sharing libertarian ideas, with a majority of militant thinking and a minority with a spiritual and cultural focus. When everyone was trying to do the best from their own view, and all of this together brought December.

The second current in the '90s, based in spirituality, arose mainly through the neo-hippy culture that came from abroad in rave parties or Rainbow Gatherings. It was connected with Reclaim the Streets from the UK. In the Greek version thereof, there was unity between the two factions, but it didn't last for long. Not because of the repression of the State but because of the inner contradictions of this union. One side thought that the other side was just lifestyle anarchists losing themselves in spirituality, focusing on meditation rather than changing the system. So there was a break, slowly but surely. Because of this, a big part of the Greek anarchist movement is very puritan in its attitude. Even though they are anarchists they can easily remind you of the Communists. They're very strict, not

35

very flexible. But all these contradictions is what makes the movement so strong, somehow. Because in the times of great social unrest all these people came together and acted together before they broke up again into different pieces.

Spirituality is not important for the revolutionary struggle, spirituality is important for changing how you view the world. If you change that it's very difficult for you to be repressed. If you are a spiritual person and connect with your inner consciousness, it comes naturally that you want to be there for other people. You feel love for them, you want them to be okay, you don't want them to have to live in a society that is repressing them so much. Spirituality also makes you effective in what you are doing. It gives you a clear mind, unaffected by hatred. A mind that is ready to act without being affected by the poisonous surroundings that necessitate the actions. Spirituality allows you to act freely, so that you are no longer a slave, neither from the outside nor from your inner complexities. Since you understand that the great game of existence surpasses any higher ideology, you are no longer definable, you are someone who changes all the time.

In the first current hate is sovereign, hatred of the structures of the system. For people who develop their spirituality, hatred is not valid at all, it's poisonous. But this doesn't mean that they're passive. This means that they act without hate but they are still there when they need to shout or fight. But they have a clear view. They understand that the real enemy is not the Other, but the ignorance that distorts our relationships.

Most of us in this second current are pacifists. But if the last resort is to fight, here the idea is that we fight. But only if it is the last option, if it is to protect yourself or to save the person beside you who is getting beaten. Only then. We are not ideologizing violence, and neither are we ideologizing pacifism. That's very important. Because you cannot stay peaceful when someone next to you is being attacked. You fight but the important thing is that you are not feeling hatred.

How do you feel about spirituality accommodating a bourgeois lifestyle?

We hate that! We are completely against that idea, we don't accept it as real spirituality. It's a way of drugging yourself. Spirituality is about developing strong philosophical systems that work slowly, or sometimes more quickly, that bring you to a higher consciousness. It has nothing to do with beads and new age shops and all this bullshit coming from the California ideology. We are against this stuff in the same way that we are against the ideologizing of hatred in the libertarian movement. That's a very important difference you can see between Greece and the Anglo-Saxon world. None of us see spirituality as something you can buy. Most of us really are searchers, freethinkers. We don't fit into Murray Bookchin's ideas of lifestyle anarchism. Actually we don't like his ideas. He was great in the '70s but after time he just wanted to make the whole movement adhere to his ideas, eventually he became just an old fart. Anything that was outside of his narrow idea of anarchism had to be placed inside a single term and abolished. We are against Bookchin, and new age, and lifestyle. We are not even post-modern. We can take ideas from Baudrillard and the rest but we use them in our own way. Anyway postmodernism is just another Western idea, it's not a global idea. It's part of the myth and ideology of the West.

People outside the movement are very affected by the connection of spirituality and libertarian ideas. Especially the young people are experimenting with new ways of living. Some move out of the cities, some go traveling, some of them find ways to travel inside their own neighborhoods and societies. This is not centralized, and it doesn't follow the approach of the main current in the anarchist movement. These people are much more loose and cool. But for example in December all of them were in the streets. They were in the councils, in the streets, in the riots, everywhere. Somehow December surpassed the classical anarchist groups in Greece.

The raves and free spaces form a part of the network where the new collective consciousness is coming together. People are making friendships, using music to express themselves, using psychedelics, or not. Many people don't use any psychedelics at all, but it's just one way to get an ecstatic view of the world. The rave culture brought many people back in touch with nature, with free love and free thinking. Of course there were some people inside this subculture who were there for business but that was a minority. Most people were there for the sacred atmosphere that was being developed inside these parties. Two generations came together and they were ready to destroy the apathy. Most of the people at these parties were pacifists, though there was always a strong minority that were into rioting, which is why many of these rave parties ended in riots. People at the parties wanted to keep the cops out, so they would attack them, and you would get riots lasting all night. In Greece the police don't attack the parties of the underground so much because they are afraid of the counterattack. They prefer to attack the parties of the pacifists. There were many attacks against them and no one fought back. This is how they destroyed the outdoor rave scene in the '90s. People were organizing raves in the forests and the mountains, but they kept getting attacked. This didn't happen to the parties in the metropolis or the parties organized by anarchists, because these people were ready to fight. And after the riots the parties didn't stop, they continued the whole time. The party was the source of the riot and something for it to melt back into.

Also in the indie rock scene, there have been massive riots at concerts. It's very important to note that in the places where these festivals took place there was no asylum, like there is in the universities. The concerts were not held in the universities, but usually in Pedion Areos Park in the center of Athens. In the last eighteen years in Athens at least eight major riots started from concerts there, and even though they had no asylum, police were only able to break up the concerts three of those times.

In Thessaloniki in 2003 there were seven days of parties organized by Void Network, leading up until the night of the big riots against the European Union summit. There were two different squats inside the campus, one led by the Black Bloc and the other by an antiauthoritarian coalition. The parties took place between these two occupations, and they kept going constantly. These were great moments. I think they prepared people for the big demonstrations and the major riots that took place. It was a very unique space for new connections and new ideas. For me this was much more important than the demonstration itself. It was a great union between the neo-hippies and the people who are all about barricades. There were many differences, and much arguing, but in the end they all came together.

There was a party in September 2006 at the Polytechnic. It turned into a massive riot with 7,000 people. There were artists from all over Europe there, playing for free. The riots started around two in the morning and kept going until seven or eight. The police would shoot tear gas and people would scatter but then come back together. This whole time the party never stopped. People would fight the police around the campus and go back to the party. There was one DJ from Germany who said it was a great moment for the rave scene. He put his T-shirt around his face and went back on stage to keep spinning.

In late 2001 there was a major party in Propilea, in front of the University Rectorate in the center of Athens. Void Network occupied the place for twenty-four hours. All the tribes came together, there were 5,000 people, 6,000 people, blocking the streets, dancing. The riot police surrounded us but they couldn't do anything, because that plaza is protected by the asylum. This was a very significant event, all these people occupying part of the city, dancing together, writing slogans on the wall. In the morning we had taken over the area of a major metro station, Panepistimio. Workers and other people were coming by and seeing this scene and they couldn't understand how it could happen, it was too far outside their reality. And this is the most important thing, creating holes in reality to show people that we can create anything we desire, surpassing these blocks in the general consciousness of society. It was really good. For me this party summarizes the whole idea of the multidimensional movement.

Lefteria ston Yiannis Dimitraki!!!

In the afternoon of January 16, 2006, there was an armed attack on the National Bank of Greece in central Athens. After a crossfire with two special unit police officers, one of the participants, Yiannis Dimitrakis, was seriously injured by three shots from the police in different parts of his body. The other four participants escaped with about $50,000, although one of them was also injured. After spending some months in different hospitals during his recovery he was transferred to the Korydallos prison of Athens.

In another self-parody of the Greek justice system he was accused of seven robberies and multiple counts of attempted homicide, with the application of the antiterrorist law. This was not the first time anarchists in Greece have gotten trumped up charges. Subsequently, anarchists all over Greece painted walls with the phrase, "Lefteria ston Yiannis Dimitraki!" *Freedom for Yiannis Dimitrakis!*

This is the letter that he sent out on June 23, 2007.

Comrades,

This letter is my first attempt to communicate and comment on what happened after the robbery of the Greek National Bank in the center of Athens on January 16, 2006. Before speaking about the actual events I would like to mention some things in respect to the motivations behind the action and the significance they have for me.

I consider that today society is like a train on a track headed for total dehumanization. We are the motor that powers the train, its engine, its passengers, and its wheels. The driver has the cruel face of capitalism and the copilot is the lazy, faceless State. The tracks are not made of rose petals, they are made of blood and corpses, bodies solitary or piled in mounds, of people who wanted to resist or change that frenetic course.

They are many: insubordinates, rebels, leftists, antiauthoritarians and anarchists; their names fill the history of this journey. I place myself between these last two categories. In agreement with my conscience and my vision of the world, what I clearly discern is that this society depends only on violence, exploitation, and oppression. A society whose purpose is the loss of human dignity in all its signs and senses. This is something we all experience every day: forced to act through the state institutions or work under a boss who exploits us.

Employment and work: words that in reality signify enslavement and prostration. Work and the added value are columns of the actual economy while the conditions in which work takes place confirm that people are treated like expendable products, like modern slaves. We see workers rotting from diseases caused by exposure to toxic substances in the workplace; they are dying in one way or another in the temples constructed by the capitalists. They have abandoned their will, their lives and their spontaneity, essential characteristics of a free person. They are working long hours for scraps. To cover the majority of their basic necessities a person is obligated to mortgage everything they have to those cold oppressors called banks and under the weight of that financial responsibility they begin to show signs of submission and servitude. If they can't pay their debts they are driven until they crack; and they end up committing suicide or humbling themselves in public in the worst forms. In order to perpetuate themselves, the State and Capital are today constructing a system that sacrifices human life on the altar of profit. And as was said before, one of the principal partners are the banks, which are nothing more than financial sharks that lend to those who will drop to their knees. The banks are directly or indirectly guilty for the plunder of the population. Taking all this into consideration we can understand Brecht's character Maki when he asks: "What is a bank robbery in comparison to the establishment of the bank?"

I want to take into consideration my actions of resistance at a personal level and an external level. All the people who know me in person know that I did everything I could to determine the conditions and quality of my life. I rejected work as a unity of mass production, another wheel of the train. I wanted to attack the bank monstrosity, knowing that I couldn't cause it that much damage. Choosing a dignified way of living, I decided to rob a bank. I consider this action, like many others, revolutionary. In all honesty I want to admit that I intended to steal the money for myself. But at the same time, as an anarchist I wanted to show support to the actions and contribute to the necessities of the movement. What I want to say is that not every anarchist has to be a bank robber nor is every worker a slave.

I started to tell my story when I was lying on the ground, injured by police bullets, unable to escape the hot embrace of the State. Despite everything, I imagine it was an impressive image, but at the same time an example for anyone who wants to involve themselves in similar actions: a crowd of blue-uniformed hunters, encircling me, the injured captive, lovingly kicking me and calling out: "We have fucked you! You're not

that big now, son of a bitch!" My back was exposed and I couldn't move nor breathe because of the bullets in my lung, liver, and elbow.

I speak about this without bitterness, I have no lament nor delusion because I didn't expect any better treatment from my enemies. Lesser criminals than I have received worse treatment. While I was being attended in the general hospital of Athens I experienced the violation of every human right. The first time my parents came to visit me they put an armed policeman between us, denying even one intimate moment with my family, and I couldn't open my mouth because of the drugs they gave me in the ICU. Later, amidst the fog of pain and drugs I realized that without permission from the hospital the police had entered my room to surveil me at all times. But I would like to thank all the hospital staff who took care of me despite their political views, and also for resisting the pressure from the authorities. The boss of the ICU informed me about my rights. He also helped me out when the clever prosecutor Diotis came. He kicked him out of the room saying he couldn't interrogate me in that condition, and I heard Diotis saying: "Clearly I have respect for the condition this guy is in, otherwise I would have removed his breathing tubes or bumped the pressure up to 50…" At that moment I understood that had the hospital personnel not been protecting me I would have had to face the infamous techniques of Diotis, carried out in many past interrogations.

After that incident the conditions of my detention got worse. I was transferred to another wing where there were always two civil cops in the room with me and two regular cops outside. Every thirty minutes another policeman came to monitor the situation and there were five or six more in the waiting room. Because of that I couldn't sleep for three or four days. I protested to the director and he responded that since I was a prisoner they could decide how to treat me to prevent a suicide attempt. They falsified the doctor's report so they could ship me to prison sooner.

Now the prosecutor has tried to charge another person with the same crime as me, just because we are part of the same anarchist scene. It's the classic scenario concocted between the police and journalists. They invented a story about an armed group of ten to fifteen people, all anonymous so they could accuse a lot more people, and then they accuse this mysterious group of six more bank robberies supposedly committed to fund anarchist groups. The end of the story is that I find myself accused of seven bank robberies, attempted homicide, and stealing money, all under the antiterrorist law. That the state has prefabricated techniques to win convictions and destroy people's reputations in a mediatic parody is nothing new.

Finally I want to say to all those who are planning our physical, ethical, and political annihilation: it's not important what dirty techniques you use, it's not important if you hunt us or beat us down, you will never destroy or domesticate us, because it is honorable to rebel. We will not lower our heads in submission.

I want to thank all of those who are showing solidarity knowing how difficult my case is.

In struggle,
Yiannis Dimitrakis
Korydallos, Greece

The Permanent Crisis in Education—Some Notes on Recent Struggles:

A DETAILED LOOK AT THE STRIKES AND OCCUPATIONS BY TEACHERS, STUDENTS AND PARENTS IN 2006–7 IN RESPONSE TO NEOLIBERAL POLICIES BEING IMPOSED ON THE GREEK EDUCATIONAL SYSTEM.

TPTG, Ta Paidia Tis Galarias: roughly translated as *The Kids of the Peanut Gallery*

Capitalist development in Greece during the '60s meant the growth of the secondary sector, namely construction and manufacturing (mainly based on the low cost of labor and not on big investments in fixed capital), the corresponding influx of peasants in the towns and the erosion of local subsistence economies. Gradually, this development created the need for a more skilled and diversified labor power. As a consequence, public education expanded, basic education became obligatory, and the population of university students started to rise. Wildcat strikes were on the daily agenda, campaigns on welfare, housing, or local issues were organized in almost every neighborhood. This was also the time when struggles for a "free and public education" began.

Reformist class struggles were back on the agenda after the fall of the dictatorship (1974) and education—in particular university education—became the main social climbing

41

"mechanism" since the '70s in Greece, as was the case in the advanced capitalist countries two decades earlier. Students of humble origin, coming from peasant or working class families, could find a permanent post in the public sector or a relatively secure job in the private sector if they possessed a university diploma (and furthermore even acquire a managerial position or set up their own successful small enterprise, especially in the construction sector). Thus, public university has become one of the most important institutions for the integration and satisfaction of "social expectations," with constantly increasing costs for the state budget.

The integration of "popular" demands helped in legitimating exploitative capitalist relations, which is one of the two basic functions of the modern democratic capitalist state—its other function being to provide for the smooth course of capitalist accumulation through the expanded reproduction of both labor power and capital. But class struggles during the '70s had the consequence that in the beginning of the '80s the state started to have great difficulties in exercising these two complementary but contradictory functions in a satisfactory way. "Social expectations" haven't been reduced even after the introduction of neoliberal policies in the '90s that aimed to resolve this contradiction through the deepening of divisions inside the working class. This is proved by the constant reappearance of struggles in the education sector.

What follows is a selection of texts we wrote during the last two years. These texts were an attempt at a theoretical analysis of the crisis of the educational system, i.e. the neoliberal restructuring process taking place for years now and the struggles against it. Apart from the university student occupations, another recent struggle that inspired these texts was the six-week strike of the primary school teachers in the autumn of 2006. Its duration and demands and the fact that some of us participated in this strike urged us to try to analyze it in the general context of the education crisis.

Although primary school teachers in Greece haven't yet felt the pressure of an alienating, standardized, and under constant evaluation labor process—like in the U.K. for example—there is a growing tendency to make school courses more and more intensive. Curriculums tend to become stricter, new teaching methods have been introduced, and quite recently new textbooks were imposed on teachers and students with a lot more difficult material than previously. The teachers' gradual loss of control over the teaching process is accompanied with the slow entry of sponsor companies selling educational programs. On top of it all education funding has been slashed as a part of a general policy of holding public expenses down.

TEN YEARS LATER

As we mentioned before, education, as the main capitalist institution that shapes, qualifies, and allocates the labor-power commodity in a continuously developing capitalist division of labor, has been expanding in terms of student population since the '60s in Greece. This development has given rise to new "popular" demands, expectations, opportunities of social mobility, and individual "successes." It has also led to the accumulation of tensions and contradictions, frustrations and individual "failures" (also called "failures of the schooling system"). Back in 1998, we participated in the movement against educational reform that went under the jarring name of "Act 2525." At that time, in the 7th issue of our journal we wrote that:

> The democratization of education that caused a mass production of expectations (and a corresponding temporary rise in civil servant and petit-bourgeois strata in the '70s and the '80s, e.g. in 1982 68.7% of university graduates worked in the public sector) created an inevitable structural crisis in the hierarchical division of labor and a crisis of discipline and meaning in school; in other words, a crisis of legitimacy that hit state education hard.

Ten years later, we are obliged to say that this crisis hasn't let up. No matter what you call this crisis—a "crisis of legitimacy," a "crisis in the selective-allocating role of education," a "crisis of expectations," or a "crisis in the correspondence of qualifications to career opportunities"—the truth is that education has been seriously crisis-ridden and it stands to reason that this situation will be maintained in the future.

The fact that state education is responsible for fulfilling a wide range of functions with great social importance dooms it to be in a constant state of crisis. To the extent that it has appropriated and integrated functions that historically were performed by other social institutions (the family, the working-class community, the workshop, the corporation), all social conflicts and contradictions manifest themselves in its terrain. Socialization is not confined to the family alone, apprenticeship as a means of imparting knowledge has almost ceased to exist as the task of the guild and individual capitalists do not have the right to organize the basic education of their workforce. As the role of state education is expanding, it is transformed inevitably into a terrain of social struggle, a terrain of class demands and mobilizations (and often, at the level of everyday life, of harsh competition among individuals). Furthermore, the fact that all these conflicts are taking place in the sphere of educational institutions makes them appear as aspects of an educational crisis and not of a crisis of exploitative class relations. From this standpoint, even if the modern school has lost its monopoly in the imparting and management of knowledge confronting powerful, and, perhaps, more alluring competitors such as the mass media and the Internet, nonetheless it retains its social role (and there is no sign that it can be replaced by any other social institutions). On the one hand it is used by the capitalist state as an instrument for the legitimization and reproduction of class relations, on the other hand it is used by the working class as an instrument for the mitigation of divisions and selection. Both of these two antagonistic objectives aim at the root of the reproduction of capitalist social relations.

43

The neoliberal attempts to restructure education that took place a decade ago in Greece had been opposed by students', pupils' and teachers' movements. In the aforementioned article, we had tried to give a theoretical account of this (multiple and, more or less, contradictory) response. One of our faults was that we took for granted that the capitalist State would be capable of weathering its crisis. By that time, the plan of the State to weather the crisis was visible; nonetheless it remained just a plan. Probing into its details, we referred to the various "educational programs that relate the EC educational directives to a postfordist organization of labor and align job qualifications with educational qualifications in order to train the future multifunctional worker-collaborator, who sees herself as a user/consumer of technological products and services." We also mentioned the role of "decentralization that is aiming not only at the fragmentation of resistance and social demands but also at the transfer of the education costs to the local communities, as well as at the strengthening of the 'autonomy' of the school unit, as a unit of 'self-evaluating, collaborating' teaching staff that self-manages the school (maybe with the help of financial sponsors)—possibly in competition with other units." Finally, we referred to the transformation of the teacher's identity from that of a state "functionary"—"a word that is rarely used today, while a few years before it indicated a prestigious identity and an obsolete social-democratic, 'humanitarian' self-perception"—to that of a "professional."

In the case of tertiary education, we had thought that the attempt to deepen the separation between workers with low qualifications and graduates of universities, as well as between graduates with low and average qualifications and graduates with high qualifications would have been successful. But one shouldn't take at face value the neoliberal propaganda in its attempt to reconcile the contradictions inherited from the period of social-democracy. It's true that in the beginning our adversaries gained several victories and, what's more, quite material ones, when they passed Act 2525 in 1997: the abolition of the teachers' list of seniority meant that there began an era when "lifelong training" and precarity would be enforced through the ideology of "meritocracy" and competition, replacing a status quo of formal equality in labour relations; in the case of secondary education, selection became more intensive with the creation of the new Comprehensive High School on the one hand and the "TEE" (technical institutes) on the other; in the case of the universities the state attempted to establish "lifelong training" through new training programs (called "PSE") imposing tuition fees.

However, there followed a series of open struggles: the movement of the unemployed teachers and the riots outside examination centers against the abolition of the above mentioned seniority list and the occupations of secondary schools and universities by pupils and students later that year. There were also several invisible reactions and refusals expressed by students, teachers and parents that whittled away the examinational monstrosity of the Comprehensive High School. The result was a relative relaxation of the selective process and a bridging of the separation between the "elite" entering the tertiary education and the "trash" graduating from the technical institutes. Furthermore, the "PSE" university programs were never really implemented and the initial plan for the abolition of the teachers' list of seniority was modified through the creation of a complex appointment system that was constituted of various lists that bypassed the provisions of the 1997 Act.

Due to class struggles, the use of EC money for setting up new university departments in the small towns in order to strengthen local revenues, and the formation and state management of a pool of reserve, complex, and cheap labor power for the tertiary sector, there has been a dramatic increase in the number of students in higher education. In 1993, only 26.7 percent of Greek citizens of an age between eighteen and twenty-one years followed higher education. In 2004, this number had risen to 60.3 percent.

In order to avoid a fiscal crisis, state expenditure on education as a proportion of the GNP remained stagnant for the last fifteen years (fluctuating between 3.5 and 4 percent). But in order to diminish "social expectations," the state had to do something more. So it changed its education strategy towards a purer neoliberal agenda. The first signs of this change of direction appeared at the beginning of this decade. Generally, this reorientation consists of two simple formulas: changes in the running of the education system (or at least a gradual movement to that direction) and inadequate state funding of education. The implementation of the first formula is visible in primary and secondary education in the planned cooperation between the public and the private sector in the construction and joint running of the new school buildings. In the future we will likely see the appearance of companies sponsoring primary and secondary schools, asserting their right to participate in the training of their future labor force. The revision of article 16 of the Greek constitution (more on this later) is also part of the same process, with regard to the universities. The reduction of public spending for the education sector is a constant characteristic of neoliberal policies. Nevertheless, it is a contradictory one condemned to create more problems than those it's supposed to solve. On the one hand, it helps the state to lessen its expenses and accelerate the process of education restructuring, claiming that it is a "social demand." On the other hand, individual capitalists (whether we refer to future sponsors of primary education or owners of private universities) have a bad reputation for being unable to go beyond their individual interests and place themselves at the disposal of the general interests of capitalist accumulation. In other words, an enterprise or sector cannot substitute the functions that historically have been assumed by the state.

In addition, neoliberals can hardly hide their ideological vulgarity. "Meritocracy," once a word meant to describe

45

a social utility, according to social-liberal ideology, has been stripped of its meaning. For neoliberals, the individual right to act as if one was a private entrepreneur leads to a historical diminution of the idea of social justice while "society" is perceived as a mere aggregate of individuals (or families-households, as Thatcher used to say) who are supposed to be in a state of constant competition. The problem for neoliberals is that such ideas undermine the basis of their political legitimacy, which in turn brings back the necessity to reinforce the State (and therefore the state provisions for education). It's a vicious circle.

The attempt to transform education into a capitalist enterprise is contradictory but constant at all levels. This attempt is visible in nursery schools with the new proposals about intensification of the curriculum and thus the earlier insertion of children in the world of evaluation, quantification, and, therefore, labor; in secondary education with the proposal—once again—from the National Education Council for a stricter selection of the students of the Comprehensive High Schools and the channeling of a part of the student population to early training through the "new" technical schools; in the new law for the universities that intensifies work in the partially and silently entrepreneurialized environment of higher public education since the '90s, threatening the unproductive (and thus surplus) intellectual proletariat with expulsion.

Visible and invisible struggles in the previous years have put limits on the capitalist valorization of public education and continue to do so nowadays. The university occupations that broke out in May 2006 and lasted for almost a year is a perfect example of a (spectacularly) visible struggle. In the second case, there belong latent processes that sabotage and undermine the imposed "innovations." E.g., the attempts to transform primary education teachers into "professionals"—executing orders from the Ministry of Education, carrying out "programs" and projects in order to find sponsors—were faced with rejection. A program called "Flexible Zone," which was supposed to connect schools to local commercial activities and was presented by the state intellectuals as an attempt to put into practice the old principles of radical and integral education, was never really implemented. Neither the talk about the "connection of school with everyday life," nor the babbling about the "abolition of the teacher-centered model" and the "development of collaboration among students" had any effect. In simple terms, most of the teachers could see that such programs would deepen the inequalities among pupils since they were connected with new evaluation systems and, after all, they would impose more unpaid labor on them. In the course of events, it became plain for all to see that the implementation of the aforementioned program was an issue of immense importance for the Ministry of Education, to the extent that it incorporated the basic lines of its policy: combination of central, bureaucratic control with decentralization, reduction of state funding and internalization of capital's logic while at the same time the participation of sponsors is encouraged in order to find resources for the realization of the projects.

WHEN THE LAW BREAKS

In this second part, we will try to summarize the struggles against capital's attempts to restructure education in the last few years. As we have already mentioned, the main weapons used by the State are the intensification of student and teacher labor, the inadequate funding of the education sector, and the stricter selection. In this manner, the State tries to respond to the crisis of the hierarchical allocation of the labor force that first manifested itself in the mid-'80s while at the same time it strives for the continuing legitimization of capitalist social relations—a combination that, let's say it once more, constantly tends to create new crises and contradictions.

The new bill for higher education, that was initially presented in the middle of 2006 (and was finally voted in the midst of the second round of the student movement in March 2007) attempted to legally institutionalize and bolster the existing tendencies toward entrepreneurialization and privatization in the universities. A series of provisions in this bill promoted the intensification of studies (for example, through setting an upper limit in the allowable years of study) and imposed underpaid or even unpaid student labor (for example, through the granting of student loans and reciprocal scholarships in exchange for part-time employment inside the university). Furthermore, university funding is getting connected with an evaluation process. Also, the attempt to revise article 16 of the Greek constitution, in order to permit the establishment of private universities, is intended to win the same end, i.e. to restructure public universities so that they are run more and more like private enterprises. Using the weapon of under funding and selective funding, the state inserts universities in a competitive environment. This has the consequence that universities are obliged to transform their activities into profit-making ones wherever this is possible. The basic criteria of their "good" operation and adequate state funding will be the size of their investments, the kind of research they undertake and their ability to impose the new disciplinary rules and regulations and encourage their students to individually invest in human capital.

Last but not least, the new bill changes the definition of the academic sanctuary. Academic sanctuary was the legal product of an earlier cycle of class struggles in Greece. It was introduced in the beginning of the '80s by the "socialist" government as an acknowledgement of the role of the "student" insurrection in 1973 in overthrowing the dictatorship and was one of the measures that intended to recuperate not only the militant student movement but the whole class movement of the '70s. Thanks to the right of sanctuary there have been constant occupations of universities for political campaigns and, to a certain extent, other social uses of university buildings (for example, university rooms in the center of Athens are used for political presentations, non-commercial parties

47

and so on without permit from the university authorities). The new bill restricts academic sanctuary, protects "the right to work," and makes provisions for specific penalties. From now on strikes by teaching or clerical staff, student occupations, etc. can be considered as actions that violate the law on academic sanctuary and as such could be repressed by the police.

The university occupation movement broke out in May 2006. Schools and departments entered into the struggle one after the other, and in a very short time almost all universities were occupied. The first round of the student movement managed to postpone the passing of the bill. The occupations started again in January 2007, when the government attempted to revise article 16 of the constitution, and lasted till the end of March. The movement managed to postpone the revision of the constitution for the next two or three years (the revision process is slow and it requires a large majority backing in Parliament). Nevertheless, the bill became a law on the 8th of March, while outside Parliament a fierce riot, lasting many hours took place.

The movement gained some concessions (not essential ones), but the new law has not been fully enforced yet. There are signs that a new movement may appear when the real enforcement of the law will commence. As far as the qualitative characteristics of the movement are concerned, it is true that occupations were more vivid in terms of student participation, organization of presentations, workshops, and so on during the first round of the movement and not so much in the second one. There were only a few minority actions that tried to spread the movement into other arenas (like for example blockades or interventions in workplaces like call centers where some students work) but the participation in demonstrations was really massive all over Greece (on the 8th of March it is estimated that forty to fifty thousand people participated in the demo).

In order to understand why this movement grew so large, it's not enough to refer only to the changes in the legislation because some of the changes affected mostly future students. We must view this movement as an expression of the accumulated dissatisfaction a whole generation of working class youth has been experiencing since the previous reforms, ten years ago. These reforms were instrumental in imposing intensified work rates in the school and in the realm of proper wage labor. It is not accidental that the mobilizations broke out in the midst of an examination period. Even if the official spokesmen of the movement never stopped babbling that the academic year "will not be lost" and the examinations will be taken after the movement, the occupations had also the character of an "examination strike," especially during May and June 2006. A lot of students, both active and "passive" participants in the movement, didn't want to take the exams before the summer vacations, asserting thus their denial of intensified work rates. Furthermore, the mobilized students raised the question of the "free" reproduction of their labor power (even if in a contradictory way) through the demand for a "public and free education." This demand was expressed more explicitly by the minority tendencies inside the movement that made the demands for "free board and lodging" as well as for "free transport for all" which were promoted with a few blockades of roads and train stations and some interventions in the metro stations.

Although the 1997 reform in secondary education had managed to discipline a generation of students for some years, this was a temporary victory. This generation could not be stopped from expressing its discontent for a life that is increasingly characterized by insecurity and fear. The students realized that the promises for a "successful career" will be true only for a minority of them. At the same time, they revolted against an everyday activity that looks similar to any other kind of work. This revolt against student labor was given a boost by a significant number of students who already directly experienced exploitation and alienation as proper wage laborers. In this context, there were interventions for better working conditions in call centers where students work. Nevertheless, this was not a dominant tendency in the movement, since most of the students depend on their parents while many others still hope that in one way or another they will become "professionals." Thus, "workers" were mostly considered as external supporters and it was mainly their parents. Of course, connection with other parts of the working class is directly dependent on the existence of struggles outside the university. For example, when a local struggle for better working and service conditions broke out at a state health center in a village near Thessaloniki, solidarity was expressed by the striking students of the Medicine School.

The strike of the teachers in primary education was called by the teachers' union during the first round of the student movement after a proposal made by the leftist trade unionists. It must be noted that there was no offensive from the state before the call for the strike. The list of official demands covered both wages and working conditions. It was a rather huge list of demands but although it came "from above," and in particular from the leftist group that took the initiative, it nonetheless gave voice to the needs of teachers indirectly.

The strike began on the 18th of September 2006 as a five-day action and lasted for six weeks. The union had no intention to continue the strike after the end of the first week, made clear by the attitude of the trade unionists in the general assemblies that took place after the first week of the strike. However, the fact that participation in the strike was very high, especially in Athens and some other urban areas (about 70–80%), as well as the fact that the ministry did not make any concessions, made it very difficult for the union to step back. At this point it may be helpful to note that some teachers in rural areas didn't participate, maybe because they have other jobs as a sideline, e.g. farming. So, although the strike was called by the union leadership,

49

in the process it became more of a rank-and-file action. Participation remained rather high in some urban areas for the whole six weeks and massive demonstrations took place at the center of Athens as well. On the other hand, participation in the assemblies was not high with the exception of some local union departments. Strike committees were organized right from the start. These committees were mainly executives of the decisions taken in the local assemblies and there was no coordination amongst them. As usual, the assemblies were an arena of various conflicts. The struggle however remained under the control of the union, partially due to the fact that the leftist group that somehow represents and brings together many radical elements in this sector took over the administration of the union during the strike.

Now, let's turn our attention to the real reasons of the strike and its militancy. Firstly, we have to stress that teachers cannot be considered a privileged sector of the working class: the entry wage of a teacher is about 900 euros while the minimum wage in Greece is about 700 euros. But the wage demands did not take precedence over all others.

The two basic demands, that were really made by the rank-and-file, were: higher state expenses for public education; and second, an end to the ongoing "marketization of school." The first demand expresses an outright opposition to the transfer of the costs of reproduction of labor power to the working class. In a way, teachers made a demand on behalf of the whole working class. The straitened conditions and the economic misery of the school is identified in the eyes of the teachers with the misery of the lack of meaning in their work. The traditional, positive self-perception of the teacher collapses under the weight of economic neglect and alienation. The fact that all this was not expressed explicitly in the demands while it was evident in a lot of meetings between teachers and parents, in some texts, in discussions and in the streets is indicative of the weakness of the rank-and-file to express itself substantially as well as of its inability to get rid of the official union spokesmen.

The protests against the "marketization of school" was the second main characteristic of the strike. The fury of the strikers was directed toward the looming financial sponsors, mystifying the fact that public education is already connected with capital and that this relation cannot be solely identified with sponsors. Overcoming this narrow point of view, teachers could expand their understanding of everyday alienation. Apart from loose words, this feeling against work wasn't articulated into a discourse and it was expressed only through the large duration of the strike. Slogans like "we will strike till the year 3000" and "we give up the next monthly wage, too" express the desire not to return to the daily alienation of the classroom. Or else it is very difficult to explain the gap separating the lengthy duration of the strike and its militancy and the more or less predictable union demands. Our interpretation of the events is further backed by the fact that this was an offensive strike: without a visible attack from the State and with a list of demands which only indirectly expressed the needs of the strikers, it would otherwise be difficult to understand why many teachers didn't want to go back to work even after six weeks on strike.

Following this line of explanation, we can better understand the wage demands. The demand for a 500 euros wage rise was a demand for compensation for the increasing deterioration of working conditions. As such it was more teacher-centered and sectoral and less a working-class demand: slogans around wages appear to say that "work has become impersonal, alienating and intensified—at least it shouldn't be so underpaid." Nevertheless, the need to come together with other parts of the working class (mainly parents but also other workers who supported the strike) could not be expressed through the demand for a good wage for the teachers (which also implies that intellectual labor is superior to manual). Common ground could only be based on common needs, that's why the initial demand was transformed into a demand for "1400 euros for everyone" in the middle of the strike and was accepted by the majority of teachers then. However, real communication with the "others" was confined to common demos with a minority of students and some meetings with parents organized by the strikers.

As we said, the strike ended after six weeks. Facing the intransigence of the State and not being able to transcend the limits posed by their social role and the union representation, the strikers did not manage to make the extra step that was necessary. But, of course this was not easy: a collective challenge and critique of the alienating and selective nature of education accompanied by a critique of the union would amount to something much more than a strike; it would amount to an insurrection.

The strike didn't win any material concessions, but were there any interesting aspects in it? Our answer will be positive in two aspects. First, the strike delegitimized to some extent a neoliberal state that claims to guarantee a "qualitative" and "public and free" education system. Second, at a more educational level, a strike of one and a half months annulled the image of a "smoothly" functioning school system. And what's more, it crashed the image of the teacher as a professional, an organ of the State for the enforcement of its ideological control and a "petit bourgeois" that, supposedly, enjoys his/her privileged position. Nevertheless, the way that the strike ended with no perspective for the future and no material gains, had negative consequences and clearly shows that a part of the working class cannot gain much if it remains isolated, however militant it is.

This became obvious early this year when the government introduced a new law which was an attack on welfare benefits and pensions. According to this new law on social security, there will be an increase of the retirement age even for mothers with under-age kids, a decrease in pension earnings and an increase in the number of stamps needed for medical and sickness insurance, something that hits mainly young,

51

part-time, and precarious workers hardest. Despite the slashing attack on all workers (students included) the resistance of teachers and students was very weak.

The supermarket expropriations were very successful

Nikos: An anarchist from Athens, active for about ten years

One action that started happening more frequently in the year before December were expropriations in the supermarkets. We would gather with a group of at least thirty people, mask up, run into a major supermarket and fill carts with food. The timing was very important. Inside the store everyone knew what they had to do, everyone stayed in a group and didn't go down any aisle alone, and we were all out of there in a minute. Sometimes people would calm the workers, saying that it was an expropriation and that all the food would be distributed for free, we were against property but we didn't want to hurt anybody. And we always made sure to get out of there very quickly. It all took just a few seconds.

In Athens we usually did these expropriations close to open air markets, when lots of people were outside shopping. That way we would not have to go far to find a place where lots of people were gathered to leave the food. After we did this a few times, when the people saw us, they would cry out excitedly, "It's them! It's them!" and they would cheer us and they were very happy to take the food. It was a nice feeling, to include all these people in our illegality. Also, they learned not to be afraid of the *koukoulofori*. The people who were masked up, dressed in black, and doing outrageous things were on their side. That was very important.

The Prisoners' Hunger Strike

On the 3rd of November, the Greek prisoners launched a major struggle that quickly spread to all twenty-one prisons in the country. Prisoners released sixteen principal demands and announced their struggle would take three stages: first, the refusal of prison food; second, full hunger strike; and third, if the authorities had still not agreed to the demands, a general uprising.

Their demands were:

1. Abolition of cumulative disciplinary charges.

2. Reduction of the sentence limit (the proportion of the sentence the prisoner had to serve, as a minimum) from 3/5 to 3/7 and abolition of the 4/5 limit for drug related crimes.

3. A 3-year reduction of all sentences to relieve overcrowding, and rejection of the new panopticon prisons that isolate the prisoners from the urban social body.

4. Abolition of all juvenile prisons, and their replacement with open structures meant to take care of youth.

5. Reduction of the sentence limit that allows 25 years of continuous detention. Reduction of the minimum detention time for conditional release from 16 to 12 years.

6. Reduction of mandatory minimums, more days of furlough.

7. Limited use of pretrial detention and shortened maximum pretrial detention to 12 months from 18.

8. Against the use of vengeful sentencing meant to kill prisoners with long sentences. Shorter sentences and greater use of suspended sentences and conditional release.

9. 24-hour full medical service and psychiatric service, improved hygiene in baths and toilets, transportation to hospitals in ambulances, not in police cars.

10. The right to paid work, classes, technical training, and access to education outside the prisons.

11. Free access to the prisons for social and political institutions, lawyers, doctors, human rights organizations and international organizations, free circulation of political and educational press with no exceptions.

12. Alternative forms of detention such as agricultural prisons and partial liberty as well as community service.

13. Increase of free visits with privacy.

14. Work and access to creative activities for all, and sentence reduction for work.

15. Right to serve their sentence in the country of origin for people from other countries, if they choose.

16. Humane and faster transportation between prisons.

In the first stage, 8,000 of Greece's 12,300 prisoners participated in the first stage. Starting November 7, 1,000 prisoners went on hunger strike, though the number soon grew to 7,000, with seventeen having sewn their mouths shut. Thousands of non-participating prisoners supported the strike and helped fellow prisoners who were in a weakened condition due to fasting. Many anarchist prisoners participated in the hunger strike, while others wrote and circulated texts in support, while criticizing the tactics of hunger striking and the making of demands. Many solidarity actions were realized outside the prisons, including concerts, huge protest marches, and attacks.

On November 20, the government caved to most of the demands, agreeing to reduce Greece's prison population to 6,800 by April, releasing all prisoners who had served 1/5 of their sentence, if under two years, and 1/3 of their sentence, if longer, without exceptions. The government announced that additionally, the law would be changed so that for all sentences under five years, the convicted person could pay a fine proportionate to the sentence instead of going to prison; pretrial detention would be limited at twelve months for many offenses; furloughs would increase slightly; accumulative disciplinary penalties would be limited but not abolished; and more people with serious health problems such as AIDS would be granted conditional release. It is worth noting that juvenile prisons, a key component in the disciplinary transformation of society under neoliberalism, were not abolished, and most of the reforms affected those with shorter sentences, thus dividing them from the long-term, non-reformable prisoners, those considered to be hardened criminals.

The Prisoners' Committee responded by calling off their hunger strike, but announcing that:

> We the prisoners treat this amendment as a first step, a result of our struggle and of the solidarity shown by society. Yet it fails to cover us, it fails to solve our problems. With our struggle, we have first of all fought for our dignity. And this dignity we cannot offer as a present to any minister nor any screw.

We shall tolerate no arbitrary acts, no vengeful relocations, no terrorizing disciplinary act. We are standing and we shall stay standing... Finally, we offer our thanks to the solidarity movement, to every component, party, medium, and militant who stood by us with all and any means of his or her choice, and we declare that our struggle against these human refuse dumps and for the victory of all our demands continues.

The prisoners gained a new ability to co-ordinate their actions

N. & Mi: Two anarchists from Exarchia engaged in solidarity for the prisoners, among other things

The most important conclusion of this struggle was that prisoners gained a new ability to coordinate their actions inside the prisons of all Greece, they gained a common platform of solidarity and they gained dignity. There also appeared this feeling, this consciousness. Vaggelis Palis and Yiannis Dimitrakis wrote a letter that explained this feeling from the terrace of their prison during the 2007 prison revolt, there they explained the amazing feeling of solidarity they gained that day when they experienced the end of all the differences and all the internal fights, the elimination of all the different nationalities, the end of ghettos inside the prison, the liberating feeling of the struggle in the terrace of your jail when all the prisoners come together as one.

To not idealize the prisoners, the important thing is that year after year thousands of people in the prisons understand that they have to fight against the drugs, the snitching, the separation and alienation, and the egotism. The prisoners

55

have to realize that all these are basic elements of the creation of the society of prisons, and they have to fight against this.

It was not important for the anarchists how they carried out the struggle. For all of us it was important how the prisoners themselves realized the struggle. Because it was a struggle for demands, the important thing was how many of their demands they succeeded in winning, and the anarchist movement was ready to struggle in solidarity with the prisoners so they could gain more. The anarchists believed they had to go further, to not relax after the announcement that the government would grant some of their demands. That they could gain much greater victories if they continued. We have to say that during the days of the hunger strike the government announced that they would release almost half the prisoners of Greece. But it became apparent at the end of the hunger strike that this will be through a long procedure that takes place drop by drop. But this still shows the power of the struggle.

We have to clarify that the political analysis and the efforts of the anarchist movement in Greece focuses their solidarity on the anarchist prisoners of course, but a big difference between them and the anarchist movements of other countries is that the anarchist movement of Greece campaigns through the publication of thousands of pamphlets and protests for the elimination of prison itself. It attacks the entire prison system. Because of this the influence of anarchist ideas appears inside the prisons, and the prisoners show solidarity to the anarchist prisoners. From the dictatorship until today there was never even a month without anarchist prisoners in the prison. The anarchist movement organized solidarity for their prisoners, the anarchist prisoners influenced the other prisoners, and the prisoners influenced the anarchist movement, without differentiating between social and political prisoners. Because when the anarchists are prisoners they fight for all people on the inside.

The Left organizations in Greece, when they speak about the prisoners they speak about improving the conditions and for the human rights of the prisoners. On the other hand, when the anarchists speak about the prisoners, even if it is a poster or pamphlet that talks about solidarity with a specific prisoner, they include mention of the liberation of all prisoners and the destruction of the prison system, so even if it has the goal of expressing solidarity with one person, it opens the way towards the anarchist proposition of society without imprisonment.

But the importance is the strategy, the way of expressing your ideas to society. Of course the prisoners agree the conditions have to improve, but when we speak to the society the anarchists are explicit about their highest, authentic goal and message. A society without prisons. In this way it becomes another anarchist struggle.

56

You Talk About Material Damages, We Speak About Human Life: PERCEPTIONS OF VIOLENCE AMONG GREEK ANARCHIST GROUPS

Panagiotis Papadimitropoulos: from Void Network

Perhaps the best manifestation of human agency, especially as far as the formation of the modern world is concerned, is that which accompanies the ideas and practices of social movements. During the course of the 20th century different groups of people have struggled for diverse political ends using different political means with the aim to transform the social order. Everywhere around us we experience the product of past and present collective attempts to bring about social change, that is to replace old meanings and forms with new ones according to the ideas, dreams, and aspirations of social groups.

Social anthropology, being particularly interested in the meanings and symbols that structure and guide social practice, has always been sensitive to the viewpoint of the weak and the oppressed because of its understanding of the workings of culture and the differential positions of power that are created within it. Especially after the mid-seventies through a series of ethnographies, such as those by James Scott, Jean Comarrof, Eric Wolf (Samuel Popkin), it approached resistance as a means of facing and critically negotiating the power that was imposed on local societies by world structures of domination and inequality. From the '70s onwards Marxist social theory detached itself from the model of "basis and superstructure" in which the emphasis was laid on the economic sphere. This change contributed to the promotion of anti-essentialist perspectives and thought with many different branches. The diverse readings of Gramsci, Foucault, French post-structuralism, and the multifarious feminist theory during the '80s engendered a new field of exploration of culture through the study of subjectivity and power. As a primary consequence, a shift occurred in the conception of culture as a social totality whose meanings are shared by all of its members. The turn was to "culture" as a field of continuous change, opposition, and negotiation of meanings.

The focus has turned on the social context and conditions in which different meanings and perceptions of social reality appear. But since this is conceived in the plural as "contexts," the conditions, the practices, and the "places" in which particular phenomena manifest themselves are not reduced to a unified structural coherence that derives from the economy, the values or some functional needs of the social system. The basic change that this theoretical move brought about has been the questioning of naturalized categories or conceptual tools, such as those of class, gender, or for that matter of society as an "objective" reality toward their dynamic conception as categories that develop historically through dominant discourses.

57

Thus, a central position in non-reductionist approaches is given to discourse analysis as a methodology that imprints and reveals with greater clarity the conceptual universe of subjects and its relation to particular institutions and social practices that construct collective or individual identities. (Scott Joan Wallash, 1988, *Gender and the Politics of History*). The understanding that identity is not something static but in constant flux is now common place. Much theoretical work has gone into deconstructing essentialist notions of identity based on sameness, replacing them with a conception of identity as multiple, plural or hybrid, and based on difference. In the context of talking about social reproduction and change in a discussion about social movements, we should follow Sherry Ortner in asking how exactly and in which conditions individuals or social groups perceive themselves in a particular way which, on the one hand, excludes alternative perceptions while, on the other, constructs acting subjects who select particular ways of action and reject others.

Perhaps a useful methodological and theoretical route comes from a creative match between discourse analysis and the theory of symbolic meaning in a perspective that views every social action and cultural form—and thus both power and the resistance to it—as constituting cultural constructs. That is, relations that are arranged through the human capacity to construct meaning, to interpret reality and communicate through the use of symbols, ones with a "life" of their own.

What I mean by this is that culture is perceived as inherently a historical process. For Ortner and Dirks the "place" where the cultural order meets with history in a creative combination is the discourse about power. Hence, they speak about "culture as emergent from relations of power and domination, culture as a form of power and domination, culture as a medium in which power is both constituted and resisted." The focus on phenomena of resistance and domination does not imply some essentialist view of culture. Power is not considered "some universal 'drive' lodged in individuals nor some elementary force transcending society and history" (Ortner). On the contrary, power is interlinked with freedom or resistance in a way that the one defines the field of diffusion of the other. It always appears in an historically specific cultural context in which man as a socio-historical being composes an entire matrix of meanings and conceptions that include a wide range of desires and emotions but also of inequalities that every time are formulated and expressed in the idiom of existent cultural meanings.

Anthropological approaches to social movements and resistance have focused on the culturally specific expression of these movements. Taking culture as a central component of movements, these approaches move beyond debates about resistance and rebellion as "irrational" outbursts by subordinate peoples or carefully calculated strategic expressions of dissent, to ones that talk about movements as cultural struggles over meaning. Generally speaking, social movements and collective action have emerged in close connection with the development of structural inequalities, marginalization, and exclusion on the one hand, and the ideas of rights, social justice, and entitlements on the other. Different groups and organizations have built platforms of solidarity and mobilization to make claims and express their grievances targeting either the state or capital or international institutions. If in the past social movements or collective action have emerged and concentrated protest within nation-states or colonial states, with the increasing interconnectedness of different locations and social spaces, currently social movements have attained global dimensions and created transnational communities.

In a context of global flows of identities, researchers like Marianne Maeckelbergh have focused on the decision making practices within the anti-globalization movement and on the ways democratic values are practiced on a global scale through network structures that support and diffuse social movements. Very interestingly, Maeckelbergh sees prefigurative practices as a strategic movement practice from which local action becomes part of global action. Eeva Berglund, looking at groups of environmentalists in Germany and Finland, has focused on the ideas about citizenship, independent knowledge and political practice that are generated through activism, and has argued that "environmentalist sensibilities that lead to activism arise out of shared experiences of loss of trust in 'official' sources of knowledge as well as unsatisfactory environmental conditions." Activism in this context has been approached as a field of social practice that contests the legitimacy of state-produced scientific knowledge, and creates transnational ideas of independence from and opposition to state or corporate power which is seen by people as hostile to the concept of a civil society. This is not to say that we can talk about universalizing models of political transformation since investigations of "civil society" discourses have exposed how such concepts as "citizenship" and "democracy" are deployed in varied forms by different actors (Gal and Kligman, 2000/ Hann and Dunn, 1995, about postsocialist countries). We should therefore agree with Berglund that "we must attend to the ways in which activists make sense of local political cultures even as they attempt to transform them and effect social change."

Closer to what I will talk about today, Jeffrey Juris has had an interest in studying activist and transnational networking in the context of the anti-globalization movement in what he calls "militant ethnography." Militant ethnography, according to Juris, involves "practice-based and politically committed research that is carried out in horizontal collaboration with social movements." Juris rightly remarks that "diverse activist networks physically express their contrasting political visions and identities through alternative forms of direct action" (2007). This action becomes visible through the communication of powerful and emotive images of protest that are diffused both by activist networks and mainstream media with different interpretations. Furthermore, Juris has also focused

59

on the Black Bloc, that is the anarchist groups that have become particularly violent during counter summit protests (Seattle, Prague, Genova, Thessaloniki, etc.). He approaches their violence as performative violence, which he defines as "a form of meaningful interaction through which actors construct social reality based on available cultural templates." His argument, with which I agree, is that Black Bloc performative violence tends to be neither random nor senseless.

On the one hand, performative violence of anarchist groups operates on an instrumental level, that of the attempt to directly transform the social environment. On the other, we may use "performative violence" to "refer to symbolic ritual enactments of violent interaction with a predominant emphasis on communication and cultural expression." In fact, the two are interlinked. In a context of political action, and following a particular perception of social reality, activists seek to effect social transformation by staging symbolic confrontation based on "the representation of antagonistic relationships and the enactment of prototypical images of violence" (Schrober and Schmidt, 2001). Very importantly, the ritualistic element seems to be ever-present, especially as far as clashes with the police are concerned. A riot takes place (and in Athens riots occur almost every week), anarchists (if they participate) decide to attack particular targets that represent the State and capitalism, they move first, the police respond, activists set up barricades, and a small scale street confrontation begins with anarchists throwing rocks or Molotov cocktails and the police responding with tear gas and, when possible, with arrests.

As Kertzer has pointed out ritual is important in all political systems and there are many ways that ritual is employed in politics. Ritual, defined broadly as symbolic behavior that is socially standardized and repetitive, is used to create reality for the people around it, while at the same time channels emotion, guides cognition, and organizes social groups. In addition, ritual does not only legitimize authority since it is also used by those who want to overthrow it. That is, there are rites that legitimize authority and rites that delegitimize it. Ritual characterizes conservation or continuity as well as change, transformation, or revolution. At the same time as all human conduct and perception of reality are symbolically organized, that is they represent not an essence of things but rather a relation between them, it follows that politics arises as a sphere of symbolic meanings, a sphere that on the one hand rests on existent habitus, while, on the other, creates particular discourses about power, ideal forms of social relations, the role of man, and the "nature of things" at large.

Symbols are means, indeed the primary means, by which we give meaning to the world around us. They allow us to interpret what we see, and of course they allow us to see ourselves in certain ways while excluding others. Perhaps the most striking aspect of this symbolic process is, as Kertzer remarks, "its taken-for-granted quality." People are not generally aware that they themselves and their culture endow the world with their own symbolically constructed version of reality. On the contrary, people believe the world simply presents itself in the form it is perceived. "But what else could you call a hippopotamus" Geertz remarks, and this, fortunately or unfortunately, is also true for anthropologists—at least in their non-academic activities. We could not get out of bed in the morning (at least for those who want to get out of bed) if we did not subscribe to this view, for if we fully recognized the extent to which our notions of reality are the product of an artificially constructed symbol system, it would be, as Kenneth Burke pointed out, "like peering over the edge of things into an ultimate abyss."

Through symbols we confront the experiential chaos that surrounds us, and create order. By objectifying our symbolic categories, rather than recognizing them as products of human creation, we see them as somehow the products of nature, "things" that we simply perceive and recognize. Indeed, as many (e.g. Cassirer and Bauman) have remarked, the very distinction we make between the objective world and the subjective world is itself a product of humanly created symbols that divide the world of fact from the world of opinion.

However, this is not to say that people or cultures can freely create any symbolic system imaginable, or that all such constructs are potentially equally tenacious in the material world. There is a continuous interaction between the ways people have for dealing with the physical and social universe and the actual contours of that universe. As Sahlins has emphasized, when symbolic systems collide with refractory social or physical forces, the potential for change in the symbolic system is ever present. Moreover, symbols do not simply arise spontaneously, nor is the continuing process of redefinition of the symbolic universe a matter of chance. Both are heavily influenced by the distribution of resources found in the society and the relationships that exist with other societies. The key is two-fold: no meanings appear outside the existent tank of cultural materials, but at the same time it is human creativity that produces change and alternative understandings by situated individuals. Though symbols provide people a way of understanding the world, it is people who produce new symbols and transform the old. This seems to be especially true for societies like our own in which, due to their complexity, everyday practices depend on a higher degree of abstraction.

Having said this, I consider the social practices that I will refer to as fundamentally symbolic action that is organized around a particular understanding and categorization of the social world, largely subversive. Although a lot has been said about anti-globalization movements in the context of a reaction to processes of globalization, my interest here is mostly on the violence performed by anarchist groups in Athens, and thus it is not necessarily or directly linked with the anti-globalization movement. Their discourse producing a particular perception of major political institutions and their function, such as the State, as well as of basic social relations and forms such as ideas around wage-labor or the commodity form have been around long before popular discourse about globalization begins. So I am more concerned with an agonistic rhetoric that characterizes anarchist discourse in Athens and that in my view both constructs identities and opens the way to the performance of violent acts, mainly in the public space, by creating a certain perception of antagonists that the individual not only has to encounter but also to win.

December has been quite unique in Athens and to some extent in the whole country. The murder of a young boy by a police officer in the area of Exarchia, well known to the whole country for its anarchist activity, led to what many saw as a spontaneous insurrection that lasted for about two weeks. Thousands of people went out to the streets, demonstrating and fighting against the police. Riots became very violent, and hundreds of banks, luxury shops, and cars were smashed and burned, as well as whole buildings. Extensive looting was taking place, while in the square outside the Parliament the burning of the city's Christmas tree, symbol of the city's prosperity, order, and normality was reported by the media as proof that the country had surrendered itself to chaos and to the destructive intentions of mindless individuals who did not know how to protest. In the first four days the riot police launched more than four tons of tear gas in Athens alone, and had to import more from Israel because they had run out of it! Barricades were set up in major avenues of the cities especially outside the squatted universities that people used as their base of operations (in Greece the universities have a constitutionally guaranteed asylum in recognition of the events of November '73, so according to the law the police cannot enter). In the context of political processes run mainly by anarchist groups, open assemblies were taking place every day in the universities to discuss means for the continuation of the upheaval. Many texts were being printed and distributed in different areas of the city.

Although it is difficult to interpret what exactly has happened there are a few certain things that I could mention. Firstly, that the death of the child was only the spark. The causes are certainly deeper and are related to specific ideas of particular people about Greek society and capitalist society as a whole, as well as to specific underprivileged statuses (e.g. a lot of immigrants participated, feeling that they were striking back in some way). Secondly, the people (people from different age groups, social classes and ethnic groups) who participated were a minority. Most people could not understand where this thing was coming from. Finally, being to a large extent a destructive force, the insurrection did not express any specific demands—besides the rage against police brutality—that made many people wonder even more about its character. It seems to me that some people (especially anarchist groups with ideological discourse and orientations) knew quite well what they were doing whereas others responded more spontaneously. But for the anarchists too the major question—an ideological one—has been what the next step would be, what this situation could leave behind as a seed. Clearly, for some this was resistance against the State. The antagonist was the State represented both in the places where commodities were being destroyed and in the riot police that were being attacked.

The crucial factor here is a powerful discursive formation, that of anarchist ideology that, largely based on Marxism, is characterized both by a specific revolutionary narrative about the social world and a specific conception of the individual. It begins with the presupposition that a better and more just society, in which social and economic equality can be attained, is possible. A belief in the self-determination of the individual and the autonomy or self-management of his community considers that hierarchically structured social relations produce societies of inequality and exploitation in which people are divided into the oppressors, those who have power, and the oppressed, those who are subjected to the control and the power of the former. From this perspective a polarized conception of the social world creates a dichotomous view of society as constituted by subjects categorized on the basis of their access to material resources that is thus equated to the power to control. In this manner, the majority of people are presented, to a large extent, as lacking agency, not being able to determine the conditions of their own existence, but being subjected to the will of individuals and institutions that manipulate them in order to further their utilitarian needs and interests.

In this context, anarchist ideology and discourse aspire to a general ideal of "human freedom" which is defined as a condition wherein the individual lives and creates according to his/her desires that, in turn, spring from a reference to the concept of self. The self should be the creator of both the community and its institutions that are presented in direct opposition to the existent ones as consolidated on the basis of man's "real" needs, that is not following economic interest which only supports a class society. Interestingly, the utopian society of anarchists is not one of absolute harmony, but one where conflict appears when people themselves decide so. This is why the nation-state is considered an artificial construct that homogenizes and unites people by force for the promotion of class and power interests of the elite. The abolition of the State comes as the answer to the issue of ideal political organization that, according to this view, must aim to the autonomy of a smaller community.

The vehicle of this fundamental social change is considered to be the mass mobilization of people, the movement to revolution which can bring "human freedom" when people realize the fetters of the State and its mechanisms, but also their own power to act shaping their conditions of life. From this point of view, representative democracy is viewed as an oppressive system of governance that maintains the distinction between rulers and ruled, and perpetuates in a sly way human heteronomy.

63

At the same time, especially among the groups I am focusing on, wage-labor is considered perhaps the most oppressive condition in modern societies and it is thus often referred to as "wage-slavery," mainly because of the restrictions it is thought to pose to "human desire," but also because according to the Marxist point of view, it reifies what is in fact a social relation. Indeed, the notion of "desire" is a fundamental one—and for the researcher a crucial factor—because it implies an essential self that differs from the social self in its will to live in ways that are not related and are contrary to the restrictions put by dominant culture. And as I said, perhaps the most important such restriction is considered to be wage-labor. Labor is identified with economic interest, which is ethically inferior in the hierarchy of values. But more importantly, wage-labor is considered to be the greatest compromise of an individual's personal freedom. From here springs the disrespect for the workplace (a place that is by definition presented as oppressive) and the will for one to physically attack it, especially when it reflects the interests of capital. In this manner, what is the workplace of some becomes the target of violent attacks by others, since these are perceived not only as spaces of exploitation and alienation but also of promotion of material-capitalist interest.

These observations concerning the anarchist ideal and discourse cannot be of much help in understanding performative violence if they are not contextualized within Greek political history, a history of intense political violence.

Towards the end of the sixties anarchist ideas began to appear in Greece as a further radicalization of the already existent social struggle and the wider left social movement that fought through severe strikes, demonstrations, and clashes with the police for social and labor rights in a society in which the civil war of 1946–49, between the national government and the communists, had cost the lives of about 70,000 people, with tens of thousands of leftists exiled to small inhospitable Greek islands. In contrast to other countries, like Spain, anarchism in Greece appears, mainly, as an urban political culture embraced by—but not limited to—the young (although its influence is also present in rural mobilizations at the beginning of the 20th century). The initial ideological influences came from the French May of '68 but also from the legacy of the American counterculture, and blended with the Greek left tradition of disrespect for a state that from the beginning of the 20th century was characterized by its nationalistic orientation, policies, and discourse and that until 1974—and especially during the years of the dictatorship 1967–1974—was fighting against what it perceived as the communist threat. Very importantly, in 1974 the Greek Communist Party was recognized as a legal political party and officially became a member party of the Parliament. At the level of ideology this change meant an important withdrawal since the Communist Party could no longer evangelize the possibility of a revolution.

Thus, towards the end of the seventies anarchists (that part of the libertarians who found the Left to be conservative both in lifestyles and in their political agenda) began to perceive the use of violence as an authentic expression of the old political and social dream of revolution and themselves as continuing and persisting with the conditions of the civil war, a war that had ended with the communists' defeat and surrendering of arms. Violence, in this context, performed not as terroristic acts by groups like November 17th, which planted bombs and assassinated people, but in the open public space during riots, or today as small scale hits on targets such as police stations or specific companies and banks by a number of people with a "teaching them a lesson" logic. Violence of this sort began to express the authenticity of intentions, "the most honest way" as an informant said, to preserve the flame of revolution. It is in this sense that violence during riots represents those who see themselves as keeping alive the dream of revolution. And as Pratt has demonstrated about anarchism in Andalusia, the moral vision of anarchists for a new social order without class divisions has given rise to a revolutionary narrative in which revolution is associated with destruction.

In the early eighties came the influence of the German movement of autonomen-chaoten and its symbols. Anarchists in Greece, now operating independently from the numerous leftist groups, began to identify themselves as "anarchist" and to use the now well-known circled "A." Most importantly, they borrow from the German movement the use of the hood/mask, as a symbol of an unexpected attack by an invisible and fearful aggressor (today most would argue that the primary reason for one wearing a mask is not to be traced by the surveillance systems of the police, thus downplaying its powerful symbolic value).

From the early nineties onwards, anarchist groups started to have an interest in influencing society more than they did in the past—they became more social and less marginal, in a sense—not necessarily with the aim of forming a movement, but more in the sense of their attempt to be politically visible during times of important social problems. A basic idea begins to take root that of the transformation of everyday life brought about both by Situationists like Debord and Vaneigem and the German and Italian Autonomia. So, in riots for instance, they begin to respond to specific central decisions and plans that came with neoliberalism after the fall of the Soviet Union, such as privatizations. But most importantly, through a public discourse that manifested itself in thousands of printed pamphlets and street posters distributed in the whole country, they further cultivated the idea of "an anarchist attack."

Now, the whole idea of the attack has great significance, it appears a lot in anarchist discourse and can enlighten us on perceptions of violence. I am referring to a widespread view that anarchists hold for themselves, according to which it is they who attack. In this manner, they are self-identified not so much as a movement of resistance—since this characterization is followed by connotations of a weak

65

position—but as a movement of offense/attack/assault. Practically this means that the police (which are perceived as a class mechanism that stands as a barrier between the people and capital) should not be the ones, strategically speaking, to make the first move, that is they should not be the ones who attack first. On the contrary, it is the anarchists who retain the momentum, that is they select the occasion, exact place/spot and the exact time of the performance of a violent act. As a consequence, they do not perceive themselves as victims of police brutality. Being the aggressor prevents one from victimizing oneself. Not victimizing oneself means that even if you "lose" there is reference to the category of an agonistic dignity—as indeed occurs—which thus increases. So, accordingly, the struggle is always offensive, thus the slogans with such strong imagery: "clashing opens passages" or "think revolutionary, act aggressively."

This is why the discourse in brochures and street posters presents themselves as the aggressors with the use of an eager rhetoric of continuous war, self-sacrifice but also open conspiratory activity aiming at the subversion of the existent social order. An example of this comes from the text that followed the attack by twenty people on a police station, burning the parked police cars and motorbikes in July 2008. To explain their position they stated: "And if some (people) continue to spin round on a roulette wheel waiting to end up on a lucky number, if some leave their lives to chance, there are others who ambush, thinking that they only live once and owe it to

themselves to draw a course of dignity in the everyday life that surrounds them choosing the role of its denier. And we are some of these people, and we organize our desires with rage and consciousness and not with blank justifications for inaction and passivity. We are the carriers of hatred for your world. Disgusted by everything that provides the sense of order and security, your police stations are always our target."

What we have to emphasize is that in this militarized anarchist discourse we find implicit the conception of the perpetuation of attack to the capitalist order and the State that leads to the idea of an ethical legitimization and higher responsibility. What is more, this legitimization of violence is, in the anarchist imagination, to be sanctioned not by present society, but from history, that is by the society of the future. Anarchist discourse does not negotiate, does not converse about the value of violent activity with those who find violence senseless or useless. This is why, during riots, whenever people from the Left attempt to persuade and prevent them from carrying out acts of destruction they fail. Indeed, holding a view of modern society as bankrupted and resembling a "desert" (a now commonly used metaphor), I would argue, creates a conviction that today's violent acts will be validated by people in a distant future, that is by future generations. In this way there is a displacement of the dialogue for recognition of violence from present society to that of the future. So, a belief that an act of revolution is an act of destruction and that nothing else from society as presently constituted is to be carried forward, creates a dialogue with the future, thus the powerful slogan that we saw during December: "we are an image from the future" in which one traces the idea that a certain violence performed against what is perceived as political targets will only be understood in the years to come. In this context, decisions about the performance of violence are beyond dispute since they represent a higher goal that cannot converse with or be compromised by present conditions, considerations or ideas. In this way, the culturally accepted idiom that could set the terms of a dialogue breaks down, or is being transcended. Hence, there is no discussion about whether it is right or wrong to burn down a store ("if in the society of the future private property will not have the same content it has today, we can, today, attack it"). Such a categorization armors individuals since it legitimizes violent activity by considering that this will only be understood in the future.

In this sense, violence is necessary for the message it sends to future generations. Since past experience informs the understanding of the present and marks possible routes of action, it is certain that the frequent performance of violence creates specific conceptions in society about the tolerable and normal limits of it, not in the sense of its acceptance but in the sense of the consolidation of an expected degree of violence, a degree that is manageable both by society and the State. Especially as far as the police are concerned, they (the police) seem to operate within a specific set of meanings that define the relation of the antagonists on the basis of a past experience of violence, an experience that is guided by and at the same time recognizes a particular ritualistic sequence in a confrontation that usually does not allow for this violence to become murderous. There is in a way, an implicit and mutual understanding between the antagonists—between anarchist groups and the police—that violence during riots must not lead to the loss of human life, which is appreciated more than material loss in the whole system of cultural meanings. This, on the other hand, could be regarded as an antithesis since a discourse of war does not account only for material damage but for human loss as well. But as we remarked, violence does not only have practical-instrumental aspects, but also symbolic-expressive ones (Riches). Going back to December, the confrontations in the streets and the heavy material damages all over Greece were followed by an attack on a riot police bus with machine guns by the terrorist group Revolutionary Struggle that aimed at the assassination of police officers as a response to the assassination of the young boy. Most of the people I talked to said that they were not sure if this was a proper reaction, since it was taking the conflict to a different level, that is taking away the legitimation of violence that had taken place in the streets. From this point of view, violence was useful and successful, that is serving the interests of a social movement that wants to gain popular support, only as long as it does not become murderous. However, those who believe in an open and continuous confrontation with the State and "its guards," those who engage in a discourse of perpetual war thought that the identity of the revolutionary is defined by him negating that the State should have the monopoly of violence. As one person told me: "why is it normal for the police to walk around with guns, while I am taken for a crazy and dangerous person if I do so? They killed a young boy in cold blood. Aren't they dangerous?"

The State employs discourses of law, order, and good citizenship and uses symbols to legitimize its authority. A different set of symbols (the violent confrontation and its targets) are used by anarchist groups to mobilize opposition and communicate a negation of what is perceived as a coercive institution and mechanism that according to a Marxist and anarchist perspective collaborates with the other major force of human exploitation that historically helped in its creation and development, namely capital or the capitalist establishment, which is identified with the State and its ordering of human life.

So far the anarchist argument follows a well known leftist or libertarian logic familiar to all of us: capital accumulates social wealth and at the same time creates and supports the State to safeguard its interests. The State does not represent or promote the needs of society but those of the capital that produce social inequality and exploitation. So, the argument goes, the State lies in its self-image and pseudo-identification with society. The problem, certainly not a social one, arises when some people believe this is so more than others and decide to act in a more, we could say, direct manner, one that is considered by most, at least in our societies, as less "civilized." Indeed, for most people, although political protest is a legitimate means for advancing certain demands and interests—social, economic, political and so forth—this must be performed within certain limits of legality established by the laws of the State. And by no means do most of us know enough or feel comfortable enough to become violent during a demonstration (to burn a few cars, to smash some banks or throw Molotov cocktails at the police or luxury shops). All the more so since this usually involves some preparation that is mostly a matter of interpretation which is linked to the multivocality of symbols (the same symbol may be understood by different people in different ways). You either feel that a Ferrari should or could be burned or you don't, you either consider it a manifestation of social inequality or a proof of higher technology and beauty, or a little bit of both, but more one than the other. Of course, what is at stake here is a basic organizational principle of our societies: that of private property and its sacredness. "No one has the right to touch what I have gained through hard labor." The anarchist understanding is slightly different: if you own a lot it means that you have been subjecting others to some sort of exploitation since someone has to be poor if someone else becomes rich. At the same time, there is a powerful idea that surrounds behavior towards objects, that of the nature of the commodity form. According to a Marxist and Debordian perspective commodities being the product of alienating social relations are themselves alienating, supporting a reified

68

picture of the world, that is a world comprised by "things" and not social relations.

Commodities are being produced by people who sell their product to those who own the means of production, thus giving up what belongs to them. What is left to them from the produced product is the paid labor, while capital is produced through the unpaid labor, known as surplus value. Alienation, here, is conceived as a process by which the paid worker experiences a sense of loss that the giving away of his product creates, and the simultaneous implicit misconception that what you buy is not yours. The products that an individual has produced with his labor return to him through consumption in which he is called to buy what he himself has produced. As Guy Debord (*The Society of the Spectacle*) has argued, especially after the explosion of the advertising industry, the commodity form is being diffused to all levels of society, falsifying all social activities and relations through the strong imagery it creates. In a society where everything can be sold, it is thought that reality is transformed into an economic transaction. Social relations are mediated by commodities as when status is acquired through the consumption of particular products. The commodity form, being diffused, is transformed into images mediated by it so that it can be sold. This, according to the particular perspective, creates the various lifestyles that the advertising industry promotes, thus constructing identities based on consumption. In this manner, the argument goes, the commodity is being internalized, that is it exists as a mediated image that guides human behavior and consumerist culture. In a world where image dominates, we begin to relate not to real individuals but with the images of the commodity. If human relations are mediated by their images, and images are mediated by commodity, then, in the final analysis, social relations are mediated by commodities.

In anarchist discourse then, it is this perception of commodities as falsifying elements of human interaction that provides legitimization to the acts of destroying commodities (and the shops which sell them) and allows individuals to imagine looting as an act by which products are being taken by those who "really" own them.

This is precisely what anarchist discourse does: it provides individuals with particular knowledge that helps in ordering the world and providing necessary material for action. And action is indeed their specialty. Without getting into detail I would say that anarchist groups appear in at least seven cities around Greece. Influenced by a different range of theoretical stances such as the situationists, classical anarchism, the German and Italian autonomia, and more recently, but less so, the so-called insurrectionists like the Italian Bonanno and the French "illegalists," they develop a discourse that conceptualizes major institutions in the way I have described.

Now, when I am talking about anarchist groups I am referring to organized ones, that is groups that can range from five to forty people (from diverse social backgrounds. Aya has remarked on the fact that the anarchist movement in Spain constituted an alliance of different economic actors, and has seen this as one of the reasons for its weakness) with specific political activity. This includes three main practices. The first is the printing and distribution of street posters and brochures. The second is regular horizontally-structured, closed meetings in which various topics and routes of action are discussed and analyzed. The third involves participation in larger open anarchist assemblies in which a great deal of networking activity and common organizing takes place on a local or national level. All three practices seem to be crucial and their coexistence is important for a sense of collective identity.

Regarding the first, with the printed material groups present their political views and criticisms in a written text that, through its distribution, is announced and communicated to society. As far as the second is concerned, the closed meeting comprises a proof that the group indeed exists and is operative through a process of dialogue between equals who see each other as "comrades." To a large extent it is the main decision-making mechanism of small collectivities, and it being closed means that certain people not only have attained a certain degree of friendship and personal contact, but also a particular way of thinking and vocabulary that excludes others—anarchists and non-anarchists alike. Coming to the third, participation in large anarchist assemblies (often held in universities) indicates participation in political processes that extend from those of one's own group and facilitates wider decision-making by people with similar outlooks and common interests. In such assemblies, which can last from two to five hours, anyone can present his views and decisions are taken through consensus, not a majority vote. This is seen by many as an intrinsic feature and a central element that distinguishes "us" from "them," that is from non-anarchist decision-making practices that are hierarchically or vertically structured. Such assemblies might be open to everyone—as when possible participation in protests is being discussed—or closed, that is by invitation to particular people and groups—as when decisions regarding risky and violent acts are about to take place.

In relation to these, they can include a wide range of targets and different practices. Banks may be smashed or burned (with molotov cocktails), as well as luxury shops and cars, supermarkets might be looted, also sabotage of surveillance cameras may take place—especially during riots—but most importantly state buildings are attacked, and finally, what is a relatively recent practice, from the last two to three years, police stations are attacked by groups of thirty to fifty people with sledge hammers and molotov cocktails, burning police cars, and smashing the building.

Mainstream media and a lot of people who find this violence meaningless and posing a danger for democracy wonder why the police cannot arrest these people. The answer is very interesting, but also very simple, and quite far from the experience of most people in modern cities. The answer is that if thirty people, and thirty is a lot of people, decide to perform a violent act against someone or something, they will most probably succeed in doing so.

What we have to keep in mind is that we are talking about small groups, both men and women, who come together in order to plan and perform unexpected attacks. But the most important element is not the accuracy of a plan—though this is definitely important—but the fact that small hits of this sort are based on close, long-lasting interpersonal relationships of friendship and intimacy. What is more, the most fundamental element appears to be that of trust. You cannot carry out a violent act with people you do not know. On the contrary, people who cooperate have done so in the past and know that they can rely on each other. And there are certain criteria and characteristics that are appreciated and valued for creating this sense of trust. A person must be courageous (i.e. bold but always sticking to the plan), must not set himself or the group to additional risk, must be able to move fast, to perform certain tasks, and also to show an ability to improvise in case something goes wrong.

What is more, setting oneself into frequent danger and risk of arrest and imprisonment, as well as the fact that experience of this sort transmits a sense of certainty about success, create a different perception of one's own position towards state repression, and most importantly a different perception of normality. It is not only that notions of "citizenship" are being challenged here. Performative violence constructs subjects with a different relation towards the emotion of fear. In this context, what is normality for some becomes a passive state of being for those informed by an agonistic discourse that guides them into social practices that most of us would consider life-threatening. From this perspective, I would argue, that since what prevents some people from such acts is the internalization of the fear of arrest and punishment that flows from the dominant discourse of an ever present and powerful state, what we find in groups like these is precisely a better management of this fear constituted through experience. This involves a powerful notion that relates to the different expectations of the people concerned: the notion that "anything is possible," that increased empowerment constructs a strong sense of agency in people who conceptualize the State as a major force of restraint of human agency and initiative. This, then, becomes a crucial factor of contestation of State power by groups that perceive it not only as coercive but also as defeatable.

It is through personal initiative for violence that individuals construct an identity of an active subject that resists perceived conditions of general passivity and apathy. The insurrectionist, the term most commonly used, is identified with the person who resists the determination of his life by an antagonistic State. In a country with a long history of intercommunal political violence, the insurrectionist constructs himself the field of conflict and steps into it by becoming either an urban guerilla or an activist.

In one of his papers, Jeffrey Juris remarks that anti-corporate globalization activists face the challenge of having to develop new approaches in the face of their mass direct actions becoming stagnant. He sees the need for sustainable organization—even if decentralized and network based—that can survive the flows of mass mobilization. On the other hand, anarchist groups in Greece do not face, in my view, a similar challenge. Their discourse and a long history of violence provide the necessary material to continue with a solid perception of the State as their main antagonist. It is this perception that being internally uncontested generates performative violence as a basic means to articulate identities that will reproduce it.

It has been said that the impact of a particular ritual is a product of its past performances. Memories associated with earlier experiences guide new enactments of rites. This is why rites have both a conservative bias and an innovative potential. This is also why December reinforced the pre-existing view among these groups that this specific sort of violence, with its spectacular characteristics, can operate as a successful political and subversive technique. To the extent that the whole country watched in awe what a few thousand people can do when they coordinate reinforces this truism.

The so-called "chaos" that anarchists create, the absence of specific—read "logical"—demands, and their rituals (violent confrontation and assemblies)—to the extent that they do not represent a particular political program—operate as crucial elements in the creation of an alternative structure. While not devoid of organization, their non-hierarchical, non-authoritarian modes as well as the fact that they do not stand for—like the organizations of other radicals—a counter-structure helps in retaining characteristics of anti-structure that are not easily contested. Acts of destruction communicate in an explicit way their utopian vision for a change that is perceived not as political but as cultural, therefore generating even stronger moral judgments and passions. At the same time, they themselves comprise an important example of the multiplicity of cultural discourses that can lead to a multiplicity of cultural experience and subjectivity within the same society.

In the cultural invention of the frequent use of violence we see not only an attempt to retain agency, but also the ways dominant discourse and power are contested. We see not a burst that reaffirms the value of maintaining the social order but a claim for its transformation. This is why performative violence might be a subversive process that challenges the preservation of existent meanings and not an element that reinforces them.

1

6

2

4

7

5

3

8

1. Greek anarchists enthusiastically particpate in the the anti-IMF demonstrations in Prague in 2000, leading to the belief that an international movement is dawning.

2–3. Antiauthoritarian Current on the opening day of the EU Conference in Thessaloniki, Greece in 2003.

4–6. Second day of the European Union Conference. Ten thousand anarchists join 190,000 activists in the anti-globalization demonstration.

7–8. From the Global No War demos of February–March 2003. With over 300,000 participants and a strong anti-US message, the Greek State is forced to minimize its involvement in the Iraq war.

74

9. Global No War demonstration in front of US Embassy in Athens.

10

12

14

11

13

15

10. From the No Border demonstrations in 2005. Anarchists from Bulgaria and Antiauthoritarian Current take part.

11. From the last day of No Border. Anarchists attack a detention camp, liberating a host of immigrants detained therein.

12-15. Photos from student struggles against the privatization of education from 2006-2007. These struggles brought a new generation into the social struggles in Greece and their radicalization contributed greatly to December 2008.

We are an Image from the Future

16-21. Photos from the university occupations. These battles built confidence and sowed the seeds of December.

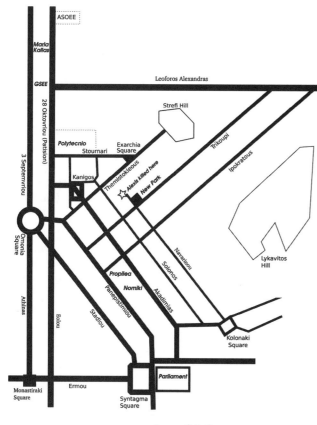

Central Athens

Chronology: December 6–25, 2008

Saturday December 6, 2008: Two cops confront a group of young anarchists on Mesollogiou Street in Exarchia, Athens. Cop Epaminondas Korkoneas shoots and kills fifteen-year-old Alexandros Grigoropoulos. Within an hour people gather and soon begin clashing with police. Some anarchists quickly make the critical decision to occupy the Polytechnic. Attacks on police, banks, and luxury stores spread to Patision Avenue, Ermou, and to the universities Nomiki and Pantio. Friends of Alexis fight off police attempts to enter Evaggelismos Hospital, where his body has been taken. Seventy luxury shops on Ermou are smashed and burnt to the ground, and a seven-floor megastore is torched. People in the cafes and bars hear the news and join in. Anarchists also occupy ASOEE university, and leftists and antiauthoritarians occupy Nomiki, the law school. By the end of the night, much of the city is filled with tear gas, police have been chased out of many neighborhoods, and multiple police stations have been attacked. News of the killing and the riots spread throughout Greece via internet and cell phone. Starting within just a couple hours of the murder, major spontaneous protests attack police stations and banks in Thessaloniki, Iraklion, Chania, Patras, Ionnina, Kavala, and Volos. Smaller demonstrations occur in Rethymnon, Komotini, Mytilini, Alexandropouli, Serres,

Sparta, Corfu, Xanthi, Larissa, Naxos, Agrinio, and countless small towns.

December 7: In Athens a demonstration of over 10,000 people immediately turns into a riot causing major property damage, burning down many corporate and luxury shops. Police attack with thousands of tear gas canisters, but are frequently chased away, sometimes even being routed by rioters. Riot police try to occupy Exarchia and residents pelt them with stones and flower pots. More banks and police stations are burned. Police are only able to carry out seven arrests throughout the day, owing to heavy and generalized resistance. In Thessaloniki 1,000 people break away from a protest march of 3,000 and attack a police station. After the leftists leave the march it continues to attack government buildings and another police station, setting up barricades and burning luxury stores. Police attack the university and theater school occupations. Police and demonstrators alike are injured in the fighting. In Iraklion and Patras there are demonstrations of 600 and 1,000 people, respectively, with the anarchists forming large blocs at the end as usual. In both cities many banks are attacked, causing the leftists in Patras to leave the march. In Corfu several hundred people protest. After demonstrators clash with police, a dozen youth from KKE (the Communist Party) and PASOK lock the university and refuse to let the protesters in, leaving them at the mercy of the riot police. There is also a large, violent demonstration in Ionnina involving 1,000 people, it is attacked by police, who

hospitalize three. Other protests and actions occur in Mytilini, Ithaki, Larissa, Pyrgos, Karditsa, Kavala, Xanthi, Volos, Serres, Sparta, Kozani, Arta, and Naxos. In some cases in small cities, groups of as few as ten people carry out bold actions like attacking police stations with molotovs and dispersing before they can be caught, as occurred in Pyrgos. In Kozani an anarchist demo of just eighty people besieges the local police station, kicking out journalists and building barricades. In other places, events unfold rather peacefully, as in Sparta where anarchists occupy a university and set up an infopoint.

December 8: Many schools and universities are closed this Monday. But rather than stay at home, students occupy their schools or take to the streets. In Athens alone, thousands of students march on and attack police stations all over the city. Meanwhile, anarchists at the Polytechnic battle police for hours and burn down all the computer stores on Stournari Street. More than 200 arson attacks occur across the city, and the huge, decorative Christmas tree on Syntagma Square is burnt down. Cops open fire on rioters with live ammo. Many police stations, banks, government offices, ministries, luxury stores, and corporate chain stores are smashed or burned completely. Dozens of cops are injured. In Piraeus all the police cars parked at the police station are destroyed by local high school students. In Thessaloniki students and extreme Left organizations hold multiple protests, and occupy the Lawyers Association building to use it as a counterinformation center. Police stations and government ministries are attacked with stones and molotovs, and a student march down the principal avenue, Egnatia, destroys every bank on the street, along with many other stores, while burning Greek flags. In Patras, anarchists occupy a local TV station to broadcast counterinformation. In Iraklion, a march of 2,000 people forces police to retreat, and at night the city is engulfed in rioting, in which many Roma, hooligans, and poor people participate alongside anarchists and students. Most banks in the city center are torched. Thousands of people, mostly students, march and riot in Chania, Larissa, Rhodes, Nafplio, Chios, Egio, Veria, Kavala, Agrinio, Aliveri, Alexandroupoli, Chaldiki, Giannitsa, Syros, Ierapetra, Kastoria, Korinthos, Kyprarissia, Pyrgos, Corfu, Xanthi, Kilkis, Trikala, Serres, Tripoli, Mytilini, Kalamata, Moudros, Lamia, Kozani, Florina, Edessa, and elsewhere. In each place between 50 and 2,000 people participate, and actions range from blockading the police station and pelting it with garbage, to pelting police with molotovs and rocks and burning down banks. In several cities, youth with the KKE try to protect the police or prevent the occupation of universities.

December 9: Cops provoke the massive crowd at Alexis's burial, shooting tear gas just as he is being interred, leading to more fighting. At the time most of the anarchists in Athens are at the funeral, yet heavy street fighting is simultaneously being carried out by non-political people throughout the city.

The ASOEE occupation successfully repels a MAT attack. Thousands of prisoners throughout Greece boycott meals for the day in commemoration of Alexis, even though they are recovering from their hunger strike. Anarchists expropriate food from supermarkets to feed the university occupations or to distribute it on the streets. Multiple police stations across the city are attacked. Immigrants are hunted by police and fascists. Fighting and protesting continues in other cities and towns across the country. There are major protests in Thessaloniki, Patras, Volos, and Ioannina, that are brutally attacked by police trying to stop the uprising. In Thessaloniki and Patras cops and fascists work together to attack the anarchists and the occupations.

December 10: The General Confederation of Greek Workers calls off the general strike it had already scheduled months earlier for that day. Tens of thousands of people gather in the streets anyway, and fighting with police resumes throughout Athens. Many workers, including air traffic controllers, walk off the job, bringing transportation to a halt. Police are increasingly assisted by fascists in Athens, while in Thessaloniki members of the KKE unmask and beat a rioter. Protests, occupations, and riots continue in other cities and towns throughout Greece. A group of about 100 Roma attack a police station in the Zefyri suburb of Athens. Total damages up to that point are estimated at fifty million euros, 554 buildings have been attacked, and twenty-seven cars set on fire. By the end the total cost of damages would quadruple.

December 11: The city hall of Aghios Dimitrios is occupied by residents. Throughout Athens students hold assemblies or fight on the streets alongside anarchists. In the afternoon, twenty-five police stations throughout the city are besieged and multiple undercover cops are put in the hospital. One hundred twenty schools in Athens are occupied by their students. Police request more tear gas from Israel; they have run out. In Piraeus antiauthoritarian students manage to kick the KKE out of the university so they can occupy it. In Thessaloniki a march of about 600, mostly anarchists, is attacked by police, but residents join them and the protest swells to 3,000, repelling police. Five thousand protest in Patras. Demonstrations, actions, and occupations continue to occur in other cities and towns.

December 12: In Athens Flash FM radio is occupied but the signal is quickly cut. A government building in the Chalandri neighborhood is occupied and turned into an infopoint. The old city hall in the same neighborhood is occupied to house an open popular assembly. Students organize a massive march in the center of Athens. They are attacked by police and fight back. Outside Parliament there is a peaceful sit down protest. Police attack the Nomiki occupation and are repelled by the people. Many cops are set on fire. All over the country, open assemblies are held in university occupations. The city hall in Ioannina is occupied. At night a massive, peaceful, candlelit protest is held in Athens in commemoration of Alexis.

December 13–23: Thousands of actions, too many to count, occur across Athens and in many other cities and towns, including occupations, counterinformation. The large scale production of pamphlets and texts speaking to hundreds of themes to counteract the lies broadcast by the media commences. Protests, propaganda work, supermarket expropriations, actions to liberate the public transportation, assemblies, attacks against specific targets, and direct communication with society on a diffuse and massive scale continues.

December 16: A group of artists and anarchists occupies NET, the major public television station in Athens, interrupting a speech by the prime minister and broadcasting a message urging people to turn off their TVs and take to the streets.

December 17: The central building of the General Confederation of Greek Workers (GSEE) in Athens is occupied by anarcho-autonomous base unions, supported by anarchists and libertarians. Roughly six hundred people participate in their assembly every afternoon.

December 21: The occupation of the GSEE ends.

December 23: Three thousand protesters march through Athens. In the afternoon a riot police bus is shot up with automatic rifles in Zografou, a neighborhood of Athens. Bulgarian immigrant worker Konstantina Kuneva is brutally attacked by unknown assailants, probably in retaliation for her activity organizing fellow precarious cleaning workers and her association with the GSEE occupation.

December 24: Several hundred anarchists stage a peaceful march through Athens.

December 25: Christmas is exploited to the maximum extent as a social symbol of peace, tradition, the atomization of social life into the private sphere, and consumption. In the official narrative Christmas marks the definitive end of the revolt; however arson attacks targeting banks, car dealerships, and government officials in multiple Athens neighborhoods as well as in Ioannina promise a continued struggle.

The World Left Behind

"There was a protest scheduled for earlier that day, the 6th of December," she was telling me, an ironic twinkle in her eye. "I remember, we had a meeting to discuss what to do. At the protest would we throw stones, or paint bombs, or just trash? We decided to throw trash. We knew that nothing much would happen at the protest, and we weren't prepared for strong clashes with the police. It was just another day. Nothing out of the ordinary could be seen on the horizon. Before nine o'clock that night, Athens was the most miserable place in the world. The same as everywhere else."

94

Suddenly I heard a bang

Lito: An Exarchia resident whose balcony overlooks the spot where Alexis Grigoropoulos was murdered

I'm not so involved in any political activities. I'm not an activist. I can only speak about the killing. I can't take a position on all the other things that happened because all these other things are very complicated and I don't have clear thoughts on them.

Exarchia has always been an alternative, counterculture neighborhood. For many years it was a frequent occurrence that something would happen on a street corner in Exarchia and suddenly everyone from the cafés and the bars and the sidewalks would pour out into the streets and run to see what was happening. Usually it was incidents between people and police, some fights, confrontations, insults, shouting matches. In the old times it happened very often. Then there was a period when this didn't happen so much, but in the last years it has started becoming more common again.

The reason that I found myself with a camera on the balcony that night was because I had always wanted to film one of these confrontations that are always taking place below my window. But every time I would come to my balcony to see what was happening, I got delayed. By the time I went back inside to get my camera it was too late, it was already over.

This happened to me many times. And the last time that it happened, I said to myself, the next time, first I'll grab the camera and then I'll go to the balcony.

And the next time turned out to be an incident that I never expected could happen. Two years earlier a friend visited me from Germany and he mentioned that the police here seem very provocative and dangerous. Even though he was a tourist, the way they behaved made him feel less safe, they made him feel endangered. And when this friend heard about what happened on the 6th of December, he wrote that he wasn't at all surprised. But I was.

All the previous times, I never got scared observing these fights between people and the police. It was part of my everyday life in Exarchia. It was something commonplace. Because the Exarchia locals express their negation of authority firmly, and they believe in it, whenever something was happening I didn't need to take a position or make a stand because it was just a part of life in this area. Of course in the ten years that I've lived in this flat, I've observed year after year a gradual increase in the police presence, an intensification. Policemen began to appear on every corner in the neighborhood, in groups, and also they were armored. Observing armored police in full riot gear carrying pistols, tear gas guns, and machine guns—was feeling more and more intense. In this period the slogan started to appear on the walls: "on every street corner there are police, the junta didn't end in '73."

On December 6 I was here in the apartment with my German friend. He was cooking in the kitchen and I was in the living room. Suddenly I heard a bang. I hadn't heard any noise before that. Nothing was happening in the streets, no shouts, nothing. Without warning there was just a bang. It seemed to me that it came from down the street, on the left-hand side. Despite the surprise, this time I remembered to grab my camera first. I was not in a panic, I didn't feel anything unusual, I just calmly got the camera and went to the balcony. I didn't think anything extraordinary had happened. I looked outside, but I didn't turn the camera on in the beginning because nothing was happening. I saw a few youths down to the left, sitting like they always do. The young anarchists are always hanging out down there, although this night there were fewer than normal. And on the right-hand side, up the street, I saw a police car parked at the corner. One moment after the police car drove off, I saw two cops coming back on foot, and this was very strange to me. I asked myself, what are they going to do? They arrived at the spot where the car had been before, and started provoking the kids, saying *come on you pussies!* When I heard this I shouted to the German guy, *come look! The police came and they're starting a fight.* He would get a chance to see this phenomenon of the Greek cops provoking a fight by insulting people. It's normal that the police speak bad to people, but this was too much. It was provocative because they parked the police car and they came walking back and shouting challenges. That's how normal people start a fight. It was like a personal fight, not the usual provocation by police.

Immediately after that they both took out their guns, both the cops. This was never mentioned by the media. And I got one surprise after another. First they came back on foot, then they started a fight by insulting the kids, then they took out their guns, and then they took aim—in a moment when there was no challenge and no threat, there was no fight or confrontation going on. And they shot. I heard two shots but I can't say if both of them shot or if one shot twice. It's possible that one of them shot twice. And they turned around and just left, simple as that, as though nothing had happened. Me, until that moment, it didn't occur to me to look to the left, to the group of kids, because it was all so incredibly strange, the behavior of these two policemen. There was no need to look to the other side because nothing was happening there. And then I heard the people in the street shout that a kid had been shot. And then I felt panic. I ran inside, grabbed the telephone and called an ambulance, and I went down to the street. I saw just one kid lying there, and I was shocked. Everybody was shouting and many people were fainting. The kid wasn't dead yet, and a doctor had appeared and was trying to administer first aid. Then the ambulance arrived and he died inside in the ambulance, I think.

I found out from other people that the first bang had been a concussion grenade. Apparently someone had thrown a plastic bottle at the police car and yelled an insult as it was passing and the police responded by throwing the grenade from the car. That's not so unusual here. It's normal to shout, everyone in Greece is shouting at each other. So I'm sure the policemen hadn't been threatened, they weren't defending themselves. Really, if a policeman feels a serious threat, he doesn't drive down to the next corner then walk back to clean up the situation. Usually when the police feel a threat or feel like they're under attack, they drive off, they get out of there. The police were not on the defensive at that moment.

I went back up and tried to watch the video on my computer, but I couldn't because I was missing some program. So I knocked on my neighbor's door and said I recorded something but I don't know what it is. Can we put it in your computer so I can see what it is? And we saw the video, and the way I felt, I had never felt that way in my entire life. We called down all the people from the entire neighborhood, everyone, we all came down onto the streets, and the energy, the atmosphere, was one of rage. It was overflowing all the streets, everywhere people were pouring out of their houses onto the streets. Everybody.

The riot police had the gall to come here, back to this corner where the first cop car had stopped, and where the shots were fired. And of course everybody started shouting at them, young people, old people, normal people, everyone was shouting at them to go the hell away.

About two hours after the shooting, it's impossible to say exactly how long but it was about two hours. The secret police came. I was back in my house listening to the radio and the TV, which were saying there were riots in Exarchia, that the police had been attacked and fired in self-defense, but this wasn't true. And the riots hadn't even started yet. And from my window I saw men without uniforms looking at the walls of the buildings around the shooting. The secret police had come to search for the shell casings and the bullets, to investigate the area. I was with my neighbor, and I told him I was going down. I wanted to react somehow to what they were saying on the news. So I went down and I said that what they're reporting on the television wasn't true. One tall old guy came up to me with a greasy smile, and said, *yes, and who are you?* And I felt an amazing fear. Because I'm very naïve, I just felt the obligation to go down and say the truth. But this guy, he terrified me. So I backed off and said, *no, who are you?* And he told me his name and his position. He was the chief of the secret police agency, and he was in charge of the autopsy and investigation. They took my name and telephone, and they asked me if I was going to come to the central police station to testify, and I said *yes.*

He asked me what happened. I brought him to the exact point where the policemen were standing when they opened fire. And that's exactly where they found the shell casings. They asked me if I had a vehicle, if I could drive myself to the station. I responded, "no" and they told me I would come with them. I said I hoped the people wouldn't bomb the police car on the way, and the chief laughed and said *have no fear.* He directed me to where a large group of riot police were gathered, and I found myself in the middle of a MAT squad. It was right at that moment that the people attacked. The chief disappeared immediately, he ran away and they left me while the people were attacking, and I saw all the guns that the police had and I flipped out. I couldn't focus on anything. I felt how powerful the people were, they were full of rage. I can't remember if they were attacking with stones or molotovs or clubs, only that they were overpowering and I had to get out of there. I ran away by myself and came back to my house.

Of course I was expecting that they would call me for an interview as a witness. But they never did. I spoke with a lawyer of the movement, Yianna Kurtovick, she's one of the members of the Network for the Defense of Political Prisoners and Immigrants. And she brought me to the examining magistrate. I had to go to find the judge because the police never called me to testify. And after I testified, some days later, they closed the whole area to make the official report to prove whether the bullet hit the kid directly or if it ricocheted off the ground. That was the official story, that the one cop had fired at the ground and the bullet bounced up and hit him.

The magistrate, the photographer, and the secretary came up to my balcony to take photographs. The chief of the secret police was down in the street. I called out to him, *Oh hello, you left me alone last time in the middle of a riot.* And he answered, *I didn't abandon you, it was you who was afraid that the rioters would burn us alive.* And I said to him, *Don't tell lies in front of all these people.*

I ran to the Polytechnic

23.10: A person involved in the anarchist movement for some years

December 6. So my friends phoned me and told me something very bad had happened. I ran to the Polytechnic. When I got there, we made sure that the story was true, that this boy had really been killed. And I began to feel that something very important was happening. Many people had begun to gather in the Polytechnic. It was clear that there would be some riots. Because it has happened before, that very young anarchists were killed in Exarchia. It happened in 1985, and there were riots. I felt like history was repeating itself. There were different trends in the Polytechnic. Some comrades said to focus our actions there, others said to go out on the streets, to attack police stations, or the commercial center. I preferred the second option. This happened. Some of us left the university after the riots had begun. We went to a police station in the center of Athens and we attacked with stones and molotovs. We were many, we were not a group of some fifteen people, we were maybe 100. Then we attacked luxury stores in the commercial center of Athens and we went back to the Polytechnic.

After I returned, some friends phoned me from Nomiki, the School of Law building, so I went there. It was occupied, there were many people there. Many were leftists, not anarchists, who were there to fight with the police. This is very unusual because the leftists have a very mechanical view of political violence. They say it's not appropriate to fight the police until the movement is mature, and they use this as an excuse to never fight with the police. They build an identity out of it. But that night I saw hundreds of these people, including people I've argued with over this very issue, fighting with the police. This made me feel very emotional, seeing these people also fighting against the police.

I slept in the Polytechnic the first night. Many people had left the building. There were only a few dozen of us left in the building. To be honest, at that moment I thought that the incident had ended. Maybe some riots the next day because there would be a big demonstration, but then things would end.

The next day there were thousands of people at the big demonstration. Some wild riots, very wild riots. We didn't manage to get very close to the police headquarters, the objective for the demonstration, but there were big riots. I went back to the Polytechnic, there were also big riots happening there. But I thought that things would end then, on Sunday.

Next day, Monday, December 8, there was a demonstration. I'm still not sure who organized it. But I think some Left groups organized this demo. I had underestimated the situation, I thought nothing would happen on Monday. But that morning strange events began to occur. School students in many parts of Greece began to attack police stations. Some friends phoned me and told me that in Piraeus, which is usually indifferent, nothing happens there, school students attacked the police station and rolled police cars over. News like this began to appear from everywhere that morning.

But I had underestimated the afternoon demo. I went to the demo at the last moment because I was very tired from the previous days, and I thought maybe I wouldn't go. When I came up from the metro, I saw tens of thousands of people. I couldn't believe it. The demo hadn't begun and already some people, very young people, unknown people, had already started to fight with police. The demo started but it began to lose its purpose as a demonstration because riots were beginning on all sides.

I've seen many violent things in protests throughout my life. I don't say this to speak about myself but just to let you know. In this demo I began to feel afraid. To be honest, the violence was blind. There were molotovs thrown inside buildings while people were still in them. I was afraid not for myself, but that something very bad would happen and anarchism could not politically defend it. I met a friend of mine, an anarchist, and I asked her what she thought and she said "I'm not sure I want to be here," and I felt the same. Around us were unknown young people throwing molotovs, fighting with the police, burning buildings, shops, everything. Many

of the shops were already closed, and in the others, the people were getting out of there.

The sense of the demonstration had been lost. It was all riots. Soon people began to break into big groups. They went down different streets, they rioted. Smashing and burning. Mostly unknown people. Young people, second generation immigrants, Gypsies, Greeks, everything. Most of them were masked. But the presence of certain demographics, like the immigrants was very obvious. After this, when the riots began to calm down in a way, I went to Syntagma Square, where I saw the big Christmas tree burning. I went to Nomiki, which was occupied by AK and some Left groups. I went there not so much because I agree with these people politically but because I was close by and thought it was safest to go there. And there were riots there too, something was happening.

At Nomiki there were many anarchists and other people, unknown people, who didn't belong to these specific groups. By cell phone we learned that riots had happened in many other places, like the Polytechnic, ASOEE, and another university three or four kilometers away. One friend phoned me, a very experienced guy, about forty-years-old, and said "I'm very afraid, some amazing things are happening here." A very experienced person. He was also in Genova.

On the 8th, Monday, the anarchists themselves were surprised by the level of violence coming from many parts of society. They felt anxious. These were the people who before were very active and very violent, and now they felt surprised and even a little anxious about society. They felt that society had surpassed them. This created anxiety among people, and I'm not talking about the pacifist anarchists.

I didn't feel so safe in Nomiki because I saw many buildings on fire in the area and I thought that maybe the police would begin massive arrests. When things began to calm at Nomiki, I thought it was a good moment to move to the Polytechnic. It was nighttime when I went there, and I saw that the streets were mostly deserted, there were only some people who had been participating in the riots. The riots at the Polytechnic had also begun to calm down, but everything was burned down. There were many people in the university, many second generation immigrants, also first generation immigrants. Many people felt a kind of disappointment. There were many people there, we did not know them, they weren't anarchists, many of them had been stealing things from the shops that were broken open and we didn't agree with this, we just thought the things should be burned. We didn't feel safe there. But there were also anarchists who said we should support them, they should be able to do what they want. That was Monday.

The following days there were occupations of university buildings and municipal buildings starting in towns around Athens. The social climate was very friendly toward the anarchists at this time.

I began to be more involved in the occupation of the ASOEE, where there were more people I know and more politically involved people. But I also had some doubts, whether it was right to be there, where there were anarchists, or to be in the Polytechnic where the subjects of this struggle were: young people, immigrants, unknown people. So I tried to strike a balance, going sometimes to ASOEE and sometimes to the Polytechnic. The anarchists organized many actions and many attacks in the following days—some things that under other circumstances, we wouldn't dare to do. But because we felt the climate around us was quite friendly, maybe we felt more safe to carry out actions like this. There was a discussion among us that in one or two days, it will all end. But the end never came. New things were always happening. New occupations in the provincial areas of Greece, attacks against police and state targets.

And then somewhere around the 20th of December, there was the assault against the Bulgarian syndicalist, Konstantina Kuneva. She was attacked to punish her organizing activities, and some other people began to get even more involved with the whole situation. People had meetings about incidents like this. It led to an occupation of the central trade union of Greece which lasted some days. And then people from the workers movement, whom we hadn't seen in the previous days, came out on the streets and to the assemblies. And sometime around Christmas, the situation began to calm down.

Homo Sacer Quartet

Flesh Machine: an anarchist magazine "on the body and its desiring machines" published in Athens

A boy resides out-of-place. Two pigs charge into the out-of-place. In the conjuncture of these two trajectories, an event is born. The boy challenges the violation of the border of his out-of-place by the pigs. The pigs park in-place and cross, once again, the limits of the heterotopia, this time on foot. The pigs enjoin the boy. The boy responds to the injunction. The pigs shoot and destroy the life that "is not worth being lived." The pigs return to in-place. The borders of the out-of-place are ruptured and urban space, from end to end, is recomposed into a thick burning network of heterotopia: *the city is on fire.*

For sovereignty, every life out-of-place is a life that is not worth being lived. The state of exception is imposed, even by suspension, on every life out-of-place, on every life that is acted not as a contemplation of privacy and its commodity-panoply, but as a social relation, as a self-constituted construction of the space and time of conviviality. The sovereign exception is not so much about the control or the destruction of an excess in itself, but about the creation or the definition of a space where juridico-political order can be perpetually validated. The state of exception classifies space and the bodies within

it. It puts them in order. It imposes order upon them. With assimilation, commodification, surveillance, and discipline. Executing the delinquent with prisons, psychiatric units, marginalization. And wherever, whenever might be necessary with bullets, with bullets, with bullets.

In a society dedicated to the production of privacies the murder of a boy can only be conceptualized in the terms of the value of his privacy, the ontological base of property: the sacred right to one's own life. This is the only way in which death can be political: as a destruction of the source of property. The destruction of property, let alone of its source, is a dreadful crime in the bourgeois world. Even, or especially when it is committed by the apparatus charged with its protection. But to destroy properties in order to take revenge for the destruction of property, that is a doubly nefarious crime: have you not understood a thing? All those tears, all the dirge, the requiems are not for a boy that attacked the power-that-safeguards-property, they are for the power that failed in its duty: the duty to defend life as the ultimate property, as privacy.

The body of an enemy now deceased can be sanitized, pillaged, transformed into a symbolic capital for the reproduction of sovereignty and finally, in the announcement or reminder of the capacity for the imposition of a generalized state of exception. An emergency confirming the sovereign monopoly on the definition of the real through the abolition of its symbolic legitimization. The sovereignty, in tears, shouts: you are all private individuals, else you are all potential corpses. And society falls on its knees in awe of its idols and shows remorse: mea culpa; from now on, I will take care of myself only, as long as you safeguard its reproduction. The return to the normalcy of the private is paved with the spectacle of generalized exception.

December 10, 2008, from the occupied Athens School of Economics and Business

I was in the heart of the catastrophe

Mrs. S.: The retired mother of a longtime anarchist, who typically votes for the conservative party

Are you sure you want to interview me? I think you'll get burned! I'm one of the people who believes in peaceful ways of doing things. It won't be helpful for this book you're writing. When I was young I was with the Socialists. We started the very first student movement back in the middle of the '60s, before the dictatorship. We were jumping on our desks in the classrooms, in the high schools, shouting for freedom and social justice. But when the Socialists came into power it was very disappointing. After the dictatorship people were in the universities, still on their desks, shouting for social justice and equality. And when we won in 1981, we were betrayed. The new government stole the money, and nothing changed. We are the betrayed generation. We took the government, but nothing happened. We won, only to lose. I don't agree with this way of protesting, destroying all the shops. But I'm a child of the '60s. We did it peacefully.

But wasn't there a lot of rioting and struggle in the '60s too?

Okay, there was, there were very big riots. The construction workers would come and gather barrels of stones to throw at the police. But the target was the police and the government, not private shops. I don't agree with damaging private property.

If we're going to protest like this, let's just start at home, open our own doors and let them do it here, smash it up and take our things. They just attack the shops because they're more vulnerable, more accessible, easier to attack, so that's why they pay the price. If people agree with this destruction, they should take the next step and open their own houses to be destroyed.

I even prefer the silent protests to these destructive ones. If you want to destroy the market, then don't buy things, don't consume. If you want to do something about the prices or the killing of the animals, don't eat meat. Try to build a majority, and bring all the people into the streets. If everyone came into the streets and stayed for three days, with everyone participating, even if they didn't do anything the impact would be very strong. They announce days in which no one should buy anything, as a protest, but still people go shopping these days. So the right mentality isn't there yet.

When the banks got smashed… ha ha, well, in a way all of us said that it was good what happened to them. They deserved it. But the problem is that this flood of destruction also claimed many small shops, many people's cars. In the moment of rioting it's difficult to discriminate. Together with the dry ones, you also burned the fresh ones. That's a Greek phrase.

As for the asylum in the universities, I don't think they should get rid of it, but I believe it has to be an asylum for the ideas—for the assemblies and public events for all different ideas, but I don't believe that if someone kills somebody outside the university they should be able to take refuge in the university to escape and not go to trial. It can't be an asylum for criminal actions. In '73, when the students took refuge in the university while they were struggling against the government, they didn't damage the universities. But now, okay in December they didn't damage the university buildings but in many other cases recently that's happened, that the university buildings have been damaged by the people taking refuge there.

Of course I think the episode in December was a healthy reaction. I could never say it was wrong for the people to rise up after the police killed Alexis. It was not only healthy, it was the obligation of the people to revolt. But I disagree with how they did it. I can't stand the violence and the destruction. The cause is right. The way they do it, I don't know if it's right or not. Also I cannot agree if you revolt when one boy like Alexis is killed, but you never revolt when a policeman dies. Me, I cannot discriminate between human beings. A policeman is a worker, he's not responsible for his actions. People much higher than him are responsible for his actions. In all the different jobs, there are people who are more evil, or aggressive, or arrogant. It's not only policemen.

I was in Ermou, the street with all the luxury shops near Parliament, early on Sunday morning, just after Alexis was killed. The whole street was still on fire. I couldn't go to Syntagma because everything was closed. The police were saying, *where are you going, lady?* They wouldn't let me pass, but I wanted to go to church with my six-year-old granddaughter. There were some major chain stores that were burned in Monastiraki, and the big banks. I wasn't scared, because most of the fires had almost burned out. Two months later I passed again and I told my granddaughter, *you see, they fixed the bank, it's open again.* I asked my granddaughter if she remembered and she said, *yes, it was all burned.*

When the police told me I couldn't pass on this side, they sent me a block down, and I went there and it was full of junkies and illegal immigrants! It was packed! I had to go through this street with my little grandchild to get to the church. It was strange. And I asked the people *what happened, is it okay?* And they told me, *everything is fine, mother, pass through,* and opened the way for me and let me pass. I didn't know that the riots had started, or what had happened, but I got to church in the end. I was in the heart of the *catastrophe.* It was very surprising, to see all those luxury stores destroyed that morning.

The first day I saw it with my own eyes, but after that most of what I learned came through the newspapers and the television. Mostly the television tries to produce fear. Through the TV the events become exaggerated. They blow it up like a balloon, and show again and again the same images, and use the same words, and this repetition causes panic. If you don't have a critical mind it's easy to get trapped in these feelings and freak out. I personally never allow myself to feel these things. I always understand that the TV exaggerates the situation and blows it out of proportion.

But yes, there were small shops destroyed, it's not only the TV saying this. On Ermou in addition to all the burned banks and chain stores I also saw one or two shops that were not big shops, they were not chains. One clothing shop that was smashed open and looted. Next time I pass there I'll go to that shop and find out who it belongs to. And in Syntagma there was an old building that was burned out completely. I don't know what that building was. I want to go tomorrow and find out. I'm curious as to why they burned that one down. It's normal that they burn the banks and the big stores if they want to hit capitalism, this you can understand. But you can't understand why they would burn the small shops, and when you see a building that was burned out completely, you can't understand why they chose this target. I guess I can understand the riots and the burnings because it's part of their fight against capitalism, but when you also have destruction of the universities and small shops and other targets, it's not clear to the people why it happened.

Do you think it will happen again, or that there will be a revolution?

The death of Alexis was only the spark. The real cause is that the whole society is bubbling. This was just the match in the dynamite store. The episode was caused by the economic and social problems that have been here for years. But if we have to speak about revolution, we speak about a general revolution, one that includes all aspects of life. But for me this is difficult to imagine because the people are alienated, they're rotten. Because of this, the people who really want a revolution are always a minority. So a general revolution that will include everybody, it can't happen. I believe that in general the people have found their places, they are *volemenos*—not comfortable but resigned, subdued, complacent. They are not satisfied, they don't agree with what is happening, but they have the minimum. And they'll stay like that instead of risking themselves or getting themselves into trouble. In the past people were more courageous, and when there were popular revolutions people were more heroic and they faced bigger problems, like starvation, or the complete denial of their human rights. So it was easier for them to revolt.

Okay, now we're going to fuck everything up

Little John: An anarchist who has been active for ten years, and is involved with one of Thessaloniki's squatted social centers, Fabrika Yfanet

It wasn't a specific squat or group responsible for the insurrection. In Greece there is a specific culture of responding to police aggression. When the police do something really wrong, there is a fast reaction: people attack police stations or other targets. At the end of August, 2007, this guy from Nigeria, Toni Onoya, was in a café selling CDs. He saw some people he recognized as undercover cops so he tried to escape by jumping down from the second floor veranda. The immigrants are always being hunted by the cops. But this time he fell on his head and died. His friends came and they tried to stop the police from taking the body before they could find their own doctor because they believed that police would falsify the autopsy and change the story. They called the media, people started to learn what had happened and they converged on the square. At nightfall there were 200 people. The police made another attempt to remove the body and this started the conflict. There was some rioting, and the next day there

105

was a demonstration of immigrants, the Nigerian community, students, anarchists, and they all attacked the police station with stones. And that was it. It ended with a demonstration in the center, some rioting, and about seventeen people arrested. This is how the anarchists here react. When there is police violence, we must respond in a direct way.

A week before the killing of Alexis we had gone to Volos because there had been another killing by police. There we were only one hundred people and we attacked the police station but it didn't get out of control like it did with Alexis. Somehow, that time, maybe because it happened in Exarchia, we all decided, *okay, now we're going to fuck everything up.*

So we met in the university to see what we were going to do. We didn't know that in other cities people were doing the same thing. We knew that Athens would explode but we didn't know it would happen in all the other cities too. Five hundred people gathered in the university and we didn't talk too much, just decided how we would respond. Some people went out and started setting things on fire. The police weren't out on the streets, they were protecting the police stations, so we were free to do whatever we wanted. There weren't more than five hundred of us in the streets.

The next day we met at twelve at Kamara, in the center. There had been no time to make a poster, we just used phones and word of mouth, but there were three thousand people there and we were starting to hear that things had happened in other cities as well.

Monday was the big boom. The high school students were in the streets attacking police stations, demonstrating. In the morning the high school students attacked the central police station for hours. And in the afternoon 10,000 people gathered, and then it was a real insurrection. And this continued for three more days. Until the end of the week there was a demonstration every day. Sometimes with fighting, sometimes not. On Wednesday there was a general strike, by coincidence. This is a periodic occurrence in Greece, a one-day strike every three months, and this one happened to fall in this week of insurrection. The government tried to cancel it and the labor unions agreed not to hold a demonstration, but just to gather, play some music, and send everyone home.

The mixture of people in the streets included students, anarchists, people who had connections with political spaces but had not been active, young people, immigrants, and political people from past generations, older people. We could see that communicating through violence and counterattack was really working. Small communities were organizing themselves to attack. They didn't need us to organize them. You could see small groups of students, fifteen year olds, faces covered, forming affinity groups like anarchists, but with no connections to the anarchists. We only tried to say, *please when you smash something be sure that it's an appropriate target.* This was a very strange role for us. All the banks were destroyed, really gutted, but no one had satisfied their urge for destruction yet, so they went on to the luxury stores. But sometimes the young people could not differentiate and they attacked a few smaller shops, which the media really exaggerated and exploited. Also, the employers used the damages as an excuse to lay off employees but they already needed to cut their workforce. They just blamed us to provide a scapegoat and to divide the people. And no one was in the streets to go shopping for Christmas, because no one had any money—you can really see the effects of the crisis. But they tried to blame that on us too.

At least there weren't many arrests in Thessaloniki. Mostly younger people who didn't know how to recognize undercover cops and protect themselves.

I don't think the anarchist movement spread in December, but its tactics spread. I think that over time, step by step, the anarchist movement in Thessaloniki is growing stronger. After 2003, with the European Union summit protests here, it sped up, then in the last years it's been moving slower, building steadily through actions, structures, communications. But I couldn't smell anything in the atmosphere that suggested it was possible for everything in Greece to blow up the very next day. Except for the prison uprisings two years ago, and then the prisoners' hunger strike in November. But before the 6th of December you couldn't understand that there were powers in society that could react in such an instantaneous and magical way. So it was all related to the anarchist movement, but we call it insurrection because it extended beyond the movement.

Fabrika Yfanet is a huge squatted social center in the eastern part of Thessaloniki. It used to be a factory, and now serves as a space for shows, political gatherings, and other events. Part of it is a house, and another part holds art spaces, workshops, a library, a bar, a climbing wall, a skate park, and more.

107

We started with 300 people, and came back with 500

Andreas: A squatter from Thessaloniki

On Saturday we received word of Alexis's death by phone. Five hundred people met in the university at once. In the meeting we shared the information we had, but it didn't end so well. We couldn't agree on what to do, and we broke in half. The smaller half stayed around the university for hit and run fighting, and the larger half marched down Egnatia, the main street of Thessaloniki, to smash all the banks and luxury shops. I was in this second group. There were also small groups of friends all over the city hitting specific targets—banks, police stations, et cetera. But this strategy, or lack of strategy, worked quite well, because the police had to divide their forces and they didn't know what to expect. A lot were near the university, fighting with the students there and defending the construction site for the new metro, so on Egnatia we didn't find any cops. We had the streets to ourselves.

Another thing: we started with 300 people, setting out from Kamara, and we came back with 500. Because people on the streets were joining us. They weren't afraid because we were doing it calmly. Yes, we were angry, we were very pissed off about the death of Alexis, but we kept ourselves under control. The banks had to be smashed, so we smashed them, but we did it calmly. One window, CRASH, next window, CRASH, here's someone who is afraid, okay, come over here, we'll move them out of the way, and then we get the next window. So no one had reason to be afraid of us, they sympathized with what we were doing and felt they could join us, so they joined us. Just normal people on the streets.

In some countries there is a critique of nonviolence. In Greece there is a critique of violence. But it's a very black and white issue. Everyone understands it is a part of the struggle, but some don't like it and others love it. There's no middle position. If you tell people you're in the middle they get confused. But I'm in the gray area. I think it's necessary to be careful with the violence. I don't say not to use it, of course you have to use it, but do it calmly, without losing control. You have to be calm. And you can do it this way at any level, no matter what degree of violence you're using.

Because we were calm people joined us on Saturday night and we came back with more people. We walked down Egnatia, attacked the police station with a variety of ammunitions, you know, and then we returned by the same street, smashing the shops a second time.

On the first day we didn't really understand what was happening. After the second day students were everywhere, setting dumpsters on fire, attacking capitalist targets. They just came from everywhere and started doing it on their own.

I see two explanations for this: one is that they were doing what they saw on the television. The other is that they have a subconscious hatred for the mechanisms that were destroying their lives.

The media were so dramatic in how they covered the riots, I think it's one of the reasons people started joining a few days later. But by the fourth or fifth day, the national media realized they were destabilizing the situation, and they tried to censor their coverage. They didn't show any more arsons, they didn't show masses of people fighting with police, and they prohibited the phrase "student riots." But the foreign media were more honest, and they were very interested in the riots, so after that Greece got all its coverage of the riots from the international channels. By coincidence there had been this conference in Athens about the role of the media in democracy, so all the international press was already in the country when the fighting started. The media were confused because they couldn't understand the general feeling and they really messed it up.

After the students came the hooligans, and after the hooligans came the immigrants, and after the immigrants every exploited person came out on the streets. You could see yuppies with ties burning banks and grandmas and grandpas attacking the police for gassing the children.

During these days there were six or seven major demonstrations, really big ones. The first contained about 3,000 people. Each of these demos destroyed a different part of the city. And all this time, there were small groups hitting the banks and attacking the police stations again and again. This is no exaggeration—at five o'clock if there was an attack on a police station, there would be another attack, by another group of people, at four past five. The cops were terrified, shouting, almost crying on their radios, yelling for backup, thinking they were going to be burned to death.

I have to tell you, the theater school occupation was very important. On the second day, Alpha Kappa squatted the theater school and then they left so the students of that school could assume the occupation—they reoccupied it together. This became a central point. There were really diverse opinions expressed there, from the radical Left to the blackest of the black.

Another building, the office of the lawyers guild, was occupied by leftists and anarchists but after the media started turning public opinion against the uprising the leftists abandoned it. So this theater school was very central. Many decisions were made there for the movement as a whole. If they called a protest for a certain day and hour, it happened. But sometimes this was problematic.

There are lots of conflicts in the movement. Some of the major conflicts are with Antiauthoritarian Movement, Alpha Kappa. First of all I think it's a bad translation. It shouldn't be Antiauthoritarian Movement but Antiauthoritarian Current. Because this word, *kinisi*, it doesn't mean like a political movement, but a flow or a current. And the antiauthoritarian movement in Greece is much bigger than Alpha Kappa. Because of the way they act they can collaborate with the leftists but there aren't many anarchists who will work with them. They make media statements, give interviews, talk with the journalists in the spotlight, you know, things no anarchists would do. They often take postures that belong to the Left, not to anarchists. And in December they made a declaration, saying that the people who loot are not anarchists. The looters are not anarchists. It's unbelievable.

But I'm talking mostly about Alpha Kappa in Athens. In each city they're a little different and there are bigger problems with the group in Athens. In Thessaloniki they're not like this. They're comrades. We have to remember that in December we were in the streets together with Alpha Kappa. We forgot about our separations and we moved together, we mixed, we weren't in separate blocs. Everyone rallied around the antiauthoritarian movement. I don't only speak about anarchists but also about leftists and autonomia.

That's how big this thing was

Anna: A student on Samos, a medium-sized island close to Turkey

After the killing of Alexis there was a demonstration in the city on the other side of the island. And all the students at my school, kids who wouldn't even get off their Playstations long enough to go down to the beach, went forty kilometers, all the way to the other side of the island to take part in that protest. That's how big this thing was. It brought the kids out of their bubbles, because we could feel it was important.

In Patras, 1000 people came out to the demonstrations

Yiannis: An anarchist from Patras

In Patras, in December, there were many demonstrations and riots. It wasn't as big as in Athens, but it was big. In the demonstrations there were maybe 1,000 people, and here in Patras there are maybe 2–300,000 people. The major thing wasn't rioting, though. We would make a demonstration and then in the evenings go and talk to the people, have discussions, give out flyers.

Because the port is here, there are many immigrants in Patras—in recent years, mostly from Afghanistan. We are friends with some of them, and they came to the demonstration. They don't have a word for anarchism, and they grow up in a society that teaches them very strongly to accept God and the State, to accept authority. But our common ground was our opposition to the police. One of these friends had no papers, he had been here for a year, and if he were arrested it would be very bad. But when the demonstration came a block away from the police station, he went with those who threw rocks at the police. I kept taking him by the arm and leading him away, saying "leave this for the other people to do," and he kept going back to throw more rocks.

Before the demonstrations we would have a meeting and decide, for example, that we would smash all the banks we passed, but if anyone went to smash a store, we would stop them. However, the media were saying all sorts of things—that we were smashing stores, that we were attacking people. It was crazy.

On Tuesday, so the third day of riots, the fascists attacked us. They were behind the police lines, protected by the police, they gathered all the stones that we had thrown, and then they attacked us. Fortunately no one was injured. But later that day they went around the streets hunting and attacking immigrants. They had knives. I don't know how many were injured. They grabbed this friend of ours also, but fortunately he got away. And they also smashed up the offices of Alpha Kappa.

111

That was the craziest moment of all December for me

Vortex: A person from Athens who was already involved in the movement when the rebellion started

We organized assemblies but no one needed them. Within an hour of the shooting people had already started smashing things. When I went out around 11:30, two hours after Alexis's murder, the fights had already started. On Akadimias I saw people coming from every direction. Since it was clear that there would be many people on the street I thought that we should create as many fronts as possible. My idea was that if different groups of people would be causing trouble throughout the center, smashing shops and then fighting the police when they came, we should start blocking the roads with dumpsters and so forth. But it became obvious that the leftists had a very different perspective. Around 12:30 that night, my little group of four people was on Akadimias, which is a big avenue, trying to block it with dumpsters and big tubes from a nearby construction site. And these various leftist groups come marching by from different streets. On our right there's this one leftist bloc marching away. Another group of leftists starts coming towards us, but they see what

we're doing and they decided to go another way. I started shouting at them not to go because four of us couldn't hold a barricade on a central avenue. And then there was this one crazy guy who had decided to start smashing a bank all by himself.

I shouted at the leftists, "where the fuck are you going?" They had gotten it in their heads that they were going to march and start a demo. But there was no demo, it was already kicking off. You're not asking for something, it's not a matter of making demands, so you don't walk around the city like it's a protest, you fucking start doing it! So I was shouting at them not to leave, but they had made up their minds to go to Omonia. But there was no protest at Omonia, I knew that the shit had already started there. So I ran up to this other group of leftists and told them we're closing down the avenue, come help us. I knew they were leftists but I thought they might have some different tactics. These guys all had their megaphones, shouting at each other what to do. "Comrades, we're going this way!" And they yelled at their herds not to listen to me and they left.

Since there were only four or five of us in the middle of a central avenue, we left. We went down Solonos Street, and there I had the idea that if we don't flip a car now then when are we going to do it? But my friends refused so we continued.

What impressed me on Sunday and Monday was that the people, especially the anarchists, were very well prepared.

112

They had gas masks, helmets, and some of them had even attached these pillows to their arms so they could block the police clubs without breaking their arms.

The interesting thing during these days was that you didn't have the feeling that you could only do things if you had your friends around. You could do it by yourself. In Omonia I was in a luxury clothing store by myself. There were 300 leftists around me just watching, but I felt very confident. You knew that things were happening everywhere so you weren't alone even if you couldn't see them. It was a strange sort of confidence. It was the moment we were all waiting for all these years.

In the fights in the streets we all worked like one collective brain connected in a mysterious way. Somehow you knew what your comrades needed to back them up. The police couldn't cope with it. They are a mechanism that works only with orders, with central decision-making. But with us, ten of us would go forward at the same time, ten of us would go back at the same time.

By Monday night they were throwing this strange tear gas that made a terrible sound, very loud. And it would affect hundreds of people within an area of many blocks. People would be blinded, they couldn't breathe. It was much stronger than normal tear gas. With normal tear gas, you have a few seconds to run away and a block later you're alright. If you weren't wearing a gas mask you'd have to pull back for a few minutes, and that was all. This new tear gas was much worse.

But we set so many fires it burned off the tear gas. This was one of the reasons to set the fires, to protect ourselves.

On Monday night at one point I circled around behind the cops, and I saw this big motorbike pull up with two guys carrying a big backpack. They started pulling tear gas canisters out of the backpack and distributing it to the riot cops, who had run out. Evidently they had called in to headquarters and these two undercovers were going around with resupplies. They left very fast.

A lot of people went to work with sledgehammers to smash windows and also to smash up the pavement into rocks for throwing. Monday afternoon there were many different teams of people who had come to create chaos. The difference between Monday's protest and a regular demo is that no one had to wait for the right time to attack. Just two blocks from Panepistimio, the starting point, people already started smashing things. There were teams of four or five people, and every team would have some tool for breaking the glass and something for setting fires. Some people hadn't even had the time to make molotovs, they just brought big plastic jugs of gasoline. People acted in a spontaneous way, but I imagine each team also had their certain tactics. These had to do more with how to care for each other and look out for each other and back each other up, because this time it wasn't a matter of selecting targets. You would pretty much burn anything that didn't look like a small shop.

I flipped my first car, that was a great joy. About seven or eight of us flipped a big jeep, quite an expensive car. Seven to turn it upside down and another to throw the molotov and that's it. And barricades everywhere. Of course you know that when you put a garbage can in the middle of the street you also light it, because even if there's no tear gas now, it will come so you'd better be prepared.

On Monday there were two hits on Kolonaki. I had this idea in the morning, before the demo. We'd already had two days of fighting with the police so I thought the evening demo would be very dangerous for us. Perhaps it would be a trap, with the police arresting everyone. It never happened like that. But my idea was that instead of going to the demo, we should make a team of about 100 people and go to Kolonaki and smash everything while the demo was starting—because I thought that all the police would be there and they'd definitely want to fuck us. But some people had already arranged that, and they had arranged it for a few hours earlier. I was lucky because I found this friend of mine, told him my plan, and he said, "you know what, we're going for it in fifteen minutes, so if you want to come…" I said, "Okay, let's go, I'm coming."

It was fucking scary for a person sitting outside, watching about fifty people all of the sudden putting on their gloves and masks. It was a light attack, though, a few luxury shops were smashed and some luxury cars were burned. But the same night, the same street got hit again by a different group of people. And whereas the first group smashed four blocks on this street, the second group smashed the whole street. We heard that it was happening while we were at Nomiki throwing rocks at the cops, and we started running. There were some immigrants with us without masks. They weren't speaking at all, they were just breaking. And we caught up with them and participated in what was left, also going into the shops to smash more things. Some people were looting as well but I was not interested in that.

The luxury street was empty because half the city was already burned down, and at that moment there was fierce fighting with the police around the universities. So there were no police, no traffic, nothing. It was really fun to see people just running along the roofs of these luxury cars, smashing them from the top, doing whatever they wanted.

At one point on Monday, we had left Nomiki because the police were surrounding it. We left the areas where there was more tear gas, went to a kiosk to get a beer, and we're coming back, passing Kolonaki. And there we saw this group of school kids wearing masks. About four or five boys, and two or three girls. None of them older than 18, wearing trendy clothes; they looked like emo kids. They're just walking down the street with masks like it's perfectly normal. And all of a sudden they started smashing shops. They didn't have tools with them, they just picked up whatever they could find and started smashing, as they were calmly talking with each other, joking around, having fun, you know? It was like a company of friends who had gone out for a drink and they were just having fun. That's how comfortable they felt there, how safe, at that moment. It was magical to see.

And then my friend shouts at them, "hey, don't leave that bank." And they look at the bank, which they hadn't smashed, and looked to each other and said, "yeah, he's right." So they found this big piece of wood, all of them together, they rammed it against the door of the bank, and the fucking thing just collapsed. It didn't break, it didn't shatter, it just fell inwards and all the bank alarms started going off.

So we decided to simply follow them and see how they were experiencing it because it was magical. They smashed a few more shops after the bank and they reached Kolonaki Square. It was just a few of them but they were acting like they were in a playground, the girls walking arm in arm, all of them smashing things on their own. And all of a sudden a police car passes. And just one of them alone starts shouting *batsi!* (cops!), like he was challenging them to get out of the car, and he grabs a rock. One of them alone started chasing the police car, the cop stepped on the gas and got out of there and the guy threw the rock. And after this they didn't even leave the scene, they just sat there in the square, talking, like nothing was happening. They were ignoring us, just sitting there. For me it was a moment of truth, to see that situation, because they weren't afraid of the all powerful law. And they had taken their masks off, put them back on, they were playing with them. This was the most luxurious square in the center of Athens. And we're watching with our mouths open.

At one point one of these guys had gone down a street where you could see the group of police stationed outside the presidential house. And he starts yelling at them, insulting them, *suck my dick you fucking cops!* Imagine a cop who is there listening to the radio about how the center of Athens is burning, but Kolonaki seems calm when all of a sudden this kid with a mask appears from the most luxurious square in the city to just taunt him, alone, without fear. That was the craziest moment for me in all of December.

If I had to summarize it in one sentence: perhaps we don't know how, but we can do it.

115

This is the spirit of the revolt

Pavlos and Irina: Two anarchists who were in the Polytechnic occupation

I heard about the shooting of Alexis from a friend, over the phone. This was already several hours later, at one in the morning. I went there as soon as I got the call, but the events had already begun. When I got to Exarchia, the streets were full of fires. People had occupied the Polytechnic after having a small assembly there and deciding to take it over. At this time, 1:30, 2:00, the cops tried to surround the campus to prevent people from gathering there. People from Exarchia Square and more people from Patision, from Omonia, were trying to approach the Polytechnic so there were fights between the riot police and the people, in Exarchia and on Patision Avenue.

From the moment of the assassination, people in that area started to take action. There was an announcement for a meeting in the Polytechnic half an hour after the murder. At the same time people were gathering at the spot where the shooting took place. Significantly, the struggle did not begin from an organized initiative, but spontaneously, as a natural expansion of the event.

Some leftists were gathering on Akademias Avenue, while people were fighting at and around the Polytechnic. Some hours after midnight, a big group of anarchists, 100–200 people, not a specific political group, but an ad hoc gathering, walked to another neighborhood one or two kilometers away, a commercial district, an area with night life, and they attacked many big shops. There were buildings that were completely burned out. This same group also attacked one or two police stations while travelling around the city. This was the first counterattack, the first initiative of people going on the offensive.

These first reactions were vital in lending a defining character to everything that came afterwards. The first reactions determine what happens next. This is why what happened in Exarchia is so crucial. From the first moment, people gathered. In the first hour a large group of people occupied the Polytechnic. And this initiative, this counterattack, gave a specific character to all the subsequent reactions.

The cops who were stationed in Exarchia were attacked. It's something that has happened before as a spontaneous response to police aggressions, or as a planned attack. It has happened frequently. In the past loose gatherings of young people would meet and decide, let's go, tomorrow night, and attack the cops at this location. It was done fluidly, not by formal organization. It's a field of exercise. This is important.

People already had all this experience. Not only the experience of organization or political discussion but also the experience of fighting in the streets. This is one of the features that enabled our successes in December.

I don't remember at what hour but at one point the cops disappeared from around the Polytechnic and all the people could come gather there. And this happened because all night more and more people were coming down into the street to fight with police. The fighting continued all night. That first night provides us a vantage point from which we can look at the rest of the insurrection. First of all I only use the word insurrection to express what period we're talking about, in December. My opinion is that we cannot determine the insurrectional when it happens, according to rules or standards. We cannot measure it. That's a sociological discussion, to demarcate when the insurrection begins and ends. It didn't begin on December 6, the insurrection was always here. In every individual or every group of people that reacted against the State and authority. What happened on December 6 in Athens and later in all of Greece and across the world was the meeting of all the insurrections, all the revolts, that could meet at this time. I don't want to see history from a sociological point of view, *now we have many people so it is an insurrection, now they are no longer in the streets so it ended.* It's not like this. With such a perspective you cannot see what is under the events, you cannot explain how it came to light and how it continues, if you see history only as numbers. And this explains how in some hours thousands of people gathered in the center of town fighting with the police. It was because the fire was already lit. The inner motive was already there. It's like a bomb. A single event that meant something to masses of people was the fuse to ignite a social power that had already been smoldering, invisibly. This explains how thousands of people met, gathered in a few hours, and could continue fighting for days, and why this expanded to other places.

December 6 wasn't the first time that a cop killed a civilian. They do it often. What made the difference, what gave a specific meaning to this event from the first moment, was that it was an attack, a straight attack. The cop car passed the area where young people were hanging out, drinking beers, discussing. And this is a place where young people and anarchists pass their time, a pedestrian street. When the cops drove by, someone insulted them, shouted something. Perhaps they threw a plastic bottle of water, I'm not sure. The cops drove on, they parked the car two blocks away where there was a bus of riot police, which is normally stationed there. They parked the car in a safe place and they came back on foot. They both took out their guns, and one of them aimed it at the group of young people, and shot two or three times. The first important feature of the event is that it was a blatant attack by the police; no one can talk about an accident. Always when they kill someone they call it an accident.

Secondly it was in a neighborhood that is in a way liberated from the police. Not totally, but they don't do what they want in Exarchia, they don't pass easily. And that's why they first parked the car somewhere out of this zone. Let's say

117

there was a mental border, a not safe place, a stateless zone, and outside of this border there is state security. This mental scheme is understood by everybody. It was a social accomplishment in everybody's minds, even the enemy recognized it. From time to time in the newspapers, in the Sunday editions where they run articles with political analysis, terrorism, or anarchists, there were articles about the *avaton* of Exarchia. Traditionally this word was only used for the holy mountain of Khalkidiki, which is a mountain where only monks can go. It has boundaries, it's like another country. Avaton is a place where you cannot step. And the State was using this word for Exarchia. In fact some journalists on the first night or the next day were saying that this assassination provided an opportunity to discuss the problem of the *avaton* of Exarchia.

They are stupid, they couldn't understand the meaning of the event and what the consequences would be. They were talking a bunch of hot air because they couldn't yet understand what would happen. Starting the very next day, everybody was selling tears, capitalizing on the grief of the assassination. Up to the president. There were some journalists saying this bullshit but the rest of the State understood how serious the situation was and everybody was trying to erase the meaning, to lower the value of the event, pretending to sympathize, because Alexis was young. And the fact that he was a young student was important because from the first moment it concerned all the youth, all the students.

After the first assembly in the Polytechnic some people left and went to start another occupation, at the ASOEE, joined by other people who weren't at Polytechnic. They did it for a political reason. They did not want to be near a chaotic situation which they couldn't control. There were also people who believed it would be better to have more occupations than one, more centers, more bases for the struggle, it's true, and some people went to ASOEE because the police prevented them from entering the Polytechnic at that moment so they went to another occupation. The fact that we had more than one occupation functioned as a factor of power, it was more difficult to attack more places. It also allowed a greater diversity of people to participate, since there were different occupations with different ways of doing things.

From the first day we were among the people in the Polytechnic who had the opinion that all the occupations must continue. That we have to keep more buildings, different bases. I'm not sure if it was the same night or the next day when there was also a third occupation at Nomiki, carried out by people of the Left and Alpha Kappa, the Antiauthoritarian Current. They have good relations with the leftists and bad relations with most of the rest of the anarchist movement. During the first night everybody was mixed, but after some hours people began to separate and clarify their political character. Some people left the Polytechnic because they did not want to be together with an uncontrolled crowd. They preferred to be in an area where they could subject all actions to a general discussion. It's not that they didn't want direct action or a violent fight, but they wanted to do it in the way they were already familiar with.

So I know that my criticism is a little hard, but I think it's true. The occupation of ASOEE had more of a Party character, not in an institutional way but symbolically, and in its ideological purity. But also I use the word Party because this strategy divided them from the uncontrolled crowds that were fighting, destroying anything in the streets. The ASOEE group participated in the marches, in many events, they also did actions by themselves, I don't say that it was a bureaucratic group, and as I said before my opinion was that all the occupations must continue, they all were important. So in the ASOEE occupation there were many discussions but among people who already knew one another, like a big family you could say, discussing different subjects. And of course the cohesion that they had between them was an advantage for many actions. They intervened in the fighting in the streets, they made attacks in the metro.

On the other hand, those of us who stayed in the Polytechnic, from the first moment, were there not because we dropped in accidentally, but because we believed that we had to stay there, to keep this occupation, for many reasons. Some of these reasons are related to the beginning of the insurrection. The Polytechnic as a place was an important factor in the insurrection. For example the people who attacked the commercial district, they started from the Polytechnic. Many

of them didn't participate later in the Polytechnic, some of them went to ASOEE, it doesn't matter. They started from the Polytechnic because the Polytechnic has a historical value. Not like a monument, but a living meaning. It's still the base, the center, of serious struggles, and a place of organizational processes, like assemblies. This meaning comes from the insurrection of '73 before the end of the dictatorship.

Because of this living historical value, the living meaning of *Polytecnio*, we had to be there, we had to keep this place. The Polytechnic is a point on the map of social consciousness that is related with insurrection. That's why not only the first night but all the first week and the days after thousands of people passed through there to fight. Many more than the number of people who stayed in the occupation. We were only a few dozen staying there, keeping the occupation running, just a few people next to the huge masses who participated in the events. In the assemblies there were some hundreds of people who didn't sleep there, didn't stay in the buildings, and during the nights, in the fighting outside the Polytechnic, there were thousands of people. And of course not only anarchists.

Regardless of the meaning of the place and the historical value of the Polytechnic, and because of that meaning, it was the gathering point for many different people, many who had never worked together or met until that moment, and they met there for a common reason: insurrection. To fight against the State. The campus and the streets around it were also the specific place designated for fighting, for violence against the

119

police and the State. The common idea was that this was our place. The place where we do what we want. You could see so many different people in the occupation and in the fights in the surrounding streets. You could see immigrants from any race or country, blacks, Eastern Europeans, anybody. You could see high school students, lumpen proletariat—people who live on the streets, junkies, hooligans, gypsies. And all ages were there. You could see all ages from the first night, the first hours, all the generations of anarchists, all the generations that had lived through struggles in the past and now gathered in the streets. You could see people who had left the struggle years ago. But they came out again this night. And the place of this mixture was the Polytechnic.

What other anarchists didn't like was the melting pot, the mixing with people from other cultures that are not very familiar or welcoming to us. And they didn't like the blurring of actions, including many actions that they didn't accept or that didn't fit their view of insurrection. This fact was one of the reasons that we wanted to be there. Because we don't understand the insurrection as an expression of the process of our ideas or a clear manifestation of anarchist organizations in society, but as a social explosion, as the expression of the needs of people who are repressed, exploited, tortured. And our work until this moment was and should be to provoke this moment, to provoke this meeting, this melting. We keep our thinking, we keep our way of organizing, our characteristics, our way to organize our own fight, but we have to be there

and to mix with all the others. This is our role, to support this, to push this. So we can say that the occupation of the Polytechnic was the most proletarian of all the occupations. It wasn't restricted to anarchists but the way of doing things and the general strategy, the way of thinking in the assemblies, was anarchist.

And that's why in the pamphlets from the Polytechnic occupation and in the poster we made you could find the clearest reference to class struggle, to a counterattack by the lower class. It was not an exclusively anarchist view of the event, on what is the State, what is the insurrection, but our discourse was very clear in announcing that the counterattack of our class begins now. From the first paper we printed, we were talking about all the people assassinated in the past, naming them, remembering them, referring also to the armed guerrillas that were killed in fights, because we are not into victimization. We said that these days of struggle were for all of them as well as for Alexis. We will take revenge for all of them. And for all of us.

On the first night, many shops on Stournari Street were smashed open. Some were looted, others were burned. Stournari is the street that goes from Exarchia Square, past the Polytechnic, to Patision. Cops were on the corner of Patision and Stournari, and higher up on Stournari, to keep people from convening in the Polytechnic. They were also behind the campus, where there is always a police bus guarding the Ministry of Culture. Normally the police attack Polytechnic from Kanigos Square and this night they did so again to try to cut off Stournari. But the cops were defeated in the street, and the shops were destroyed—all the big shops and some smaller ones, but most of the little shops were not touched. The biggest computer shop in this street and one of the biggest in all Greece was smashed open and burned completely. Many floors, a tall building, all burned. And it was burning slowly, so the arson was well done. I think it is not usable now, I think they will have to demolish it. This particular building was burned on purpose because this company was part of a consortium that wanted to build a technological park, like Silicon Valley, on a mountain near Athens, in a place where there is forest now.

The next morning Stournari and all the smaller side streets were a surrealistic place, a magical and unimaginable scene. You couldn't picture it if you hadn't seen it. The whole street covered with stones, pieces of metal, anything that could be thrown. Burnt cars. Cars flipped over. Smoke. It was like a moonscape. Very quiet, that morning. Only a few people passing by to see the scene or take photos. But you didn't see anyone going to work, no one went to open their shops. It was like time stopped there. The feeling was great. Tranquility. It was like this the first morning, and all the mornings of the first week. People were passing by going into the occupation or coming out. Like it was our place, it was free. A specific political and military situation, a balance of power, in which one neighborhood, one street, was liberated. It was ours. For days.

It was a place of no control. It's not like the police came to write up the damages. For one week, there was no State there. In the rest of the city the police were on the streets, but only in big groups, in defensive formation, or they were hiding. But here it was ours. And just one and a half blocks away, there was a bus of riot police guarding a ministry building. They never left their post. They were attacked many times, with a variety of methods, but they didn't budge. Very surreal.

Next day, Sunday, was the first march. It started near *Polytecnio* and went towards the police headquarters, at Leoforos Alexandras, not too far, but away from the center. This march contained many people, and much energy. It was an unstoppable attack, from the first moment. Many people started destroying all the symbols of capitalism. They were burning corporate offices, supermarkets, banks, car dealerships, for example Ford was burned totally. And the cops were not there at first, they were waiting near their headquarters. As soon as the people saw the cops on Leoforos Alexandras guarding the headquarters, they attacked. But the cops managed to break the march and push it back, and there was continuous conflict. The people didn't scatter, but they were steadily pushed back. At this point the police were trying to disperse people, not to make arrests. They used incredible amounts of tear gas. Sunday's march was the first mass outlet of destruction in the city. Some leftists and Left parties called the Sunday march, I think also with Alpha Kappa. But everybody went there. People from all the occupations, anarchists generally.

121

The people from the political parties were not in control, they did very little.

Sunday night, after the protest march, thousands more came to the Polytechnic to fight with police, thousands of people. This happened from Saturday to Wednesday, but Sunday night was the night of the rage outside the Polytechnic. The people were uncontrollable. You cannot describe it with words, the rage that was expressed there. Against the cops and against anything that symbolized authority. It was pure rage. When I went out from the university into the street on Sunday night, I saw a large group of people in front of one of the computer shops throwing anything they could find, along with dozens, maybe hundreds of molotovs, into the same shop. For a long time. It didn't follow any plan, it was just uncontrolled rage. And then they went to find the police at Kanigos Square. In Kanigos there is also a ministry building so you could always be sure to find cops there. These nights we went out from the occupation to go fight, but we didn't have to do anything because everything was done, it was done by others. Fighting and rioting was not the exclusive specialty of the anarchists.

Many people, anarchists and others, were coming from other countries to experience the insurrection. There was a hooligan from Poland who heard the news and on the second day he took a plane to Athens, came to the Polytechnic, and he stayed there until the last day of the occupation. It wasn't only a political familiarity that attracted the people, it was the mind of the insurrection, the common potential of every exploited person. On Monday there were events in the whole country. Even in the little islands far to the east, near Turkey, the students made attacks on the police stations. And also in an area in the northwest of Athens where many gypsies live, on the second day they participated in the insurrection. They didn't come down to the center but gathered in their own area and burned a bank, looted a big store, and attacked the local police station. They set fire to a stolen truck, jammed down the gas pedal, and drove it into the front door. Then they shot the building up with hunting rifles. It's a hard place, there are bad relations between the cops and the gypsies. They also have lost people to police assassinations in the past.

Next day, Monday, the minister of education decided to close the schools and universities so that the students could not gather. They had estimated that they would have a problem with the students mobilizing, and they thought they could stop them like this. But on Monday morning the students swarmed around their closed schools and started carrying out actions spontaneously, everywhere. Everywhere in Athens and throughout the entire country. You could hear about students who were blocking streets, making protest marches, others who were attacking police stations with stones. And we're talking about people who didn't have any contact with us and who hadn't been in the center of Athens the previous two nights. These were random people all over the country who gathered and did things. It seemed like the entire student body of some schools were coming down to the Polytechnic. On Monday morning I went to Patision Avenue with some other friends, some comrades, to distribute pamphlets. It was the first pamphlet that was written in the Polytechnic occupation. Students were arriving in groups thinking that the Polytechnic was the place to gather and find out how to get involved. They asked us what we would do and when, and where.

I will add a personal experience to illustrate the atmosphere there. At one point a march arrives, with a large mass of students. They had come from many kilometers away, not a very poor neighborhood either, but middle class and upper middle class. And when they arrived at Patision outside the historical door of the Polytechnic, where the tanks attacked in '73, they blocked the avenue without asking us what to do. And they started shouting the common slogan, *batsi, gourounya, dolofoni!* Cops, pigs, killers! Watching this scene, I became ecstatic. And I understood at this moment that the thing now has departed. It has gone beyond us. I don't say it surpassed us. Many people use this word, but I don't believe this. Maybe it surpassed them because they didn't believe this could happen, but the insurrection surpassed this way of thinking. I am one of those people who was sure that insurrections will happen, and soon. And I am one of the people who believe that revolution also will happen.

So when the insurrection came here, it wasn't a surprise. The moment changes you, every experience in this situation becomes a new part of you. But it's not unexpected. It's what you expected but you've just never seen it before and now here it is in front of you, all around you. And in this moment, in front of this scene, I was ecstatic, thinking that these are our people. It's not only our small circle of comrades. Now that which is hidden in everybody, every single person, will be expressed. It was in this moment that I understood that now the event goes forward. It's free to advance, it can't be stopped now.

Monday afternoon was the first march in the center of town. Everyone was there. It was the biggest march of the week. And it was this afternoon that the center of Athens was burned.

From the first moment, people started attacking. Burning buildings, central banks, state buildings, big shops, chain stores, department stores. And looting. Below Omonia Square, let's say Omonia is the border between the high city and the low city, where normal society meets the underclasses. Immigrants, junkies, homeless people, they always gather below Omonia. When the destruction began, it spread through Omonia Square, and many people who weren't in the march started to destroy and to loot. Many of the people arrested this day, a big percentage of the total arrests, were immigrants from this situation. When the riot police came there, they found dozens of people inside the shops. They were hanging out, choosing things, not just breaking, burning, and running, like we were.

The attacks of the Monday protest spread beyond the march, destroying the bordering areas. One friend went to Kolonaki Square after the march, and he saw a group of young people, ten people hooded and masked, in the richest square of town, smashing shops. My friends continued to Skoufa Street, that goes from Kolonaki Square to Exarchia, and here they found another group, students, coming up towards Kolonaki, and these two groups joined and started to smash all the shops on the street. This also shows how the insurrection works. Many people, including anarchists, have a mechanical way of understanding how things work. They cannot understand how the State cannot control certain situations, why the State cannot repress Greek anarchists, why they cannot stop violence in the marches. Many anarchists understand the State as something that can only increase its power. The insurrection of December demonstrates how this mechanical understanding is not real, it's not valid. It's only the projection of the State's own mentality. A mentality concentrated on control, the idea that everything can be controlled. It's a reality that many of us accept. Me too. I opposed this way of thinking, yet I also had a view of a strategy planned in advance, a prepared way to begin the insurrection.

But in the insurrection of December I saw how a plural subject can be more clever than any individual subject. When we are in a situation that involves many minds working together, in the midst of action, the group is more intelligent, more fluid. The insurrection of December is evidence of the intelligence of anarchy. On Monday afternoon in particular we did not have any plan or single strategy, but precisely because of this the State and the cops could not control us. The situation was too chaotic for them. They cannot stop an enemy that is everywhere or anywhere. They cannot stop an enemy that doesn't have a single objective. When they attack in one area, they lose another area.

In the fights outside the Polytechnic, I saw how a thousand people or fifty people could attack the riot police, working as a single body. We could fight without having an organization, a structure, prepared before the action, because all of the participants could understand the fight and the moment from a holistic point of view, a point of view centered in the group. The group existed not because before we had an assembly but because everyone at that moment understood himself as a part of a group. And it is more effective than their model because in our model everyone simultaneously has a vision of the entire situation and everyone feels the responsibility to take any initiative he can take to support the common objective.

On the third night, Monday night, thousands of people, mostly students, came to the Polytechnic after the march. You could see people as young as 12 years old, breaking, destroying, throwing stones. All the generations were there. This night at the university saw the greatest participation in the riots and the character of the conflict was visibly a little bit different than the nights before. Sunday night was the rage, but on Monday night… you could see a spirit of collectivity. There were many students but also immigrants and anarchists and junkies and others, all of us thinking collectively. There were groups coming into the Polytechnic to rest, others going out to fight, a continuous chain. A large group of people, many of them girls, were inside the Polytechnic breaking the masonry to make stones, collecting things to throw. They were working like a factory but nobody told them what to do. They were like the ants of revolution. We didn't have to do anything, our group that was keeping the occupation running. We were at the doors just checking that nobody got caught, nobody got left alone. Or we would throw the gas canisters back at the police.

In these events, there was a generation who educated themselves, who passed through a rite of passage. This is a generation that will be in the streets for the next ten, twenty years. I believe that. It's a very powerful experience for a young person, if this was your first experience in the streets. It's not so easy afterwards to go back to normality. Once again we see the importance of the occupation of the Polytechnic. It was an opportunity for all these people to gather and fight in the streets.

One of the occupations, that of the central building of the General Confederation of Greek Workers, happened during the second week. It was started by some comrades who were already organizing base unions. They weren't explicitly anarchist unions, but antiauthoritarian workers unions. Some of these comrades had also been in the occupation of the Polytechnic. Their approach was to emphasize a class

analysis, but not as a formulation of economic demands or a discourse focused strictly on work. They were representing themselves as workers in revolt, talking about the insurrection, the prisoners. They wanted to mobilize working people but inside the insurrection. Not in a divided program, in a limited struggle for solely economic demands. The truth is that this effort didn't achieve the mobilization of many workers, or the creation of mass events, but they provided a basis for some struggles that are beginning now, directed at problems of work but seizing the spirit of the insurrection. Konstantina Kuneva participated in the assemblies of this occupation, before she was attacked. When she went with her union to ask for solidarity from the General Confederation and to spread their text about the brutality of their bosses, the General Confederation asked them to denounce the occupation. And of course Kuneva and her union refused.

Afterwards they occupied the central offices of the railway, which contracts the private companies that employ the cleaners represented by Kuneva's union. And her union refused to cooperate with the Communist Party union or any other party. They were protesting with us, with the people who supported the insurrection, anarchists and the base unions. Another Left party offered Kuneva a spot on the list of candidates for the European Parliament and she refused that too. And in the workers' marches there were also violent conflicts, attacks on banks, fights with the police. The insurrection provided a basis for bringing anarchists, antiauthoritarians, and autonomists, closer together with working people who are ready to fight.

As the days passed, violent events continued, but they were not as massive as before. In Exarchia and the Polytechnic, people continued to carry out violent struggle. One week after the assassination there was a meeting right on the spot where he was killed. All the anarchists went there, and we started fighting the cops. There was an attack on a police bus and the police station of Exarchia, and then the fighting went on all night around the Polytechnic. Some anarchists in the university occupation, we believed that we should take the initiative to call for a major march. Until then none of the marches had been called by the anarchist occupations. And we believed that we should call a central march, as the occupation of the Polytechnic, to send a political message against the State but also to society, of what we are and what we want. That the insurrection is not only anger, but also a political objective. We did not want to represent the insurrection but to give a clear political stance of one major group that was participating in the insurrection and that supported its goals and proposals. But we encountered resistance from many comrades in the occupation and outside of it. There were not enough of us in favor of this proposal. It's not a matter of numbers, but a matter of synthesis. We felt we couldn't take the initiative, being such a small part of the anarchist movement. If we had gone into the streets thousands of people would have come

but we did not want to monopolize that role, even though we believed it should be done. And it didn't happen.

In the discussion inside the Polytechnic our proposal was absorbed by another one calling for a day of global resistance against state violence, and the assemblies of the Polytechnic and ASOEE adopted this call-out, for the second Saturday after the assassination of Alexis. On December 20 protests and actions took place in more than forty countries, and over 100 cities. It wasn't the first day that there were events outside of Greece. From the very first days of the insurrection things started happening in other countries, like occupations of embassies, marches, in Germany, London, France. The ASOEE occupation called for a march that morning, and the Polytechnic occupation called for a gathering to take place at night at the spot of the assassination.

So on the 20th we started a violent fight that spread once again to the Polytechnic. On this night we didn't have the thousands we had two weeks before, but all the anarchists were there and they were prepared. I mention it because it was the first time that we took the initiative, the decision to call for an offensive action well in advance. We didn't hold a march somewhere, or go off in a spontaneous group to riot. This time we decided to do this, to converge as a movement in order to go on the offensive. And this night was the first time the State started talking about suspending the asylum and invading the Polytechnic. It was the last day of mass violent struggles. They could accept spontaneous fighting but they did not want to accept something on that scale planned in advance. It was a publicly announced attack, and they didn't want to tolerate that. So they started a lot of discussion and propaganda about invading the Polytechnic and taking away the asylum. But they didn't do it, because they weren't ready to manage it politically, and I don't know if they are ready now or if they will ever be ready. Also because they were afraid of the fight; they couldn't invade without spilling blood.

But after this night they revoked the university's asylum and said they could invade at any time; if there were any more attacks they would invade. It was a psychological tactic. Previously we had decided to hold a concert the following Tuesday, and despite this government pressure we decided to continue with our plans and also to transform the concert into a response to the government's threats. We did it, although some comrades disagreed with us because there were so many people who were physically exhausted and people who couldn't understand that our power was not our numbers inside the occupation but the social meaning of the occupation. There were people who thought that we had to announce a definite date for ending the occupation. And there were many comrades who didn't want to hold a central march because they were afraid of the repression. They couldn't understand that it wasn't just some anarchists against the State but that what we were doing was embraced by many people. We wouldn't have been alone.

So we held the concert, and two days later, one day before we had scheduled an end to the occupation, some professors came to the assembly and told us that the cops were ready to invade and they would come in one hour. This had also happened the Sunday after the attack, the 21st. We ignored the warning. It was repeated the next day, and this second time they were really trying to pressure us—the leftists, the professors, the syndicate of lawyers, everyone was pressuring us and waiting for the police to invade the Polytechnic. We said that it was a psychological game. They knew we didn't want to leave and that we had an internal conflict over this question, so they wanted to exploit the event politically. They wanted to be able to say that they pressured us and we came out, so they won. In response to this pressure we decided to stay longer. The same night, during the assembly, we made a pamphlet and published it, just a few words saying that they will not pass, we will not let them take the Polytechnic, we don't give in. Just ten minutes after we published the pamphlet on Indymedia and had it read over the anarchist radio, the professors came again and said *okay guys, excuse us, the information was wrong, the minister had been pleading with us to stop the occupation*, and we responded, *okay, when the prime minister calls us up to beg, maybe we'll discuss it.*

An important characteristic of the occupations, besides the violence, was how they were following an anarchist model. No organ could make decisions for the occupation besides the general assembly. This wasn't an assembly of students but of

127

all the people participating in the occupation and the fights. For example the occupation of the architectural school in the Polytechnic, they had their own assembly and they supported the general occupation, but they didn't have any authority over the occupation as a whole. The different schools weren't separated, it was a unified occupation. Some leftist students tried to separate the different schools, and in the first week we tried to work with them and give them space to do their own activities but they kept trying to bypass the general assembly and occupy areas of the Polytechnic just for themselves, to cut it up like a cake, in a very underhanded way. And of course they were thrown out.

After the first days of the insurrection we said that the occupation must take on another role, to be a center of speech, of discussion, of the distribution of ideas. We made some pamphlets and some posters but we didn't have the time and the energy to do so many things because we were tired. A few people were keeping the occupation going, day and night, and we had to do many things. But all things considered we published a lot, as did other anarchists throughout the city. At the end of the first week, we opened the dining hall of the university, a very luxurious establishment because it was new. We opened it and started cooking every day for everybody. We used it to feed the struggle, every day. There was a group of people who were working there. We had cooks and other people who went there to clean. I for example didn't cook but I cleaned. And every day we had food for everybody, not only people living in the occupation. Poor people were coming there only to eat. To keep the restaurant stocked, groups of about thirty people formed up every day to go to supermarkets, fill-up shopping carts, and take the food. And other things were expropriated as well, like fire extinguishers and the sound systems.

It was important because having this tool, this ability to feed ourselves, affected our living conditions. But it was also like a womb of the world that we want to create inside the insurrection. But also there were people coming to steal food from the occupation. I don't want to give a bad impression, but it's okay to admit this because it was our decision to mix with everyone in the insurrection, and out of all these people who came together there were many who carried within them the culture of the enemy. So there were people who came to steal mobile phones and computers to sell for money. I don't have a problem with this but when it happens in an insurrection it doesn't advance the struggle. So that's why we put an end to this phenomenon after the second or third day, because some people were coming only to steal things. After that, anytime somebody wanted to enter the gates of the campus with looted items—there were people carrying boxes of stolen goods, computers and other things—we didn't allow them in unless they gave us the objects to throw in the fire. We told them *you have to choose: you or your computer.*

I think that people were ready to go until their own personal limits. The intentions of the insurgents were not so limited; they wanted the destruction of the State, or at least the destruction of the police. If they had the means to attack further, they would have done it, many of them. But they fought until they were physically exhausted. The police didn't stop us. We stopped. But the external limits were numerous. One of them is that we haven't constructed our world. And I don't believe anymore that in one night we will change the world. I'm not a pacifist but now I believe that as we were saying in the assemblies of the Polytechnic, if the revolution doesn't come now, if we don't push this insurrection to a real revolution, it will not be because we don't have the power but because we don't have our world. And that's what we're building now. The truth is that already in the first week we were discussing revolution. It may seem very romantic, very fictional, very fantastic, but seeing the potential of the struggle, we knew that revolution was an open prospect, a possible future. We were ready for everything. And I'm not sure if they could have stopped us, even with the military.

I think it would have been a serious problem for the State to deploy the military. I read somewhere, I'm not sure if it's true, that the generals told the government that the army at that moment was not ready to take on such a responsibility, that if we engage the army we will lose the army. It's a problem for a democracy to pass to an open war. It may be efficient in the immediate moment, in a military way of seeing the conflict, but it would destroy the entire basis of State domination of society, all the links. The internal links, let's say, between society and democratic domination. Particularly in Greece. For example in Italy they have a tradition with fascism, with the domestic use of the military, that is not wholly rejected by Italian society. We also have a tradition with dictatorship, we have a nationalist movement, but the dictatorship was not popular and in general the intervention of the army in social and political life is not legitimate for Greek society.

There are many factors that gave birth to the insurrection, factors that go far into the past. Why it happened in Greece, for example. Why in Greece anarchists have so much liberty to act, now as well as before the insurrection. Why it's so easy for people here to use violence. Greek history plays an important role. In the past century, after World War II, we had a guerrilla movement that never surrendered. The civil war didn't end in negotiations, with a peace agreement between communists and nationalists as in Italy. Here we had a civil war that continued, and even when it ended its spirit continued by other means. The spirit of civil war never ended in Greece. And in this period, violent struggle was always legitimate. There were always people struggling, not only anarchist militants, not only revolutionaries, but a large part of Greek society. Here, struggle is legitimate. This is one factor. A living tradition, that goes from one generation to the next, expressed in new ways.

Another factor is that the anarchist movement in Greece is very young. There were anarchists in Greece at the beginning of the 20th century but they were all repressed by the

Communists and they disappeared. The movement we have now began after the '70s. This movement from its beginnings linked up with society. It wasn't just an ideological, a closed thing. It was not just philosophical or alternative. It carried the tradition of the struggle and the violence, the tradition of Greek society, the traditions of the anarchists, of direct action, and also the concentration on expanding throughout society the revolt and direct action and self-organization. And year by year it created this potential. That means much work was done years before, with a variety of methods, working in neighborhoods, violent struggle against the State, everything. That made this unity, this synthesis.

In the '80s, the first years of an organized anarchist movement in Greece, the anarchists were calling demonstrations and violent marches but as people who were fighting in the '80s dropped out at the end of the decade, due to repression and other factors, there was a big change. And in the '90s anarchists weren't very numerous, they generally didn't organize many marches and many of them participated in the protests of the leftists. But at the end of the '90s, as more people joined the anarchist movement, this new generation began to stay in the movement. The first generations were lost, they left, but those of us who started to fight in the '90s are still in the streets. The movement started to construct a history. The cause of this shift, I think, was a clearer political vision.

From the beginning of December's insurrection, from Monday night, the State took exceptional measures to protect the members of the government. The ministers were all assigned armed escorts and were sent into hiding. They put some military units on readiness, to come down to the city if need be. They had the soldiers equipped with plastic bullets. The cops in Athens were already shooting plastic bullets, but this wasn't new. A year earlier I was shot with a plastic bullet in a fight near Exarchia. We know that in some military units the officers were making propaganda, psychologically preparing the soldiers to deploy against the insurrection. There were rumors that if the street fighting had continued for three more days they would have sent in the military. But those of us fighting in the streets, we weren't afraid, we weren't discussing it as a possible end to the revolt. Of course the insurgents weren't ready to fight against an armed force, but nobody came into the street with the belief that there was a point we could not pass, that there were limits. We just fought, and we were ready for anything. And this is the spirit of revolt.

Their Democracy Murders—The Polytechnic University Occupation

On Saturday, December 6, 2008, Alexandros Grigoropoulos, a fifteen-year-old comrade, was murdered in cold blood, with a bullet in the chest by Epaminondas Korkoneas of the special guards' police force in the area of Exarchia.

Contrary to the statements of politicians and journalists who are accomplices to the murder, this was not an "isolated incident," but an explosion of the state repression that systematically and in an organized manner targets those who resist, those who revolt, the anarchists and antiauthoritarians.

What we are seeing is an increase in state terrorism. It's expressed in the upgrading of repressive mechanisms, the continuous armament, increasing levels of violence, "zero tolerance" doctrines, and the slanderous media propaganda that criminalizes those fighting against authority.

These conditions prepare the ground for the intensification of repression, attempting to extract social consent beforehand, and arming state murderers in uniform who are targeting the people who fight—the youth, the damned who are revolting in the entire country. Lethal violence against the people in the social and class struggle seeks everybody's submission, serves as exemplary punishment, and is meant to spread fear.

It is the escalation of the generalized attack of the State and the bosses against the whole of society, in order to impose more rigid conditions of exploitation and oppression, to consolidate control and repression. An attack that is reflected every day in poverty, social exclusion, the blackmail to adjust to the world of social and class divisions, the ideological war launched by the dominant mechanisms of manipulation (the mass media). An attack which is raging in every social space, demanding from the oppressed their division and silence. From the schools' cells and the universities to the dungeons of waged slavery with the hundreds of dead workers in the so-called "working accidents" to the poverty embracing large numbers of the population... From the mine fields at the borders, the pogroms and the murders of immigrants and refugees to the numerous "suicides" in prisons and police stations... from the "accidental shootings" in police blockades to violent repression of local resistances, Democracy is showing its teeth!

In these conditions of fierce exploitation and oppression, and against the daily looting and pillaging that the State and the bosses are launching, taking as spoils the oppressed people's labor force, their life, their dignity and freedom, the accumulated social suffocation is accompanying today the rage erupting in the streets and the barricades for the murder of Alexandros.

From the first moment after the murder of Alexandros, spontaneous demonstrations and riots appeared in the center of Athens; the Polytechnic, the Economic and the Law Schools are being occupied and attacks against state and capitalist targets take place in many different neighborhoods and in the city center. Demonstrations, attacks and clashes erupt in Thessaloniki, Patras, Volos, Chania and Heraklion in Crete, in Giannena, Komotini, Xanthi, Serres, Sparti, Alexandroupoli, Mytilini. In Athens, in Patision Street—outside the Polytechnic and the Economic School—clashes last all night. Outside the Polytechnic the riot police make use of plastic bullets.

On Sunday the 7th of December, thousands of people march on the police headquarters in Athens, attacking the riot police. Clashes of unprecedented tension spread in the streets of the city center, lasting until late at night. Many demonstrators are injured and a number of them are arrested.

From Monday morning until today the revolt spreads and becomes generalized. The last days are full of uncountable social events: militant high school students' demonstrations ending up—in many cases—in attacks against police stations and clashes with the cops in the neighborhoods of Athens and in the rest of the country, massive demonstrations and conflicts between protesters and the police in the center of Athens, during which there are assaults on banks, big department stores and ministries, the siege of the Parliament in Syntagma Square, occupations of public buildings, demonstrations ending in riots and attacks against state and capitalist targets in many different cities.

The attacks of the police against youth and generally against people who are fighting, the dozens of arrests and beatings of demonstrators, and in some cases the threatening of protesters by cops waving their guns, as well as their cooperation with the fascist thugs—like in the incidents of Patras, where cops together with fascists charged against the rebels of the city—are the methods in which the State's uniformed dogs are implementing the doctrine of "zero tolerance" under the commands of the political bosses in order to suppress the wave of revolt that was triggered last Saturday night.

The terrorism by the police occupation army is completed by the exemplary punishment of those who are arrested and now face severe accusations leading to their imprisonment: in the city of Larisa, eight arrested persons are prosecuted with the "anti" terrorist law and were imprisoned facing charges for "criminal organization." Twenty-five immigrants who were arrested during the riots in Athens face the same charges. Also in Athens, five of the arrested on Monday were imprisoned, and five more who were arrested Wednesday night are in custody and will be taken in front of a prosecutor next Monday, facing felony charges.

At the same time, a deceitful propaganda war is launched against the people fighting, paving the way for repression, for the return to the normality of social injustice and submission.

The explosive events right after the murder caused a wave of international mobilization in memory of Alexandros and in solidarity with the revolted who are fighting in the streets, inspiring a counterattack against the totalitarianism of democracy. Concentrations, demonstrations, symbolic attacks on Greek embassies and consulates and other solidarity actions have taken place in cities in Cyprus, Germany, Spain, Denmark, Holland, Great Britain, France, Italy, Poland, Turkey, USA, in Ireland, Sweden, Switzerland, Australia, Slovakia, Croatia, Russia, Bulgaria, Romania, Belgium, New Zealand, Argentina, Mexico, Chile, and elsewhere.

We continue the occupation of the Polytechnic School which started on Saturday night, creating a space for all people who are fighting to gather, and one more permanent focus of resistance in the city.

In the barricades, the occupations, the demonstrations, and the assemblies we keep alive the memory of Alexandros, but also the memory of Michalis Kaltezas, of Carlo Giuliani, Michalis Prekas, Christoforos Marinos and of all the comrades who were murdered by the State. We don't forget the social-class war in which these comrades fell and we keep open the front of a total refusal to the aged world of authority. Our actions, our attempts are the living cells of the insubordinate free world that we dream, without masters and slaves, without police, armies, prisons and borders.

The bullets of the murderers in uniform, the arrests and beatings of demonstrators, the chemical gas war launched by the police forces, the ideological attack of Democracy not only cannot manage to impose fear and silence, but they become for the people the reason to raise against state terrorism the cries of the struggle for freedom, to abandon fear and to meet—more and more every day, youth, high school and university students, immigrants, jobless people, workers—in the streets of revolt. To let the rage overflow and drown them!

THE STATE, THE BOSSES, THEIR THUGS AND THEIR LACKEYS ARE MOCKING US, ROBBING US AND KILLING US!

LET'S ORGANIZE, COUNTERATTACK AND SMASH THEM!

THESE NIGHTS BELONG TO ALEXIS!

CONCENTRATION FOR SOLIDARITY TO THE ARRESTED AT EVELPIDON COURTHOUSE: MONDAY, DECEMBER 15, 2008, 9AM

IMMEDIATE RELEASE OF ALL THE ARRESTED

We are sending our solidarity to everyone occupying universities, schools, and state buildings, demonstrating and clashing with the state murderers all over the country.

We are sending our solidarity to all comrades abroad who are mobilizing, transferring our voice everywhere. In the great battle for global social liberation we stand together!

—*The Occupation of the Polytechnic University in Athens, Friday, December 12, 2008*

All the kids felt so much power yelling at the cops

Alexander, Thodoris, Vlasis, & Kostas: Two students and two graduates from Exarchia High School

V: Some years ago I became politically active. I'm influenced by the place where I grew up, Exarchia, and by my family. My mother was also a political activist. Those of us in the neighborhood, we've experienced lots of political events that helped us deepen our political understanding.

I was in a house a few hundred meters from the crime scene. The assassination took place at about eleven o'clock [sic] and I heard about it half an hour later. I went immediately to Exarchia Square. There I found that the atmosphere was tense, and already a lot of rioting had happened even though there weren't more than thirty people on the spot. When I got there the people assured me it was true, Alexis had been murdered, and altogether we made our way to the Polytechnic, where there was asylum. The cops blocked us from entering the university so we went back to the square. We were waiting to see what we could do but our goal was to get to the campus. At that point a group of about forty other people attacked the riot police really hard, throwing stones

and molotovs, and they opened the way for us to go to the university. When I arrived at the Polytechnic I was amazed to see that even though there had been no call for a meeting there were thousands of people gathered, mobilized just through phone calls. The sheer numbers made it possible to attack the cops in a powerful way.

It was the first time I met people from all ages, from fathers on down, in a confrontation with police. All of them put Alexis in the position of their own children—they put themselves in the shoes of his parents and they made it personal. It was the first time that we saw so many people of different ages attacking the cops with such limitless determination and hatred. And they all had gathered there in just a few hours.

A: Before December we were in the streets. Most children of Exarchia were influenced by the political activities that were taking place in the neighborhood. But from the period when we were protesting and participating in the student movement (2006–2007), we took it up a level to the more violent activities during December. It developed strictly from the student struggle. The way of organizing also changed. It was no longer demonstrations following a specific course but something that was happening everywhere in the city.

So that night I was getting ready to go to a party and the news spread around. I don't remember how but it was very vague, no one knew what had happened, they just knew some shots were fired, someone was hurt, but not necessarily killed.

My mother came down to my room and told me not to go out because police were shooting and things were burning. An hour later I called a classmate of mine and he told me to come down to the square, the square was on fire and a boy got shot. So when I went down there was already a big riot, and cops, but the cops were farther away, in the outlying areas. The riots were spread all around the square, three and four streets away there were garbage bins burning and no cars on the streets. You had to wonder how everyone came there so quickly.

T: Before December I was not personally informed about political ideas and I didn't participate in any political activities, even though I lived in Exarchia. During December I spoke with my friends more deeply about political ideas, and I started to participate more.

I was in my house when I heard about the killing on television. Even though I was not the type to go out in the streets, I felt depressed because I hang out with my friends in this exact place, and I realized it could have been me. The first day my parents didn't allow me, so I didn't go. The next day I started to go to Stournari with my friends, and I continued going every day. The scene was completely different than normal. You had the impression that you were in a war, a battlefield. It was mostly young people. That made me think, how there were so many really young people who came down into the streets just to confront the cops, throw stones, smash shops. I also saw that the neighbors in Exarchia were speaking with the demonstrators and that was good. Any type of person could come down for this reason. We were welcomed.

K: I'm a graduate of Exarchia High, now I'm a university student but I still live in Exarchia. Before December I was already participating in political activities and riots and violent confrontations with the cops, but what opened my eyes is that another assassination happened just like with Michalis Kaltezas so many years before, and nothing had changed in society. We were at the same point. And through this understanding your horizon opens up. You can see all the injustice of society, and from this moment you fight against it however possible. And I am still doing it.

On the 6th I was with my friends outside of Exarchia. I came down half an hour later, passing by Nomiki. I saw there were already barricades and riots in Exarchia, and I stayed there for the next few days participating in the riots. I met with my company of friends, we already had an affinity group that we ran with in the demos, never following a bloc or an organization. It was just me and my friends making actions. So immediately we put this into practice again, we met and attacked the riot cops. I stayed until eight in the morning, then I took a look at the TV and what they were saying about the assassination, I went to my house and ate, and then I came back. From that day on you didn't have anything else in your head except that it was a boy that could have been me. There was no possibility of a nonviolent response to this situation,

145

so the violent practices were the only possible ones in my mind. The only reason that you were coming to the streets was to burn, smash, and fight against cops, against the whole copocracy. It was the only possible response.

When the State steals something from you and doesn't give it back then you demand it and take it back with violence, so that's why the use of violence was the only way.

A big difference between these days and previously is that previously in the demos there were some people in the front fighting with police and most other people standing back, but this time everyone was at the front, rioting and fighting police, and no one was standing back. Me personally, I was helped by my parents because they never told me to stay at home. They were also inhabitants of Exarchia and felt angry, too.

V: I want to tell you about Alexis. In the beginning, he mostly just came to Exarchia on the weekends. Personally, I was closer with his friends, but whenever we met we said hello. Generally speaking, he was a calm person, polite, but he had a passion to know more and more about the political activities and ideas. His friends were mainly active in the Network of Autonomous Student Groups that was formed during the student movements. It was a choice of his to hang out in Exarchia. As most of us who hang out there, he had a strong anti-cop feeling. He had a lot of reasons and a lot of arguments against the police, he could analyze the police as an oppressive machine in Exarchia and in society. He was never violent,

before, when he confronted the police. Our experience from meeting with him contradicts with the testimony of the cop's lawyer and the cop himself, who said that Alexis was one of the most violent people in Exarchia. To conclude, I have to say that all his friends, even if before they were pacifists or leftists, afterwards they transformed into the worst enemies of the police.

A: The first day of the week, Monday, most schools were open and functioning but no one was focusing on the lessons. The children and teachers were all discussing how to react, and talking about taking to the streets. It's not true that the schools were closed on Monday, maybe some were, but most of them weren't. It was the day of the funeral—Wednesday I think—that the schools were all closed across the country. We did go to class a little bit but the murder was the subject of the day. Since there was a riot close to the school many people left. Most people weren't participating in these things before the murder, they were only looking forward to their holidays, but that week you saw many people who had never protested before going down to the square to express themselves violently.

V: On Monday I was at my house when I found out about a demo that was organized by all kinds of students from many schools around Athens. The meeting point was at the spot of the murder. The moment I got there I saw thousands of young people there for Alexis. We were all wondering how the cops could be investigating whether the bullet that killed him ricocheted. Everybody was sure that if Alexis shot a policeman, they would never investigate the possibility of a ricochet, they would just charge him for murder. Everyone was angry about this hypocrisy. In my mind there was a great plan orchestrated by the State and the media to cover it up.

A: I thought it was funny when the students of two schools met in front of the neighborhood police station and the cops looked so weak in front of all those angry students. That day they were ashamed, saying sorry, and they weren't attacking or being aggressive as usual. And all the kids felt so much power yelling at the cops, and throwing rotten fruit at them, those wild oranges that are all over the street in the winter.

There was a riot at Syntagma Square and I had never smelled so much tear gas. Some people fainted. Others were prepared, with masks. Lots of people were getting out of there, screaming, crying, from the gas, but the police did not chase them, they just surrounded the square. Then the huge Christmas tree caught fire and burned slowly, from the bottom up. A lot of cops gathered at the base but they didn't know what to do. And there were a lot of people clapping. Me, during all the days of December I worked my job from six in the afternoon until midnight and then I went directly to the riots at the Polytechnic, everyday.

V: In the first few days I was in the Polytechnic but in later days I went to Nomiki, where we made some amazing actions. The cops were running after demonstrators there and we were up on the balconies of the school throwing molotovs down on them, burning many of them. You could see them burn.

T: One day I left class at noon and went to the center, where I found myself in a very strange situation. There were some huge people with masks taking part, but for me it was obvious they were cops. I saw that they burned a bank van but when they took out the old man who was driving they beat him badly. I was almost sure these guys were from the secret police. Other days I saw these same people and they were behaving very strangely, going around in a small group with hammers, smashing irrelevant, random things, scaring neighbors, and causing trouble.

A: You always see this, people acting like junkies or anarchists but causing troubles and then later you see them in front of the police station talking with the cops. Many secret police do this. There were photos of this in December, with groups of hooded people talking with policemen behind their lines, planning.

V: All of us believe that there was a plan, a set up, made public by the journalists and put into practice by the State. In other words the journalists created a debate with a dead boy on one side and the destruction of small properties on the other, and the State put it into practice. They got undercover cops to play demonstrators and smash small shops and kiosks, to produce a conflict between the social elements.

A: Even though on the TV everyday they said the streets were full of young boys and girls being irresponsible, smashing and burning small businesses and cars, I never once saw any young person smash these kinds of targets, it was always old athletic men. So it was a self-fulfilled prophesy. They wanted to turn public opinion against the riot. They wanted parents to tell their children to stay home so the case could go to trial like any other case, without all the people in the streets.

K: During the funeral thousands of people gathered to honor Alexis and without any reason the State stationed the riot police very close to the funeral. It was ridiculous and provocative to see the same cops who killed him, the riot police, just in front of you while the funeral was happening. And the police provoked people and shouted things at them. They were singing a humiliating song during the funeral, going "Where is Alexis? tra-la-la! tra-la-la!" It was a spark that made the whole thing explode. Then cops from all different units came to the graveyard, on motorcycle, on foot, riot police, so riots started all around the cemetery. There was panic because most people did not know how to respond to such a situation, they were normal people, old people, and they weren't prepared.

At that moment some motorcycle cops took out their guns and fired into the air, producing more panic. After December there were many situations when the cops took out their guns. In some demonstrations there were some cops from the special branch, the ones with masks who have the license to kill, and they were brought down to confront young people. I read that in Australia after the cops killed a boy they were disarmed and given tasers, but here after they killed a boy they started using their guns even more. It became normal.

V: Many times during the insurrection, members of leftist political organizations or people representing mainstream parties would come to student assemblies and try to force them to release statements against the riots. I felt the opposite, the need to express solidarity with the people who got arrested because it is unbelievably hard to have to deal with a murder and at the same time with people from the movement going to prison.

For me December was very dynamic. There was no political party or organization that could use it to become more popular. Everyone who was in the streets was a total militant, using violent practices without identifying themselves with the anarchist movement, but at the same moment they were standing miles away from the leftist organizations. The leftist parties and organizations, they tried to do the same thing that they always do in social movements, they tried to push the political views of the students and change the appearance of the communiques to make it look like the student movement was adopting their own political program. For me it is a sick idea to step on a dead body to announce your political ideas.

But there are also people who use the anarchist movement to just act like hooligans, without any ideological background.

K: During December the leftists were behaving as always, they do nonviolent demonstrations to beg for something from the State. This time they were begging for an apology. On the other end the anarchists always believe—and this time much more so—that the State is stealing something from our lives and they go out in the street to take it back. I feel the same way, and the majority of people in these days believed it too.

A: I don't think anyone was influenced by the parties because they weren't listening. I didn't spend time watching TV during this period. It is obvious that no one on the streets belonged to the Right but at the same time they didn't belong to any organization.

V: However there were some people who exploited these moments, like fascist groups that used this time to make connections with the police and attack the insurgents. This is normal in social movements.

A: It looked like a battlefield, those riots. You could see the Golden Dawn, the neo-nazi group, with the cops, protecting each other, and against the anarchists. They weren't trying to hide it, everyone could see.

T: Me personally, I am an Albanian immigrant. One day in December I was coming home from the gym with two friends, one from Bulgaria and another from Greece. We passed the police station responsible for killing Alexis and the MAT encircled us so no one on the outside could see what they were doing. I had my hands in my pockets so they hit my arms and shouted that I should stand at attention in front of them. They asked for our papers and we said we were immigrant students. Immediately they turned to my Greek friend and said, *What the fuck, you keep company with these malakas?* And they arrested me and the Bulgarian boy. My mother came to the police station to get me out and when she showed them my papers they saw that I was from the south of Albania, where there is a Greek minority, they suddenly changed their tune. They told her to be careful that I don't keep company with Bulgarians and other immigrants. I said to the cop that before he told my friend not to hang out with me because I was an immigrant and he said I was lying.

Me personally, I have many friends from all kinds of countries like Ethiopia, Bulgaria, all over the planet. We have big problems with the copocracy because the cops and many normal people treat us like shit, like we are nothing. If the

149

cops ask for your papers you'll have big problems. Any time you meet with the cops they behave really bad, they treat you like you're already a criminal, and they behave the same way with all of us.

A Black Immigrant's Cry of Despair

The Voice of the Black: Text written by black brothers in the occupation of ASOEE, December 19, 2008

For me, a black man, freedom stops at my apartment's door. And I call the Greek youth, who are concerned about equality and the rights of all people. For this reason, I join you and your noble struggle, because we know that you do not ignore how the police are squeezing us in all the corners of the streets, in front of the bus stations, even in front of our houses.

Conscious youth, Greek people, I don't say something that you don't already know: in front of a policeman I don't have any right but to obey up to the point where:

- he will take my residential card
- he will kick me because I display my merchandise
- he will take away all my personal belongings indefinitely
- he will hit me whenever he wants

Conscious youth, Greek people, I feel like I am in the 17th century, the century of barbarity, where it is possible to shoot a little boy, like Alexis. We join with your struggle and we express our deep condolences to his family and to the Greek people.

These Days Are Ours, Too: from the Haunt of Albanian Migrants

Following the assassination of Alexis Grigoropoulos we have been living in an unprecedented condition of turmoil, an outflow of rage that doesn't seem to end. Leading this uprising, it seems, are the students—who with an inexhaustible passion and hearty spontaneity have reversed the whole situation. You cannot stop something you don't control, something that is organized spontaneously and under terms you do not comprehend. This is the beauty of the uprising. The high school students are making history and leave it to the others to write it up and to classify it ideologically. The streets, the incentive, the passion belongs to them.

In the framework of this wider mobilization, with the student demonstrations being its steam engine, there is a mass participation of the second generation of migrants and many refugees also. The refugees come to the streets in small numbers, with limited organization, with spontaneity and impetus informing their mobilization. Right now, they are the most militant foreigners living in Greece. Either way, they have very little to lose. The children of migrants mobilize en masse and dynamically, primarily through high school and university actions but also through the organizations of the Left and the far Left. They are the most integrated part of the migrant community, the most courageous. They are unlike their parents, who came with their heads bowed, as if they were begging for a loaf of bread. They are a part of the Greek society, since they've lived in no other. They do not beg for something, they demand to be equal with their Greek classmates. Equal in rights, on the streets, in dreaming.

For us, the politically organized migrants, this is a second French November of 2005. We never had any illusions that when the peoples' rage overflowed we would be able to direct it in any way. Despite the struggles we have taken on during all these years we never managed to achieve such a mass response like this one. Now is the time for the street to talk: the deafening scream is for the eighteen years of violence, repression, exploitation, and humiliation. These days are ours, too.

These days are for the hundreds of migrants and refugees murdered at the borders, in police stations, and workplaces. They are for those murdered by cops or "concerned citizens." They are for those murdered for daring to cross the border, worked to death, for not bowing their head, or for nothing. They are for Gramos Palusi, Luan Bertelina, Edison Yahai, Tony Onuoha, Abdurahim Edriz, Modaser Mohamed Ashtraf and so many others that we haven't forgotten.

These days are for the everyday police violence that remains unpunished and unanswered. They are for the humiliations at the border and at the migrant detention centers, which continue to date. They are for the crying injustice of the Greek courts, the migrants and refugees unjustly in prison, the justice we are denied. Even now, in the days and nights

151

of the uprising, the migrants pay a heavy toll—what with the attacks of far-righters and cops, with sentences of deportation and imprisonment that the courts hand out with Christian love to us infidels.

These days are for the exploitation continuing unabatedly for eighteen years now. They are for the struggles that are not forgotten: in the downs of Volos, the Olympic works, the town of Amaliada. They are for the toil and the blood of our parents, for informal labor, for the endless shifts. They are for the deposits and the adhesive stamps, the welfare contributions we paid and will never have recognized. They are for the papers we will be chasing for the rest of our lives like a lottery ticket.

These days are for the price we have to pay simply in order to exist, to breathe. They are for all those times when we crunched our teeth for the insults we took, the defeats we were charged with. They are for all the times when we didn't react, even when having all the reasons in the world to do so. They are for all the times when we did react and we were alone because our deaths and our rage did not fit pre-existing shapes, didn't bring votes in, didn't sell in the prime-time news.

These days belong to all the marginalized, the excluded, the people with the difficult names and the unknown stories. They belong to all those who die every day in the Aegean Sea and Evros River, to all those murdered at the border or on a central Athens street; they belong to the Roma in Zefyri, to the drug addicts in Exarchia. These days belong to the kids of Mesollogiou Street, to the un-integrated, the uncontrollable students. Thanks to Alexis, these days belong to us all.

Eighteen years of silent rage are too many.

To the streets, for solidarity and dignity!

We haven't forgotten, we won't forget—these days are yours too, Luan, Tony, Mohamed, Alexis…

Invitation to the Open Popular Assembly of the Liberated City Hall of Aghios Dimitrios

On December 6th, 2008, the special guard Epaminondas Korkoneas pulled out his gun and murdered a citizen, a fifteen-year-old kid. The rage that everyone feels is huge, despite all the attempts by the government and the mass media to disorient public opinion. It is now certain that this insurrection is not only homage to the unjust loss of Alexandros Grigoropoulos. There has been a lot of talk since then about violence, thefts, and pillages. For those in the media and power, violence is only what destroys the proper order.

For us however:

Violence is to work forty years for crumbs and to wonder if you will ever retire.

Violence is the bonds, the stolen pensions, the securities fraud.

Violence is to be forced to take a housing loan that you will pay back through the nose.

Violence is the managerial right of the employer to fire you at will.

Violence is unemployment, temporary employment, 700 euros a month.

Violence is the "industrial accidents" that happen because the bosses cut costs at the expense of worker safety.

Violence is to take psycho-medications and vitamins to withstand the exhaustive work schedule.

Violence is to be an immigrant, to live with the fear that you can be thrown out of the country at any time and to be in a state of constant insecurity.

Violence is to be simultaneously a wage worker, a housewife, and a mother.

Violence is to be worked to death and then to be told "smile, we are not asking that much of you."

The insurrection of high school and university students, of temporary workers and immigrants, broke this violence of normality. This insurrection must not stop! Syndicalists, political parties, priests, journalists, and businesspeople do whatever they can to maintain the violence we described above. It is not just them, but we too are responsible for the perpetuation of this situation. The insurrection opened a space where we can finally express ourselves freely. As a continuation of this opening we went forward with the occupation of the City Hall of Ag. Dimitrios and the formation of a popular assembly open to all.

An open space for communication, to break our silence, to undertake action for our life.

Saturday, December 13, 2008, 7:00pm, open popular assembly at the Ag. Dimitrios City Hall.

NO PROSECUTION—IMMEDIATE RELEASE OF ALL THOSE ARRESTED

—The occupation of Aghios Dimitrios City Hall

153

I thought the revolution was coming

Katerina: A Thessaloniki student sympathetic to the anarchist movement

December... it was amazing. Everyone was in the streets. I couldn't understand what was happening. I thought the revolution was coming, I really did! There was so much energy, all the normal ways of living had ended and it was all in the streets. There was a lot of violence, lots of burning. It was very frightening. There was a rumor that they would send in the military. I got scared—after the 3rd or 4th day I shut myself in my apartment. I didn't have television, no radio, no Internet. I would just go out on my balcony sometimes to look out in the streets, to see if everything was alright. I expected to see soldiers some morning.

But in December I learned that the TV is the most powerful weapon they have. The most important. It's the only one they need. To make people afraid, to make people stay home, to misinform people, to turn people against the revolution. Now I think everyone has gone back to their old lives, to the normal way of doing things, thanks to the TV.

I want to eliminate everything that represents the alienation of our lives

Maria: An anarchist poet

It was after midnight, the first night, the people didn't know what was going on. And I was explaining to people that the cops had killed someone. There were about forty police on the street, there outside Monastiraki metro station, below Acropolis. The cops looked at us, the drunk people, the normal people, the posh people who had gone out to drink whiskey and dance, and it was the first moment that they heard that the cops had killed a young boy. Suddenly the cops tried to arrest one person who was crossing the road. I was getting really angry and, with my friends, we were all saying we have to do something, we can't let them take him away. So I went toward the cops, pushing against their shields. One of them shoved me back. I felt a pain in my chest and I knew that I didn't have the physical power to push him back. I dragged one of my male friends in front of me, and I pushed him ahead of me, using him like a shield. My friends were my shield. Of course, he was hit by the police. I felt guilty but it wasn't that bad. So I'm shouting, swearing at the MAT. My friends grabbed me and told me it's over, they gave up trying to arrest the guy.

Later, but still at the beginning of the revolt, I think in the first week, at the main commercial place in Athens, Psiri, we smashed the shops and the ATMs. One bank building was burned. Another time I came up against the MAT in a big demonstration. I was in the front line without any protective gear, but I was wearing my passion for freedom to fight face to face with the police. Of course, when my comrades hit the riot police with their clubs, and the riot police threw tear gas, I ran because I didn't have a mask or a club. But I had the love of my comrades and the will to eliminate the first layer of the apparatus.

Another day I was carrying the molotovs in a bag. I couldn't throw them because I didn't possess complete hatred, the psychological and emotional power to set someone on fire. But it's not that I couldn't have this power, it's that I consciously choose not to. But carrying this bag, I felt responsible for the actions that would happen with its contents. I had volunteered to carry this bag in order to sneak in molotovs and deliver them to specific people. It's an important role. The tear gas canisters and the first molotovs were being thrown. And I'm there with a bag reeking of benzine, and I got afraid and wanted to throw the bag away but my boyfriend says to me, keep the bag, keep the bag. I held onto the bag, which I knew was a medium for the continuation of this struggle. I waited for my fear to subside, and I continued. I kept going until I found my comrades and handed out our weapon, our answer to the enemy.

During the revolt I realized that I would play the role of carrying weapons for the movement, for the demonstrations, for the actions, but that I would not personally carry out the burnings and smashings. I believe that beneath the ashes of Capital will be born our new dreams. Sometimes I walk in the streets of the metropolis, I walk in the streets of my village, and I am aggravated by the big commercial centers, the luxury shops and the mundane bars, and I want them to disappear. I want to smash them apart, to burn them, to eliminate everything that represents the alienation of our lives. That is why I do what I do, and even though I personally am not strong enough to go face to face with the police, I know that I play an important role.

155

Before the revolt, all the Greeks were enslaved

Sofia, Vasilis, Bill, Irini: The owners of a luxury boutique near Nomiki

V: Before December, for many different reasons, it seemed that there was a lot of wrong-headedness in the government, but the majority of society was self-centered. Each person was focused on their own survival.

S: It's not that Greek culture or the social context caused all this egoism. For many years the government and the economic system forced people to behave like this, to only pursue their self-interest. The system puts a knife to your throat and it seems that you don't have any other choice but to run for your survival. You're so trapped you become like a volcano inside.

I: Before the revolt, all the Greeks were enslaved. Everyone was running the rat race, or almost everyone. I already knew some anarchists personally, and I had the best opinion of them.

V: I never realized what their active role in the social context of Greece was, even though I knew some anarchists personally. Possibly most of the people who entered the anarchist movement did so as a negation of society. I don't think it was an intellectual process for them or a personal cultivation, but rather negativism. There was a big gap between what I was reading in the university about anarchist theory and the experiences I had with the anarchists in the center of Athens.

B: An educational process is essential to changing society. The authorities consciously mis-educate people to keep them submissive. If suddenly today society transforms the economy into an egalitarian system, perhaps everything would collapse in chaos. That's why the cultural side of the anarchist movement is so important, not the violence. But I think most of the property destruction in December was caused by criminals.

S: Over the last few years I have made some new friends who are anarchists. Their opinions have influenced me, and now I believe that there is a very important role for anarchist movements in all societies, that it can be very beneficial during a period of abusive authority, or under a government that creates problems rather than solving them. I believe that anarchy cannot exist because societies are so huge and they surely need laws and rules and forms of control. The role of the anarchists is to express the voice of the voiceless, the anger of the people, to feel the social pulse, and to express criticism against the authorities. In a way I feel that the anarchists try to do what Jesus Christ expressed—I'm going to bring down the world in seven days and then in seven days I'm going to bring it back. And to do this you have to cultivate a very high consciousness. You have to be a saint to achieve this goal. It seems utopian.

V: Now let's talk about why we created this boutique here in the center of Athens. I studied archaeology, but in the end I decided with Irini and Sofia to create this boutique to live like a simple man, to have a regular life. I don't have capitalistic ambitions.

I: Liar!

V: It's important to explain that we want to live a normal life.

I: I don't want to live a normal life at all!

V: She's a diva! Anyway, this was before December. It's important to mention that the biggest longtime riots took place in front of our shop, on this corner, Solonos and Massalias.

I: We met in the drama school, Sofia and I, and this shop was born out of our friendship. It is a creation of joy.

S: I studied business administration before going to drama school. The first step was our friendship, and that we love clothes. And of course we have to admit that our goal is to profit. Profit in order to survive. It's a job. But if we worked hard we had the chance to become our own bosses, and this helped us realize that we were assuming a major responsibility not only to ourselves but also to society. When you are your own boss it's up to you to sustain what you are doing through all the difficulties, through the economic crisis, to not let it fall apart.

B: If you look at our stories you will see that each one of us worked two or three jobs and also had two or three identities—we had different aspects of our lives. Often when we speak about who we were. I choose from these three identities who I would like to be, not who I actually am. All this is a matter of surviving.

I: I was in a hospital working as a nurse, that's my night job, and I saw on TV that the cops had killed a fifteen-year-old in the center of Athens. I was wondering why this happened and all the excuses that I found on the TV were that the boy shouted at them. And I was wondering if it was possible for the cops to kill someone for cursing at them.

V: I was on a bus and I heard on the radio that a child died, killed by cops, and half of my mind said, *so what?* And the other half of my mind said, *if I don't react, the prison of our lives will expand.* I was feeling strange. My intuition told me that something was going to happen, but I didn't know what.

B: I was in the north of Greece, and I felt surprised when I found out, and hopeful in the same moment. Surprised that we had come to the point where a fifteen-year-old could be assassinated, and hopeful because I saw that in just half an hour in the middle of nowhere in northern Greece people were gathering and reacting to what had happened. I said to myself that society is still alive, it still has some sensitivity.

S: I was in my house, which is in the richest area of Athens. For me it was not a surprise, I was expecting it. Children are dying every day, everywhere. The only thing that surprised me... it's like when you hear about people dying from cancer, it's just a disease. But when it comes into your house and someone from your family gets cancer, then you realize what cancer is. Likewise, when this assassination happened in our society and the revolt occurred here as a reaction, I felt that now we are one family. And in this way the reaction has meaning, it unites the society. So my first reaction was to call an anarchist girl I know and to ask her, *what is going to happen?* From the beginning I was expecting the reaction. But I could never imagine that all these thousands of people would appear from nowhere. I was expecting that only the anarchists would react. So my friend says that they are going to gather,

and I said to her I'm coming down to the center to switch off the lights of my shop because I knew that total chaos would ensue. Because of my personal links with some anarchists, I knew that total chaos was a certainty.

On Sunday I called this friend again and I asked her what was happening. She told me not to come down to the center alone, because everything was out of control in the whole city. So I just switched off the shop lights and went back to my house. On Monday people attacked the shop. At the same moment, I was 300 meters away in the demonstration. And that's when our personal experience begins. It's like schizophrenia.

B: Dr. Jekyll and Mr. Hyde.

S: In the demonstration, I felt that the police showed tolerance, like they felt guilty so they were waiting for the wave to pass over them. In the beginning the police were allowing the people to express their anger, and this led to many people from the demonstration starting to smash everything around. The police thought it would all end soon but it only snowballed. All kinds of banks and shops were being attacked. At the same time many of the demonstrators, faced with this uncontrollable situation, started to lose the unified meaning that brought all of them out in the street and they began to feel fear or alienation. I found myself happy because the cynicism and the smug security of the authorities had been shattered, but the social protection of the State was also broken down.

158

The State could not protect anything. Everything collapsed. The entire market collapsed, as did this idea, this statue of the State as protector. On the one hand I felt happy because the State collapsed and became naked before the eyes of all the people but on the other hand I felt completely handicapped, because since the State couldn't protect my shop, I couldn't protect it either. I felt exposed and powerless.

So at that point I started to feel like a hostage, because I wanted to be in the demonstration, to shout and watch the State collapse and see things change, but on the other hand I needed to protect my shop. It's like when the Palestinians in the '70s hijacked airplanes to defend their right to exist as a nation—suddenly I felt like I was inside this airplane and I agreed with the Palestinians but at the same moment my life was threatened, my livelihood was used as a tool for another cause, a cause I already agreed with. And I felt scared.

I: When I first heard about the riots I felt perfectly enthusiastic and I really enjoyed it. If something good will appear through this burning, burn them all. But really all of it, burn everything, even my shop. And even the moment that my shop was smashed, I still continued to believe that it wasn't a problem, that it would be much better if they burned everything, all the big corporations, the banks, the parliament building, everything. So that nothing would remain. But this is not easy at all. People have to decide what will be burned and what won't be, and they decide on the basis of what is accessible.

So the big malls in the suburbs continued to function during these days because it was very difficult to attack them. They are far away and well protected. As a result, Capital benefited. I cannot believe that it was the anarchists who did all this. That's why I continue to respect them.

V: On Monday Sofia called me and said that our boutique had suffered serious damages. I was shocked. *What are you going to do?* Sofia asked me. I didn't know. *Come here quickly, we have to protect the store! Are you coming?* I replied: *I don't know, I need to think.* At this time I was in bed, watching TV constantly, like a statue without life or breath, without a goal. Our shop had only been open for two months. My dreams were dying. How could I react as a human being? As a member of society? Who was I? On Tuesday morning, I chose my role: I decided that this store was me and I would protect it in the same way I would protect my thoughts and ideas as a human being. Everybody assumes that to be the owner of a shop means to be a capitalist, but I wanted to avoid the capitalist idea of ownership.

On Wednesday morning I was in the demonstration with a group of actors. We went to Syntagma, and then split up and I decided to come back to the shop. At Panepistimio, it was like the silence before the storm. And I saw a big mass of people running towards Nomiki, where our shop is. I realized that I had to run there myself, with this mass of people, because I couldn't explain to the police that I wasn't one of them if I got caught alone. Inside the group I suddenly saw a friend of mine. We ran to the law school. All those thousands of people were trying to go inside the university. I continued running to my shop. The girl started to shout at me, *where are you going? They'll arrest you! Come inside and protect yourself.* And I said to her, *I'm going to my shop.* Suddenly we found ourselves looking at each other and freezing. And in this moment I felt completely crazy, because I didn't know who I was.

All the other nights we were here in the shop, protecting it. One night there was a huge fire on the corner, a barricade. One junky, a real obvious heroin addict, came up slowly and put a wooden chair in the fire at the barricade. And then he shuffled up to me and Sofia and he asked us, *Hey you guys, can I ask you something? Oh, no, no need.* And we imagined that he wanted to ask us for money. He came back and said, *Okay, whatever, I'll ask you. Maybe it's possible to stay with you here in the university, together with you and your fellow students? Because I don't have any other place to stay.* And we told him, of course you can stay, go inside the university with all the others and stay with them. In a way I felt angry, because I thought this person didn't have any understanding, that he wasn't participating in what was happening. While I was thinking all this he was looking strangely at me. And he asked me, *Are you a cop?* And we said, *No way.* He started to walk away down the middle of the road. Then he turned and asked, *Do I look like a junky?* And Sofia said, *No no, you underestimate yourself.*

S: I was together in the demonstration with my anarchist friend. And there was one young boy holding a molotov. Some guy in his mid-thirties went up to him and told him not to hold the molotov with bare hands, better to use gloves. And the young boy said, *You can't tell me what to do, I'm not a kid.* And this made me think that the young people are full of rage, they are very suppressed, and all this was a revolt of the younger generation against the older generation. Then I felt a little sad. I thought that in the same moment that we can talk about global revolution, we are faced with a generation gap, with people just revolting against their parents. This struck me as immature. We continued walking and we saw an old woman on the corner carrying shopping bags, going to speak to some young people and tell them not to destroy everything mindlessly, not to destroy the National Library or things that were irrelevant to their struggle. And the young people didn't shout at her, they just politely said: *Of course some people make mistakes. But you give us this advice standing outside the demonstration. Come inside the demonstration and with your knowledge you'll help make it all better.* My friend pointed out to me that these two generations met on the street and they spoke to each other, they changed each other. In the end people are not isolated in their private, distanced worlds; they share their opinions.

Some days later the rioting stopped, but the important thing that remained is that the people met each other and they shared their opinions. In this strange way it looked like the ancient *demos,* the old direct democracy, where everyone met in the streets and shared ideas and opinions like the ancient Greeks.

V: The story is continuing. Not the history, the story. You're very lucky to be writing this story because it's not the end, maybe it's the beginning.

One day we jacked a fire engine, got on the CB radio, and said, "tonight, you motherfuckers, we will burn you all"

Transgressio Legis: An insurrectionary anarchist group in Athens engaged in counterinformation and direct action

Our group began in early November, and our main subjects of interest were support for prisoners (social and political) and, practically speaking, direct actions centered around attacks. Practice rioting. In the first month there was the general hunger strike by the prisoners, with 5,000 participating in prisons all around Greece. Then there was the demonstration in Thessaloniki for Vaggelis Botzatzis and the three wanted comrades. After this we were in a period of critical thinking and evaluation. The campaign was a big success in influencing prisoners; most of them participated, and they captured the attention of all Greek society. It became known, and the news spread internationally. On the other hand the mass media of Greece buried the story. They did not focus on the efforts of the prisoners themselves, they focused on the different organizations and political parties that participated as intermediaries between the prisoners and the government. In

161

the period that we and other groups were busy evaluating this campaign, suddenly everything was interrupted by the sound of three bullets in Exarchia.

The assassination of Alexis created parallel opportunities for many different courses to be realized by society in general. It made openings for masses of people to adopt practices that in other circumstances they would never adopt: the lootings, the burning, especially the attacks against the police. On the other hand there were people who had been preparing and carrying out such actions for many years. And through the continuity of these attacks over the last few years and the powerful propaganda of the government and mass media against these actions, society knew from the first moment that when they come down to Exarchia, they would find people who would help them to smash, burn, and attack. When society felt the need to revolt, they knew from the beginning where they could find people who would help them respond to this brutality, as equals. It was the same in Thessaloniki and other cities. So because of all this, all the people with different grievances, everyone who was fed up with the scandals and problems of the last years, the people who were fed up with the low salaries, the people who couldn't stand their schools anymore, the immigrants who couldn't stand the brutality and insults of the police anymore, all these people knew where they could find comrades who would help them to revolt. The people were witnessing the attacks by anarchists for many years and they knew that there were specific points in the city where they would find comrades to help them fight back.

The assassination was the straw that broke the camel's back. Especially for students, but also for the anarchists and the activists and immigrants and precarious workers and all the people in the society who were oppressed and exploited. The most important development was the occupation of government buildings and universities, they would function as starting points, as places to prepare the riots, as well as counterinformation spaces. Some very important moments in December were the result of decisions made at general assemblies, not just the initiative of small groups. Like the burning of *Tiresias,* the central archive of the treasury, where they keep all the information relating to people's debts to the government or to the banks. Another important moment was when the policeman who killed Alexis was brought to court. One hundred people attacked the convoy he was in with molotovs in a very well-planned action. It was particularly difficult because it took place in front of the central courthouse while there were a ton of police protecting it. And it was a great success. Then there was the initiative to attack the metro stations, breaking the ticket machines, writing graffiti in all the stations, and spreading thousands of pamphlets demanding free transportation as well as criticizing the meaning of public transportation as travel from home to work and back home, like a *poleodomic,* an urban symbol of obedience to the compartmentalization of life in jobs and houses.

And we can't forget the attack on the Ministry of Environment and Urban Planning. The entire building burned to cinders. This was in solidarity with the people of Lefkimi, a town in Corfu, who for the last year have been fighting hard against the police and the government to keep a new garbage dump from being built in their area. In the riots the cops had killed a woman, one of the protesters. So they burned this ministry building completely. After this action, which became very public because of all the announcements that appeared in the blogs and Indymedia and other Internet sites of the movement, the people of the town sent a letter of thanks for the solidarity actions, an official announcement of thanks. These were just some of the actions that happened in the first ten days.

An important part of the spirit of December was that tens of thousands of high school students appeared in the streets all around Greece, most of them for the first time, even as young as twelve and thirteen years old. Many of the students occupied their own schools and then used them to prepare street protests and attacks against police stations with molotovs and stones. There were times when twenty-five different police stations were simultaneously under attack by high schoolers. This produced the image that a civil war was occurring just like sixty years ago, but instead of being between the communists and the right wing, it was between the youth and the government. In addition to the student occupations there were occupations of government and municipal buildings all over the country, carried out by old people, young people, and workers. It was a meeting of many social elements. Many of these other people didn't become as active, they didn't participate as much as anarchists were hoping they would, but it was a great moment, this meeting.

It was very empowering for us that solidarity actions took place all over the world. Many of these actions took place in countries where it is very difficult to carry out direct actions and the feeling that comrades in these countries were taking action for the Greek movement gave us the power to do more here. And we want to say thank you. This solidarity also produced a great fear among the governments of the planet, demonstrated for example by how Sarkozy revoked the law to privatize the universities to avoid general riots in France.

163

There were also many funny incidents in December. Perhaps the funniest was on the 10th of December. We jacked a fire engine and were driving it around. We got on the CB radio and radioed to the dispatcher, we were saying, "tonight you motherfuckers we will burn you all!" At the time the journalists had been saying hysterically that the anarchists were burning everything to the ground and the fire department couldn't stop the fires, so this was a great joke. And the girl in the station was saying, "Please get off this frequency because we are getting lots of calls and we can't coordinate all the different fire engines around the city." She was begging. At the same time that all this happened, the symbol of Christmas consumption, the big Christmas tree in front of Parliament was in flames. Journalists were shouting on all the channels that 300 anarchists broke through the line of riot cops and are going behind the Parliament to burn down the house of the prime minister, and this was true. The Ministry of Foreign Affairs was facing molotov attacks, the main commercial street of Kolonaki was being completely burned at the same moment, and during all this the regime was in a complete panic and they were spreading rumors on the TV that we were under the threat of dictatorship and the only solution would be to call down the army and restore order.

The attacks against the police were very heavy. The molotovs came down like rain. We weren't using small beer bottles anymore, we were making molotovs with big wine bottles. We had no more fear. There was a very strong feeling that we had the moral right to attack the government and the police. There were many normal people in the riots who were helping us in every way. When they saw comrades with molotovs, they were telling us where the police were. They protected us from the police the same way, giving us warnings. And when the rumors started to spread that the military would be called into the streets, we were wishing it would happen so that what we have been talking about for all these years, the civil war, the class war, would become a reality.

We personally participated in the riots of '91 and '95, which were the biggest riots in Greece over the last few decades. But for us, December was the first time that people felt so courageous and enthusiastic. And this feeling was spread among nonpolitical people, it didn't matter if they were anarchists or leftists or political activists, it was the general feeling of society manifested by pure and deep hatred against the police. Whoever saw police uniforms saw a target, and this expanded from one side of the country to the other.

During the riots, the incredible thing is that people appeared and took on important roles when up until that moment they had been *volomeni,* people who were complacent and had their basic needs met, like a car and television and a house. Even these people felt that this was a great moment for Greek society, and they felt an urge to come down to the streets and take part in the riot. In a practical way this enabled everything to happen.

Our cause has always been to produce chaos. What many people say is a utopia, we have experienced it in our lifetimes. And as we have succeeded in living it once, we are 100% sure that it will happen again on a global scale. And this certainty exists because the simple people who maybe vote for the conservative party or live their normal lives, there comes a moment when they realize that the only way to succeed in their lives is to lose, to lose their normal lives, and the moment they realize this they come into the streets in the most powerful of ways and fight alongside the initiators and provokers of these fights. And then we have to take care to allow these people to become the vanguard of the struggle, and not us.

We Are Here / We Are Everywhere / We Are an Image from the Future

Ego Te Provoco December 11, 2008

If I do not burn
If you do not burn
If we do not burn
How will darkness come to light?

—**Nazim Hikmet, "Like Kerem"**

Clenching fear in their teeth the dogs howl: Return to normality—the fools' feast is over. The philologists of assimilation have already started digging up their razor-sharp caresses: "We are ready to forget, to understand, to exchange the promiscuity of these few days, but now behave or we shall bring over our sociologists, our anthropologists, our psychiatrists! Like good fathers we have tolerated your emotional eruption with restraint—now look at how desks, offices and shop windows gape empty! The time has come for a return, and whoever refuses this holy duty shall be hit hard, shall be sociologized, shall be psychiatrized. An injunction hovers over the city: "Are you at your post?" Democracy, social harmony, national unity and all the other big hearths stinking of death have already stretched out their morbid arms.

Power (from the government to the family) aims not simply to repress the insurrection and its generalization, but to produce a relation of subjectification. A relation that defines *bios*, that is political life, as a sphere of cooperation, compromise and consensus. "Politics is the politics of consensus; the rest is gang-war, riots, chaos." This is a true translation of what they are telling us, of their effort to deny the living core of every action, and to separate and isolate us from what we can do: not to unite the two into one, but to rupture again and again the one into two. The mandarins of harmony, the barons of peace and quiet, law and order, call on us to become dialectic. But those tricks are desperately old, and their misery is transparent in the fat bellies of the trade-union bosses, in the washed-out eyes of the intermediaries, who like vultures perch over every negation, over every passion for the real. We have seen them in May, we have seen them in LA and Brixton, and we have been watching them over decades licking the now long white bones of the 1973 Polytechnic. We saw them again yesterday when instead of calling for a permanent general strike, they bowed to legality and called off the strike protest march. Because they know all too well that the road to the generalization of the insurrection is through the field of production—through the occupation of the means of production of this world that crushes us.

Tomorrow dawns a day when nothing is certain. And what could be more liberating than this after so many long years of certainty? A bullet was able to interrupt the brutal sequence of all those identical days. The assassination of a fifteen-year-old boy created a displacement strong enough to turn the world upside down. A displacement from the seeing through of yet another day, to the point that so many think simultaneously: "That was it, not one step further, all must change and we will change it." The revenge for the death of Alexis has become the revenge for every day that we are forced to wake up in this world. And what seemed so hard proved to be so simple.

This is what has happened, what we have. If something scares us it is the return to normality. For in the destroyed and pillaged streets of our cities of light we see not only the obvious results of our rage, but the possibility of starting to live. We no longer have anything to do than to install ourselves in this possibility, transforming it into a living experience: by grounding on the field of everyday life, our creativity, our power to materialize our desires, our power not to contemplate but to construct the real. This is our vital space. All the rest is death.

Those who want to understand will understand. Now is the time to break the invisible cells that chain each and everyone to his or her pathetic little life. And this does not require solely or necessarily one to attack police stations and torch malls and banks. The time that one deserts his or her couch and the passive contemplation of his or her own life and takes to the streets to talk and to listen, leaving behind anything private, introduces into the field of social relations the destabilizing force of a nuclear bomb. And this is precisely because the (till now) fixation of everyone on his or her microcosm is tied to the traction forces of the atom. Those forces that make the (capitalist) world turn. This is the dilemma: with the insurgents or alone. And this is one of the really few times that a dilemma can be at the same time so absolute and real.

UP AGAINST THE WALL MOTHERFUCKERS! WE'VE COME FOR WHAT'S OURS...

In these days of rage, spectacle as a power-relation, as a relation that imprints memory onto objects and bodies, is faced with a diffuse counter-power that deterritorializes impressions allowing them to wander away from the tyranny of the image and into the field of the senses. Senses are always felt antagonistically (they are always acting against something)— but under the current conditions they are driven toward an increasingly acute and radical polarization.

Against the supposedly peaceful caricatures of bourgeois media ("violence is unacceptable always, everywhere"), we can only respond: their rule, the rule of gentle spirits and consent, of dialogue and harmony is nothing but a well calculated pleasure in beastliness: a promised carnage. The democratic regime in its peaceful façade doesn't kill an Alexis every day, precisely because it kills thousands of Ahmeds, Fatimas, Jorges, Jin Tiaos and Benajirs: because it assassinates systematically, structurally, and without remorse the entirety of the Third World, that is the global proletariat. It is in this way, through

166

this calm everyday slaughter, that the idea of freedom is born: freedom not as a supposedly panhuman good, nor as a natural right for all, but as the war cry of the damned, as the premise of civil war.

The history of the legal order and the bourgeois class brainwashes us with an image of the gradual and stable progress of humanity within which violence stands as a sorry exception stemming from the economically, emotionally, and culturally underdeveloped. Yet all of us who have been crushed between school desks, behind offices, in factories, know only too well that history is nothing but a succession of bestial acts installed upon a morbid system of rules. The cardinals of normality weep for the law that was violated by the bullet of the pig Korkoneas (the killer cop). But who doesn't know that the force of the law is merely the force of the powerful? That law itself allows violence to be exercised on violence? The law is void from end to bitter end; it contains no meaning, no target other than the coded power of imposition.

At the same time, the dialectic of the Left tries to codify conflict, battle and war, with the logic of the synthesis of opposites. In this way it constructs an order; a pacified condition within which everything has its proper little place. Yet, the destiny of conflict is not synthesis—as the destiny of war is not peace. Social insurrection comprises the condensation and explosion of thousands of negations, yet it does not contain even in a single one of its atoms, nor in a single one of its moments its own negation, its own end. This always comes heavy and gloomy like a certainty from the institutions of mediation and normalization, from the Left promising voting rights at sixteen, disarmament but preservation of the pigs, a welfare state, etc. Those, in other words, who wish to capitalize political gains upon the wounds of others. The sweetness of their compromise drips with blood.

Social counter-violence cannot be held accountable for what it does not assume: it is destructive from end to end. If the struggles of modernity have anything to teach us, it is not their sad adhesion to the subject (class, party, group) but their systematic anti-dialectical process: the act of destruction does not necessarily need to carry a dimension of creation. In other words, the destruction of the old world and the creation of a new comprise two discrete but continuous processes. The issue then is what methods of destruction of the given can be developed in different points and moments of the insurrection. Which methods cannot only preserve the level and the extent of the insurrection, but contribute to its qualitative upgrading. The attacks on police stations, the clashes and roadblocks, the barricades and street battles now comprise an everyday and socialized phenomenon in the metropolis and beyond. And they have contributed to a partial deregulation of the circle of production and consumption. And yet, they still comprise a partial targeting of the enemy; direct and obvious to all, yet entrapped in one and only dimension of the attack against dominant social relations. However, the process of production and circulation of goods in itself, in other words,

167

the capital-relation, is only indirectly hit by the mobilizations. A spectre hovers over the city torched: the indefinite, wild general strike.

The global capitalist crisis has denied the bosses their most dynamic, most extorting response to the insurrection: "We offer you everything, forever, while all they can offer is an uncertain present." With one firm collapsing after the other, capitalism and its state are no longer in a position to offer anything other than worse days to come, tightened financial conditions, sacks, suspension of pensions, welfare cuts, the crushing of free education. Contrarily, in just seven days, the insurgents have proved in practice what they can do: to turn the city into a battlefield, to create enclaves of communes across the urban fabric, to abandon individuality and their pathetic security, seeking the composition of their collective power and the total destruction of this murderous system.

At this historical conjuncture of crisis, rage, and the dismissal of institutions at which we finally stand, the only thing that can convert the systemic deregulation into a social revolution is the total rejection of work. When street fighting will be taking place in streets dark from the strike of the electricity company; when clashes will be taking place amidst tons of uncollected rubbish, when trolley-buses will be closing streets, blocking off the cops, when the striking teacher will be lighting up his revolted pupil's molotov cocktail, then we will be finally able to say: "Ruffians, the days of your society are numbered; we weighed its joys and its justices and we found them all too short." This, today, is no longer a mere fantasy but a concrete ability in everyone's hand: the ability to act concretely on the concrete. The ability to charge the skies.

If all of these, namely the extension of the conflict into the sphere of production-circulation—with sabotages and wild strikes seem premature—it might just be because we haven't quite realized how fast power decomposes, how fast confrontational practices and counter-power forms of organizing are socially diffused: from high school students pelting police stations with stones, to municipal employees and neighbors occupying town halls. The revolution does not take place with prayers toward, and piety for, historical conditions. It occurs by seizing whatever opportunity of insurrection in every aspect of the social; by transforming every reluctant gesture of condemnation of the cops into a definite strike at the foundations of this system.

Off the pigs!

The media as part of the counter-insurgency

Ego Te Provoco: Four members of a counterinformation group in Athens

We are a group that creates counterinformation addressing existing issues, against the ideological war being waged by the State and Capital. We make brochures, posters, a newsletter. We intervene in the discourse around current affairs and also carry out a permanent campaign of ideological sabotage of a more general nature.

In the first four days it was very different, until the funeral, because the media were not unleashing their full counterinsurgency strategy. They were not able to have a consistent approach during December. For example leading journalists were saying this was a rebellion and a just rebellion, and other journalists were complaining that rioters were attacking irrelevant shops, thus implicitly suggesting that there were relevant shops, that it was justified to smash banks or certain other shops. They had no consistent approach. In the West there is a consensus between news agencies about how to report things, like condemning them or not reporting things from the grassroots. But in Greece that consensus does not exist because all the channels compete to report the most exciting stories, and the channels reflect different interests. Some news channels want the government to collapse and they want the next government to adopt a certain policy. So, objectively speaking, some of the media were actually helping us. They did not have this consensus that they would leave all their differences behind and defend the State. Instead they were working on a micropolitical level.

In the main right wing newspaper you could see the conflict. One line of articles was dead against the squats, arguing that they should all be evicted, and then there was another article arguing for the legalization of the squats, funding them and turning them into art centers. But this government would never do it. The conservative party is very old-fashioned, very uncool. It's all about repression, not about assimilation. It's a good thing the Socialists weren't in power in December, because they're much better at that kind of thing.

Another example is the surveillance cameras on the street. They were installed by the Socialists for the Olympics. Many were not functioning so the right wing party says they want to put them all in operation and now the Socialists are crying their heads off saying this is fascist. Rather than acknowledging, okay, this is a tool of the State and it will make us all stronger, instead they are playing at being defenders of human rights. There is no consistent policy.

The killing of Alexis and the uprising made people listen; they were much more interested in counterinformation.

Usually when you hand out leaflets one out of three people takes it but in December people would queue up to take it, they would demand leaflets from you. Our need for counterinformation started about three days after the beginning, when we realized that it was an uprising and we had to produce a counterdiscourse. One of the main things we tried to get across is the fact that the State doesn't kill an Alexis every day because the State kills hundreds of immigrants and Third World workers. So one of our main foci was, you know, Greek society was so upset about the death of this white First World boy but doesn't give a shit about the immigrants killed a few blocks down the street or the trafficked Russian women getting raped. The other thing we put forward was a discourse against democracy, because many people were saying, what kind of democracy kills children, we need more democracy, and we were trying to deconstruct this whole notion of democracy, to claim that this murder is not an exception, it is the rule of democracy, the rule of the nation-state, the rule of capitalism.

In the beginning the media failed in their counterinsurgency work. Everyone failed in the beginning. They tried to project the fear of the ruling classes onto the general population, but it no longer applied. During the uprising we would be masked and carrying big iron sticks but people would still come and sit with us and take leaflets from us. It had become a completely normal figure, the *koukoulofori*.

But after about four days they began to make their coverage more effective. Shop owners began to demand more protection from the police, because the media focused a lot on damage to private property. In contrast in the beginning the shop owners said they weren't going to discuss a few smashed windows, because someone had been killed and that was more serious.

This is how the media worked as part of the counterinsurgency: first through the segmentation of the insurrection. The school children were presented as good and justified, and strictly represented by a single aesthetic, as peaceful. They did not show the students rioting. Then there were the anarchists who were taking advantage of the situation to create chaos, and theirs was an aesthetic of violence, their only activities were destructive. And finally there were immigrants, who only wanted to loot. All of these were extracted from the mass that took part in the insurrection, they were identified as separate, even as identifiable groups, and they were all assigned specific attributes.

Next, the media consistently and repeatedly claimed that the movement lacked demands. They were always talking about this lack of demands. So they placed the movement on a continuum of irrationality. It was simply an issue of rage, which the State would tolerate to a limited extent, because after all a child had been killed, but there had to be an end to it and after that things had to go back to normal. They still say that there was a lack of demands and this reduces December to a sentimental explosion. The state representative specifically instructed the media not to refer to it as a social uprising. The foreign media really portrayed the uprising as related to the economic crisis, which in reality it was not because at the time there was no real economic crisis in Greece.

Only the Left groups responded to the pressure to make demands, to dialogue, and I felt that they couldn't handle the demands they were putting forward because even within the Left there were people who were very active and taking part in the riots—the base. So the heads of these groups were demanding to disarm the police, to lower the voting age to sixteen, for the government to resign, but they couldn't control their base, they couldn't mobilize people for their demands.

In one of our leaflets we said, you are demanding from us that we enter the logic of demands. It's a logic of exchange, a capitalist logic, that if you meet our demands then we will give you peace, but we've gone beyond the time of peace.

On Thursday we learned that twenty-five police stations in Athens were attacked by students, and immigrants had conflicts with the police by themselves and attacked shops. This was crashing down every demand, the motion was spreading in many places. There were thousands of demands, not just one list.

Finally the media functioned as a force for counterinsurgency by spreading fear. They repeatedly reported rumors that a woman had burned to death in her building as a result of the riots, even that bus loads of anarchists and immigrants were travelling through the countryside to smash up all the provincial villages.

What they're trying to say now is that it's not the anarchists but that society as a whole is crazy, it's snapped and everyone is becoming violent and breaking the law. Today there was an interview by the president of the general union of industrialists, he's president of the big milk-producing company, and he said, look, the government is shit, it cannot control anything, and the opposition is useless. What we need is social cohesion. There has been massive propaganda against violence. Some days if you were only listening to the radio and didn't go out in the street you would think you were in Somalia. There was a cacophony of shootings and armed guerrillas, bank robberies, rapes, an image of decay and chaos. And the ex-minister of public order, from the opposition, went in public and said that Athens has turned into Baghdad. So they're playing on this Middle Eastern archetype of everyone on the street with bazookas. They try to put it all together, that everyone has lost it.

Crime has not gone up, just reporting of it has gone up. When Kolonaki was attacked, it was front-page news for a week, as if it were a disaster. But it had already been attacked several times before and it just got a small mention. It was obvious as well that during December they had no filter for separating things, distinguishing, as a strategy, between acceptable actions and unacceptable ones. They furiously condemned everything, even some artists going into a theater and

171

dropping a banner against spectators; this was denounced disproportionately as fascist, as a sacrilege, in the same way they would rant against a ministry being attacked.

I know people who were in the army and they were put on yellow alert. They said they had talked with other soldiers and if they had been sent into the streets they would have given the arms to the people and there would have been a massacre—of the police. They even distributed a text. This led to a new regulation forbidding all political texts in the military. The government could not have called in the military because they would have mutinied. The government could not control the rebellion in a military way. It was a political issue, not a military one. If there was even one more death the situation would really have gone out of control and they couldn't risk this. It already was out of control, but I mean there would have been people shooting down cops during the demonstrations. The government had internal disagreements and it was obvious. In the high ministries they were insulting each other as malakas, so the government did not have cohesion. The ruling party only had a majority of one in parliament. Both the government and the police were seen as completely illegitimate by the general population and of course there was one part that called for repression but the more realistic members of the government dominated in the end. So there was a more communicative and political resolution of the whole thing. Calling in the army would have been a great mistake for them, this would have been the worst thing they could have done.

After some rioters looted bows and arrows from this weird specialty shop on Omonia the media were reporting that the demonstrators had looted an arms shop and were marching on parliament, which would have required calling in the army. Segments of the elite were testing it, to see if it would catch.

The occupation of the national TV

Vortex: A person from Athens who was already involved in the movement when the rebellion started

NET is one of the three national TV stations. It's broadcast all over the country. What happens there, everybody sees it. And the whole thing took place on Tuesday, December 16. If I remember correctly, the idea was proposed by this friend who knew people working within the media industry, and knew how it functioned. They know both how to use complicated equipment and also a few of them knew their way into the specific building. I'm not sure if the whole thing can be called an anarchist action because not everyone who participated was an anarchist. Most of the people were definitely libertarian, and a lot of them were artists. People who worked in film, actors, documentarians, but all of them very moved by the killing of Alexis. And some of them had only started becoming active after the killing. So we started meeting in this basement for about a week trying to organize the whole thing. It wasn't easy because we had to be very precise with our moves. The goal was to interrupt the three o'clock news program, which is their major broadcast. Everyone is at home for the afternoon break at that time so we considered this to be the best moment. The

difficulty was deciding who was going to do what, how many things we were going to do and who is going into each room. We had three main targets. One was the control room. It controls the studio, and from there you can see what's going on inside the studio. The other target was the master room. From there if something goes wrong they can cut off the signal. And the third target was the station president's office.

We had to be certain which room was on which floor, and some of the people who had a way in and out of the building gave us the necessary information. We made various maps on big sheets of butcher paper stuck up on the wall so we could memorize the basic plan of the building. It was vital not to look hesitant when we got there, so no one would stop us and ask us where we were going. A good map was absolutely necessary to the action. You can't go in looking like someone who is in there for the first time. When you're familiar with the location, you walk with certainty. The psychology of the action is very important. There were some older people involved in the action and they were the most hesitant. As the day came upon us, they started doubting our chances for success, and that caused problems during the discussion because they raised stupid questions.

The three rooms were on three different floors. We had to be very precise with the timing, down to a precision of seconds, more or less. The people who entered the master room would be the first team, so that the technicians there would have no chance to switch off the signal when they found out what was going on in the studio. We said that this team should get into the master room thirty seconds or a minute before the people who entered the control room. We had decided that the people who would enter the studio would not talk, they would just hold up a couple of huge banners. The news anchor would get out of the way, and all of a sudden you would see banners from inside the studio. One of them said, *Don't just watch us. Everyone get out in the streets,* and *Freedom to the Prisoners of the Insurrection,* and a small one said, *Freedom to Everyone.*

Both of these teams included people who knew how to use the equipment. You also had to have a person who knew how to use a TV camera. We had decided that the people holding the banners, about ten of them, would wear masks if they wanted to. But not all of them did because the people who had decided to be in front of the cameras were not hardcore anarchists, most of them were artists. Perhaps they saw it as more artistic than subversive. But in any case none of them had the aesthetic of *koukoulofori,* the masketeers. At first I thought it would be a good idea for everyone to mask up, but I saw that the whole action was successful and I saw that these people were sure of themselves. So you know, if you don't mind I don't mind. And it was a courageous act.

The third team would get into the office of the manager, with the goal of calming him down—because he has TVs inside his office and knows exactly what's going on inside the building—and not let him call the police. This team failed. The others were very professional, but this team failed. This guy could not be calmed down, and we had decided not to use violence. He went crazy and ran out into the hall, screaming.

We didn't go in from the main entrance because you had to leave your ID there, but there was a side entrance that they used for equipment. Because there were about fifty of us, which is a big number, we had decided that we would enter in pairs within a time period of two hours. So people started going in already from one o'clock, so we wouldn't draw attention. We all had to be dressed well, quite formally. I wore a suit, nice shoes, nice trousers. And we also said everyone should have some sort of prop with them, a folder, a CD, papers, something to signify that you're going to deliver something at an office, that you're there for a reason.

I was in the team that took the master room, and our team had to be quick and if need be a bit… I wouldn't say aggressive, but we had to let them know that we knew why we were there and we weren't joking around. So the goal was to get in and tell them to get their hands away from the control panels. There were some big guys in this team. We had to look scary. I did the talking: don't touch anything, get away from there, blah, blah, blah.

The goal was to stay on the air about five minutes, which was very ambitious. And we hoped that by that time the helicopters wouldn't have come and we'd have enough time to leave the building. There was a big cafeteria on the first floor of the building where we would all meet afterwards and all exit the building together, making sure we weren't leaving anyone behind. Each team was responsible for knowing if they were all there.

I got to the building around two o'clock, going in with another guy from my team. We entered through the side entrance and we went straight to the cafeteria, which we knew the location of, thanks to the maps. We already knew how to get there, which way to turn, et cetera. And by 2:30 I think everyone was there, and everyone was in the cafeteria, all pretending not to know each other. After quarter past two, it was basically only us in the cafeteria. Before that were lots of other people from the building, because it's a big building. But we were all acting, being normal, being social. We had decided not to go in at three when the news started but to let them broadcast for ten minutes. First everyone had checked out the rooms they needed to go to be sure it was all according to the map, and then went back to the cafeteria. A lot of people were visiting the toilets because they were stressed and had to pee.

At seven or six minutes past 3:00, everyone was outside their target room. So at 3:09 I put on my gloves, because I didn't want to leave fingerprints, and we crossed the hall, and got in. Well there was a problem, we got confused at the last second whether that room was the right one or whether it was another one, so we were a few seconds late. When we got into the master the second team had already invaded the control room, just seconds before. We were lucky because the people in the master were busy with something and they hadn't realized it yet. I had learned professional names for the equipment

so I could pretend I knew what I was talking about. What I had to say was "Nobody touches the master, keep your hands away from the PLF!" I still have no idea what a PLF is. There were only two people in there, and one of them grabbed the phone. I grabbed his arm and said, "No, you're not making a call for the next few minutes. No one is going to get hurt, we're only going to be here a few minutes, and then we'll go." It was important to let them know we were friendly.

The people who were working in the control room completely freaked out when our team came in and replaced them at their seats. The director started screaming, someone had to calm her down. We didn't stay for five minutes, in the end only two minutes or a little less, because there was another room, it turned out, that could interrupt the signal. And we hadn't known about that. That was an element of misinformation. So after a minute and a half they put on advertisements. The lucky thing was that because we had decided to invade at ten past 3:00, they were broadcasting a live feed from the Greek Parliament where the prime minister was talking, and all of a sudden there was a fade in, fade out. One second the two pictures were together, and then the PM disappeared completely and you could only see the people with the banner.

When the commercials ended we saw from the monitors that our people were leaving the studio, so we said "thank you," and left. The whole time we didn't use any elevators so we couldn't be trapped in them, we took the stairs down, met in the cafeteria, and threw flyers into the air as we left. The

175

general manager continued to freak out completely, and he went live and announced that they had been attacked by a group of anonymous people.

Some of the people holding the banner were known artists. While we were leaving people were coming out of their offices. Everyone in the building has screens so they had seen what had happened. And they came out to see who we were as we were leaving. Some of them were quite happy with us. I think they might have even clapped, but I don't remember.

Outside of the building there were two police officers in the yard. They saw us but they didn't do anything, because there were fifty of us. Someone in our group went to calm them down to make sure nothing would happen, saying that it was all over and we were leaving. One of them tried to make a joke, saying "No problem. It's good to see that you can do things without being violent." We all stayed together for a block and then we scattered.

A similar action happened in Patras. And a week before, there had been a similar proposal in an anarchist assembly, and some people argued against it, not wanting to be part of the spectacle and to put ourselves between advertisements. Most of them did not favor such an action but when they saw it happening I think they changed their minds. It was a very impressive thing. Afterwards this video got replayed on all the other channels.

Call for a New International

One of many texts released anonymously on the Internet

Politicians and journalists brag around, trying to impose on our movement their own failing rationality: we revolt because our government is corrupted or because we'd like more of their money, more of their jobs.

If we break the banks it's because we recognize money as one of the central causes of our sadness, if we smash shop windows it's not because life is expensive but because commodity prevents us from living at all costs. If we attack the police scum, it's not only to avenge our dead comrades but because between this world and the one we desire, they will always be an obstacle.

We know that the time has come for us to think strategically. In this Imperial time we know that the condition for a victorious insurrection is that it spreads, at least, on a European level. These last years we've seen and we've learnt: The counter-summits worldwide, student and suburban riots in France, the No-TAV movement in Italy, the Oaxaca commune, Montreal's riots, the offensive defense of the Ungdomshuset squat in Copenhagen, riots against the Republican National Convention in the USA, the list goes on.

Born in the catastrophe, we're the children of all crisis: political, social, economical, ecological. We know this world is a dead-end. You have to be crazy to cling to its ruins. You have to be wise to self-organize.

There's an obviousness in the total rejection of party politics and organizations, they're part of the old world. We're the spoiled children of this society and we don't want anything from it. That's the ultimate sin they'll never forgive us. Behind the black masks, we are your children. And we're getting organized.

We would not make so much effort to destroy the material structures of this world: its banks, its supermarkets, its police stations, if we didn't know that at the same time we are undermining its very metaphysic, its ideals, its ideas and its rationality.

The media would describe last week's events as an expression of nihilism. What they don't get is that in the very process of assaulting and harassing this reality, we experience a higher form of community, of sharing, a higher form of spontaneous and joyous organization that forms the basis of a different world.

One could say our revolt finds its own limit in the very fact that it only creates pure destruction. That would be true if, beside the street fights, we hadn't set up the necessary organization that requires a long-term movement: canteens provided by regular looting, infirmaries to heal our own wounded, the means to print our own newspapers, our own radio. As we liberate territory from the empire of the State and its police, we have to occupy it, to fill it and to transform its uses so it can serve the movement. So the movement never stops to grow.

All over Europe, governments tremble. For sure what scares them most are not local copycat riots but the very possibility that the western youth finds common cause and rises as one to give this society its final blow.

This is a call to all those who hear it:

From Berlin to Madrid, from London to Tarnac, everything becomes possible.

Solidarity must become complicity. Confrontations have to spread. Communes need to be declared.

So that the situation never goes back to normal. So that the ideas and practices that link us to one another become actual bonds.

So that we can stay ungovernable.

A revolutionary salute to all our comrades worldwide. To all the prisoners, we'll get you out!

177

In London, the response was immediate

Em: A Greek person who has been involved for years in anarchist and grassroots struggles and has lived the past four years in London

I've been involved in squatting and setting up social centers, participating in local projects, housing campaigns, and more general campaigns throughout the UK. I wasn't so much a part of the Greek community here. My political milieu was British.

In London the response to the killing of Alexis was immediate. At first it was mainly Greek people, but also some Brits and Poles. Personal connections, Greeks and others who had friends and contacts in Greece, enabled this fast response. Also the Internet and Indymedia. The first actions happened on Sunday, the very next day. What we could do was limited by police repression, which is very well developed in Britain. But it was also limited by the fact that some of us were already burnt out.

Our goal was to raise the political cost of what was happening in Greece. We knew what our goal was, in that sense it was clear, but in another sense it's not so clear, not so straightforward, because it was also an emotional response. That's an important part of it. We were reacting emotionally to what was happening in Greece. But I think we achieved our goal. Our actions made themselves felt, and they were very much appreciated in Greece. They made them feel that they weren't alone. We should never underestimate the emotional factor. The people in Greece were not having an easy time. What was happening was exciting but it was also extremely difficult and stressful and frightening. To know that they weren't alone, that there was support, was very important for them.

I consciously decided on the 6th of December to organize solidarity actions in London, and I stayed there until the 15th. Then I came back to Athens and stayed here until February, and I decided I had to move back to Athens. The city has changed. So I went back to London and got my things and came back here. But since the 6th of December I've been running around constantly, organizing things. It's been my entire life.

Mostly we organized protests and blockades—blockading the Greek embassy and the offices of the Greek tourist organization. At the first official protest, Monday the 8th, five people got arrested while blockading the embassy. Two days later there was another one but no one got arrested. On Sunday the 15th of December there was a big protest in Dolston Station in North London. This was the first action in collaboration with the British anarchist scene. It was a hard thing to bring them in contact. I was one of the only ones trying to get the general anarchist movement in touch with the Greek enclave. There are only a few active Greek anarchists in London, but lots more who identify as anarchists though they aren't active. They only show up when it's something related to Greece.

Even the Stalinists had a protest in front of the Greek embassy, which was surreal, because the day before the chief secretary of the Communist Party in Greece renounced the uprising and the violence. So I went up to them and told them to piss off.

There were other solidarity actions all over Britain—Bristol, Cardiff, Edinburgh. Some of these actions exceeded what was normal for protests in Britain. Seeing what happened in Greece had a positive effect on the movement. The people felt inspired again, and empowered. The solidarity actions themselves were typical, they weren't anything special. Sorry for being so cynical but I want to be realistic. The actions themselves weren't so special, and they were quite small. But you could see that people were more enthusiastic. Greece helped them to reclaim a dream that they had kind of lost. It's what happened in any other European city that is experiencing repression. They found a dream and said we can do it, they regained their confidence. And now you saw what happened in the G20 [protests in London in April, 2009, where anarchists stole some of the spotlight from the world leaders by fighting with police and smashing some banks]. They got inspired in many ways.

Many people are scared of returning to normality. I have no problem with this because what changes is the way you perceive things. Greece is a time bomb after December. Even if it doesn't happen right now, it will happen. Everyone knows that. I think it will take the police killing someone else to create another insurrection, but that could happen. I had a friend badly injured in a protest in February. They threw a stun grenade at him, it exploded on his shoulder, and it burned him badly. If it had hit him in the head he could have been killed. The police are stupid. They're very scared, but they're stupid, and violent, and they could kill someone again.

In Barcelona, we quickly organized a solidarity protest

Pere: A squatter and anarchist who participated in the solidarity protest in Barcelona on the 20th of December

A week ago, after we first heard about Greece and kept hearing about it and understood that it was real, we quickly organized a solidarity protest. With all the rage and urgency and excitement, the people managed to get past the police for the first time in a long time in this fucking city. They smashed up some luxury shops and banks, nothing heavy but better than we've had in a couple years, and then scattered. A couple people, I think they were from out of town and didn't have anyone looking after them, got arrested.

On the 20th of December, the day of international solidarity, we organized another protest. Seven people had been arrested in Madrid after the solidarity protest there attacked a police station and they were facing heavy charges, so this protest was for them too. About three hundred people convened in Plaça Universitat, where we always convene, and where the police are fully practiced in surrounding us and controlling us. By Plaça Catalunya the *mossos* started signalling their

aggressive intentions and evidently no one wanted to fight. On Indymedia they'll write about how weak the movement is, but they never come to a protest prepared to start a fight. What, this is something the magical masses initiate, some insurrection that comes about through a scientific dialectic or mystical process? The mass is just another person standing next to you, waiting for you to start something. I had brought some paint bombs, not much, but early on my compañeros ran off to avoid any inconvenience so I never had anyone to watch my back so I could throw them.

Anyway, the march started running, more or less, as the cops came up hard behind us. All they had to do was look at us like they wanted to beat us, and we dissolved. On the way a few people were causing a little damage to cash machines, spray painting a little, but it was hard to do more with the cops breathing down our necks and the fleet of a dozen riot vans behind them. At Urquinaona we hooked back left, as usual, and ended up on Passeig de Gracia, where it was easy for the police to surround us, in this case right in the middle of a big intersection. At least we were blocking up traffic?

Then one cop fell into the fountain there, got himself all wet and hurt his leg, and no one had even pushed him. He just fell in! Naturally we all started laughing our asses off, saying how stupid the cops were, congratulating Comrade Fountain. They were seething. The injured cop was helped away, they waited a minute, glaring at us, and then started pushing and beating us from all sides. Anyone who got close enough felt their batons. A few of us pushed back but we paid for it in bruises. At least we didn't let them arrest anybody, but they were mostly interested in pushing us to the side of the road. At this point there were only a hundred of us because so many people started to scatter early on. Some of those came back to watch, and at one point the police picked through the crowd and grabbed anyone they thought was an anarchist, pushed them in here with us.

The fucking cops were pushing on all sides until we were packed like sardines. I knew the paint bombs were bursting in my backpack and I just hoped the paint wouldn't start leaking out. You could see a few people dazed, their heads bleeding, while others screamed at the cops to let an ambulance get in. They kettled us up tight for a while, maybe half an hour or more, and then let us go. But there was one injured woman, I couldn't see so close, and they wouldn't let the medics get close to her, so more scuffling started, someone threw a glass bottle, they attacked again, and everyone scattered through the city while they hunted us. I think a couple people got arrested. I walked all the way home to avoid using the metro, just in case, and all through the city police cars were tearing around looking for us. And we hadn't even managed to do anything.

Many foreigners have been killed

Adams: A Sudanese refugee who runs a refugee aid center in the Omonia neighborhood of Athens

I think I found out about the death of that boy, Alexandros, on the TV. The demonstrations were started by Greek people. As foreigners we didn't play the main role in what happened in December. But ultimately the demonstrations were used by many people in need, people who were angry with unemployment, with not having papers, angry with the police, or just frustrated by the whole situation. So they joined the demonstrations, but for their own purposes.

In the center of Athens there was looting everywhere. Like I said, many people were using the occasion for their own motives. Of course as foreigners we were afraid of taking part in any violent actions in a protest or another situation because we have no power here. They could find a dead body after all the riots, what's his name? It turns out to be an immigrant and it doesn't matter. No one would hear about it. They can kill us much easier than they can kill Greek people. Many foreigners are wanted after December. They accuse foreigners of carrying out the robberies, the looting. Many Greek citizens complained about the thieving and the arsons and property damage. The media put the blame for that on us.

187

The police are violent in general, all the time. Many foreigners have been killed at the borders and the asylum centers. These feelings of resentment toward police behavior had grown very strong, so people used the occasion of the riots as an excuse. But the Greek people were making a serious revolution to change the system. Since then things have gotten better. Now the police behave better and they treat us better.

What I saw was very limited. I didn't go out at all to the demonstrations. The streets were full of tear gas, especially in Omonia. But how I saw it, the problem occurred suddenly and from there everything happened automatically. The Greeks meant to create change, they were organized, but the foreigners just took advantage of the situation.

Since December I don't notice any change in our relations with Greek people, four months later. I have lots of contact with humanitarian organizations, but it's all the same. And I don't feel any difference in attitude from the Greek civilians even though the media blamed the foreigners for the looting. But in the demonstrations everyone was mixed together, so how can they say who did it?

I can't say if other foreigners have made contact with Greek anarchists or if they came together in December. Individually of course it happened but in terms of organizational contacts, there has been nothing. And I can't judge if Greek sympathy for foreigners has increased or not. There are many good people in Greece, but they are afraid of us, especially of us Africans. I don't know why, maybe because we have black skin or something. But if we came near to them and talked with them it would be good. But how can we do this when we are so far apart?

Here we are refugees. We don't know about the situation faced by the immigrants. Their problems and our problems are very different. Many refugees have no papers and they are not learning about their rights like the immigrants do. Many refugees are thinking about the problems back in their own countries. Or they are worrying about their papers. The majority of us have no papers: we only have deportation papers. Many refugees will be killed when they are sent back. The refugees have been coming to Greece more recently, since about 2003, but the immigrants have been coming here for longer.

I've been here since September 2004. That's when I went to the police and asked for asylum. If you're very lucky you get a pink card which says you have requested asylum and this gives you some rights, but most of the time they refuse to give you that card or take your name. And they almost never grant asylum, even if you get a pink card.

This center is the Association for Sudanese Refugees. The majority of us are from Darfur. We established this center to organize ourselves and be in contact with humanitarian organizations, to make bonds with Greek people, to help each other, provide access to lawyers, medical care, aid organizations, and free food. We raise awareness for the problems faced by refugees. And we help out the newcomers when they arrive. When a new person comes, we show him where to get food. So this is the place where someone can find us, exchange ideas, understand our situation. We also have an entertainment program. You can watch TV, we eat together, drink tea together, smoke nargileh. It's social.

It's very difficult to get into Greece and once you're here they don't let you go to other countries in Europe. They make you stay here. Many people are trapped, forgotten in Athens. There's no work, many people have no money, no where to go, people are dying here.

And on the streets they are constantly checking papers and putting people in jail. There is a guy I know who is constantly being arrested. In the past three years he has only been in the streets for 7 months. He has no valid papers so when they find him in the streets, they arrest him and lock him up for the three months. Then he'll get out and be on the streets for a month before they arrest him again. It's completely crazy.

The minister wants to clean up this neighborhood to increase tourism. So the police come here all the time. There's no social support. The only solution they have is a police solution.

The leftists are good. They are doing things, making protests, and they cover the city with posters. But after that nothing changes. We don't get papers, they don't stop the deportations, they don't let us work, they don't follow their own laws for asylum seekers. Nothing. They've signed international conventions that have protocols but they never follow the protocols. The only thing they do is send the police.

Open Letter from the Soldiers

Anonymous Greek soldiers

Hundreds of soldiers from the forty-two districts state that:

We refuse to become a force of terror and repression against the mobilizations; We support the struggle of the school and university students and the workers. We are soldiers from all over Greece. We are soldiers who, very recently, in Hania, have been ordered to turn on and bear weapons against university students, workers and combatants in the anti-militarist movement. Soldiers who bear the weight of the reforms and "tactical maneuvers" of the Greek army. The soldiers who live daily amongst the ideological oppression of militarism, of nationalism, of un-remunerated exploitation and submission to "our superiors."

In the army barracks, we learnt of yet another "isolated incident": the death, at the hands of an armed police officer, of a fifteen-year-old named Alexis. We heard it in the slogans carrying over the exterior walls of the camp like distant thunder. Weren't the deaths of three of our colleagues in August also called "isolated incidents"? Haven't they also called the deaths of each of the forty-two soldiers in the last three and a half years "isolated incidents"? We believe that Athens, Thessaloniki, and a growing number of Greek cities have become areas of social

189

agitation, environments in which the resentment of thousands of young people, workers, and unemployed people resounds, while we are dressed in army uniform and "working attire," guarding the camp or running errands, being servants of "superiors." We have seen, as have university students, workers and desperately unemployed people, their "clay pots," "accidental backfirings," "bullet deflections," as well as the desperation of precarity, of exploitation, of lay-offs and of prosecutions.

We hear the rumors and insinuations of the army officials, we hear the threats of the government, made public, about the imposition of a state of emergency. We know very well what this means. We are living it through an intensification of work, and the increase of our tasks, intense conditions with a finger on the trigger.

Yesterday we received the order to take care and "keep our eyes peeled." We are asking: whom are you ordering us to be careful of?

Today we have been ordered to be prepared and on alert. We are asking: with whom do we have to be on alert? We have been ordered to be ready to bring the state of emergency into action.

There has been a distribution of arms shipments amongst certain units in Atica [where Athens is situated], accompanied by orders to use them against the civilian population in the case of threats (for example, orders were given to one unit in Menidia, close to the attacks against the Zephiro police station). There has been a distribution of bayonets to soldiers in Evros [along the Turkish border]. They are aiming to inspire fear in the demonstrators by setting out squads in the area around the army barracks.

They have moved police vehicles to army camps in Nauplia-Tripoli-Corinth for safekeeping. There was a "confrontation" on behalf of Major I. Konstantaros in the recruits' training barracks in Thiva regarding the identification of soldiers by shop-owners whose property had been damaged. There has been a distribution of plastic bullets in the Corinthian recruits' training barracks and the order to fire against citizens if they move "in a threatening manner" (against whom?).

A special unit was ordered to the statue of the "Unknown Soldier" just in front of the demonstrators on Saturday, the 13th of December, and soldiers from the Nauplia recruits' training camp were put into action against a workers' demonstration. They are threatening citizens with Special-Ops units from Germany and Italy—in the role of occupying forces—thus revealing the true face of an anti-worker / authoritarian EU.

The police shoot with the objective of present and future social revolts. In order to accomplish this they are preparing the army to take on the functions of a police force and they are preparing society to accept the return of an army of Reformers' Totalitarianism. They are preparing us to oppose our friends, the people we know and our brothers and sisters. They are preparing us to oppose our past and future workmates and classmates. This series of measures shows that the leadership of the army, the police with the consent of Hinofotis (ex-member of the professional army, currently vice-interior minister, responsible for the internal "unrest"), the army headquarters, the government, the EU directives, the small shopkeeper as an angry citizen and the far-right groups are looking to use the armed forces as an occupying army (isn't it called Peace Corps when it's sent to a foreign country to do exactly the same thing?) in the cities where we grew up, in our neighborhoods, in the streets through which we've walked. The political and military leaders forget that we are part of the youth. They forget that we are made of the same stuff as a youth which is coming face to face with the bleak wasteland of reality inside and outside of a military camp. A youth which is furious, un-subjugated and, even more importantly, fearless.

We are civilians in uniform. We will not accept being turned into free tools of fear that some are trying to implant in society like a scarecrow. We will not accept being turned into a force of repression and terror. We will not oppose the people with whom we share the same fears, needs, and desires, the same common future, the same dangers and the same hopes. We refuse to take the streets, under the name of any state of emergency, against our brothers and sisters. As young people in uniform we express our solidarity with a fighting people and we state that we won't turn ourselves into pawns of a police state and of state repression.

We will never fight our own people. We will not allow, in the army corps, the imposition of a situation which brings back the "days of 1967."

The Treaty of Varkiza is broken

Eliza: An anarchist in Athens active for nearly twenty years

There's this word in Greek, *Dekemvriana*. It comes from December, but it means something like "the events of December." Journalists were using this word a lot during the insurrection, even though it originally refers to December 1944, when the Communists revolted against the British-installed government. The guerrillas kicked the Nazis out of Greece after they lost at Stalingrad, so when the British arrived nearly the whole country was already liberated. But Stalin had made a deal with the West that Greece would belong to the British sphere of influence, so they instructed the KKE leadership to hand over their weapons and accept the new government. The Communists never mention this.

So in December 1944, there was a protest march by many people who didn't know about this deal made by the leadership, and they went to Syntagma. There, British troops surrounded the square and opened fire. So the Communists started the guerrilla campaign again, this time against the British occupation. The leadership of the armed group later surrendered, signing the Treaty of Varkiza—Varkiza is a suburb of Athens. And one of the popular slogans that appeared in graffiti on the walls in December was: "The Treaty of Varkiza is Broken!" So you see, things go in circles.

The Logic of Not Demanding

A.G. Schwarz

December was not the first time we have burned them, and it was not the first time they have used these same lies. "Senseless violence!" the politician cries out, dabbing at the tears with a flag that on one side shows the national colors and on the other the standard of all humanity. "These protesters have no demands, they are only acting out of anger," assures the Two Face, who holds a club in one hand and an olive branch in the other. The media runs up with a podium named The Middle Ground and, placing it directly between these two characters, concludes neutrally, even sympathetically: "They must not know what they want. We'll have to tell them." And a curtain flies up revealing a panel of experts, economists, sociologists, humanitarian activists, and don't forget the fascists, and they begin to develop the lie and weave it into the most captivating shapes, but it all starts with this one premise.

The police know that we propose solutions to their violence because they use the literature seized from our homes as evidence in the trials against us. The politicians know we envision a world without their authority because we talk about it in the communiques that accompany the bombs placed outside their houses. The journalists know we criticize their control of culture and information because they fancy themselves investigators and we put these texts for free on the Internet. And what they all know is precisely what they refuse to say in those embarrassing moments when they must admit that we exist: they have no place in our future. We are going to destroy them.

So they talk about us like a rabble of confused children, hoping to deafen the people to our words. And they also hope to fool the foolish among us into translating our words into a language they can understand. The language of demands. The revolutionary dream, reduced to a few pragmatic points that might ostensibly serve as the first steps in the long march through the institutions. Snap! The trap springs shut.

Carl Schmitt, the influential German political theorist, jurist, and unrepentant Nazi, whose work was later taken up by the neoliberals at the University of Chicago, said that government was not a monopoly on violence, but a monopoly on decision. This seems true. In fact, the State permits and depends on private violence in the form of patriarchy, racism, employment conditions, fascist street gangs, and so on, in order to maintain itself. What the State requires, in order to maintain power, is the prerogative to decide, in increasingly miniscule spheres of life, what is allowed and what isn't; to decide the course of the country and post facto legitimate and regulate the initiatives taken by the capitalists. And when some social power contests the reigning order, the State must be involved in the resolution. The pacifists are wrong when they say that violence is the government's strong suit. If they ruled through violence they would never have legitimacy. In fact, the government's strong suit is communication. It is to occupy the central position, the role of mediator and protagonist, in any decision. It will make itself feared if it has to, but above all it survives by making itself heard and making itself necessary, to the point where people cannot imagine a solution to a social problem that is not tailored first and foremost to the needs of State.

This is exactly why anarchists, in December and at other times, refuse to make demands. We will not dialogue with the State, we will not sit down to chat with Capital. We will not tell them what we want because they already know: we want them to die. But not only this; we want to be the ones to destroy these institutions, with the help of as great a part of society as possible, in order to win the ability to create the world anew in the interests of all its inhabitants.

It is oxymoronic to make demands of something you wish to destroy completely, because the request for change transfers agency from you to that thing that receives your demands, and the very act of communication grants it continued life. Our attacks aim to destroy authority, to open up spaces in order to recreate life, and to communicate with society. We do not wish to communicate with the State.

If a rebellion does not communicate demands, it is not because it is senseless, but on the contrary because it is intelligent. And if the people think that it is senseless, this is only because we have not succeeded in challenging the media's role as narrator, we have not distributed enough counterinformation to contradict their lies.

But one day, if we do our work well, the people watching the TV will hear the commentator say: "They have no demands, they do not know what they want," and they will only smile and think how stupid these charlatans are, playing the same old tricks year after year.

Not this History But this Rage Is Ours

Statement from anarchists in Ankara, Turkey

Since the revolt started we have felt the rage of the comrades across the water and the continuous developments of the world we carry in our hearts. In the incoming mail we've learned of the devastation of the banks, the symbol of Greek capitalism. The anarchist voice rising up so near echoes in our neighborhoods. Having taken a deep breath, we feel that our century is starting now.

After the global call to action announced on December 12 from the Athens Polytechnic Assembly, we started to make our own arrangements. This week several groups told us they had heard the call, and wanted to support it and join us in the action. Dtcf Toplumsal Cinsiyet Karşıtı Platform, Ehp, Sgd, Genç-Sen, and Sdp ve Genç Kurtuluş all support the action of Ankara Anarchy Initiative and have prepared their own banners.

Youngsters practiced a street theater piece, a reenactment of being killed by police bullets, for all their sisters and brothers, for Alexis.

We were in front of the Greek Embassy of Ankara on December 20. We went to the embassy on two city buses. The driver of one of the buses was warned and threatened by plainclothes cops at every station. And the driver changed the route. But we were ready to get around the measures taken by police in front of the embassy building and in the streets. In order to cheat our way out of the traps of the State we got off the bus two stops before our destination and started a longer march to the embassy. As we expected, we saw that the guards of capitalism were waiting with their tanks and buses—we with our flags and our banner, which stated:

"BÜTÜN DEVLETLER KATİLDİR

ΟΛΑ ΤΑ ΚΑΤΗ ΕΙΝΑΙ ΔΟΛΟΦΟΝΟΙ"

We waited for the second bus. When it arrived we marched to the embassy. The police tried to prevent the march. Having approached the embassy, we made our press statement with the accompaniment of our slogans, which included:

Body of Alexis, Flame of Rage;

Body of Engin, Flame of Rage;

Body of Dilek, Flame of Rage;

No Independence Alone, All Together or None of Us

A Thousand Salutes to Those Who Fell and Fight in Athens

Rage, Revolution, Anarchy!

The State Massacres!

All States Are Murderers!

Athens Rage; Thessaloniki Rage; Komotini Rage; Patras Rage; Alexandropoli Rage; Crete Rage; Cyprus Rage; Istanbul Rage; Ankara Rage; Rage Everywhere;

Anarchy Everywhere!

After the press statement, the young anarchists took the stage for their street theater. They finished by shouting: "All The States Are Murderers; Rage!" Anarchists then threw bulbs filled with red paint at the embassy and shouted, "We brought you thousands of years of anger and the blood of our sisters and brothers you've murdered." The police got their fair share of the red paint, the representation of the blood of our murdered sisters and brothers. We frequently raised the level of tension but the guardians of capitalism didn't dare intervene.

The action continued with a forty-five minute march to Kızılay (Ankara's city center). Along the march, which was accompanied by 300 riot police, we encountered many curious people who asked us questions. We received their support when we told them that we were coming from the embassy and we were marching for every single person who has been murdered by the State, and on that day actions were carried out all over the world to remember our brother Alexis who was murdered by police in Greece.

When we arrived at Kızılay, we finished the march in front of the monument of human rights by telling people about the action in front of the embassy. Then we threw the last paint bombs at the police.

Approximately one hundred anarchists in Ankara honored the global day of action on December 20, joining people in cities all over the world.

Forgive or forget?

Never ever!

Viva Revolucion, Viva Anarchy!

—Ankara Anarchy Initiative

To Those Who Rise Up in Greece

ABC Wellington

The Anarchist Black Cross of Wellington, New Zealand stand in solidarity with you and support all actions you take in these difficult times.

It is horrific news to us, that police murdered a young member of the community. We don't need to mention the brutal repression that you must face when resisting this state crime and terror, only that we are aware of much that is occurring. We share the rage against the police, government, and capitalist institutions, in all nation-states, and we applaud the resistance in the streets of many Greek cities.

Nor do we need to mention the way the mainstream media has handled this, only that we are using our own channels to get the truth out, and in countering the propaganda.

From the November anniversary demo of the student uprising, the hunger strikes of thousands of prisoners in the same month, to the many stories of successful direct actions which take place throughout your country; everywhere people are inspired by the movement in Greece and it is hoped that the call for solidarity spreads widely throughout the global networks and takes many different forms, including tactical unity in revolutionary struggle in our home countries, internationally and in building relationships of permanent solidarity, mutual aid, and cooperation.

There are many of us who support your struggle, even when it may not seem so obvious. It is our hope that things soon become better for all of you. That through your continued efforts, you succeed in your goals, in a permanent state of peace from prisons, police, governments, and capitalists.

Stay strong and keep up the spirit of total resistance without surrender!

Solidarity.
ABC Wellington, New Zealand

A Bedouin Anytime! A Citizen Never.

Ego Te Provoco

Having by our late labours and hazards made it appear to the world at how high a rate we value our just freedom (…) we do now hold ourselves bound in mutual duty to each other, to take the best care we can for the future, to avoid the danger of returning into a slavish condition

—Levellers, "An Agreement of the People," 1647

Let's look beyond the tear gas, the batons, and the riot police vans: the operation being conducted by the bosses since December 6th doesn't comprise a mere combination of repression and propaganda; rather, it is the application of a series of methods aiming to renegotiate social peace and consensus.

From the Communist Party, which views the revolting people as puppets of Syriza (the euro-left parliamentary party) and of the CIA, all the way to Socialist Party politicians moaning that Athens resembles a city of the Eastern Bloc, what with its streets empty of consumers. From the archbishop of Thessaloniki, who begs his flock to go shopping, to the city's international exposition offering free parking to Christmas shoppers, they all share a common goal: the return to the normality of democracy and consumption. Thus the day after the revolt, which happens to be Christmas, the demand is raised that we must celebrate at all cost: not only in order

for some tills to fill up but in order for us all to return to our graves. The day after holds the demand of the living dead that nothing disturbs their eternal sleep any more. It's a moratorium legitimizing the emptiness of their spectacle-driven world, a world of quiet and peaceful lives. And the generals of this war hold no weapon more lethal than the appeal to that absolute, timeless idea: democracy.

The word democracy, developing as it does ever more densely from the demagogues of calmness, aims at the social imaginary—the collective field of structuring desires and fears. Everyone knew, well before the assassination of Alexis, that the oligarchy of capital had given up on trying to even seem democratic, even by bourgeois standards: economic scandals, blatant incidents of police violence, monstrous laws. Yet this fact is not, neither here nor anywhere else, worrisome to the bosses. This is precisely because the functioning of the establishment under such terms ("Is it democratic enough? Is it really democratic?") reproduces the capitalist oligarchy. The same oligarchy that builds around itself a wall of scandals, regrets, resignations, demands, and reforms—preventing, in this way, the questioning of (not the democratic qualities of the regime but) democracy as a system of social organizing. Hence bosses can still appeal to this higher value today, this axiomatic mechanism of the political, in order to bring us back to normality, consensus, compromise—in order to assimilate the general spontaneous rage in the sphere of mediation, before this rage can organize its revolutionary potential. A revolution that would swoop all

197

intermediaries and peaceful democrats—bringing along a new form of organizing: the commune.

Amidst this ludicrous climate of shallow analyses the salaried officials of the psychological war point at the revolted, howling: "That's not democratic, that ignores the rules under which our democracy functions." We are speechless in the face of what we would until recently have considered impossible. Even if having the intention to deceive, the bosses of this country have said something true: We despise democracy more than anything else in this decadent world. For what is democracy other than a system of discriminations and coercions in the service of property and privacy? And what are its rules, other than rules of negotiation of the right to own—the invisible rules of alienation? Freedom, rights, equality, egalitarianism: all these dead ideological masks together cannot cover their mission: the generalization and preservation of the social as an economic sphere, as a sphere where not only what you have produced but also what you are and what you can do are already alienated. The bourgeois, with a voice trembling from piety, promise: rights, justice, equality. And the revolted hear: repression, exploitation, looting.

Democracy is the political system where everyone is equal in front of the guillotine of the spectacle-product. The only problem that concerned democrats, from Cromwell to Montesquieu, is what form of property is sufficient in order for someone to be recognized as a citizen, what kind of rights and obligations guarantee that they will never understand themselves as something beyond a private citizen. Everything else is no more than adjusting details of a regime in the service of capital.

Our contempt for democracy does not derive from some sort of idealism but rather from our very material animosity for a social entity in which value and organizing are centered around the product and the spectacle. The revolt was by definition also a revolt against property and alienation. Anyone that didn't hide behind the curtains of their privacy, anyone who was out on the streets, knows it only too well: shops were looted not for computers, clothes, or furniture to be resold but for the joy of destroying what alienates us: the spectacle of the product. Anyone who doesn't understand why someone delights in the sight of a destroyed product is a merchant or a cop. The fires that warmed the bodies of the revolted in these long December nights were full of the liberated products of our toil, from the disarmed symbols of what used to be an almighty fantasy. We simply took what belonged to us and we threw it to the fire together with all its co-expressions. The grand potlatch of the past few days was also a revolt of desire against the imposed rule of scarcity. A revolt of the gift against the sovereignty of money. A revolt of the anarchy of use value against the democracy of exchange value. A revolt of spontaneous collective freedom against rationalized individual coercion.

I don't care if I don't take even one more picture, I just want to be okay with myself

Kostas Tsironis: A photojournalist who works in Athens as a freelancer for foreign press agencies

I said I would never give this story to the international media because I got no support from them in December, but I'll speak to you. I like to speak about it person to person.

On Saturday when the murder happened I was drinking with a friend of mine, it was his name day celebration. I was a little drunk when I got home and I heard on the news that they had killed Alexis in Exarchia and there were big riots, so I took my cameras and I went outside to walk and cover it. I wasn't responsible for the coverage but I did it on my own initiative. I spent the first night at Nomiki, which had been taken over by the demonstrators, and early in the morning I left, went home, slept a bit, sent some pictures to the newspaper I was working for, and went back onto the streets. Three o'clock was the big demo. It started at four. The demo was headed for the headquarters of the Greek police, and I was in the front.

When the police and the crowd started fighting, I wasn't wearing a gas mask so I was affected by the tear gas and I went away from the riot, back behind the police lines. I was in the flower beds, puking because of the gas.

Then I stood up and I saw the first policeman holding his hand up, making like he was shooting a gun. So I took out the camera to take a picture, and I saw the gun, the real gun, that another policeman was holding. He was threatening the demonstrators. This was less than a day after Alexis was shot, and here they were drawing their guns again. They did not know I was there because I had been down below the flower beds, puking. The whole thing happened in two seconds. I held down the shutter, took about twenty pictures—this is one of those professional cameras that takes pictures very rapidly—and then I left immediately. The area was full of police, and I remember that they saw me as I was taking the pictures. I thought I had to find a way to escape from the police lines and get to the demonstrators, where it was more comfortable for me because I knew I would be able to get back home and not disappear somewhere.

I did not say anything to anyone about the picture. After a quarter of an hour a lady came to me and introduced herself as a journalist from a Greek radio station, it was supposed to be the station owned by the same corporation as *Eleftheros Typos*, the newspaper I was working for. I did not recognize her. She asked me if I knew about a photographer who had the picture of the cop waving his gun, and I knew she was a cop.

I then asked a colleague to accompany me to my motorbike so I could leave. We went to the newspaper, I had the memory card with me, so I had to think about the situation and decide what I was going to do. I couldn't send the picture to a press agency due to my contract with *Eleftheros Typos* so I found the chief editor and talked to him in his office. I asked him two questions. First: *If a photojournalist has documentation, during these days with all that is happening, of a policeman pointing a gun at the demonstrators, what would you advise me to do?* He said, *This is a big story, and of course you have to publish it.* So I asked him if the newspaper would publish a picture like that and he told me, *of course*, because it's breaking news. So I told him I had this picture, I printed some copies for him, and he told me not to tell anybody. So far I had only gone to his office. No one else knew about the photo besides me, my one colleague, the chief editor, and the police of course.

He said he'd have a meeting with the other editors of the paper and they'd talk to me later. I said, *If you don't want to publish it let me publish it somewhere else.* He said, *No, you can't do that, you are working for us.* So that was the first time I thought he would probably want to keep it and not publish it. After their meeting, he told me he couldn't run the photo in the Monday edition, because they were not sure it was a real gun or whether the policeman was pointing it at the demonstrators. I told him, *I was there, I saw it, I know it's a gun, I can give you a bigger print with better resolution so you can even read the gun's serial number.* I gave him the print, and he said, *Okay,*

we'll see tomorrow, we'll have to call an expert to make sure it's a gun. I left thinking that was the end of me, I'm not going to work as a photojournalist in Athens again. I did not want to hide this picture, I wanted everyone to see what was happening in Athens.

He called me at midday Monday, while I was working, and the expert confirmed that it was a gun and that you could see what type it was. And that you could see a shell casing, in other words that it was loaded. And in the last picture you can see one of the policemen is pointing at me. So the editor said it would be published on Tuesday, and told me to give the story so the captions could be written. And I left. There was rioting again, much harder than the first day.

I came back around eight o'clock in the evening and I saw the art director. He showed me the front page, and right on the cover was my picture with a caption. This was the main story for Tuesday. It continued on the inner pages. I remember it even had the exact time of the incident, down to the second, 18:36:36. I remember reading that off my camera. He asked me if I wanted to put my name below the picture. I asked him what he advised, and he said that if I didn't want to have problems with the police, I shouldn't include my name. But the police all knew who the *Eleftheros Typos* journalist was covering riots.

I was editing my Monday pictures when I heard the art editor screaming. I asked him what was happening and he said the chief editor just called him up and told him to remove the picture and the whole story. This was ten at night. That's when I knew I was trapped.

Later the pictures appeared in the international press and Indymedia, and now *Eleftheros Typos* is suing me, saying I released the photo.

On Tuesday morning the photo was not published on the front page but it appeared in the inner pages because they knew it had already gotten out and they did not want a scandal for suppressing it. At midday they called me up and fired me, allegedly for breaking my contract. I left the equipment and left the newspaper. No one said goodbye, it was very funny, I think they were afraid. The president of the Press Photographers Union of Greece was a colleague of mine, we worked together. He was the one who was supposed to defend my rights and he did nothing. He was also the guy telling me to publish the pictures.

For me, that's when the party began. I had to think about what was happening. I was fired, but it was okay, I didn't care, because you cannot sell yourself for money or because you want to have good relations with the government. So I was free then, I could work however I wanted and publish whatever pictures I wanted. And that day an independent Internet news site, Television Without Borders, called me up for an interview. I told them the story and they published it. The next day everybody knew about the story. These were the first days of December—really mean riots and a tough situation—so I started feeling afraid for myself. What would

happen with the police? I have to work with them sometimes. Sometimes I work with the demonstrators, taking pictures if they let us, but I don't like to work with the police because they hate us. I have many photos of them ready to hit us or break our cameras.

Well, once I had my camera broken by a rioter. This summer I saw him on the beach on one of the islands, and I recognized him. We were both naked. I said, *You broke my camera, you bastard!*

I was very afraid during December. I did not know what was going to happen next. Every day became more violent, and there was more police brutality. With all these stories of journalists dying and their bodies being found ten days later... I was waiting for that. You were expecting anything. We might have another murder. Or another cop might start shooting, or some protesters will take out a Kalashnikov and start shooting, which actually happened.

Around Christmas I could not log in to my Gmail account. When I contacted Google they told me how to log in and change my password. They said my password had been blocked because in the previous days there had been 50,000 attempts to crack it. They said they didn't think my email had been broken into but that whoever was responsible wanted to disable my email account so I couldn't communicate through it. I was also maintaining a blog through this email, so I couldn't upload photos or communicate via email during this time.

Until I got fired I was taking pictures and thinking how I could protect myself. Once I was fired, I was just living what was happening. I was part of the demos. It was my purpose to be out there every day on the street, it was something like a liberation. I had been trying to strike a balance between my eyes and the public's eyes, but after I was fired I did not have to keep this balance. I was able to take sides, to define my position.

I don't believe that if you have the camera you show the truth. You show your truth, what you believe. So I don't want to say that working as a photojournalist I show the one and only truth. I can tell the truth with my eyes, with what I see and what I do. So for me holding a camera was like participating in what was happening. I don't want to say that if the police see me with a camera they won't gas protesters or beat protesters or take out their guns, or do all the other things they do.

I don't believe that the mass media will liberate us, even though I work for them. But you know in Greece we've only had private television for twenty years, before that it was only national television. I have witnessed all this period. When the first corporate channel broadcast I was twelve years old. I've seen the way they treat news, the way they try to manipulate people. I studied sociology, and before I saw the media from the outside, as an observer. Now I work for them, and what I believe about the future is that free networks can spread news and information, and this happened in December in Athens.

If there is a possibility for real news to spread around, this should be the work of the free networks and not the work of the big news corporations. But in this specific circumstance, the way the picture got out was through AP and AFP. In this case, it was good that the international media published the picture. But I can still criticize the way they work, especially in situations like Iraq, with embedded reporters. For example AFP spread my photo worldwide, but they did not announce worldwide that I was fired. They had to keep a balance. I don't believe mass media will change the way we live for the better.

The most interesting part of the story is not about taking the picture or how they fired me, the interesting thing is what happened afterwards, when the police called me to testify and I went to the headquarters of the MAT because they were conducting an investigation into who pulled the gun. They called me up, I went there, I saw two fat policemen sitting there, and they said: *Ah, I know you, I've seen you at demonstrations.* They offered me coffee, and their first question was, *How did you make this picture, how did you manipulate the image?* They wanted to make the investigation in order to close it. They did not ask for pictures because in the pictures you see the exact number of the policeman on his helmet and they did not want to know who it was. They took it easy on me because they didn't want to make a real investigation. After two hours of writing and erasing, they asked me to swear on the bible. That's what the policemen regularly do but I was not obligated to so I refused.

I left the building but they had forgotten to ask me to sign my statement. Now, while I was inside the building they were calling me by a fake name to protect my identity. But as I was leaving, I was in the street and there were dozens of riot police getting ready to board their bus and go to where the riots were happening. So I was waiting among them, and one of the policemen came out yelling my name, "You forgot to sign your declaration!" in front of all these armed riot cops who knew the name. And he brought me the paper to sign in the street. He gave me a pen, took a riot shield for me to write on, to use as a hard surface, and I signed it against the shield. I wished I had a picture of that, for myself. In any case, they identified me to all these riot cops by calling me by my real name, as though to say, *Now you'll recognize him in the streets.*

Of course the police knew me from the past. Two years ago, the first week I went to work for *Eleftheros Typos*, was during the student movement, 2006–2007. One day outside the Polytechnic I took a picture of a rioter throwing a molotov that exploded in the air. He was in motion so his face was blurred and therefore he could not be identified. It was a very nice picture. At the newspaper they said: *Oh, what an amazing picture, congratulations, we'll put it on the front page.* I wondered what was going on, because it was just a picture of a guy throwing a molotov. Anyways, they published it on the front page, just like they said. Two months later, May 2, I was in the office, the day after covering the First of May, and the phone rang. It was a policeman asking to speak with me. They said they wanted to show me some pictures and asked if they could come. I said, *Do what you want.* They must have been outside the building because five minutes later two guys came up. They showed me the front page from two months ago, and said they were conducting an investigation and wanted to know if I had another frame where it was possible to make out the rioter's face, or his belt, or the type of shoes he was wearing, anything that would help them arrest this guy. I said, *You're joking, coming into the newspaper asking for this. That's not my job.*

In the meantime I was looking for other people to be witnesses. The chief editor, a different guy than the one in December, came in and asked what was happening. I told him, and he kicked them out and the next day published it in the news that two policemen came to ask for pictures to make an arrest and we kicked them out. We don't give pictures to police. The background to all this is important. *Eleftheros Typos* was a hardcore right wing newspaper when Iana Agelopoulos bought it. She's the rich person who brought the Olympics here, she was on the organizing committee. So she wanted to give the newspaper a democratic face. What happened with the policemen was a very good opportunity for them to show that they were not the same newspaper as in the past. It's interesting to see how the editors and owners of the news use the news to show what they want, to give themselves a democratic profile, and other times they cover it up to protect government interests.

In December many left wing journalists from left wing newspapers told me, *Come on Kostas, this is not a big story, who do you think you are, Che Guevara? You have to talk to the mainstream media about this story, and not talk on the Internet about these things.*

I don't care if I don't take even one more picture, I don't care if they kick me out, I just want to be okay with myself. I had an opportunity once in a lifetime to say that, and I did. If I had hidden the picture I could have made a lot of money, getting paid to not publish it.

I'm also the only photographer who has photos of one of the immigrant detention centers. Previously I had tried all the legal means to get photos of a detention center and I never could. But one day I was invited to take pictures of a new detention facility on one of the islands. I wondered what was going on. The first guard we met there tried to block our entry, and then the person accompanying me took out his phone and said, *I can call up the ministry right now and next week you won't be working here anymore.* So the guard let us through. It was all very strange. I had half an hour to take pictures. It was a newly constructed camp, like Guantanamo, with three policemen guarding 600 immigrants. Everything was electronic.

The story came out on a Tuesday, and on Monday, the day before, Greece got a fine from the EU for one million euros a day for bad conditions in the camps. Then I realized, *Oh, that's what I was doing there.* To show that it was very clean, state of the art, and the prisoners had telephones and everything. Because the government already knew it would get the fine they wanted to generate some good news coverage.

The funniest day in December was about ten days after I was fired. I was in a bloc… I don't want to say "black bloc," but… it was like a black bloc. I was taking pictures, and one of the protesters came to me and told me to leave, because they didn't know if I was a policeman. I laughed, but I did not want to say *I* was that famous photojournalist, so I left. And as I was leaving I heard them shout a slogan, the same people who had just kicked me out. "It was unjust to fire Kostas Tsironis, Cops, Pigs, Killers!" which rhymes in Greek. Then the next line was "We're going to hire Kosta Tsironi, *Batsi, Gourounya, Dolofoni!*" I didn't go back to let them know it was me, because I was laughing so hard. I thought that even if I give up my camera tomorrow, it's okay, I've done my life's work now.

Another funny moment from December: one day there was a cordon of police outside Parliament, facing off with demonstrators. One demonstrator goes up to give the police flowers, and the media all swarm in to take the picture. But the cop refused to take the flower. So the police chief came up to him and said under his breath to take the damn flower, and the policeman takes it, and in that one moment when all the photographers are snapping away at the flower in his hand, he lets the flower drop. He was so confused. There were 2,000 demonstrators waiting to attack, all these journalists like hunters taking a picture when they give him a flower. It's schizophrenic.

I spent New Year's Eve outside the prison. There was a protest. I was there to cover it in case something happened, but for me it was also like participating. And then December ended, well for the media it ended but I don't believe it has ended. December was like a small child being ignored by everyone as they sit around the table, and this was the moment when the child shouts out, *I am here, you have to respect me.* We are here, you can rob us with credit cards, this economic crisis, you can underpay us, but you cannot kill us, we are here. And they get afraid of that, and you could see that they got afraid. Also the policemen. I don't hate the policemen, I don't want to say that all the police are bad, but policemen in December were afraid. I think that for one moment they thought the whole society was against them.

In December I got a network of support, friends from school I had lost contact with who got in touch with me and were talking about what had happened. There were people all around me who felt the same way about things, who felt that it was important, so this showed me I was not wrong, and I could go back out in the streets. After I got fired the first thing that came to me was fear, but after I got all this support I was not afraid, I knew it was okay. My best friend told me, *Don't be afraid, this is our story.*

Journal entry of one of the insurrectionists

In trying to write a quick, retrospective chronicle of what I lived through from the 6th of December until today, Christmas Day of 2008, it is certain that I have forgotten and omitted a lot. I don't know if the insurrection is continuing or not, although it looks like it has calmed down. It is certain, however, that those of us who lived those moments have changed. We have been transformed forever. The ferocity of our attacks in the city and on the temples of the commodities, the battles with those who stand as an obstacle in our attempt to destroy authority and its symbols, the joy of razing everything that stands in our way, the moment we're not thinking but acting, will be engraved in my memory forever. As will be the courage of my friends and comrades who showed more bravery and decisiveness than I did by staying for eighteen consecutive days inside the Polytechnic. The insurrection is not a utopia, viva la anarquia!

205

These pages are dedicated to all those who did not speak with words, who for political reasons or security reasons did not want to give an interview, who did not want to define the insurrection by any words that were not written on the walls of the city, or carved out with deeds.

Their actions have spoken much louder, anyway.

1

1. Ten minutes after the assassination of Alexis Grigoropoulis by the Greek police on Dec. 6 2008, people began attacking police, banks, luxury shops, corporate targets, and State buildings all over the country. For the next month countless people in thousands of actions kept the insurrection alive. Images, videos, and communiqués came pouring out of Greece, spreading via the internet, mass media, and the underground press. Through the work of hundreds of amateur and proferssional photographers the memory of this struggle will live on, planting a seed of liberation in us all. These days are for Alexis. These days are for all of us.

2. The policeman that shot Alexis. One of the two pigs that took part in the assassination.

3. The radicalization of a new generation through demonstrations, riots, and attacks on police stations.

4. The funeral of Alexis Grigoropoulis.

5. The occupation of universities became the center of the struggle. The banner reads "Assassins / Law School Occupation." The Polytechnic, Law School, and School of economics in Athens, the School of Theology and the entire University campus in Thessaloniki, and the Parartima building of the university in Patras being the most notable.

6. Powerful demonstrations, rioting, and attacks on government buildings took place in large and small towns.

We are an Image from the Future

7

9

11

8

10

12

7–12. Arson attacks, street barricades, open demonstrations, and university assemblies were the main arenas for organizing the struggle during the revolt.

210

15

14

13

16

13–16. Numerous international solidarity actions took place around the world during December. Greek Embassies were occupied, pamphlets and information were passed out, and demonstrations organized. These acts of solidarity energized those in Greece and worried elites across the planet, as the messages of the insurrection illuminated both the problems and the hopes of people in their own societies.

We are an Image from the Future

17

18

19

17. This van acted as both barricade and billboard. The graffiti reads: "Burning City / Flower in Bloom."

18. Demonstration.

19. The place of Alexis's murder. The banner reads: "We Don't Forget, We Don't Forgive / Alexis You are with Us, 06/12/08."

Chronology: December 28–March 4

December 28, 2008: Friends, colleagues, libertarian syndicalists, and anarchists concentrate outside the Athens hospital where immigrant worker and union organizer Konstantina Kuneva is in intensive care.

December 30: The offices of the Trade Unions Center in Thessaloniki is occupied in solidarity with K. Kuneva.

December 31: A thousand anarchists gather outside Korydallos prison to celebrate New Year's Eve with the prisoners, shooting fireworks, playing loud music, chanting, singing songs together with the people on the inside, and calling for the liberation of those arrested in December and for freedom for all prisoners.

January 1, 2009: Coordinated arson attacks in Athens, Piraeus, and Thessaloniki target banks and car dealerships during the New Year's celebration. In Thessaloniki protesters attack police with rocks, and police respond with tear gas.

January 5: A few masked gunmen open fire on a riot police unit guarding the Ministry of Culture and Information in Exarchia, seriously injuring one cop. Revolutionary Struggle later claims this and the 23 December attacks. In their communique they critique capitalism and call for an armed uprising.

January 9: A student march in Athens planned to commemorate the 1991 killing of Temponeras gathers ten thousand people and turns violent when police attack the anarchist bloc, which fights back. Many protesters and bystanders are injured by police. In Thessaloniki, anarchists trash the offices of OIKOMET cleaning company in solidarity with their employee Konstantina Kuneva.

January 10: The Assembly of Media Workers and others occupy the office of the Editors' Union of Athens Daily Papers to protest their distortion of the struggle and open a space for counterinformation and alternative media.

January 17: Thousands of people protest in solidarity with December's prisoners in Larissa, the only city where the anti-terror law is used against high school students participating in the riots. The terror charges are subsequently dropped.

January 20: Anarchists in Thessaloniki raise 13,000 euros for a seventy-four-year-old woman whose kiosk had been burned down in local riots two months earlier. In Athens, one hundred anarchists attack a fascist anti-immigration protest in Aghios Panteleimonos, a neighborhood where neo-nazis and fascists will become increasingly active in the coming months, creating their own neighborhood assembly.

January 23: Anarchists and people from the extreme left protesting in solidarity with Konstantina Kuneva attack police guarding a government building in Athens. Farmers block the highway between Athens and Volos, as well as other national highways in northern Greece, protesting the low prices set for agricultural commodities by the European

Union. The same week, 1,500 farmers in Crete occupy the Iraklion airport in protest.

January 26: Underestimating the continuing power of the revolt, the mayor of the city orders the cutting of the trees in Patision Park in order to turn the park into a parking garage. The felling of the trees sparks several days of actions and riots, including attacks on two police stations. On the second day, neighbors, including anarchists and leftists, take over the park and occupy it permanently, replanting trees. SYRIZA attempts to separate the struggle for the park from its context, such as persecution of immigrants in the neighborhood, and turn it into an isolated issue to win votes. They are subsequently pushed out of the assembly that had formed in the park.

Elsewhere in Athens the Assembly for Health, composed of doctors and nurses who participated in the insurrection, occupies the Red Cross hospital cashier's office for four hours to allow everyone to get health care for free.

January 28: The National Opera Hall of Athens is occupied by artists. The daily assembly draws 600 people and discusses the connections between art, philosophy, and insurrection, and every night the street outside is closed down by thousands of people dancing and playing improvisational music. The occupation lasts until February 7.

February 2: In Athens, hundreds of people take part in a torch-lit demo organized by the neo-nazi group Golden Dawn, which is aesthetically modeled on the early marches of the Nazis and Mussolini's blackshirts. Police protect the march from an anarchist counterattack.

February 3: Antiauthoritarian armed group Sect of Revolutionaries attacks an Athens police station with gunfire and a grenade. Later in the day, farmers in Piraeus clash with riot police.

February 8: Over 2,000 people, mostly Afghani, Iranian, Pakistani, and Balkan immigrants, gather in Aghios Panteleimonos, invited by the activist initiative "We and For All of Us, Here and Now." The event is a huge celebration and feast with speeches and music by immigrants, also attended by many Greeks showing their support.

February 12: The Initiative of Health Industry Workers occupies the entrance and cashier of AHEPA hospital in Thessaloniki, allowing everyone to receive free health care that day, and distributing a text against the privatization of health care.

February 17: Sect of Revolutionaries attacks the TV channel ALTER, shooting up fourteen cars belonging to station journalists, denouncing their manipulation of events and promising that next time, they will pay a visit to their homes.

February 22: Legendary outlaw Vassilis Palaiokostas makes a daring escape from Korydallos prison with a helicopter, along with an Albanian accomplice. This is the second time he has escaped from the same prison this way. Anarchists throughout Greece subsequently begin making stickers and buttons featuring a lone helicopter.

February 24: Unknown assailants, probably fascists or paramilitaries, attack the social center of the Network for the Defence of Immigrants and Political Prisoners, in Exarchia, with a hand grenade while a meeting is taking place inside. Fortunately no one is injured.

February 27: About sixty students from the high schools of two rich Athens neighborhoods attack the Athens American College, the private high school where the children of the elite are educated.

March 3: A group of about twenty anarchists, taking advantage of Carnival by wearing masks, carry out a major arson attack against the train station of Kifissia, the richest neighborhood of Athens, causing sixteen million euros in damage. The attack was in solidarity with Konstantina Kuneva, who worked cleaning the trains. The same day, after Patras port police beat an Afghan immigrant who is trying to hide on a truck going to Italy, immigrants riot and clash with police.

March 3: A large protest march in response to the fascist attack against the immigrants' social center battles police and destroys several banks and luxury shops in Athens. The offices of neo-nazi group Golden Dawn are burned to the ground.

Alexis Grigoropoulos Street

The corner of Mesologgiou and Tsavella, where the *batsi* shot down Alexis, has been transformed. It was always our turf, always the place where we hung out and where the mere presence of the police was an insult. But now it would be considered an act of war. The corner was turned into a living memorial—not a sacred temple purified by ritual and prohibition, but a beloved spot defended by our profane presence. Graffiti was everywhere. People started making stencils with the face of Alexis, to remember. Then we took down the old street signs and put up new ones: *Odos Alexis Grigoropoulous*. The street of Alexis Grigoropoulos. People brought candles, and a memorial was started in a little glass box right on the corner. Those candles burned for months. We did not let them go out. Then a plaque was put up on the wall, a huge, well done, beautiful one with his photo and an explanation of what happened there on that spot. We won't forget. We'll carve our rage and the history of our struggle into the very walls and streets. These streets, our streets.

Koukouloforos

Extracts from the newspaper, *The Hooded One*, printed in Thessaloniki, with a 50,000 print run.

THE INVISIBLE HAVE A FACE

We were shadows. Shadows in what you refer to as "everyday life." Countless invisible figures you walked past in the streets. Faces that reminded you of something but you were never sure of exactly what.

The pint of beer on the bar that is full again.

"I've ordered a pizza half an hour ago but the delivery boy isn't here yet."

Supermarket shelves and shiny floors.

"Where is the girl to empty the ashtrays?"

Put your helmet on, your raincoat, drive your motorcycle across town.

"Position 146, how can I help you please?"

Behind the stalls, folding clothes, in the aisles organizing books on the shelves.

"It seems a bit tight around the waist."

In front of computers answering phones.

Circling small ads "female wanted, person with former experience needed."

And sometimes queuing outside OAED [the Employment and Unemployment Offices].

"Signing checks every Monday-Wednesday-Friday."

Stage programs, seminars, "new job vacancies."

Never here, never there. In constant motion, in an endless nerve-racking stand-by.

Selling ourselves out, our whole lives in order to survive. Always present, always invisible, alien in our own cities.

And suddenly a shot…

"Have you heard the news? They murdered him, the bastards!"

"Who did they murder?"

"They murdered that boy, man!"

Murder. Violence. This word rings a bell. Yes, it does…

Early morning, wake up for work. The stamps they didn't give me. The rent that I need to pay every month. Suddenly hitting the brakes and the creepy sound of crawling on the road. The nights that I stay in alone. My boss calling—fuck… I need to be at work tomorrow. My struggle to get paid for the hours I've worked. The peering eyes of the customers on my body when I serve them. Counting my stamps—can I go on the dole? Classified ads. The clock at work that seems to be stuck and my boss has just bought a new car. And in all this the sound of a shot. He was murdered. All in the streets, man! Rage. Rage for the killing, rage for our everyday death.

We meet in the streets. We yell at their faces together. We build roadblocks together. We break pavement apart and we put the stones in our pockets. Tear gas is suffocating but we go on. We continue, all of us who until yesterday spoke a different language, all of us who until yesterday were invisible. We go on because after this nothing will be the same again. Away from all those who tried to represent us, away from politicians and syndicates who speak a strange, foreign language, away from all those media experts who still wonder where we all came from.

We have no demands. No, we don't. We fight for every reason in the world. We want back the life that everyday they are stealing from us. The violence of the cop who shot the boy is the condensed violence we suffer everyday. It is against this that we revolt. We are not shadows anymore, although we started as such…

TO LIVE IN COMMUNISM, TO SPREAD ANARCHY

To live in communism, to spread anarchy. It is not the first time that cops commit murder, so it is not the first time that people revolt, attack the police, or burn down banks. But this time things are different. The rage that broke loose inscribes its own history. Yes, it is an uprising. And what is characteristic of uprisings is a gut feeling that nothing will remain unchanged, that nothing will be the same again. That's how we feel. History is condensing, new forces are being released, and authority becomes frozen. The immediate question is how we go on since we are no longer the same. What do we do when there is no bank left to be broken, no police quarters untouched, where do we meet again after the riots, how do we go on relentlessly, as we used to, toward bringing down capitalism in the world? Since the first night of the murder, Athens Polytechnic School was occupied by hundreds of people. Since December 8 ASOEE has been under occupation as well. This is a part of the first announcement from their blog: "As a piece of social-class conflict, the occupied University of Economics and Business constitutes an open space for briefing and co-formation of collective action on the streets. At the same time we consider very important the occupation of academic institutions as spaces of rearrangement and self-organization of our forces against state repression, so that no one will stay on his/her own in the struggle that has burst out against the State. For this reason the occupation of the University of Economics and Business stays open and calls for an assembly on Monday the 8th at 20:00. We declare that the occupation will last until the release of each and every one arrested by the police across the country."

The School of Theater in Thessaloniki is occupied on Saturday night after the riots on Aristotelous and Egnatia streets. From its blog: "After the demonstration in Thessaloniki on Saturday night in response to the murder of Alexandros, antiauthoritarians occupied the School of Theater in

217

Thessaloniki to cater to the need to counter-inform protesters in the city. From the start the MAT tried in vain to invade the building. The next day after the assembly, the occupation was reinforced by drama students and by people who do not belong to any political associations." The Salonica School of Theatre has become a center for convocation, exchange of ideas, a space to organize action. The following day, the Lawyers' Association of Thessaloniki building was squatted as well. There, a number of assemblies have taken place, mainly by students, and it functions as a counter-information center until the cross country strike day on December 10—when unprecedented occupations, without any specific demands, will overtake many state schools and academic institutions.

On the 12th of December the town hall of Aghios Dimitrios in Athens was occupied and calls for a public assembly were made. From their blog: "We are revolting. We function on a directly democratic basis because this is the only way that we want to live. We've taken our lives in our hands. We will get rid of our bosses and help the prosecuted to get rid of their charges. We use this public building as an open center for counter-information, as a meeting place where people who have decided to change their lives come in great numbers to co-form ideas and actions." Three hundred people attended the first assembly. Actions were planned, current events discussed, people from different generations came together, individuals from various social backgrounds met, and cultural events and Greek language lessons for immigrants were organized. From the beginning the Association of Public Servants of Aghios Dimitrios Municipality stood in favor of the occupation and is actively involved in its defense. It is the first time ever that the town hall is truly open to the neighborhood as a vivid political space. There is no point mentioning here the predictable reactions of the mayor and the cops.

On the same day the former town hall-KEP (Citizens' Information and Service Center) on Halandri Square was squatted. One blog read: "The sorrow and the rage that we all feel cannot be expressed by zapping from the couch in front of the TV. We decided to squat the former town hall-KEP on Halandri Square, the meeting place of town hall officials, and transform it into a place for counter-information and discussion on future actions. We invite the residents of Halandri, and the ones of nearby areas to defend this squat and take part in open, egalitarian, non-guided, co-forming procedures." A public meeting was called every day at around 7:00pm, while a number of actions and demonstrations are supported. On Monday the 15th the town hall of Sykies in Thessaloniki is occupied. A public assembly is announced that same afternoon. The main slogan on the banner that covers the face of the building demands the immediate release of all people arrested by police forces.

What matters is for these examples to spread, for people to start directing their own lives, to question the very idea of representation, of responsibility, of getting politically comfortable while belonging to a party. Now is the time. Now, when everything has changed. The spontaneous occupations that started in many academic and non-academic places—not necessarily by students—provide the possibility for meeting each other. But they cannot accommodate us anymore. That's why we need to squat town halls, empty houses, public buildings, and transform them into places for meeting and organizing. More places like that must be created, more places must be liberated, new spaces for communication and resistance must be founded. All anarchist squats should look into how they can make their actual space more accessible to their neighborhood. Schools must close down and be transformed into places where the possibility to overthrow capitalistic-nationalistic education can be realized. Working places must be blocked by workers and the meaning of employment must be discussed and reinvented. The idea of direct organization and solidarity must be carried into every collective. We don't need bosses, we are not in need of guidance, we don't care for any kind of representatives. It's time to start living in communism. It's time to start living in anarchy. To create the communes of the future.

The Spirit of December Spread Round the World

A.G. Schwarz

I have heard many anarchists from other countries ask, "Why weren't the Greek insurrections generalized to other countries, and what could we have done to make them spread?" Most often, the question was not asked in a constructive way, but posed to suggest that the local movement was worthless because the insurrection was not generalizing. I have to say that this question strikes me as ignorant. A vital fact that anarchists must come to terms with and work their way around is that insurrections usually do not jump national borders. In the early years of the 20th century there was arguably more common consciousness among the lower classes of Europe that mitigated national divisions. Nonetheless, the much more extreme situation in Russia, which passed from insurrection to revolution, did little more than encourage pre-existing movements in other countries. It did not spread. The same is true in 1968. A rebellion here certainly encouraged a rebellion there but things always kicked off in response to local situations. The insurrection in Greece came from years of experience preparing society and antiauthoritarians themselves

219

to fight back with everything they had, and that experience obviously cannot follow the photos of the riots as they race across the Internet.

Formed in part by the summit-hopping of the antiglobalization movement, many anarchists forget that we live in a reality very different from most people. We are friends with anarchists in other countries or we at least know that when something happens the anarchists in other countries will stand in solidarity with us. In other words, we have emotional ties. I won't minimize the importance of theory, but I will put it in its place: most people do not risk their lives in struggle on the basis of theory but on the basis of empathy, love, courage, and rage. When an anarchist in Spain hears they have shot an anarchist in Greece and the comrades there are rioting, the insurrection has already come to her heart: she feels rage and a desire to join in the fight; an empathy and even a love for the living comrades who are pushing that fight forward in spite of the repression; and on the basis of these feelings and with the support of comrades in her own town she will find the courage to act. But everyone else in Spain, though they might hear about the assassination on the television, though they may think badly of the Greek police and even sympathize with the rioters, they will not understand how it applies to them. Because solidarity is based on affective bonds.

The nation is not only a trap created by the compulsory education of the State and the cultural institutions of capitalists to divide and conquer the lower classes, although it is that, too. In the absence of State and Capital the nation is a fictive community united by a common language, culture, and history; it is a context in which common experiences can take place and it is therefore also an affective universe. In other words as the world is not homogenous and there are many languages and cultures, there will also be nations (as distinct from nation-states, which is something else entirely). This is why insurrections are sparked off by local events, rather than spreading between nations: because it is much easier for people to identify emotionally with someone whom they see as belonging to their larger community. The high school students who started burning dumpsters in Patras did not personally know Alexis, but they saw him as "one of us." High school students in Italy are unlikely to make that connection because they live in a different cultural context and the death of a Greek high school student, even if it reaches them emotionally on some level, does not have the significance of constituting an attack on them. The common experience of the oppressiveness of high school or the oppressiveness of the police does not overcome these cultural differences.

Western anarchists, on the other hand, make up a common cultural group and in some senses we even speak the same language. We are something like a nation in diaspora, so repression against one of our communities in another country will make sense to us and will affect us emotionally. But we would be wrong to assume that other people are like us in this regard.

And we may even be overestimating the limits of our own solidarity. When immigrants in Omonia rioted in June 2009 after a cop ripped up a Koran in a racist police raid, shockingly few anarchists took part. The tearing of a Koran was interpreted by many immigrants as an attack on their identity, their difference, and thus their very survival. Greek anarchists seemed to interpret it as a religious squabble, much the same way that Italian high school students might fail to understand what the killing of a Greek kid has to do with them.

After nation or culture, a second factor seems to be proximity, but I think it is actually a matter of signals. The immigrant neighborhood in Athens below Omonia is full of people who are not culturally integrated into Greek society, people from many different nations, whose experience of life does not resonate within the national context. In other words they are excluded. Yet they became participants in the December rioting on a massive scale, especially on Monday when the riots kicked off right in their neighborhood. Looking at it from a map, it seems that the insurrection spread geographically. Yet there are many culturally distinct groups that might not join an insurrection even if it is occurring right next to them. The Broken Windows theory of policing used by the authorities may propose a better explanation. Acts of disorder (such as broken windows) provide a signal to the people that authority is weak and further acts of disorder will be tolerated. The State itself implicitly recognizes that authority is a provoca-tion and by showing weakness it invites counterattack; thus everyone carries within them the seed of insurrection.

The massive rioting on Monday provided a clear signal that everyone with a vendetta against State and Capital (and this includes a majority of the population, potentially anybody from whatever class who has not sold themselves out so completely) is free to take revenge. This idea of the importance of signals of disorder explains why people in different cultural groups with no physical proximity to the rioting, for example the Roma community outside Athens who attacked a police station with rifles, also took part in the insurrection if they had any personal cause to hate the authorities, because the signals of local disorder are also spread via the media. And this is one reason why people living under other governments, no matter how much they personally were affected by the killing of an anarchist youth, did not riot with abandon. The signals of disorder were absent, because other governments were not directly weakened by the situation in Greece.

A substance that lies behind both of these factors is the emotional, the subjective. The masculinized, depersonalized, and bureaucratic politics of the Left have long succeeded in removing emotional concerns from our concept of revolution, but you cannot have a liberating revolution while ignoring the emotional half of human existence. All you can have are square-jawed calls for sacrifice issued by a manipulative leadership and a convenient confusion between freedom that exists on paper and freedom that exists in the heart. It is only through the recognition of this subjective, personal, and emotional revolution that people can fight for themselves and recognize the constant attempts to recuperate the struggle through appeals to a false common good. This is not to say that struggle must be individualistic, but that only individuals who are free to feel their needs and desires can participate in a liberated collective capable of overthrowing authority and creating free communities.

Many of the things that happen in Greece could technically be carried out by anarchists in other countries—we have the numbers, the materials, and the proficiency—except that we are afraid. A striking feature of the insurrection and the anarchist movement in Greece is the centrality of courage. But courage is largely a social phenomenon. There are always some people who have a little more of it, who are able to make the first strike, even if no one is behind them, but these people will never be a majority, nor should they be (how terrible the world would be with so many impetuous jackasses running about!) In general, humans being social animals, courage is fostered firstly by peer group support, and secondly by broader community sympathy. If you have enough comrades to act with you, or if you are an anonymous member of a like-minded crowd, you can perform superhuman acts you never would otherwise. And if you are in a group of fifty anarchists facing a hundred well-equipped riot police, you are much more likely to kick things off if you know that all the bystanders are cheering for you, then if you think they would

disapprove of your actions or tell the police which street you ran down after it's all over. The mood on the streets provides another vital signal that directly affects the morale of the police and the morale of the comrades. Take the same fifty anarchists and the same hundred cops, and put them on different streets with different moods, even if no bystanders actively intervene in the situation, and you end up with entirely different outcomes.

But courage is also a matter of practice. The first time you do something is always the scariest. And if you only do an illegal action after meticulous planning—not that planning isn't necessary in many scenarios—you will not learn how to act spontaneously, how to react to the immediate situation, which is a crucial skill for anarchists to have. The December revolts were not planned, they were not prepared by some assembly or vanguard party, but they were prepared for. The insurrection would never have flowered at that moment if the Greek anarchists had not readied themselves to react, and they did this by developing proactive affinity groups united by trust, common politics, and practical experience together; and by carrying out dangerous actions with varying levels of preparation, from spontaneous (reacting in the heat of the moment) to minimal (deciding to do something in just a few hours or the next day and just going and doing it) to meticulous (with intensive planning). This capacity among hundreds or even thousands of anarchists was built up in the years before December, and it allowed them to react immediately upon

Alexis's death and define the character of the revolt in all the days to come. If they had needed to hold a meeting first, a long debate, do reconnaissance, weigh other options, and have the first counterattacks ready a week later, Alexis's murder never would have been avenged.

Additionally, because in the previous months and years Greek society was accustomed to seeing occasional attacks on police stations and banks carried out by anarchists, this form had entered the social consciousness and was ready and available for all the tens of thousands of high school students, immigrants, and others who needed some tool, some expression to their rage. If all they had seen in their worlds were peaceful protests in response to the aggressions and insults of State and capitalism, that is probably all they would have organized in response to the murder. There would have been a few scuffles with police to vent the worst of the rage, and the rest would have to be buried inside them, weighing them down even more and stealing more of their dignity, preparing them for adulthood, for integration, for retirement.

Now it should be clear how the spirit of December can spread internationally. The insurrection of the comrades in Greece can animate us and rejuvenate our hope. It can invite us to study their situation and identify what made it possible, so we can go on building the foundations in our own corners of the world. We can also use it as an opportunity to increase the internationalism of those around us, by holding protests and memorials so our neighbors can consider the possibility that what the police do in Greece is important to us too. But it is counterrevolutionary to pull out our hair, as so many comrades have done, to lash out and insult our local movements for not being able to spread the insurrection, for misinterpreting the geographical limits of the insurrection as evidence of weakness or laziness in other parts. December is an opportunity to rejoice, to boost our morale. How terrible that some hotheads blogging endlessly on the Internet have used it as an opportunity to drain us of even more self-confidence. The opposite is needed.

The December insurrection arose from very specific local circumstances, and it was allowed to arise because people believed it could, within an anarchist movement that did not and does not consider itself special. The insurrection will arise where we are, and we can help it along in a number of ways.

* By understanding that insurrections are not controllable, and they do not follow ideological lines. They are an opportunity for all the oppressed and exploited to fight back in their own ways, but that in this fight, many different people can meet one another, if they are willing.
* By understanding that insurrections usually do not topple governments, but if people do not base their hopes exclusively on the simple act of rioting, they will see that after people are physically exhausted and the fighting in the street stops, if the movement chooses to it can build off those experiences, lay deeper foundations, use the change in the social balance of

power to open autonomous spaces and build the beginnings of an anarchist world, and move closer to stronger insurrections and to revolution.

* By organizing attacks against authority and developing a capacity for spontaneous reaction, so that anarchists prepare themselves for insurrection and make it more likely that an event blooms into an insurrection, and so that society itself is prepared to accept the reality of struggle and counterattack.

* By starting now to find whatever communal and antiauthoritarian traditions exist within our society and expanding on them to counteract the effects of capitalism on culture and to create a popular culture that supports violent resistance, distrusts authority, and cherishes communal values.

* By intervening now in ongoing social conflicts, working respectfully with other non-institutional actors in these conflicts even if they are not anticapitalists, and forcefully opening spaces or employing methods that transform the logic of the struggle from the mediating loop of conservatism vs. reform into one of authority vs. people.

* By building infrastructure and vital capacities (skills, habits, traditions) that reflect and cultivate the world that we want, not as alternatives but as beachheads, so that when we are able to force the police off the streets we will have something creative to move forward with, and so that in the meantime we can give substance to our dreams in a way that sustains hope and sustains us in our struggle, which is hard and long and cannot be fought just for pie in the sky.

These are some of the ways that we can be ready to seize the event and help it expand to its natural shape, a swelling rage and creative collectivity that knows no boundaries and denies logics of control, an explosion that will start to burn away the old world and leave us open ground for the planting of the new one that we carry with us, if only we are courageous enough to seize the opportunity with both hands.

Konstantina was the first to join the union

Maya: A colleague of Konstantina Kuneva, interviewed by a Bulgarian comrade

Konstantina Kuneva is a Bulgarian migrant worker in Athens. She is also the secretary of the Union of Housekeepers and Cleaners of Attika (PEKOP). She worked in ISAP, the state-owned Athens-Piraeus Electric Railway Company, which hired hundreds of cleaners through contract with OIKOMET, Kuneva's direct employer. She had a clash with her employer when she demanded that the entire Christmas bonus be paid to herself and the rest of her colleagues. She also denounced illegal payment procedures, and visited the occupation of the General Confederation of Greek Workers office in Athens. On the 23rd of December, she was attacked in front of her home by unknown assailants who threw sulfuric acid in her face and forced her to swallow acid. She was admitted to the hospital in a critical condition. She lost one of her eyes, and suffered severe burns to her face and internal organs.

What is the current condition of Konstantina Kuneva?

One of her eyes is fully lost and her other eye received a tissue graft. Her vision is weak, but she is able to see outlines, shadows and some colors, meaning that up to now the eye is recovering well. The problem is with her internal organs. The acid that had been swallowed, or possibly the acid fumes that had been inhaled, has subsequently damaged her esophagus. Two days ago she had a serious operation—the doctors implanted an artificial esophagus so that she would be able to eat on her own. It is possible that some complications may arise and thus we are waiting to see how things develop. In the beginning nobody went to visit her, apart from her mother. We wanted to leave her alone so that she could decide when she was able to see us. A few days ago I visited her in the hospital... She is unrecognizable. All her face is burnt, and she had a few plastic surgeries. Probably more will be done in the future. She is a bit better, but of course her face is not what it used to be. Basically Konstantina is doing okay and is very strong psychologically. She is aware that there is a lot of support outside, which is very important. She gets information all the time, her lawyers talk with her and with her mother.

Are there any direct charges or evidence against the attackers?

That's a difficult task. Konstantina saw two of them and she gave testimony and described them, but these are faces she hadn't seen before. And since she saw the attackers, they took care that she will not be able to see, because even if they are found she will not be able to identify them. But when they had thrown the acid she chased them. Can you imagine what a spirit she has? I would have totally lost it, but Konstantina got back on her feet and ran to catch one of them and told him: "Why did you do that to me? What did I do to you?"

How did you feel when you found out that Konstantina was brutally attacked in such a way? Did you get scared?

Of course. This was a warning against everyone who works in that company to keep our mouths shut.

And why did they choose Kuneva?

Because at this time Kuneva was a member of the PEKOP union and since she held an elected position in a trade union they cannot fire her. This protected her. In all other cases they would simply kick you out and that's it. The problem with Konstantina was that her employer, whatever they attempted, couldn't sack her. And Konstantina blamed the state-controlled organizations, pointing out that they were an obstacle. They tried to buy her—they offered her a high position in the company, working as the person responsible for the shifts, which is very highly paid. She refused and went on with her syndicalist activities. So they understood that they could neither buy her off nor kick her out, and thus they decided to stop her in the most brutal way, to physically silence her and blind her.

What are the actual accusations against OIKOMET pressed by your syndicate and how did the conflict grow?

The Greek legislation is a bit confusing—there are many new laws and sub-laws and everyone reads them in any way they want. Companies like OIKOMET are private and they have a contract with state-owned companies and get money from them to hire workers and to organize the work on site.

In this way state money is poured into private hands. Legally in Greece there should be a six-hour working day without any break. For an eight-hour working day there should be a 20 minute break during the shift. But there is that other law, according to which private companies can negotiate directly with the worker and thus come to an agreement about the working conditions. For a six-hour working day and five-day working week there is a heavy-labor insurance due to the worker. But if they have an oral agreement with their worker, the private contractor can set a thirty minute long break. In this way, instead of 30 working hours per week, the worker gets around twenty-five and for that the worker no longer gets heavy insurance but a standard one instead. At the same time the State is obliged to pay for heavy-labor insurance as it is stated in the contract. And the money goes to the private company. In fact the whole situation started to unravel from that point onwards. Konsantina began to look for information and we are now putting that together.

If there is any form of complaint from a worker to a state institution regarding the way legal and labor relations are being controlled, they immediately warn the private contractor and the worker gets sacked. In order to impede the intervention from Kuneva's syndicate, the private company created its own workers' trade union. This means that if there are any problems related to the legal and labor relations, they say that the company trade union does not see any problems and that they would take care of everything. This is where the problems started.

The company trade union initiated propaganda amongst the workers: "Look girls, we have a problem with Kuneva's trade union, they want to shut down the company and you will lose your jobs." When you tell 300 people that they will lose their jobs they get scared. But at the end of the day, after all the fuss, they stopped the breaks and now we have heavy-labor insurance. Subsequently the company trade union started to control the workers and to threaten them, saying they have no right to any break at all and that if they see them taking a break, even a really short one, they will fire them. This is why some of the girls got scared and decided they would prefer not to have heavy-labor insurance, but to have a 30 minute break instead. De facto now we are divided between two fronts. It is normal that if you're working for six hours you take a 5 minute break for a snack. The shifts are in the morning and you get hungry at some point and you need to have something to eat, but those breaks are informal. And in the end we are cleaners, not doctors, we are not in the operating room.

Are your colleagues also migrants?

We are an International—from Greece, Romania, Bulgaria, Bangladesh.

Do you think it is possible to stop private contractors like OIKOMET?

Really hard, since it had become one and the same thing with the state organizations. It has been three months since we have started trying to cancel the contract. Even only for

what happened to Konstantina—it cannot be proven who did it, but there was information that the company is involved.

How did you decide to come to work and live here in Greece?

I came to Greece in 1995. At that time there was a crisis in Bulgaria, there were no jobs, so we came to Greece and settled in Athens. Firstly we started to work in one house. Here there is this system to take care of elderly people and to live with them. Initially I came with friends, and I didn't know the language. Much later my family moved to live here, now my family is here as well, everyone is here. My daughter graduated, my son is working here. None of us has Greek citizenship, but we have work permits.

How do you spend your day?

As anywhere else. The things I have to do after work are the same as in Bulgaria. After the night shift I have to cook, to wash.

How was PEKOP founded?

The union was created in 1998 (even before we came) out of the need to protect workers' rights. Konstantina was the first to start looking for such an organization, she found the address and joined. Initially we were afraid to join, since everyone who did lost their jobs. But after what happened to Konstantina there was a huge wave and people started to look for help and to get together, to overcome their problems.

What are the next steps before the syndicate, how do you see its future role?

227

We will start to unite. It is hard to call it a unification, but at least we will start to work in that direction together. We have to help each other and all the trade unions that are scattered by party interests have to start to work together to protect the interests of the workers.

Do you think youth and student organizations should be actively involved?

Not only that they should, but they absolutely ought to, because this is their future, too. If they do not secure some solid ground for the future, tomorrow it will be way harder. And no one is going to just grant that to you. This is what I learnt from the life here—you have to fight for every single thing. Maybe you are not going to achieve it, but when one day you wake up you can say to yourself—I didn't achieve it, but at least I tried.

What does your family think of your activism?

They are afraid...

Have you been threatened personally?

No, because I do not hide. I am very straightforward and direct. Konstantina possibly made one mistake—she went all alone. On the one hand she did not want to harm the others. On the other she was thinking that she would be able to achieve something legally. At that point there weren't many followers and to be honest there weren't many people that would have followed her. And practically it turned out that it is not possible for an individual to break through.

At the end of the day how do you evaluate what happened up till now, do you think you won after what had happened to her?

We won. We won a faith in the future, a faith that a human being, even alone, can shake up a large organization. This means that we just have to work in that direction. No one should consent to being oppressed.

What is going to happen on the 2nd of April in Greece?

There is a call-out for a general strike of the workers in the public sector in Greece. Probably everything will be blockaded on that day. From that point onwards there is going to be a huge wave, something is going to change in this world. I see that most of the wealth of humanity is concentrated in the hands of very few people. Years ago profit was in fuels, after this in the drug and arms dealing. But now most of the profits come from cheap labor. And it seems that this is the future direction, to profit by exploiting people, treating them like labor units. I suppose that the activity of all international organizations should be directed towards this problem. I think that this financial crisis is created on purpose, to make the workers scared that they will lose their jobs and to use their fear to pass new laws. And this is everywhere in the world. I never expected to live at such a fast pace as I do now. But there are things to be finished and I do it mostly for the young.

We need to make it obvious that it is easy to attack

Ego Te Provoco: Four members of a counterinformation group in Athens

After December there wasn't any time for reflection or self-evaluation because there was so much urgency, there was so much to do. But December didn't just end one day, other things kept turning up, like the Kuneva case, so around New Year's Eve there were occupations and violent protest marches for Kuneva. December has still not ended. There are also the prisoners of December, the occupied parks… It's a continuing process. The revolution did not freeze. And several collectives that were created in December are continuing their discourse and their actions. Even this building [where the interview is taking place], the Patision squat, is an outgrowth from the occupation of ASOEE and the relationships that formed there.

All this has been an opportunity to test out a new way of living. From my point of view, I've seen a lot of interest in reclaiming public life. People want to leave behind the private life, the dominant privatization of lives. They resist it and try to express themselves publicly, and this has been a place where we could hear opinions we hadn't heard before, from people we hadn't known, and do things with them and help them build the new structures. The ASOEE occupation was

a real revelation. A week before no one could have guessed that we would be able to work together in such a harmonious way. These were mostly people who knew each other for many years. Still, I didn't believe that we could do anything with them, plus a lot of people you had never seen in your life. But together we managed to organize the building, cook and clean, print, discuss, and plan external actions—sabotage, coordinating attacks between one hundred people. Then one or two hours later executing those attacks with minimal mistakes. This was unprecedented.

Even though the majority of revolutionary means used by the movement are quite old or established—like squatting, or blogs, or the attacks—through December they have proved quite useful. There has been a transvaluation of the old methods, and they have received a tremendous new impetus, and many more people are using them. A year ago squatting was not thought of as an offensive action, but now they are offensive, they are a form of attacking, and this is because of the relationships that they are developing internally.

And the same goes for the attacks, the violent attacks. The violent means that we used during the uprising were very popularized. The children were attacking police stations. Supermarkets were being looted, and people who had never used these methods before were able to try them out. The atmosphere was not so dangerous, so a lot of people could take part. If you count the battle hours of people who are now eighteen or nineteen years old, their accumulated battle hours are probably more than I tallied up from 16 to 28, because we'd always have to wait for November 17 and the leftist protest march, and that was it. That's the practical side. The theoretical side is that during the general assemblies, in amphitheaters full of 500 people we were talking openly about violent attacks, which had never happened before. This prepared people for the notion that it might get dangerous, so people started thinking about it more. And there was no hierarchy that declared some people were good enough to cook and clean and make leaflets and some invisible group was capable of making the attacks. No: everyone cooked and everyone cleaned and everyone made attacks.

It was amazing to see people involved in these violent attacks in a way that was previously unimaginable. There was an acceleration. Being involved in the planning and execution of an attack became a normal thing, whereas before it was a closed issue.

There has been an increase in individuals' discourse and actions while the loose periphery is coming more to the center and getting involved in the central procedures of the movement. Many more people are getting involved in critical discourse and counterinformation, and also violent attacks and sabotage. People are taking things more seriously in general.

Before December it was up to a few groups to carry out counterinformation so each group was very significant and unique, but now it's so diffuse, coming from so many corners of society. It's important to retain the images of December to hold on to the courage and also to retain the memory, because the State wants to erase this. So we use the imagery of December to help keep the violence generalized. Personally I am deadset against creative forms of counterinformation. I think this is playing the game of the spectacle. The situation is so serious and everyone recognizes it, there is no need to use tricks. We're not an advertising company, we're a revolutionary movement and we'll say it straight. And people are ready for it. Before, if people didn't take a leaflet from us it was not because it wasn't shiny but because before December there was no perspective, they couldn't see an end to the tunnel and the tunnel wasn't so intolerable to them. But now it is intolerable and they see a way out. Something has to be done and something can be done, in their eyes, so we don't need marketing tricks to communicate with them.

The goal of counterinformation is to remind people of the reasons why one should attack. If one is convinced of this he or she will find the ways. Secondly, reminding people that this happened across the country and they did not manage to kick us off the streets; it was not repression that ended the uprising. And third to make it obvious that it is possible, it is easy to attack. And this is obvious from the fact that actions happen all the time.

While the regime is militarizing itself, we should on the one hand keep attacking it to show that it is vulnerable and it's not achieving the state of security that it claims, and on the other hand to produce a discourse against the state of security as such, to challenge its reasons for coming into existence. Greek society is allergic to military solutions, and the government is making a big mistake. You have a big uprising sparked by a police killing and what's their solution? More cops. Very smart. Alexis was killed by a cop from the special branch, and all the rhetoric repeated the idea of insufficient training. Now they're putting these special cops in their new Delta Force, to deal with an even higher level of violence, and they're just getting one week of extra training. They're shooting themselves in the foot.

Security is not the main value of this society, although since the '90s they've been trying to make it so, talking about immigrant criminality to provoke fear. Then there were the Olympic Games and the security that went with it, then the new police corps and the cameras. The Greek state is mimicking the Western metropolitan areas. But Greece is a different society, so it's completely idiotic. They have no idea of what a society is; they're completely mechanistic, they say it worked in New York so it can work here. To them there are only individuals, there is no society; they're Thatcherites. Greeks have a hundred different reasons to oppose cameras that people in London may not have. People here are breaking a hundred laws every day, running red lights, not paying for the metro. So this kind of security might be a nice word in the coffee shop but when the cop comes to make you pay the traffic ticket you're going to become very angry. In London they

would say, this is good because I did something wrong, so I should pay the ticket.

From the view of the antagonistic social movement there are two interlinking ways of dealing with this. One has to do with countering the antiterrorist discourse of post–9-11, asymmetrical threats, and the immigrants. The other part has to do with countering the demand of security in everyday life. So on the one hand the demand for security is in itself a strategy of counterinsurgency. In this sense it prevents insurgency, it engineers a pacification of society, each one in his little house, don't mind public affairs, just mind your own business. And on the other hand it prepares the State in terms of its ideological artillery and its material artillery and preparation on the street to be ready to counter any kind of challenge to it.

One way of countering this phenomenon is to demonstrate that this is an enterprise of war, a strategy of war by the State against society. But it's a very different situation here because in the UK or the US the man in the street is convinced that there might be some rotten elements but the State in itself is good, that it's there for your own good. In Greece no one believes that. There is a complete and utter mistrust, all politicians are lying bastards, all they do is steal the budget money, but the people tolerate it because they can't do anything else. There is no civil society in Greece. No social contract. There is a long relationship of imposition, and it is experienced as such, even though in reality it's a relationship of complicity that is experienced as one of imposition. So resistance is a great

231

value and compliance and conformity are utterly disgraceful in public discourse. They stink of the junta. The imaginative construction of Greek society draws from values of resistance. Of course complicity is still a part of the social reality here. But in Britain the real society is complicit and their ideal society is a complicit one as well.

Traditionally, we are against using the media to communicate with the public. It is an issue that has been resolved for many years in the anarchist scene. There used to be collaboration with the media, until the early '90s, but no more. Theoretically the argument is that you cannot fight alienation with alienated means. You cannot claim that journalists are the scum of the earth and snitches, and at the same time be using them. And on a higher level it's the question of the spectacle, of whether you could actually use the media. Even if there is an article of yours in the newspaper, it will be next to another article so yours becomes just a piece of information, it supports this whole idea of democratic pluralism. Cooperation with the institutions is always an obstacle to the development of autonomous structures. Our relation to communication is based on face to face relation in the street. Often we also challenge the use of Indymedia, which creates this fiction of sharing things, this imaginative community, but materially there is no sharing or community. Many people consider Indymedia to be a part of the spectacle.

We finally understood that many people supported us

Andreas: A squatter from Thessaloniki

In Thessaloniki things started calming down around the 15th of December. There were still really big demos but less violence. We started organizing a solidarity movement for the prisoners of the uprising. We didn't start the solidarity movement and the protests for the prisoners until the situation had relaxed, because we didn't want to signal the end of the uprising, and we wanted to use it as a new rallying point so all the groups could gather and stay involved even though the fighting had stopped. We had about thirty people arrested in Thessaloniki, not so much. But it was very hard to find out who was arrested, because so many of the people who participated had no connection with the anarchists, they had never participated in the movement before. And we couldn't just call up the jails to find out who was arrested because they only give this information to the lawyer of the prisoner. And lots of arrests were random. Immigrants walking down the street with a new mobile phone could be arrested on suspicion of looting and nobody would know. There were thousands of mobiles stolen during the uprising, so they made these kind of arrests frequently. We learned that they had an order to arrest people whom it would be hard to find out about, people without connections, because this would terrorize the movement. So it was hard work finding out the names of everyone who was arrested.

The situation after December has not really changed. It's like it was before. To say that the many people who adopted our practices had some sort of a social awakening is to have a negative view of the people who weren't active. I believe that before December many of them maybe listened to us and agreed with us. What happened in December is that finally we understood that many people supported us but just didn't have a way to enter, to join in.

In Greece there is no historical tradition of neighborhood assemblies but now it is starting everywhere. The assembly provided a neutral place for people to come and shape the decisions from the beginning. A place like Delta [a squatted hotel in Thessaloniki], it's not so open because from the beginning we already had a specific project, a specific politics in mind. But these assemblies and these new occupations provide ways for other people to join in.

December helped us see another weakness in our movement. We weren't thinking about the future, about what the world might be like three or four months later. We were just doing the things we were already used to doing from all the years of struggle that had come before: burning banks and attacking the police. But you can only burn the same bank so many times before you have to stop. I tell you, all the banks were burned. In December we were not mature enough for planning. We were in a situation in which any plan was possible—we could have destroyed the TV transmitters and abolished television, we could have taken down the cell phone infrastructure, we could have squatted Parliament, but we did not make those plans and we did not realize how important it would have been for the future.

We saw our weaknesses. Rioting for five days showed us that violence alone doesn't get us anything unless it has content. There was an organizational gap. December provided us with a new theoretical experience. We can see our structural gaps. Squat radio stations are being set up throughout the city. We're going to set up a print shop. We're creating the structures we need.

The most important thing about December is it made the movement understand the people, and not vice versa. It made us understand that they need a place to stand, a way to participate. You can see anarchists who used to be antisocial talking about social acceptance. And you see the nonviolent groups talking about rioting and attacking the police. A coalition, an atypical coalition is being created here in Thessaloniki.

The myth of Sisyphus

Panagiotis Kalamaras: A publisher of editions on libertarian culture

For me, without the antiglobalization movement we would not have what we have now in Greece. Many people went to other countries, they saw what was happening, they read the literature, and the numbers grew and the movement developed a certain internationalism—especially after the European Forum protests in Thessaloniki. Genoa [the G8 protests in 2001] was very important, many Greek anarchists were in a black bloc in Genoa. They saw what happened with the police, with the Left, and they told people back here about it. They went to the IMF protests in Prague, and then Thessaloniki in 2003. Some people say they were just revolutionary tourists but for me this is a major mistake. These protests provided a great school for the movement, people learned a lot.

Before we had influence but we didn't have the numbers. Now, since December, the anarchist movement begins to have the numbers. Not just in Athens but in other cities as well. We're not just speaking about hundreds we're speaking about thousands. The major difference between December and the major movements that occurred in the '80s and '90s was that in December it was an anarchist revolt. This was the big

difference. Also this time it happened everywhere in Greece. In other strong periods of movement the anarchists were fewer, it was mostly leftists. And now a lot of people use an anarchist practice. I'm not the only one who says this, I even see this in leftist publications. You'd have to be an idiot not to recognize that this is the situation. In previous years it was the anarchists who made attacks on police stations. Now everybody does this. It doesn't mean that these other people who attack police stations are also anarchists but there is an influence, there is *osmosis*. Now we will see if this will have an effect on everyday life. We will see. We are only at the beginning. But in December it was clear: ordinary people acted like anarchists.

There is an ethical problem I want to talk about. Maybe it's too philosophical, but… The leftists say if I fight for revolution I will have a better life. Another way to look at it is that you don't need the result, you say I'm going to fight because my fight is right and maybe there won't be a revolution because our enemy is stronger than we are but we will fight anyway.

Like the myth of Sisyphus, even if God will knock down the stone, I will roll it up the hill again, I will keep trying. In a way the anarchist movement is very Kantian without being aware of it, because Kant says you always have to fight for what you believe is right no matter what happens. There are a lot of people on the Left who only believe in results. They decline to fight for revolution because they lost the civil war. And when the Socialists came into power they went with the

Socialists and joined the government. But the anarchists here don't have a history of losing and they believe that ethically they are the winners. But this presents a problem because you also need an outside judge to judge you. If you always judge yourself you have a problem. In a way history can be a kind of judge. We have the problem in Greece that the anarchist movement is very self-referential. We don't critique ourselves with the eyes of the others, we critique with our own eyes.

When there is strong social conflict, you raise the tension of the attacks

Transgressio Legis: An insurrectionary anarchist group in Athens engaged in counterinformation and direct action

After the first days of paralysis, the State recovered its powers and this manifested in two ways. First with numerous random arrests, and second with all the propaganda about the looting of small shops and the pressure to return to normality, the idea that society could not stand this situation any longer. On the other hand the movement started to get more organized to provide solidarity for the hundreds of people arrested, and another important move against the return to normality was the occupation of the General Confederation of Greek Workers. And this countered the propaganda of the State that the workers did not participate in this struggle. After many different events and assemblies and talks inside the building, the General Assembly of Insurgents for Solidarity with the Prisoners of December was formed inside this occupation. Initially this assembly brought together 500 people, mainly from the anarchist *horos,* the scene. They organized the first actions of support for prisoners with posters and texts and

235

protests, including the magnificent protest outside Korydallos prison. There were around 900 people gathered there for New Year's Eve. This was the first time there was such a large New Year's Eve noise demo, and it was similar in other cities. Later there was a large demonstration in Larissa, where many of the juveniles facing charges under the anti-terror law were being held.

The next move of this assembly was the organization of the big demonstration in solidarity with the prisoners of December, on January 24. About 3,500 people came. At the end of the demo the police attacked without provocation, very brutally. But because of the inner polemics and disagreements among the groups participating in this general assembly, many groups including ours left and because of this we believe that the solidarity movement lost force. Then there was a wave of armed attacks. Some comrades believe this caused an ideological counterattack by the bourgeois press and the government, but it also scared the political elite, the economic elite, and the media elite. And as the massive actions faded away, a strong second wave of government repression appeared. The dialogue to end the asylum in the universities, the effort to criminalize masks in protests, to criminalize insulting cops, when this had become a popular activity in December. The fear of crime and immigrants and poor people and junkies. So what does society need? Security. Total security. And this is the dominant political dialogue at this moment.

According to our analysis, it has been a traditional strategy going back many years that when they have taken prisoners or when there is strong social conflict, you raise the tension of the attacks and sabotage and vandalism. Our opinion is that we should intensify these tactics. Other groups believe that now is the time for more public and political presence. In our analysis this is faulty because the great disagreements between different anarchist groups don't allow us to organize massive political appearances, like what was happening in December. The social spirit of December is no longer obvious, it no longer has visibility, so it's up to small affinity groups to sustain the spirit of December by continuing arson attacks. We believe that there is no holistic logic or strategy we can all follow because of the variety of opinions and tactics and strategies. No one wishes to produce one general anarchist opinion or organization or solution. This is the basic characteristic of all these years of anarchist action in Greece.

Of course whatever move the government makes after December, the anarchists will respond. And fortunately our responses will be wildly diverse. On the other hand what remains unchanged since December is that each group has its own analysis, makes its own decisions, and carries out its own response. In a way we carry on like December never happened. We don't have a plan for the distant future. The strategy of the elites will provoke the specific response of the lower classes. We'll respond in the ways we know how, but if

236

new social phenomena appear, then we are ready to invent our new responses, analytically and practically.

The war is continuing. Our generation has the opportunity to see incredible things happen to the societies of this planet. And it is up to us to see if the fascists and the leftists will capture the hopes of the people or if the anarchists, through our struggle, will offer society an escape route through the fires and cataclysm of liberation.

We want to occupy the media and use it for the movement

Assembly of Media Workers: About a dozen members of a group of media workers, and students of media and communications, including a wide range of the political spectrum, from the Left to anarchists

We occupied the offices of the Editors' Union of Athens Daily Papers. Our inspiration was the occupation of the General Confederation of Greek Workers in December. The idea was that we as workers in the media could occupy the office of our bosses.

Our group was started by students in the School of Mass Media and Communications. Within the school there had already been a room occupied for ten years now, that was used as a political gathering point and a foundation for our movement. As people finished school and were getting jobs in the industry they didn't forget about their background; they kept coming back to the students here. So there was an *osmosis* between the students and the working people. This was especially important during the student occupation movement of two years ago. The workers started a group last year, that consisted mainly of a blog with writings about the media industry. And we also started to go to the demonstrations of journalists, we met some people who were working as freelancers, started talking about the precarity of freelancers as a working problem. The idea arose to create a non-hierarchical, self-organized syndicate of freelancers who wanted something different. This failed. The fact is that freelancers in Greece do not work that way as a choice but the bosses want people to work as freelancers in order to have more flexibility. They don't hire you as an employee, they make you do the same job as a freelancer. It's a form of outsourcing. But in this case they don't hire people from other companies, you're just an individual worker, even though you're essentially working for a specific newspaper or whatever. So you have to pay your own social security.

In December the media did an awful job, as always. They tried to divide the movement into the bad anarchists and the good students. After December the media used more aggressive tactics to scare people with the spectre of terrorism, to make them afraid so they would stay at home. But those of us who are in the movement and in the media have to point out some exceptions. There was one photojournalist who published the famous picture of a cop on the streets facing protesters and drawing his gun, just after the murder of Alexis. The journalist was fired for this photo. So we have to emphasize that what the media produce depends on what the bosses want, and what they want is to profit and to send the right political message.

Anarchists in Greece generally want no relationship whatsoever with the media or reporters. In the last ten years many photographers have been attacked by demonstrators and TV vans have been burned. And okay, the media have a central role in state propaganda today, and in spreading fascism. They present anarchists as bad people wearing masks, the "known unknowns." There was a legend circulated by Greek TV in December that all the riots were provoked by anarchists. Their representation in the spectacle is as "the known unknowns," everybody knows them but nobody knows who they are, they're an antisocial element that cannot be pinned down. So the anarchists respond ironically, "Yes, we're the same 300 people since November '73."

Since December they haven't been using this term because no one believes it anymore. Now they say *koukoulofori,* the masked ones. The State's main point is that these unknowns have names and addresses and we had better find them soon. The media and State cannot accept that there is anarchy in Greece and real people behind it. It is essential for them to make people believe that these anarchists are vicious criminals with ulterior motives. In their minds anarchists cannot exist, so it is obvious to them that they are manipulated by something. The Communist Party says they are police provocateurs, and nationalists say they are manipulated by some external element trying to destabilize Greece.

Our group participated in the revolt in December, in the occupations and mobilizations that were happening. At the first demo of the year, in January, the cops were very aggressive and beat lots of people, including journalists and lawyers. This provided an opportunity to occupy the newspaper editors' offices in order to talk about the labor problems of journalists, to criticize what the media were saying about the revolts, and to address the general precarity of all workers in Greece. The two main purposes of the occupation was to produce counter-information and to denounce our problems as workers, the firings, the precarity, the aggressions of the bosses. The occupation lasted six days.

One of the main reasons we occupied these offices was because we knew that anarchists had no connections with the working class. The workplace did not play a large role in the rebellion of December and one main aspect of our action was our desire to get close to the working class, as we belong to it. We wanted to create some link or bridge, to show that these ideas are not opposed, that there is not such a big gap.

The movement received our action ambiguously. Some people said journalists don't deserve to be a part of the movement and some people were more tolerant towards this occupation. The first two days were very complicated because people of the movement who had a bad impression of journalists came in contact with people working in the media who thought of themselves as part of the movement. The crowd there was very diverse. That was part of what made it unique but it also caused problems in terms of organizing. People were trying to formulate different methods of organizing because some people were really radical and others less so. There were two lines, one of people coming from the movement and another of people coming from the media. Some people came to the occupation because they wanted to work on counter-information, against the media and against the spectacle, and the people coming from the media wanted to do something against the bosses, and the job situation.

Counterinformation is a key movement issue and we are a small part of that. Indymedia is another part of it, as are the people who publish magazines or newspapers. My personal view is that blogs and other forms of communication had a central role in December, facilitating instant reactions, instant responses to what was happening on the ground. Many people were trying to inform others and that worked really well in December. From the first night there were demos and attacks on police all over Greece because everyone knew what had happened in Athens. Due to the Internet and telephone and also the mainstream media the access to information was expansive. There were attacks in the most remote parts of Greece. I think high school kids saw it on TV so they got the idea to do it themselves. In a sense even the mainstream media has a positive role sometimes, in an impressionable kind of way: their coverage made an impression and some people wanted to know more. It's not that they gave the rebellion and the attacks a positive spin, but it would have been worse if they had stayed silent.

But counterinformation is necessary to actually produce discourse. And for this we employ classic methods, such as open assemblies, pamphlets, blogs, posters, demos, occupations.

Our assembly is now debating the role of the media. We don't yet have a common idea on how to "despectacularize" the media. We believe in counterinformation, we believe that the media uphold capitalism. Most of us want to occupy the media, or rather the means of production of the media, and use them for the movement. Indymedia is one direction. The other direction is, since we know from our studies how the public sphere is created and how the mechanisms of the State work, to expose the methods of brainwashing, of ideological suppression.

Another big discussion begun during the revolt centered around the use of videos. We don't have an answer to this question yet. Some people said we must use videos, while others feel that they are a medium that creates the spectacle. The most obvious objection is that the cops will get hold of the images and get our identities, but it's more complicated. It also has to do with the fact that the videos are being edited by the TV channels so you can't be sure if it will be used in the wrong way. People do not trust the medium of videos and audiovisual materials because it has been used primarily against us. As a squat we tried to make videos, one at the demo on

January 16 and the other at the Patision Park. We also tried to work as a counterinformation team at one demo. It was experimental. But some people strongly opposed us in this.

Then there is the debate about television. Is it possible to have a radical self-organized TV channel? It would be the same thing but with different political content. Some of us believe that within capitalism the media cannot be used to promote revolutionary ideas. There are some radio stations, but they are counterinformation, pirate stations, they don't have bosses, they self-organize with assemblies. I think the media industry is a capitalist machine that can't be transformed within capitalism. But if we occupy them it can produce good results. During the revolt there was a group that occupied NET, the national TV station. But this action was an interruption of the program, it was not a program promoting revolutionary ideas. I think that would have been a total failure.

TV is different from radio because you're dealing with images. It would be propaganda on your behalf, using the spectacle to your benefit. But that's a debate we haven't really gone into because it's so complicated. The TV is much more infused with the ideologies of state and capitalism than the radio or newspapers. Also the relationship you create with the audience; they are rendered more passive, it doesn't matter if they're watching a demonstration or a football match. It's naturally reactionary. To perceive yourself as a viewer means you are not an actor. In capitalist society we are alienated and

240

we become spectators of our lives, our lives become strange to us. For example I can't imagine someone who tries to shoot photos during a demo instead of fighting with police.

These are some of the problems we are wrestling with. Journalists questioning their role as journalists. It's pretty self-annihilating but also creative if you think about it.

December's Riots as Mediated by the Image of Mass Media

Leandros Kyriakopoulos from Void Network

"It is the historical and structural definition of consumption that, by way of [a] 'lived' level, it *exalts signs on the basis of a denial of things and the real.*" This quote comes from the French philosopher Jean Baudrillard as he was meditating on the culture of mass media and the ways in which visual consciousness adjoins the image. In these few pages, the devastating thinking of this mediator will be the vehicle for a reflection on the events that followed Alexandros Grigoropoulos's death, as mediated by the visual and printed screens of Greek and international mass media. Reading the *sign* of Baudrillard, one could say that "riots" is a micro-event in the contemporary news reports, *permanently* interlocked with others of its like, such as the war in Afghanistan, a typhoon in the Philippines, sports events, and the weather forecast. This technique of mass exporting (and producing) events, like a collage, is based on the pathetic exaltation of them. This is the denial of the real through the multiple repetition of a reactualized exemplar. *If the impossibility of an "outbreak" is proposed, then this "outbreak"*

241

is being ritually sacralized by the media through the consumption of its image in the "up-to-the-minute" news reports.

The Greek and the international media identified the riots that followed Grigoropoulos's death as an "insurrection," strongly referring and comparing them with other historical events, such as the Parisian May of '68 and the riots at Columbia in the US during the same period. The headlines of known newspapers are very indicative of this: "The whole world is inspired by the insurrection of Athens" or "The dynamic of the youth's insurrection has awaken the citizens." On the 13th of December—a week after the riots had begun—all the Greek media had comments on the foreign press' reports about the situation in Greece: "The revolt of the spoiled: European youth are rising up as they see the end of their privileges." Titles like this on the front pages of the German and French press are the result of a correlation between the events of Athens and those of Berlin and Paris. Social injustice, suffering, and anger are incarnated in the image and are being combined with the archetypical paradigms of the modern expression of opposition and political disobedience (such as the Parisian May of '68). At the same time, the media's images carry the terror of violence as it cataclysmically intrudes in everyday life and disrupts the State's efforts for an "equitable modernization of the civil society."

This essay is not concerned with the political management of December's events by the mass media. It can be said though, that the range of comments extends throughout

the political spectrum—inside and outside the political correctness of the parliament.[1] Every attempt at assembling December's events through the image—even the "friendliest" one—embraced by the media's logic of consumption, becomes suspect as a result, since the sign at stake—named in a holistic way as "outbreak"—is manipulated with certain contents which were not previously subject to that logic. That happens because of the turning of the events into up-to-the-minute daily news that corresponds to the *technical essence* of the media, that is the disarticulation of the real into successive and equivalent signs, and their combined modulation with other ones. This is evidenced in daily news reports such as: "the economic policy of the Minister of Finance," "the problematic state of Exarchia," "the state of alert of the Ministry of Domestic Affairs," "the limits of police violence," "the change of political attitude," "the major issue of European integration," and "the common question of global democratic governance."

What is shared then, between media's portrayed images and the emotionally stressed eyes of the viewers, is a corpus of signs and references based upon the camera's representation and the state, legal, and political reformulation of the embodied lived experience of the riot's participants. In this corpus of signs, the intractable materiality of "youth," "anarchist," "masked face," "foreigner," "unscrupulous vandal," is

---

1   The well-known national satiric comedian Lazopoulos, said during his most popular TV program: "I would recommend to these kids to destroy everything, do not sober up!"

shifted from the dark and imponderable body of the street, towards politically familiar, ideology-bound platforms from which the question of the "outbreak" and its virtual answers can be addressed. Thereby, mass communication excludes the corporeal experience of the polyphonic event of the riot, while at the same time it creates a common ground from which a compromise can be made among all the eyes staring at the dramatic images, toward the same ambiguous demand of this "outbreak"; namely a change to a more humane social world. Therefore, the reading of the new contents by the virtual collective of all those driven by the same ambiguous exigency sacralize "outbreak" as something profane that needs purification through an eligible "answer."

This "answer" though is not articulated, yet is always at stake in every effort for defining, commenting, and situating December's events by the mass media. This rephrasing of the "outbreak" with its presaged answer implicitly provides a reassuring social narrative (which at the same time ascribes blame): that "modernization of the State" and "just democratic governance" entails the progressive withdrawal of violence from everyday life. What is really at stake then, in the mass media's discourse about December's events, is not Alexandros Grigoropoulos's death by the armed hand of the police and the riots triggered off by this death, but the capability of the State to handle this domestic crisis.

A month of continuing reports and live broadcasts is encapsulated in three stances that, after a year, makes Greek political life conform to the universalized rational norm of its parliamentary spectrum. The first concerns the criticism by the main opposition party, the Socialists, against the government that is "incapable of protecting the citizens," the second is the attack on the small party of the progressive Left (SYRIZA) by the liberal, the Communist, and the right-wing parties, because of its "unwillingness to confine its political range within parliamentary legitimacy." As for the third one, it involves all the parties and it is the commitment to terminating domestic terrorist political movements. Mass media say that December's "outbreak" changed a lot of things in the political life of this country. I believe that these stances are the legacy of the power of images in the collective thinking of the Greek citizen-viewers.

The Greeks' involvement in December via the image and discourse of the media indicates their consent in the deciphering of the media's message. And if "the medium is the message," then this deciphering is not about the "outbreak" but about the media themselves. That is, the viewer is being unconsciously called upon to decipher the deep discursivity of the media—the realist representation of the camera with its applied objectivism—before and beyond December's events. Thus, mass media's image incarnates December's riots while evading their embodied character, and re-writes them through an evenly up-to-the-minute agenda for collective reception. And as these riots are sacralized by the viewers for being the "outbreak" of a social and economic privation that troubles Greek society for many years now, they are sacrificed all the same when one attempts to find an answer in their actualization.

The new neighborhood assemblies

Mi: An anarchist of Exarchia

It is very early to draw conclusions about the messages and the lessons that we learned through the insurrection of December. Maybe it will take months or even years to understand what we did because we're still in the heat of the moment. One characteristic of December was the occupation of government buildings, municipality buildings, universities, and municipal cultural centers. The goal of all these actions was to organize the participation of the inhabitants and local people in the center of the different cities and also in the suburbs. In the city centers and in the universities, the occupations arose from political actors, from the libertarians or anarchists or autonomists, and also ultra-left movements, and inside these occupations the majority of participants were already politically conscious. On the other hand the vast majority of people who participated in the occupations in the suburbs were local people who hadn't been active before. Even though there were also politically conscious comrades there, the great majority of the participants were people who appeared in the movement for their first time. All these assemblies in the suburbs used the name, "Open Assembly of the Inhabitants of" whatever area, or "popular assembly." Because parthenogenesis does not exist, many of these assemblies arose from campaigns and meetings and struggles around specific local themes that predated December.

The second important characteristic of these assemblies is that for the first time struggles that started in the center of Athens—like the response to the assassination of Alexis or the attack on Kuneva, or the solidarity with the prisoners, or general talks that took place during the insurrection in the occupation of the Polytechnic or Nomiki or ASOEE or the General Confederation of Greek Workers building—became subjects for discussion and struggle in the assemblies and neighborhoods all around Greece. The central point of these assemblies was no longer a local problem, but a general subject that connected all these assemblies all throughout Greece. And this was apparent in a slogan that you could find in all the different assemblies, "Let's take life back into our hands." This means that we have to carry out a global struggle that includes all the different sides and activities of life.

In many areas of Greece where popular assemblies had never existed, new ones appeared for the first time, possibly started by neighbors who knew each other. To get a good picture of these assemblies, imagine that during December and the beginning of January, between 150–500 people in each neighborhood were taking part. And they organized many different demonstrations for Alexis, for Kuneva, for the prisoners, they printed many different posters and pamphlets,

and also organized concerts and attacks on police stations or other local targets.

In the neighborhood assemblies people always prefer to talk and debate for hours and even days, sometimes to even avoid making a final decision at all, in order to seek consensus and avoid stooping to holding a vote. Sometimes this is chaotic, sometimes it is a lengthy procedure, but it allows everyone to express his or her own opinion and to find a place within the general spirit. Another important characteristic is how the general assemblies functioned as welcome centers where you could find announcements and calls for help for all the different initiatives that appeared inside the assembly. The initiatives were not created by final decisions coming from the assembly, but rather they were the initiatives of members that were accommodated by the general assembly. There were no decisions about what would happen and what wouldn't. All of it was happening. Thus, these assemblies allowed important anarchist principles such as consensus and the empowerment of individual initiative to pass to people who were not anarchists but adopted the practices and theories and principles of the anarchist movement.

There were other actions that had previously been unheard of. The refusal to pay for public transportation and attacks on the ticket machines, the occupation of the Opera Hall that worked as a meeting point between the artists and the society, and gave the artists the chance to express their new ideas developed during the insurrection. To even mention

245

all the actions that took place you would need a catalog of the hundreds of blogs created during the insurrection by all these different assemblies and initiatives. These blogs were very important instruments for visibility and direct public announcements. There was no need anymore for any kind of mediation or intermediary, in the form of the media. And all of the groups produced thousands of posters and pamphlets that created direct public dialog in the streets.

Another important initiative that started after December was the Assembly for Health. It is an assembly constituted by workers in the health sector, including doctors, pharmacists, and nurses. This assembly tries to expose the great problems of health care as a social problem and not a medical problem. To break the barriers between the specialists and the laymen, the doctors and the patients. The first actions of this assembly took place in two huge public hospitals where the members occupied the lobby, liberating it and giving everyone a chance to have free health care for five hours. The idea behind these actions was to announce to all society that health is a social gift and that it is irrational to expect people to pay for health care.

It is also important to mention the assembly for solidarity with Kuneva. It gathered a large number of people who participated in the insurrection. With demos, occupations of state buildings, and the smashing of private cleaning companies. And the arson attack on the metro station of Kifissia, one of the richest areas of Athens, that caused 12 million euros in damage.

In the suburbs, after the occupations of all these municipality buildings and cultural centers and central buildings ended, the assemblies have continued to exist though they no longer have a central building as a reference point and they don't gather such a large number of people. But in three different suburbs, Petralona, Nea Filadelfia, and Brachami, they now have permanent occupations for the assemblies. The health workers' assembly participates in the occupied building in Petralona. A new horizon has opened up in terms of building anarchist social struggles as they try to create solutions for health as a social problem, and to offer free health care to the people of the neighborhood. And meanwhile the already existing social centers and squats have been empowered, and host intense activity every day.

These assemblies that we mention here, and all that we have left out, created an entire galaxy of actions, attacks, protests, confrontations, pamphlets, campaigns, posters, and critiques. All this appeared after the assassination of a fifteen-year-old boy but it spreads its light across the planet by creating itself, creating new people, new comrades, new actions, new visions, new practices, and the future of the movement itself.

Kill the Sexist In Your Head—the menses flow

A communique released by an Athens anti-sexist group

During the insurrection, the slogan "Cops, cunts, you kill children" was often shouted. One of the times when we reacted, one of the "insurgents," to our disgust, said: "Learn to shut up. And if you do not know how, we will make you shut up."

We didn't shut up, though.

It was not enough for us that already:

• Capital exploits our bodies. In employment, in the unpaid work between the four walls of our homes, in entertainment (for others).

• The nuclear Greek family wants us as housewives and rabbits, intending for our bodies, even within our own personal space, to reproduce: "the future of this country."

• We have to put up with the motherfuckers, the bosses at home and at work, and their culture of hunter and prey, their pick-ups and propositioning, their whispers and their harassment in the street and on the buses.

• All manner of liberal experts reassure us that "equality" has been achieved. Of course! With equal rights to wage slavery.

On top of it all, we have comrades and compañeras who call the cops "pussy." This specific slogan is an attempt to denigrate the cop by comparing it with a pussy. Why does this word denigrate the cop? The word "cunt" (and the body part itself) is already denigrated in the social hierarchy of gender. This relationship is reproduced everywhere. Now also in the street!

Language reproduces and maintains the space in which the authoritarian gender relations are normalized. Without this space provided to them daily, these relationships fall into a social vacuum, and thus are challenged.

In the dominant language, and in the language of the street, the "ardent desire" for sexual exploitation ("we will fuck you, pussy" etc.) undermines social liberation.

Hey! go further.

The subordination of bodies to violence and to the symbols of the ruling class can not be reversed with hidden hierarchies.

Aside from the cop...

Also kill the sexist in your head!

—The menses flow, the body asks for rebellion.

The Limitations of Anti-Sexism

Sissy Doutsiou from Void Network

During December 2008 anti-sexists were arguing about the sexist behavior of comrades and youth in the streets who were shouting the slogan "Cops, cunts, you kill children." This argument opened a discussion in which a female group, participants in the December rebellion, expressed their opinion, through posters and communiqués, that many anarchists are sexists and the "movement" has a problem with sexism. This initiated a conversation among some Greek anarchists about what is sexism, what can be called anti-sexism, and how you can fight effectively against sexism. This conversation was one more fragmented dialog that happened in the occupied universities and in the streets behind the barricades in the few moments of calmness while we recovered from the tear gas burning our eyes and lungs.

When the clashes ended and the various collectives directed their energies into many different actions and projects I found myself still thinking and trying to better understand this sexist/anti-sexist debate that took place, and envision a possible anarchist standpoint. I found myself trying to bring together my experiences from participating in many different anarchist groups in England over seven years, my thoughts about anti-sexist comrades in international meetings against the G8 or EU summit, and in squats and social centers across Europe during tours and travels. Through rumors spread mainly by anti-sexists and nonviolent demonstrators it seems that many people believe that Greek anarchists are macho, sexist, and lacking in their theoretical understanding of sexism.

My goal in this essay is to use these international reflections in addition to my experiences during the social insurrection of December 2008 to offer some thoughts about an anarchist perspective on sexism and anti-sexism. The differences between societies in terms of culture and norms of behavior make the topic a vast one. The different cultures of resistance, scales of confrontation, targets of disobedience, perspectives, terminologies, and political agendas of this world make it impossible to speak in general about sexism and anti-sexism in the global anarchist movement. Many things I say here express the thoughts of male, female, and homosexual comrades here in Greece, while other comrades are in disagreement. I hope these thoughts can open a creative debate.

Of course not all anti-sexists are the same, but I am directing this criticism at what I see as a major part of the anti-sexists. My major problem with these anti-sexists is how they characterize certain people as sexists and the criteria they use.

Each comrade has to change her everyday life first and then, as the next step, to share her experiences and visions

248

with her friends, her community, and her society. Of course, we have to eliminate all the elements of capitalism, puritanism, sexism, greed, and apathy. The anarchist society—as we imagine it, and work, and think and plan for it—is a different society from the one we live in. It could be said that anarchy is utopian—it is a network of honest human relationships free of the traps the elite have used for centuries to dominate us. Anarchy is a network of compassion and mutual aid without the taboos and limitations of organized religion, capitalism, and the State. Anarchy is the evolution to a more joyous form of life approaching the greatest possible freedom for all— the earth, the animals, humanity—where the people are not forced to follow one definite, obligatory way of life in order to survive.

A part of the fight against today's oppressions is the fight against sexism. But let's not make a distinction between sexism within the anarchist movement and sexism in society because we are still part of this dominant society. Similarly, though we reject the role of consumer and buy as little as possible, we are still socialized in Western capitalist ethics and still participate in the reproduction of Capital, even at this minimum level.

Many anarchists believe that we first have to fight against sexism inside the movement and then to fight against sexism in society in general, or even if they do not adopt this argument, their practice reflects an almost exclusive focus on internal sexism. The same people believe that if we destroy sexism within ourselves, then the anarchist movement will be more open and more powerful, and above all more revolutionary. These anti-sexist warriors think that one of the weaknesses of the revolutionary movement is that it is still not inclusive for revolutionary women. Additionally, they mention the suppressive and condescending attitude prevalent in meetings towards women who do not say anything in public but rather limit themselves to communicating in informal, personal situations.

These women don't speak except to respond to the kind of questions they are supposed to know about. The situationist Françoise Denevert, in her essay, "La Critique ad Mulierern" (1975), describes and remonstrates these silent women who, accidentally engaged in theoretical discussion, look worriedly from the edge of their eyes in search of acceptance from their boyfriend or a close male friend. They will never dare to admit their ignorance of a subject under discussion, and entangled in a confusion of thoughts or repeating what they heard someone else say, consider the difficulties they have as something to be ashamed of. Paradoxically, these same silent women, according to Denevert, are often eloquent writers, who themselves frequently comment about the discrepancy between their ability to express themselves in the written and spoken word.

In reality, the ability to speak and to write depends on the experiences of the person. It depends on self-cultivation, on socialization, on courage. There are men who are not good

249

speakers at all, and there are women who are not good speakers at all. We cannot say that men are good speakers and women are not; nor can we say that women are more sensitive than men, as it depends on which women and which men we have met. We cannot limit our analysis inside the anarchist space as there are friends outside of the anarchist space who are not sexist, just as there are friends in an assembly who are misogynists.

There are different women, there are different men, and there are people who are different independent of their sex. The characteristics of a personality are not sexually segregated. Passivity is not only a female characteristic and ribaldry is not only a male characteristic. What is traditionally defined to be masculinity and femininity are complementary and can appear in both men and women.

If we accept the complaints and arguments of the anti-sexists, automatically the "silent women" are recognized as having greater sensitivity and are unable to speak in public not because of the behavior of their male comrades but because of their sex. The anti-sexists lump together all the women who don't speak in an assembly without taking into consideration the differences between these women. So, the "silent women" and the watchers of the silent women are colonized by the theory of anti-sexism and see their selves the same as sexist society sees them. As Françoise Denevert was saying these women are colonized by the spectacle of their self, and they are colonized by the theory of anti-sexism. They enslave themselves in the obedience of the "silent woman."

In our struggles we must be aware of the injustice capitalism imposes on us, as the first step to realizing that something is wrong. But sometimes we see the enemy in a person, a theory, or a situation which is only a vessel for the sexist culture that shapes and oppresses them.

Sometimes after reading an anti-sexist text, we start thinking that our boyfriend is a disgusting, sexist pig who victimizes us, in the same way that after reading a psychology book we start diagnosing ourselves with imaginary paranoias.

Women can build an identity upon the historical oppression they all share, and base their very respect for one another on this shared history. Some women—feminists and anti-sexists—ask for recognition of woman as a political category. And this is not only in the liberal political groups but also in the anarchist scene. Judith Butler expresses a view that "the representation of the category 'women' is always exclusive, resulting in resistance to the domination that this representation claims. The category 'women' is constituted by a political system, including 'the State,' then a politics that takes this category as its foundation assists in the continual production of a hierarchical gender division. Feminism should understand how the category of 'women' is produced and restrained by these systems rather than seeking emancipation through structures of power."

Also, woman as political category can seek recognition of her liberation through an open assembly. But there

250

is a difference between creating an assembly structure that recognizes women's right to equal participation and allowing or expecting individual women to demand and seize the space for their equal participation. If we say that women are not capable of the latter, aren't we the ones putting them in a weaker position? There is an important difference between being emancipated and empowering oneself. There is a difference between recognition and demand. There is a difference between respecting a woman because she is a woman and respecting her because she is a respectable person.

Louise Michel[2] put her revolutionary beliefs in practice because her sexual identity did not prevent her from doing what she thought was right. She didn't want a special place just because she was a woman, she wanted to be recognized as a person regardless of her sex. She was consciously indifferent to existing agreements and compulsions based on her sex. She was recognized for her political importance thanks to her abilities, her radical nature, her courage, her decisiveness and her consistency in realizing her theory, and not because of her sex.

The revolutionaries are acrobats on the rope of theory who always fall, reaching too far in their quest to turn everything into politics. There is always the possibility of approaching anti-sexism and feminism as a class war and anti-capitalist issue only so that it is certified as a "valuable" political struggle. On the other hand, there is the possibility of approaching feminism and anti-sexism just as individual women and men with bad personal moments and sad experiences with our partners.

The anti-sexists aim for the permanent destruction of gender inequality in revolutionary activity; in other words, their aim is to destroy the roles that alienate both sexes and to clarify the limitations these roles impose on the revolutionary experience. They mean to destroy the contrast between femininity and masculinity as a difference that comes from gender as a social construction. But femininity, masculinity, and everything else are in the culture. Believing that femininity is just an element of the alienation of women and masculinity is only an element of the alienation of men leads to the possibility of losing our sexiness and our sensuality.

Judith Butler, in her 1993 interview by Peter Osborne and Lynne Segal in London, says that "One of the interpretations that has been made of *Gender Trouble* is that there is no sex, there is only gender, and gender is performative.[3] People then go on to think that if gender is performative it must be radically free. And it has seemed to many that the materiality of the body is vacated or ignored or negated here—disavowed,

251

---

2   Louise Michel (1830–1905) was a French anarchist, school teacher, and medical worker who participated in the Paris Commune. She treated her writings as emotional processes and not as intellectual ones. Her basic and most compelling feature was her ability to provoke both spontaneous anger against injustice in demonstrations and spontaneous assistance and mutual aid in wider society.

3   The difference between performance and performativity is that a performance presumes a subject but performativity contests the very notion of subject.

even. (There's a symptomatic reading of this as somatophobia. It's interesting to have one's text pathologized.) .... how it is that sex itself might be construed as a norm. Now, I take it that's a presupposition of Lacanian psychoanalysis—that sex is a norm. But I didn't want to remain restricted within the Lacanian purview. I wanted to work out how a norm actually materializes a body, how we might understand the materiality of the body to be not only invested with a norm, but in some sense animated by a norm, or contoured by a norm."

We can also see somatophobia as negating the care of our body because of the recognition that this care is governed by some norm. The acceptance of beauty, of sexuality, of the visible differences of the two sexes serves only as a capitalist alienation, taking away from the individual their very own individuality and connecting them to the undercover ideology of the capitalist norm.

An individual under capitalism presupposes the use of a capitalistic object and the application of such abstract concepts as alienation, passivity, and an implicit admission to let capitalism penetrate inside his body and mind. The individual, as an anarchist, classifies the penetration of the alienation based on the frequency and the character of the use, of the consumption of an object, of a product, and not on the consciousness of the use of the product.

The consciousness and the choice to use, to consume a product, seems much more an alienated choice and not an understanding of the very real distance between the object itself and the use of the object under capitalism. Everything seems to be lost in a relentless theorizing and an almost totalitarian relativism imposed by postmodern discourse and the need to define ourselves in the framework of yet another standard theory with the familiar standard enemy and standard allies.

The women who want to look the same as the supermodels and as the sex kittens on the magazine covers and the men who want to reproduce the hard and "macho" sexy man of the soap operas and newscasters relive "the society of the spectacle as simple promoters of the culture" (G. Debord). Yet the women who express their aggression towards men in order to show that they are not subjugated by any man, or the men who avoid an honest aggressive dialogue with women because they must behave gently otherwise they would be sexists, or even anarchist men and women who locate erroneous behaviors and explain them as sexist behaviors ... all of these are the dolls that merely confirm the spectacle of the anti-sexist theory. Truly anarchist men and women take every effort to avoid merely confirming the sexist spectacle and to fight against it, even if they have a lot of taboos, problems, theoretical dead-ends, and many both written and unwritten political agendas.

A woman can be an accomplice to the "masculinity" that she allows to be imposed on her. All women (both in the West and in the East, although in the East they will face humiliation and even torture) have the ability to demand their time to speak, to put their thoughts and their ideas into practice, to swear at a man when they don't like his behavior, to humiliate a man if they think that this man humiliated their gender or themselves.

On the other hand, Simone de Beauvoir in her 1976 interview with John Gerassi said that a secretary or the wife of a worker could not enjoy the privileges that she enjoyed as a woman because these women did not abandon their female nature and their life was defined, determined. Beauvoir as an existentialist accepts the principle that existence precedes essence. Therefore, she believes that no one is born a woman, but becomes one. She said that these women must be aware of their dependence and then they have to believe in their own force and the women who have an interest in cooperation with the male-dominated society must be made aware of their betrayal; however, Beauvoir's position supposes that only the women who are well educated are able to understand the social phenomena. Does this education come from a certificated institution? Of course not. All women can feel and enforce their freedom without reference to their job, class, age, and sexual desires.

We should not present the "silent women" as passive, innocent women because in this way these women are forced to not believe in their own thoughts and finally, feeling weak, to express only a childish anti-male identity based on intolerance. We should be careful that our theories do not turn the emancipated woman into some sort of compulsory asexual or "bitch" that just builds her identity on some immense

illustrative narrative of her politicized problems. In this way, she will never understand what exactly made her a "silent woman," and as an oppressed woman she will always be trapped in the explanations and excuses of an oppressive sexist society, never thinking deeper about her own limitations, fears, and insecurities.

Our theories should also not stereotype loutish men as oppressive men, because in this way the loutish men will only become more certain of the effectiveness of the patriarchal structures and repressive mechanisms that they reproduce as men. Cast as a group and not as individuals with unique whims, these men will not be able to understand that their behavior produces suffering not only for others but also for themselves. "Normal" identities and even identities that are based on going against these normal identities are attached to the fetters of the bourgeois morality or some caricature of revolutionary morality. The first morality is the passport for the reliable slaves of the State and the other is the passport for the reliable revolutionaries who have been conquered by the morality of the bourgeoisie, as they define themselves in negation to their bourgeois morality. But we don't want any kind of passport or permission to follow revolutionary ideas. Even if there were an anarchist morality, we would be the heretics.

A claim for a morality that would be suitable for all is an illusion. What is fair for one person can be restrictive for another. An "objective" morality that treats all individuals the same without taking into consideration the particularities (the

253

enormous difference between people) is a slave morality. Each individual can make up their own morality and their own criterion for dignity, within the twin limits of schizophrenia and freedom.

Each identity group can define a "self." Experiences, participation, and actions with different groups create certain idiosyncrasies. Various expressions of our self can coexist and these give us the ability to explore new phenomena and social relations. Any kind of ideology that is incapable of understanding social phenomena only makes us objects of that ideology. Throughout the ages a socially aware person has been able to express vastly more intelligence and sensitivity in understanding social phenomena than a person entrenched in ideology. An activist acting in multiple struggles across identity groups is then far more capable of enacting revolution as compared to one who has a constructed identity in a specific group. This is the multi-expressional activist.

It is necessary for every person as an individual to resist, struggle, demand, and scream for their freedom. Nobody should be more respectful in relation to others. We don't want men who will continue to express their macho status at any price nor women who will mourn because of their treatment by men. Using our political consciousness, we need to know and *feel* that men who dominate or behave badly with women are legitimizing the existing structures of authority and contributing to a wider net of domination which holds people back.

Sexism refers to when someone, woman or man, believes that his or her sex is superior or the opposite inferior, proficient or incapable, valuable or worthless compared with the other gender. Sexist behaviors confirm and continue to apply male and female stereotypes, and are influenced by and reproduce these impressions and beliefs. But we should not forget that the leveling of differences is disorienting since it disrespects the particularities. It is impossible to simultaneously sustain basic sexist personal characteristics and try to eliminate the inequality between the two sexes. At the same time we want to be ourselves, to keep expressing our unique individuality. As Emma Goldman said, "the mass and the individual, the true democrat and the true individual, man and woman, can meet without antagonism and opposition." In her opinion, women have the right to love and be satisfied sexually but if women are the only ones to emancipate themselves while the whole society doesn't change, these women would remain without an appropriate partner.

If women are released from their bonds while the remaining society is imprisoned by its bonds then their emancipation would not last. Liberation is not only for women. When we smash all barriers, liberation and emancipation will be the path to total freedom, liberation from obedience, the standard of morality, and the power of authority. We say this just to remind ourselves to avoid the traps of the heroic woman.

Sexism has spread everywhere, in every way we relate. Our comrades are not sexist but the authoritarian logic that anti-sexists borrow in order to distinguish them as sexists is sexist. Who exactly are sexists and who are anti-sexists? Are these roles absolutely separated? Where are the borders of sexism and anti-sexism? The agreement on these distinctions, as these distinctions are created by our social norms, is sexist.

The slogan of identity politics is "the celebration of difference." Yet it is a celebration of complacency. That identity is something fixed and everlasting is an illusion. It is absurd to demand rights through the validation of victimization. I agree that there should be a "celebration of difference" but from another route to another destination. We can celebrate all together or we can celebrate as individuals who constitute themselves with the characteristics that the society and the state provide us. Identity needs to be analyzed philosophically and politically. Anti-sexism bases its dialectics on cultural categories (macho men and oppressed women) constructed, maintained, and used by the dominant culture. The definition of a specific denigrated sex, race, or social-economic class maintains the homogeneous culture of the dominant moralism, the specific categorization that something detectable reflects the common sense made by the statists, the sexists, and the racists. Marginalization doesn't end with the creation of marginalized groups. The division creates two groups, two categories. The division occurs when we deny the struggle of a group based on identity but it also occurs when the sup-

porters, the participants, divide themselves and name their comrades as enemies.

Creating two opposite groups means that in theory and in practice, there is a conflict between them that must be solved. All behaviors are scanned by the undervalued sex. This is necessary as the sexists don't notice the behaviors of their sex object since they are hypnotized by stereotypes of the two sexes. The anti-sexists examine every manner, every timbre and tone of the voice, any expression of the sexist and patriarchal macrocosm.

Language shapes us, composes us, and forms us. Language is based not on words per se but on the use of this word and the meaning of it at a specific time and place. However, the anti-sexist hysteria with language, with both creating new words and not using certain words, only makes those feel guilty who express themselves using words in a colloquial manner. This leads to a dead-end even if it is simple and convenient to base the effects of sexism on just words. Phenomena such as metaphors, irony, and exaggeration abound in language. The meaning of a sentence cannot be captured solely by the definitions of the words that constitute the sentence. Those purporting to be anti-sexist only end up as jailers of semantics and detectives of the prohibited colloquial expressions.

In practice, the participants of an identity group, and especially some anti-sexists, keep watch over their members, their comrades in meetings, and in everyday life by imposing a certain identity, a fully determined behavior code that

255

implicitly presents a united homogeneous identity. Some anti-sexists posit men's behavior to be a direct result of stereotypes from the sexist society, analyzing people as a definite result of a definite cause. Many of them are also essentialists, ignoring the complexity of social relations and homogenizing individuals in order to fit them into categories, without taking into consideration cultural, psychological, and historical differences, or allowing the individual to occasionally exist unburdened by any political analysis, to just be a person rather than the alienated product of inhuman social mechanisms. What we say and what we think are uncertain and chaotic.

The lace around us is so tight and we want to loosen it. The fashion, the lipstick, and the high heels, the expensive dresses and the modern styles are obligatory. However, a girl can decide to wear a short white dress, high heels, and red lipstick and have political consciousness. An anti-sexist would likely consider this girl to be stupid and not take her opinion seriously. Now, who here is sexist? Once trapped in anti-sexism, we found ourselves hidden under a rough exterior and we lose our femininity.

The Church teaches fear, humility, decency, frugality, and submissiveness as important elements of a faithful Christian. The Church teaches the inferiority of women, presupposing that women fall easily into sin, so that she has to be a faithful believer and loyal supporter of the authority of men, like her husband, her father, her brother. How many of us have Christian parents, how many of us heard stories about Jesus and the Virgin Mary? Most official religions are oppressive towards women. We—men, women, transsexuals, homosexuals, hermaphrodites—have thousands of years of patriarchy and submission to confront and a heritage of elitism, feudalism, and the whole industrial society to eliminate from our minds and our memories.

For hundreds of years patriarchal societies have not just given birth to obedient, submissive women. These very same societies have given birth to wild, liberated beings, to goddesses and orgiastic women, revolutionaries and poets, dreamers and wild witches. The past cannot be separated from the present; it will always leave its mark on the structures of today. In order to open the path to the future, we need to fight the obstacles we have inherited from the past and not the past itself. The unfinished battles of the sexual revolution leave us with habits, behaviors, and beliefs from the conservative society of the beginning of the 20th century. To overcome this conservatism, we need to identify which of these characteristics are actually obstacles rather than trying to erase all reminders of the past, as many anti-sexists do.

At the same time as the church enforces an antisexual Puritanism, capitalism sells—through all kind of media and advertisements—cynical hedonism and egoist sexism as symbols of social status and the modern way of life. So, naturally, it is easy for people who want to fight sexism, in their effort to avoid cynical capitalistic sexism, to reproduce puritanical attitudes or asexual ways of life. On the other hand, it is possible for those who choose to fight against Christian morality and puritanical social codes to trap themselves in an egoistic, sexually extreme life and self-approved fetishism accompanied by an inability to create and sustain long-term love relationships. These are two problems that we have to face day after day in our struggle for erotic, joyous love relationships.

Comrades can adopt a puritanical opposition to sex and sexuality, and so embrace censorship, control, and suppression against pornography and all kinds of eroticism. This repressive behavior is rooted in systems of values that will need years, decades, and even centuries to be uprooted. Only then will sexism cease to exist. But my dear, today we cannot be non-sexist in a society where there are institutions of hierarchy and there are relations of power and domination. The oppression and opposition to our dreams come from all the dominant, authoritarian social mechanisms rather than simply masculine men, patriarchal behaviors, and sexism.

Anarchist women and men need to see gender-based injustice as an expression of the dominant culture's ethos and avoid hypocrisy with an anti-sexist logic. We need to deconstruct the dominant reality, the substructure of this civilization. We need to deny the morality of the present time and the meanings of the words.

We need to move beyond understanding sexism as an individual issue or singularly as an institutional, social or cultural problem. Sexism is a social problem and an individual issue simultaneously. Society and the individual feed each other, having a reciprocal relationship. Are not single-issue struggles a part of the whole? An analysis and political struggle based on some "objective" feature only creates groups that are categorized by these traits (gender for sexism, race for racism, class for classism, nationality for nationalism). Identity politics only reinforces identities that are maintained, rationalized, validated by the sexists, the racists, the nationalists, the rulers.

We want to reverse the entire dominant culture. Identification and association with a group are not sufficient. Divided struggles based on identity cannot destroy the dominant reality from its singularity.

Joshua Gamson, a sociologist, argues that there is a dilemma: if the ethnic/essentialist maintenance of boundaries and the queer/deconstructionist destabilization of boundaries make sense. Gamson believes that queer politics reveal the limitations of essentialist gay and lesbian identity politics that inherently strengthen binary divisions, including the divisions between man/woman and hetero/homo that are produced by political oppression. But, he says that "the deconstructionist" strategies remain quite deaf and blind to the very concrete and violent institutional forms to which the most logical answer is resistance in and through a particular collective identity. To borrow a saying of sociologist Jeffrey Weeks, "operational identities are necessary fictions."

The capitalist system is sexist, it promotes an "objective" norm of beauty. Capitalism is all about profit and destroys the planet with the industries that produce consumer goods.

257

Capitalism sells water, food, art, philosophy, our radical history, love, and sex. Capitalism uses the human body as a piggy bank. Capitalism uses images of a happy family or of a man who loves a woman to sell merchandise, private education, and bank loans. Capitalism uses our sexual desires to sell cars, shampoos, and toothpastes.

Our everyday decisions and practices sustain state institutions and markets that reproduce this world. Our obligation, our participation, and unconscious need to be a link in the chain of production keeps this system alive. All these days and years in offices, schools, universities, shops, and supermarkets keep this society functioning and expanding. Our discipline increases the greed of this system. Our struggles against sexism, against racism, against homophobia, against social apathy, and obedience to fashion, mass media and egocentrism, are all parts of a struggle for cultural and social change.

Confronting certain individual behaviors is synonymous with confronting the regime. The revolution is a constant process of mutation and a conscious decision to define the conditions within which we live. Each of us, as an individual with her friends or her lover, needs to make the first jump beyond this given reality. As radical individuals we are rabid for the destruction of this world; when we fight we are fighting for our lives. We decide to fight for total freedom motivated by our dreams and not by the decisions of some assembly or group. Sometimes loyalty to a group, to a collective, can

become compulsive but the loyalty to the beat of our heart is above all politics. There will always be men and women and children who will be very impudent or kind, raunchy or shy, vulgar or polite, saucy or gentle, nymphomaniac or asexual.

Capitalism would still not be threatened if we stopped being sexist, but if we quit our jobs and dropped out of the universities then the capitalist system could collapse. Even if these actions did not cause it to collapse, we would have more time to dedicate to the procedures of the war against the State, more time to dedicate to our cultural revolution, more time to dedicate to the barricades, more time to dedicate to the cultivation of ourselves (to understand the phenomena and have critical thought) independently of wage slavery and time spent in the classrooms. This is time that we don't give to friends, to lovers, to assemblies and squats and demonstrations and fights and projects, these hours that we offer to the system, the hours that we don't share with loved ones are our chains.

Some people think that the biggest problem of the Greek anarchist movement is that it is sexist. As a Greek anarchist woman I think the biggest problem is that the anarchist movement cannot explain to society how an anarchist world could function. We don't have applied anarchist social economics.

As we cultivate ourselves, we cultivate the community around us in a cycle of constant interdependence. We, as anarchists, must be aware of struggling against the dominant cultural ethos, to live and experience life, with our limits. We fight for the vision of our dreams and the breadth of our visions. We fight authority wherever we meet it.

Sexism outside and inside capitalism will corrode as we appear in every neighborhood, in every march, in every rebellion, both small and large. We will confront issues, start conversations and critiques, and share ideas and dreams so that we will not see anti-sexism as a separate issue, separated from the whole body of revolution.

We are fighting for gay and lesbian power as we fight for the elimination of the State. We fight for identity and gender issues as we fight against repression and exploitation. We fight for the freedom of transsexuals as we fight for our freedom. Maybe we are not transsexual, and maybe in our country a girl can kiss another on her red lips, but in Uganda, Morocco, and Saudi Arabia it is illegal and dangerous and you could be put in prison for a kiss like that. In our country it is not illegal to be homosexual but in many countries your parents can have you committed. We fight for women's liberation and we fight against sexism.

We grow up in a sexist society that imbues us with the idea that women are inferior to men. Anti-sexism is not just about fighting against forms of sexism like violent rape, domestic violence, and overtly sexist words, it is also about challenging our relationships, the ideas that create a rape culture, the way that the people are socialized, our needs, our desires, our passions.

Anti-sexists challenge the ideas and behaviors that promote masculine sexism and alienated women, both in personal relationships and in social and political groups. But we have to remember that the relationships are not so simple, they are always complicated.

We are human, and men exist and women exist, as different as all of us are different. Some people are shy while some aren't, some people are charismatic while some aren't. Some women are sensitive and some aren't, some men are fat and some aren't. Some humans have a dick and some others have a pussy... some women shave their pussy and others do not. Some women are more masculine and some aren't, some men are more feminine and some aren't. Some men are more "macho" than others and some are not "macho" at all. Some women are nymphomaniac and some unorgasmic.

Masculinity and femininity is a personal trait, a personal relish. It is matter of taste if someone likes a macho man or an effeminate man, just as it is a matter of taste when a man likes a teenager or an adult, a BDSM mistress or a willing slave. Masculinity and sexism are different. Some masculine anarchist men gain a superficial understanding of the sexism in society by reading about women's liberation and feminism, and fight for anti-sexism within the anarchist movement. But it is a pseudo-analysis and pseudo-politics when we try to analyze and separate the anarchist movement from the whole society, a micro-logic for a micro-analysis. The anarchist space is not somewhere else, it is not a different planet so we cannot analyze its own community, separate from capitalism. The anarchists are not saints living on holy mountains, living in foreign lands far from their grandmothers and fathers.

259

We can have self-criticism about anarchist spaces without paralyzing ourselves. The women who I know participate and contribute as much as they can and as they want in the movement, before, during, and after December. No comrade stops them, no one disrespects them, no one interrupts them in a meeting because they are women. People interrupt a woman in a meeting as they could interrupt a man if they don't respect or don't agree with what they say, not because of their gender. There are not masculine and feminine discussions, there are not masculine direct actions, and there are not separations and exclusions for girls and boys in their participation. If there is a particular majority of one sex, that doesn't mean the resistance takes on the characteristics of this sex, as each sex is flexible and influenced by the other sex. There is no masculine or feminine participation in resistance: there is only resistance. Women are not treated as a weak gender and they don't have a secondary role in the street fights, in arson attacks, in meetings, and in decision-making.

Dualism separates reality into two parts, the good and the bad. The anti-sexists are the good ones and the sexists are the bad ones. Anti-sexists focus on the authority of men as oppressive, but anarchists have to fight against the oppression of authoritarian society in total. The anarchists fight against alienation, exploitation, and power as a whole as expressed through decisions, hopes, activities, and plans of each member of this society. A part of this fight is the fight against sexism.

The whole world—our friends, our parents, our trips, our acid-trips, our readings, our listening—influences us. We choose to free ourselves from normality to become the most extreme of beings. We want to break through identities established by society, by tradition, and even by anarchist spaces. This deconstruction does not have to lead to nihilism; we can deconstruct these identities in order to arrive at a new synthesis, new understandings, and new horizons.

We encourage women to participate in actions and events as we encourage men and kids and grandmothers to participate in them. Is it mostly men or women who are taking up speaking engagements? Who talks at meetings? Who facilitates meetings? Who does the work of the organization, and then, who gets credit for it? These questions can be answered but this becomes mere statistics. In the world of chaos theory, the statistics of normality don't work!

"Join The Resistance…Fall in Love."

We want to celebrate our fluid identities and not a newly constructed political identity. The anarchist movements fight against sexism but they are not identified with a separate anti-sexist ideology. We can define what sexist behavior is but not what an anti-sexist behavior has to be. The anarchist activists fight against sexism but not through a separate ideological identity of "anti-sexists." The society maintains sexism as long as we don't fight against authority, exploitation, and alienation.

Now there are more social centers in Thessaloniki

the evenings there is usually cinema, some documentaries or films, maybe a presentation. It's nice, you should come.

Adriani and Flora: Two students of the Aristoteleous University of Thessaloniki

We really started to become active in December. Two years earlier, during the student movement, we voted for the occupation in our assembly but we weren't really active, you know?

December was incredible. All the people were out in the streets, it was unstoppable. There was a lot of destruction. I'm from the part of the movement that is against the destruction, but... it was good that it happened. It made it clear that it won't be tolerated when the police kill a young boy.

Now there are more social centers in Thessaloniki, I don't know how many exactly, but many. I like to go to Buenaventura. It's like a social and cultural center. Yfanet is nice but for normal people it's not so open. Delta, Yfanet, they're older buildings, a little bit dirty. They have a different feeling, a different aesthetic. But Buenaventura is a new building and it's very nice, very clean. It's also run by anarchists but it's open, it's easy for normal people to come to. They have lots of events, like free language classes. I take Japanese lessons there. And in

Many people were saying that they want Bulgarian society to be "like in Greece"

Jana : An anarchist and blogger from Bulgaria

Initially the mass media demonized the Greek anarchists and tried to present them as terrorists and so on. Once it was clear that the revolt went beyond anarchists the mass media attempted to understand what was happening. Most stories were absurd—referring to ancient Greece or the "hotness of the southern blood." There were some liberal understandings—the "economic crisis" argument and a struggle against corruption.

Many people here in Bulgaria were sympathetic to what they understood as a greater level of concern for social issues in Greek society. I do not think those people were sympathetic because of what had been shown in the media, which as I said was often contradictory, incomplete, and very simplistic. Neither was it for any reasons people developed themselves, separate from the media interpretations. I think there was much sympathy because people would project their own beliefs, ideas, and anger onto what was going on. People saw Greece as a rebellion against the injustices they perceived themselves. For example, the liberals saw it as a rebellion against corruption, the nationalists/patriots saw that the Greeks cared for the children. Many people in Bulgaria are also angry at the isolation, alienation, and ultra-individualism of this society, even though they would express it in different language, depending on their politics. I think people were happy that someone was rebelling and jealous and self-deprecating that it doesn't happen here. This kind of self-hate is common here: "In foreign countries it is always better."

In order to organize solidarity we were translating and trying to spread information on the Internet. We translated everything from sites like the *Voices from Occupied London* blog.[1] Many people we didn't know before were very interested and the website hits went up dramatically. Some people even joined to help with translations.

As for any real solidarity, the leftist student group *Priziv,* whom we work with, organized a small event. There was a discussion in Sofia University and then a small solidarity protest. There were only thirty or forty people, but this is normal for here. It was peaceful and there weren't many police. They didn't bother us when we stuck our posters on the door of the Greek Embassy, even though the protest was unpermitted, which is unusual.

The fascist reaction to the Greek rebellion was quite interesting. At first the fascists just demonized anarchists on

---

1   Ed: This blog was perhaps the most important point of translation and diffusion for Greek texts in English, and also responsible for some of the translations in this book.

their websites. They said, *you see what the anarchists are doing,* saying that anarchists do not respect property, they are lazy they have a destructive ideology, and that they do not respect police authority. But once they understood that this was not going to stop after a few days they stopped writing shit on their websites. Probably most of them felt angry that they weren't in revolt like the Greeks.

In December a student in his twenties was killed in a fight on the student campus in Sofia. He was attacked by a group of drunk guys who beat him to death. The students politicized his death. They were under the strong influence of the images coming from Greece. There is a high level of everyday violence in Bulgaria and it is not the first case of a similar murder, but usually people do not pay much attention. At least the attention is not manifested in the public sphere, but is limited to individualized complaints. Many young people felt, for nationalistic reasons, that the Bulgarian youth should care more about Bulgarian children, like the youth in Greece. Leftist students tried to show that this murder, as well as the very high levels of violence on the student campus, is linked to the heavy process of commercialization that is going on there. The Sofia student campus has the most clubs and bars in the whole city. They are mostly owned and used by the mafia and people inspired by the gangster, macho lifestyle— one that praises brutal violence as a way to assert oneself into the patriarchal and strongly conservative social order—and is extremely widespread in post-socialist capitalism.

The family of the boy who was killed also saw structural reasons for the death. They called out for action against the conditions that allowed it to happen. Some of the leftist students met with them.

The murder was also politicized by one right-wing populist student group, SROKSOS. They were using some of the slogans that were coming out of Greece, which they had probably read in the texts that we translated, along with ultraconservative slogans like "we are the oldest state in Europe."

In December a demo was organized by both the leftist and the populist group. This may sound stupid and maybe it was a mistake, but I support the leftists in their decision to cooperate with the populists at that time, because they managed to push more radical demands and to identify commercialization (which is heavily linked with the mafia lifestyle) as the structural reason behind the high levels of destructive violence. Also at that moment it was not clear how conservative SROKSOS actually were. The demo was organized in cooperation with environmentalists as well. It went okay, even though one of the fascist parties tried to infiltrate and lead the protest—but they couldn't in the end, because people wouldn't allow them to do so. Many people joined the demo, which I think would not have happened without what was going in Greece at the same time. Many people were saying, the conservatives as well, that they wanted Bulgarian society to be "like in Greece," as people were often putting it.

Another demo was announced for the 14th of January, again co-organized by the students and the environmentalists. Soon we understood that the conservative students unilaterally decided to cooperate with the fascists and the leftist student group left the organization. The right-wing populist students decided to play the national vanguard calling out for "national" protests, completely void of meaning, just empty talk, to be interpreted at will. We, the anarchists, published a declaration that we were not involved, as well as a warning of what was going to happen on the 14th, and some of the press published our position. It was good that we made it, because there were already many stories in the press demonizing anarchists and scaring people with some mythical Greek football hooligans that were coming to return the favor after some Bulgarian anarchists helped in the Greek riots. We also met with the environmentalists to warn them, but they were a bit naïve and they didn't take us seriously. They didn't really think SROKSOS met with fascists, and obviously the fascists don't define themselves as such. This time they were disguised as a "sports organization," though SROKSOS clearly knew who they were cooperating with.

At the so-called national protest there were a lot of people, thanks to the empty, nationalistic language that was used in the mobilization. On the 14th there were all kinds of contradictory groups and demands—neoliberal political elites, fascists, environmentalists, some fanatics who were demanding that old people should not have voting rights, students demanding nationalization of the student campus and so on. It was absurd.

The fascists were separated into some kind of a nazi black bloc; they use this kind of style here, copying it from the German national-autonome. In the end there was a big nazi riot all over the center of Sofia. Its images attracted a lot of media attention and often it was interpreted as a continuation of the Greek revolt. The images they would see probably confused them even more, as the Bulgarian nazis wear black outfits and try to imitate the anarchists. In the *Guardian* or somewhere there was that article saying this was the first credit crunch riot spreading from Greece to other countries. Some people have a very simplistic understanding of politics. They think some economic indexes change in percentage and afterwards riots automatically follow. I am not saying there are no structural reasons for people's discontent, but discontent can go in many directions. Also there are many reasons for anger. It is not as the liberals, who mainly see corruption, nor as the traditional Left, who can only see economic crisis and degradation, would have it.

The next step is to create the places where all the people can meet

Little John: An anarchist who has been active for ten years, and is involved with one of Thessaloniki's squatted social centers, Fabrika Yfanet

In the last few years at Fabrika Yfanet, we've to developed structure necessary to organize open events. We've mostly done ideological work: publishing texts and forming groups that took on a specific theme, organizing actions and discussions, participating in demonstrations, communicating to others about how we organized. And direct action of course. The space is basically a political social center. It's not just a social center where people can be creative or come to fulfill certain needs, although this is a part of it. The difference is that the assembly of Yfanet is also a political assembly that involves itself in campaigns, makes political posters—we have a presence in the city.

You could say that lots of young people started to get involved through Yfanet. In recent years the anarchist movement has spread ideas about different ways to resist, and I think that offering this allowed December to happen. But in Thessaloniki, after December, you didn't see lots of young people coming to the social centers wanting to get involved. Part of the reason is that Yfanet was a bit closed at this time. People were at meetings in the universities and here we only had small, closed meetings, so as a building or a structure it didn't work for the masses. It worked for a smaller group of people who needed it. But in general Yfanet is an open place. You see many different people going there and they can see that it's a place that's open for them too. Maybe they don't participate in the assemblies, but going there has become normal for them and we can communicate without alienating them.

I think the State has begun its counterinsurgency, yet we don't understood what has happened. We can't find the time to discuss it calmly, so I don't know. There are a lot of questions we still have to answer. Since December so many people are talking about anarchists, they want to know what anarchism is, so for me the next step is to create places where all the people can meet—maybe on the basis of a common need. It can't be a one time thing, it must be a response to a need people experience every day, or a response to something that oppresses us every day. A new strategy that came out of Athens that is inspiring lots of people is to initiate local, neighborhood assemblies.

In December this cinema was squatted, Olympian cinema, in the city center, and all sorts of people came there to talk with anarchists, to participate. It was strange because we weren't ready to propose anything, we were there just trying to organize a meeting. But all these new people came and it turned into an interview with the anarchists: Why this? Why that? What do you want to do? This shows that people wanted to do more and to find ways to participate. We weren't ready for this, and next time we have to do it better.

So we're starting with neighborhood assemblies, getting used to talking with people from outside the movement. We're doing this in our neighborhood now, near Yfanet. We had to find a neutral place, not a squat, where everyone would feel comfortable. I think that maybe in five years it will be working great. Ha! It's also happening in a few other neighborhoods. And other people are starting new social centers, like one in the western part of the city where there has never been anything. And this is all the product of December.

But the State wants to stop it. In the newspapers today it said that law had to be brought to the squats and the police had to be able to enter them to see if illegal activities were taking place. And they tried to connect it to the student occupations. In the newspapers they confused everything—the students, the anarchists, random crimes happening near the universities. They try to blame it all on the occupations to scare people so they'll want the police to come protect them. They want to criminalize the squats and the anarchists. It could be a preparation for some kind of repression.

The Rebellion, the Workplaces, and the Rank'N'File Unions: EXTRACT FROM "THE REBELLIOUS PASSAGE OF A PROLETARIAN MINORITY THROUGH A BRIEF PERIOD OF TIME"

TPTG

To discuss the reasons why the rebellion did not extend to the workplace—a question often asked by comrades abroad—we need first to be more analytical about certain segments of the proletariat. From our knowledge, those workers who can be described either as "workers with a stable job," or non-precarious, had very limited participation in the rebellion, if any. For those stable workers who actually took part in the rebellion, to try and extend it to their workplaces would mean engaging in wildcat strikes outside and against trade unions, since most strikes are called and controlled by them. In the last twenty years many strikes have been called in the public sector (education, public utility services, some ministries). These past struggles have shown that the workers were not able to create autonomous forms of organization, and move beyond the trade unionist demands.

Occupations of workplaces have only taken place as defensive struggles against closures or relocations, mostly of textile factories. But even those, as well as most strikes, in the previous years have by and large ended in defeat.

Capitalism in Greece is characterized by a low concentration of capital resulting in small firms where even fewer than ten people are employed and almost no unionism exists. The precarious waged workers, one of the main subjects of the rebellion, who mainly work in such places, do not consider them to be a terrain of proletarian power and mobilization. In most cases they are not attached to their job. Possibly it was their inability or even unwillingness to mobilize on the job that made young precarious workers take to the streets. Moreover, like we said before, this first *urban rebellion* in Greece was, like all modern urban rebellions, a violent eruption of *delegitimization* of capitalist institutions of control and, what's more, a short-lived experience of a *communal life against separations and outside the workplaces*—with the notable exception of the universities and the municipality of Aghios Dimitrios. In the case of precarious workers, extending the rebellion to their workplaces would mean wildcats and occupations and nothing less. Given the practical possibilities there and their subjective disposition, such activity was both unfeasible and undesirable.

However, many rebels realized these limits and tried to make such a leap. The occupation of the central offices of the General Confederation of Labor of Greece (GSEE) stemmed from the need for workplace action and to undermine the media coverage of the rebellion as a "youth protest at the expense of the workers' interests." Besides, it offered an opportunity to expose the undermining role of GSEE itself in the rebellion. The initiative was taken by some members of the rank'n'file union of couriers, who are mostly antiauthoritarians. However, during the occupation it became obvious that the rank'n'file version of unionism could not relate to the rebellion. There were two, although not clear-cut, tendencies even at the preparation assembly: a unionist-workerist one and a proletarian one. For the unionist-workerist tendency the occupation should have had a distinct "worker" character as opposed to the so-called youth or "metropolitan" character of the rebellion, while those in the second tendency saw the occupation as only one moment of the rebellion, as an opportunity to attack one more institution of capitalist control and as a meeting point of high school students, university students, unemployed, waged workers, and immigrants, that is as one more community of struggle in the context of the general unrest. In fact, the unionist-workerist tendency tried to use the occupation as an instrument of the union, and the idea of a base unionism, independent of political influences, in general. This didn't work. That's why some of them remained there just for two days.

As far as the rest of the "independent" left unions are concerned, things were even worse. There was only one assembly of trade unionists in the Faculty of Law on December 10th where several left bureaucrats stressed the need for a "political prospect" in the rebellion, meaning a political and unionist

267

mediation expressed in a list of populist demands. They rejected any proposals for violent action and pompously called for general assemblies and agitation at the workplaces for a general strike after one week—needless to say that nothing of the sort was ever tried.

In January the media workers that had participated actively in the rebellion occupied the offices of the corporatist journalists' trade union. The Union of Editors of the Daily Newspapers of Athens (ESIEA) is the main journalists' trade union in Greece. It includes journalists from the major Athenian newspapers, many of whom are at the same time employers because they are TV producers or they own newspapers, while it excludes those journalists who work with precarious contracts or are hired as "freelancers." The occupation of ESIEA focused broadly on two issues: the first was work relations focusing on the widespread precariousness in the media industry and the fragmented form of union organization of the media workers; the second was the control of information by the official media, the way the revolt was "covered" by them and how counter-information could be produced by the movement.

After the end of the occupation the same people created an assembly of media workers, students, and unemployed that organized a series of actions at various workplaces against layoffs, or attempted layoffs, and "covered" demos and other activities of the movement in a way that was against the dominant propaganda. Many members of this assembly are former students of the Faculty of Mass Media and Communication

and took part in the students' movement against the university reform in 2006–07. Others had for years worked to create a new union that would include all the media workers. Right now workers in the media industry are organized in fifteen different unions (photographers, journalists, cameramen, clerical staff etc). The idea is to create a union that will include all workers, regardless their position, from cleaners to journalists, and their labor contract, from full-time employees to "freelancers." Recently they tried to coordinate their activity with that of the laid off workers of the newspaper *Eleftheros Typos*.

On December 23rd in Petralona, an old working class neighborhood in Athens, a Bulgarian immigrant cleaner, Konstantina Kuneva, the General Secretary of the Janitors Union (PEKOP-All Attica Union for Janitors and Home Service Personnel), was the victim of an attack using sulfuric acid by goons of the bosses while returning home from her workplace, a railroad station of the ISAP public utility (Athens-Pireaus Electric Trains). She was seriously wounded, losing the use of one eye and of her vocal chords and she is still in the hospital. It's worth mentioning that she had also visited the occupation of GSEE since her previous activities had led her to a confrontation with the leadership of the confederation bureaucracy. The attack on Konstantina took place a couple of days after the end of the occupation of GSEE and that was one of the reasons why there was such an unprecedented mobilization of people. After the attack, a "solidarity assembly" was formed.

Using direct action tactics they organized a series of actions (occupation of the headquarters of ISAP, sabotage of the ticket machines so that the commuters could travel free, demos). The assembly, despite its internal divisions, played a vital role in inspiring a remarkable solidarity movement that expanded throughout Greece demanding not only the prosecution of the perpetrators and the instigators but also the abolition of subcontracting altogether. We should add here that outsourcing cleaning services has become the norm for public sector's companies and these companies do not hire cleaners any more. Contractors are now the employers of thousands of janitors, mainly women immigrants, who clean hundreds of public utilities, hospitals, railroad stations, schools, universities and other public buildings. However, regarding the character of cleaning sector jobs, these were always precarious and until recently it was regarded as normal and natural for a woman to be a janitor or home service worker. Moreover, by equating subcontracting or precariousness in general with "slavery," the majority of this solidarity movement, mainly comprised of leftist union activists, is trying to equate certain struggles against precariousness—one of the main forms of the capitalist restructuring in this historical moment—with *general political demands* of a social-democratic content regarding the State as a "reliable" and preferable employer to private subcontractors and thus putting the question of the abolition of wage labor *per se* aside.

More old people and leftists are coming closer to the anarchist ideas

Elina: An unemployed anarchist from Agrinio

Agrinio is a small town of 80,000 people with a radical history in western Greece. The anarcho-syndicalists were very active here, and there was a major tobacco strike in the '20s. And this is the city where the Anarchist Union started. I think that was the '70s but I'm not very good with the chronology. The anarchists in Agrinio thought that all the anarchists should come together, and also that they should be more social. This was at the time when other anarchists were taking up arms, like ELA (Popular Revolutionary Struggle). But the Anarchist Union failed. They had their assembly in Agrinio and Athens and Thessaloniki but in the other cities it stopped working. Later there was the Anarchist Federation of West Greece, it was mostly anarchist-communists, and Agrinio participated, but this also failed.

There were riots in Agrinio in December, of course. There were demonstrations with four hundred, five hundred people, and they smashed the banks. Lots of high school students participated, as well as the anarchists, including anarchists of the older generations and from the villages around Agrinio.

This is what made December a rebellion, the fact that it came to all the small cities and the villages. Otherwise it would have just been a huge demonstration, a huge riot, in Athens.

Most people, normal people, were glad when they saw the smashed banks. My aunt went out to see the broken windows because she said it made her happy. She was calling all her friends on her mobile phone, saying "They smashed all the banks here! And here too!" all full of joy. But in a small village you can't smash so many things since you usually know the person who owns it. Because of this there were some conflicts between Alpha Kappa and the Black Bloc anarchists here, with some people telling others not to smash certain shops.

After December you can see the difference. The thing didn't stop with the demonstrations. Right after December antiauthoritarians of Agrinio made a new social center, it's the second one, there already was one anarchist social center. The antiauthoritarian group Aura of Freedom, along with a cultural hip-hop collective, rented a building, painted it, fixed it up, and started hosting events. And some of the young people who became active in December are still participating. But it's not just young people, some older people are participating as well. A colleague of my mother teaches classes in the new social center. There are also two new pirate radio stations, Radiourgia and Kokkinoskoufitsa. Kokkinoskoufitsa means "Little Red Riding Hood," actually. It was the name of the pirate radio station here in the '80s and '90s so in a way it's been reincarnated in the struggles of our times.

I think the major result of December in Agrinio and maybe other villages and towns in the countryside has been that more women and men in their 30s and 40s, people from the generations of our grandfathers and our fathers, and also more leftists, are coming nearer to the anarchist and antiauthoritarian ideas.

Now I really know what terrorism means

Lito: The Exarchia resident who filmed the killing of Alexis and became the principal witness in the trial of the two cops responsible

I remember telling myself some years ago that I lived in a military camp, with all the police around Exarchia. Now I say that I live in a war zone. What happened in December, I never believed that it could happen. For me, there was always a limit, a final line, and when the police crossed it, there was a qualitative change. Everything changed. Everyone understood that there was a certain horizon to the situation and beyond it everything was different. We have passed this horizon. It is not a conflict anymore, it is war.

For a month after the killing I felt rage, but also an unbelievable silence. It was the first time in ten years that Exarchia has been silent, dead silent. It was very disconcerting. Now I've had some time to think about everything but in the very beginning I was completely exhausted from talking about it, all the questions. I put my video on Indymedia and from there the TV stations picked it up. Soon journalists were calling me constantly, and I was seeing my video everywhere. For the first few months I was in a very strange state. I was never calm. I was in a state of shock for a month. Now I feel more better, but whenever I hear a certain sound… the stun grenade that the police threw a few minutes before they killed Alexis triggered a security alarm in one of the shops, or maybe a car. So during the entire video you hear this security alarm going off in the background. I kept seeing my video everywhere, it was on the TV and everything, and when I hear this specific alarm on the other side of the street, the feeling of the shooting comes back to me. I really want to go ask them to change the sound of their alarm because all the memories come back to me. It's unbelievable that a sound brings up these feelings it took me one month to recover from.

The assassination of Alexis was the last straw. There is no more tolerance for the police. The killing was so outrageous, so far beyond the limits. The people reacted and still continue to react. They are empowered by the rage that was expressed at the time of the killing. There were many other problems too, besides police brutality. These problems continue, but the people don't tolerate them, not anymore.

I don't know if Exarchia is more autonomous now than before. The people, the ones who are active, they try. And me, I always feel autonomous, but now I really know what terrorism means. From the day they killed Alexis to the day when the guerrilla group attacked the police, the police did not appear on the corner where Alexis was killed. But when Revolutionary Struggle made this attack, the first thing the police did was to occupy the spot where Alexis was shot, and they stayed there for twenty-four hours. This was the riot police, with helmets, guns, everything. And when they came at midday, I was on the balcony and one of them looked up at me. I think because during this whole period the telephone was ringing, journalists were calling and trying to find out where this video had come from. When the one cop looked up at the balcony, I gestured like, *what do you want?* And he jabbed the guy at his side and pointed me out, and I felt completely terrified by the way they were looking at me. That night, I heard some neighbors talking, and then crying, and the cops were sitting right on the spot where Alexis died. I came out to see what was happening, and because I couldn't see I peered out discreetly over my balcony and one of the cops saw me. I felt terrified so I crept back inside but the cop came down below my balcony and made eye contact with me. I thought they would raid my apartment. So I went to my neighbor's house. I was terrified.

This is what I call terrorism. It's impossible to just sit on my balcony looking down into the street. Another time, in February I think, there was a car burning down in the street, and the police again came and looked up at me, and I got scared and went back inside my house. The policeman shouted up to me, *So you're hiding, eh?* And then I realized, *What the fuck, what is happening, why do I hide?* So I went back to the balcony and I started taking photographs. And the police started taking photographs of me.

You can see everything from this window. That's why I'm thinking of putting a camera there, for the policemen and also

for these young people who do many things without thinking about why they do it. Because everywhere there are a few people who can make a small mistake and everyone else has to live with the consequences. Some people say that this is Exarchia, the only thing to do is to burn the shops. But this is not the truth. There are many possible reactions outside the dogma of burning and smashing.

So I'll be in the trial of the policeman who killed Alexis. I was worrying about how I'll feel toward the defense lawyer, because he's defending a very bad person. Then I started to worry about the outcome of the trial. If this cop ends up with only two or three years in jail, I don't know how I would react. How do you react to the decision of a trial like this? Many terrifying things are happening, we hear about them and see them on the news, but it is very different when you see it with your own eyes. It is not just words, it is reality for you, there is no doubt, there is no distance from it. The assassination is such an absolute truth, it is like if you stole something from me, in front of my eyes, and then tell me it never existed. It is not something you just heard about from somewhere else. And I fear very much that if they find this cop not guilty, maybe my reaction will get me thrown in jail. I think about this all the time, as I prepare to testify.

1

2

3

4

5

6

Many people remained active in the months following December. These struggles kept the revolt alive throughout 2009. Endless meetings, assemblies, gatherings, parties, and film screenings coincided with arson, solidarity demonstrations, antifascist struggle, occupation of squats, and struggles around sexuality and the legalization of drugs.

1. Occupation of the television station. The banner reads: "Stop Watching. Come out in the Streets. Freedom for all of us. Liberation for those Arrested."

2.–3. Syndicalist activist Konstantina Kuneva. Before and after she was attacked and burned.

4. Attack on the national train company—Kuneva's main employer—that resulted in 16 million Euros in damages.

5. Demo attended by anarchists, communists, autonomists, and Leftists in support of Kuneva.

6. Occupation of the General Confederation of Greek Workers building. The banners read: "General Strike. Occupation. Self-organization of the Workers Will Be the Graveyard of the Bosses. Workers Re-Occupation of Syndicalism."

7. Anarchists organized demonstrations in front of prisons and government buildings. Keeping up pressure until all arrested were freed. Banner reads: "Not Even One Step Back: Liberation for all Prisoners of the Insurrection."

8. The Assembly of Health blockaded a hospital reception, arguing for free health care for all.

9. Patision Avenue park slated for demolition by the mayor of Athens but reopened and rebuilt by locals. The new, self-organized park is still there.

10. Demonstration in support of the arrested.

11. A local newspaper office in the countryside. It was attacked for humiliating the movement.

12. Farmers from Crete fight with police in the port of Piraeus.

13. Demonstration in Thessaloniki. The banner reads: "Magistrates, Politicians, Cops, Academics, Contractors, Journalists, Bosses: Keep Your Hands Off Our Lives!"

14. The occupied Opera Hall. Lively assemblies took place here covering the arts, philosophy, and politics.

15

16

15.–16. Daily assemblies created a public space for thought and action. .

Chronology: March–October 2009

March 7: In Exarchia, 4,000 people rip down the wall around a vacant lot destined to become a parking garage, tear up the asphalt with jackhammers, plant trees, and create a free park fifty meters away from the spot where Alexis was killed.

March 9: In separate incidents in Athens, a group of youths smash two banks in the middle of the afternoon, while early in the morning a homemade bomb explodes outside a Citibank branch, causing extensive damages and no injuries.

March 13: Fifty masked anarchists smash dozens of luxury shops in Kolonaki, the wealthy downtown district of Athens, in broad daylight, distributing flyers in solidarity with anarchist prisoner Yiorgos Voutsis-Votzatzis, and disappearing before police arrive.

Mid-March: Spectacularizing the Kolonaki attacks, the media go into overdrive presenting the anarchists as a threat to order. The government announces several new security measures, including announced changes in the law to aid the criminalization of protests, the arrival of police consultants from Scotland Yard, and the creation of Delta Force, a new police corps that will patrol on motorbikes and function as a rapid response force.

March 21: After hearing about the assassination of prisoner activist Katerina Goulioni, women prisoners in Chania and Thiva revolt and occupy their prisons.

March 30: The various squatted parks, social centers, and assemblies of Athens convoke thousands of people in a major protest march, starting at the new Navarinou Park in Exarchia and ending at City Hall.

March 31: Anarchists occupy the President's Office of Athens University at Panepistimio, hanging a huge banner from the front of the building calling for solidarity with all squatted and self-organized spaces throughout the country, on and off the universities, as well as for university asylum.

April 1: Kouzina Collective appears in Athens, serving free food in public. The same day, in Iraklion, three hundred people hold a demonstration in solidarity with those arrested in December.

April 2: During the national general strike day, 50,000 people demonstrate in the streets of Athens while major demonstrations take place in other cities. In the middle of the demo a group of anarchists smash the Athens offices of OIKOMET while members of Kuneva's union, with protection from anarchists and autonomists, occupy the offices of the train company, forcing them to cancel their contract with OIKOMET and give the cleaners permanent contracts directly with the public transportation company.

April 4: Members of the neighborhood assembly of Petralona (Athens) along with the Assembly for Health, occupy PIKPA, a two-storey former hospital, in order to establish a social center that will be used for many events and as a facility to provide free health care for the neighborhood.

April 15: The British College in Thessaloniki is attacked with a gas canister bomb in solidarity with the people arrested and repressed in London and Nottingham around the G20 protests, during which one older demonstrator was killed by police violence.

April 16–18: A string of arson attacks in Xanthi targets the house of a police informant, the ATM of the central bank, the luxury car of the city's bishop, and the car of the chief justice of the city.

April 25: 5,000 people take over a pedestrian street below the Acropolis for a DIY punk concert, one of several massive public, open air free festivals, concerts, and illegal raves to occur throughout the spring and summer.

April 28: 3,000 people march from the occupied park in Exarchia to the occupied park on Patision in opposition to the new anti-protest law criminalizing wearing masks or insulting police officers. Along the route, many CCTV cameras and banks are smashed. One thousand people, mostly anarchists, march in Thessaloniki in support of the occupations.

May 9: The neo-nazi group Golden Dawn, together with the MAT, hold a protest against immigrants in Omonia. Anarchists who try to attack the protest are pushed back by riot police, and fighting occurs around the Polytechnic.

May 12: A branch of Eurobank in Athens is destroyed by a bomb. The same day, an arson attack targets the national electricity company in response to the deaths of two workers.

May 18: A barrage of simultaneous arsons in eleven different areas of Athens target a shop selling police uniforms, a police training school, a surveillance systems corporation that works with police, two shops that sell guns to police, the central office of a private security company in a wealthy neighborhood, a Suzuki exhibition that provides the police with motorbikes, two private motorbikes and two private cars of cops parked outside their houses, and an exhibition of Skoda, a company that provides the police with vehicles. The communique was signed by "Enflamed Shadows." In the preceding days, similar attacks also occur in Thessaloniki and in Hania.

May 20: Police raid a café in Athens where many migrants gather. During the raid they tear up a Koran. Over the next two days immigrants organize several demonstrations and attack the police with stones. Hundreds participate, and police respond with tear gas. Sixteen are arrested, one, a Syrian immigrant, for throwing a molotov at a police station. Seventy-five cars, five shops, and one bank are damaged or destroyed.

May 27–31: 40,000 people participate in B-Fest, a week-long festival on the campus of the University for Fine Arts that includes concerts, raves, and a multi-day international conference that features anarchist and autonomist speakers from other countries, such as Noam Chomsky (via video feed), Bifo, Class War editors, and Michael Albert.

May 28: The Anti-sexist Faction commits an arson attack against two high-end brothels, "not for them [the sex workers] but for us." Their communique also mentions the trafficking of women.

May 29: The offices of fascist party LAOS are smashed in the city of Pyrgos. Similar attacks against LAOS are carried out in several other cities over these weeks, accompanied by accusations that they coordinate with paramilitary groups inside the police to repress the social movements.

June: Fascists in the Athens neighborhood of Aghios Panteleimonos stir up racism against the strong immigrant presence in a local park, situated near a church that was giving aid to undocumented people. The fascists instigate a right-wing neighborhood assembly that occupies the park and kicks out the immigrants, protected by the riot police and supported by the Minister of Public Order. Shortly after the Minister speaks at the right-wing assembly, fascists attack the nearby anarcho-punk squat Villa Amalias with firebombs. On the 9th of June, anarchists manage to fight off the fascists and open the playground, but they are subsequently attacked by police. They injure one cop, but five are arrested.

June 4: A police station in northern Athens is attacked by ten hooded anarchists with molotovs. Meanwhile three banks in different parts of Athens are firebombed at the same time.

June 7: Early in the morning, a group of hooded assailants attack a police station in Patras with molotovs and escape on motorcycle.

June 8: A bank in Thessaloniki is torched with a gas canister bomb.

June 11: About twenty hooded anarchists attack a group of police in Exarchia with molotovs and escape on foot.

June 17: In Athens the Sect of Revolutionaries assassinates a policeman who was guarding the home of a prosecution's witness in the terror trial of members of ELA. In a subsequent communique, they threaten to target politicians and journalists, and include "everyday life" and "normal people" in a long catalogue of enemies of the revolution.

July 2–4: In response to the collaboration between the State and the neo-nazis, the Interior Ministry, the political office of the ex-Minister of Public Order, the offices of an advisory think tank for the military, the Institute for Immigration Policy think tank, and the car of the president of the Constitutional Court are targeted in a barrage of arson attacks claimed by "Combat Groups for the Elimination of the Nation."

July 7: 3,000 people in Athens and one thousand people in Thessaloniki march in solidarity with immigrants. Fascists attempt to attack the Athens march with molotovs. Demonstrators blockade Patision Avenue outside ASOEE, burning dumpsters and fighting with police and fascists into the night.

July 8: The last remaining prisoner of December, Thodoros Iliopoulos, is denied bail on the grounds that he is an anarchist and a "danger to democracy." He goes on hunger-strike in protest.

279

July 10: A riot police bus is fired upon in Athens, forcing the cops to abandon the bus and run for their lives.

July 11: The Conspiracy of the Cells of Fire carries out a bomb attack against the home of a former interior minister and warns that the new national intelligence chief could be next. Dozens of fire bombings have already been claimed by this anarchist group. In contrast, most other anarchist fire bombings and attacks were claimed by groups that disappeared after signing their name to only one or two communiques.

July 12: A large refugee camp in Patras is mysteriously burned to the ground during a police operation. The city subsequently bulldozes the remains, preventing its reconstruction.

July 14: Villagers near Chaldiki block the road to Scouries, which a major gold-mining corporation wants to exploit and destroy. In Athens, protesters attack the central tower of the National Telecommunications Company with black paint, with the support of many workers there, after the company sues the Polytechnic University for hosting the Athens Indymedia server. Protesters claim the company is taking cues from LAOS politicians who want to gag radical dissent.

July 22: Police defuse a bomb placed by the Conspiracy of the Cells of Fire in front of the Chilean consulate in Thessaloniki, in memory of Mauricio Molares Duarte who had recently died while carrying a bomb meant for a police target in Santiago.

August: Dozens of actions, from gas canister bombings to radio station occupations, occur all across Greece in solidarity with the last prisoner of December, Thodoros Iliopoulos, who is still on hunger strike. Thodoros is subsequently released. Also, the occupied social centers all across Greece continue to maintain and also defend themselves, and the occupied parks expand, with the planting of more trees and flowers, the construction of playgrounds and tile mosaic walkways, becoming more beautiful than any park the State has ever produced....

August 10: Eco-anarchist group "Animals' Revenge" rescues 7,000 mink from two different fur farms in Kozani, in northern Greece, causing hundreds of thousands of euros in damages.

August 21: Major forest fires begin just north of Athens and burn for four days, destroying 40,000 hectares of forest, olive grove, and shrub land. Many people understand that these fires are set intentionally by real estate developers.

August 25–31: Anarchists and leftists hold a No Border Camp, amidst an extreme police presence, at Mytilini, on the island of Lesvos, near Turkey.

September 2: Revolutionary Struggle bombs the Athens Stock Exchange, calling in a bomb threat first to avoid casualties. The building is heavily damaged by the huge blast.

September 5: Athens police chase some people painting graffiti into Exarchia, where a crowd gathers attempting to stop the arrests. Delta Force arrives and they attack anarchists throughout the neighborhood, yell at neighbors, smash things in the occupied park, and generally behave like hooligans. They arrest five people though all are later released with charges dropped. Police kick one of the detainees until they rupture his lung.

September 23: A suspected cell of the Conspiracy of the Cells of Fire is caught by police in Athens after the explosion of a small bomb in front of the house of an ex-minister of finance and PASOK member, just days before PASOK wins the national elections. Three men and one woman are arrested and given terrorism charges. One is released on provisional liberty awaiting trial, with the terrorism charges dropped. Six other people are wanted by police. In the months since December, the group had claimed responsibility for 160 attacks.

October 2: The Conspiracy of the Cells of Fire take responsibility for a small bomb placed close to the stage where the current prime minister and candidate for ND is giving a major public speech, just two days before the election.

October 4: PASOK win the national elections, which had been called largely in response to the political crisis of legitimacy exacerbated by December, and the December revolt proves to be a major election topic. 30% of eligible voters abstain (compared with 26% in 2007), PASOK takes 43.9% of the votes, ND takes 33.5% (their lowest polling ever), KKE takes 7.5%, LAOS takes 5.6%, SYRIZA takes 4.6%. The Green Party, with only 2.5%, do not win enough votes to enter Parliament.

October 7: Three days after the elections, prime minister-elect Giorgos Papandreou (son of the legendary former Prime Minister) says in a public speech to his new ministers, "We must be like antiauthoritarians in authority... our main target is to bring equality to all genders, races, economic classes, and nationalities, bringing together all differences," revealing both how much the real antiauthoritarians had influenced the political structure, and also hinting at the strategy of the Socialists for recuperating the revolt.

Meanwhile, anarchists and the extreme Left riot nearby in Istanbul, Turkey, in protest of the International Monetary Fund, while World Bank president Robert Zoellick declares an end to the days of elitist decision-making without input from developing countries, mirroring the PASOK rhetoric.

October 8: At midday, about thirty koukoulofori in Exarchia smash out the windows of a half dozen corporate targets, including the National Bank of Athens and a fascist bookstore, as well as a few luxury vehicles, disappearing before the arrival of Delta Force, units of which had been parked nearby.

That night, hundreds of police invade the neighborhood, searching some 200 people, eighty-one of whom are taken to the police station and eight of whom are arrested (for poverty-related crimes). They also search sixteen automobiles and twenty-six cafés. The next day, the new minister of public order, who some years earlier was responsible for torturing suspects in order to bust and imprison several members of 17 November, says on television that the purpose of the raids is not to go after the anarchists but to arrest the vandals and hooligans and establish police authority in Exarchia. The massive and aggressive police presence, raids, and arrests continue. The last time it was like this, recall the old timers, the Socialists were also in power; it was after the 1989 riots sparked by the acquittal of the cop who killed anarchist Michalis Kaltezas, and then the police occupation of Exarchia lasted for three years.

October 10: In the afternoon, several hundred residents of Exarchia and anarchists hold a protest against the police occupation, angrily confronting a line of riot police guarding a government building, but deciding not to attack. The neighborhood assembly of Exarchia has decided to permanently resist the repressive measures. At night, on Strefi Hill above Exarchia, four thousand young people take over the park for an unpermitted free festival with DJs, VJs, and bands. At one point Delta Force makes a threatening show of force but leaves without provoking a fight.

The neighborhood assembly continues holding protests twice a week, bringing thousands of people together to march from Exarchia Square to Parliament and back, vowing to continue until the police presence is removed. The struggle continues...

Alexis Grigoropoulos Park

On Saturday, March 7th, 1,000 people converged on a vacant lot that for years had been surrounded by metal construction barriers several meters high, stealing the space from public view and public use. Going on fifteen years, the city government had promised to turn the lot into a park and still had done nothing. Recently the owner of the property, which was valued at 9 million euros, decided to retract their offer to allow a park there and were formulating plans for construction. A confluence of neighborhood residents and anarchists from all over Athens acted first. In one day they tore down the metal barriers and began the process of creating a park, ripping up the asphalt, building benches and planting trees. One of the participants tells with glee: "For years there had been these walls here, no one was used to thinking that there was an empty space behind them. And the day we tore it down, you see neighbors walking by, they come upon this open space and start looking around them, checking the street signs—they were lost in their own neighborhood. We transformed this place." A visitor exclaimed: "You know what the best part is? It's seeing all the old people look at the park and how happy they are." "No," interrupted a Greek anarchist. "The best thing is that we fucked the city out of 9 million euros."

We intervene in the daily flow of things to interrupt it

Daredevil : An active participant in Exarchia's new squatted park

Before December I wasn't directly involved. I followed what was happening and went to some protests but there was no strategy. It was just solidarity for other people's actions. There's a lot of small anarchist groups that do a lot of actions and they created the conditions for December to happen, but what happened exceeded these groups. They made some sort of a network and this network was very helpful, at least in the beginning. They started by occupying the national university, the economic school, the law school. They provided some sort of a basis for people to come and meet. The anarchists were more involved and they were more active before December. They also had street knowledge, they know about conflict and fighting. And the young kids, they picked it up very fast and in two days they were experts too but it was vital that this knowledge was present beforehand.

Two crucial events happened during this time: the death of the young kid and the attack on the lady, Kuneva. For Greek standards this was very brutal. It's unheard of. A lot of people felt like they had their backs up against the wall. That's why we saw such a powerful eruption of outrage.

At some point we formed a group, but this group didn't have an identity. It was part of our strategy not to have a name, not to have anyone speak for the group. I operated together with other people but I cannot speak for anyone else. What was important is this decision that we took not to have a name or identity.

Often the strategy of the State and the authorities, is to separate the different groups, to differentiate anarchists from students from workers, so they can play one group against the other. Or they can represent a particular group as, for example, artists, so everyone who is not an artist, it doesn't involve them. But when we did things that got in the news they didn't know how to label us—students, anarchists, youth. I think that this has worked very well.

Sometimes we organized things in cooperation with a group that already existed, a group that was more visible, more broad. For example here there is a group of residents. With the park we did all the work but they took all the credit. This was a civic group, more open, so they couldn't be tagged as anarchist or whatever. This worked well for us. We did this a couple times, three times, with a big festival in Exarchia, for example.

We don't want to be in touch with the media, so we get in touch with more mainstream groups, and they can get in touch with the media. For me this strategy has worked.

283

What's new is that now a lot of people are united and doing things, but this is still mostly around action. There are a lot of ideological differences but there is some sort of unity around the action. Like for example here at the park. I think this is a new development, since December. This is a small country and everyone knows one another. The different groups have some solidarity but also they have differences, they were fragmented. But now you have osmosis, people going from one group to another. It's much broader.

In December we talked with some people about this strategy of autonomous zones and I think a lot of people liked the idea. There's a lot of new squats, a new discussion about this situation. It also happened after the student riots of 1991: there were lots of occupations and now it's happening again. But there are many different approaches. For example there was the occupation of the National Opera, that lasted for ten days. It was very big. And by Greek standards it was a very open squat. Lots of people came in who wouldn't feel comfortable going to other political spaces. There were people from the whole political spectrum. Lots of discussions, it was quite interesting. At the beginning you saw they all came from different backgrounds but slowly a connection began to form.

The park is wonderful. It's very open, anyone can approach it, there's no inside and outside. In the Opera there was the dynamic of one big group using the place and one smaller group that ran the place. There was a tension.

The starting point for our strategy was *parenvoli*, intervening and breaking the normal routine. We intervene in the daily flow of things to interrupt it. The first intervention lasted one minute, then ten days, and now a more permanent interruption, with this park. These actions were done by different people, but what's important is that it goes from smaller to more permanent. It's part of the strategy that the same group of people doesn't do everything, so more people can participate and more people can relate. And the authorities never know who is doing it. One minute they thought it was fourteen-year-old kids and the next minute they thought it was veteran anarchists.

To occupy the park we worked with a civic group. They had been thinking about it for a long time, and for 6 months already they had been pressuring the municipality and the owner of the lot, which is the Union of Mechanical Engineering, to turn this place into a park. Some of our people who also participated in this civic group decided that it would be a good idea to make the park ourselves. In the beginning we didn't have this whole thing in mind, we thought maybe we would just make some holes and put in some trees, and you can see now how it's grown. But this is only because people put in so much work. They put in time, brought tools, and did so much. The park built itself. Some people provided the spark, and so many more people showed up and made it happen. And now it operates through its open assembly.

If someone comes along, uninitiated in this way of doing things, of organizing assemblies, he would think it is completely chaotic—nothing could possibly come of this. But the truth is that from this seemingly chaotic environment a lot of things can happen and they work really well. They're well organized, no mistakes, no big conflicts. This is a lesson for new people but also for us, to believe more and more in this way of organizing and this way of acting. The idea that you don't need some sort of leader to tell you where to go and what to do and who is responsible. You must prove this through action, not just say leadership is superfluous but prove it in action. And I think that on many occasions since December we have seen this.

Where do we go from now? There's this dilemma: do we do things that bring in more people or do we do the things that we like and if other people like it too, so be it, something like that. But I'm not sure how to do it. We need some kind of combination. We should hope that the things we like and do well appeal to other people also. Because we don't want to dilute our principles or our activities. There is this idea that we have to create the life that we want, parallel to a direct conflict with the authorities. We must build a new reality on the ground, of what we like and how we want to live. Like this park: we have to build it ourselves and organize it in some autonomous way, period.

In my view, all the different aspects are related. Hitting the police, throwing molotov cocktails, these are different from creating a park and different people participate, but they fit well together. It's a multifaceted struggle. The strategy of the opposite side tries to distinguish between everything, to turn you against the others. But the same people, different people, same time, different times, it doesn't matter. We're all together.

The big question we face now with the park, is that if you take the best scenario, that the municipality is willing to compromise with the owners and give them some money so that the park can legally remain, then the municipality takes ownership of the park. How can you guarantee the autonomy of the park so it doesn't just become another city park? This is uncharted territory. I'm sure that in other times and in other countries there were similar experiences so we must look to history. We are formulating a new language to describe these experiments. Currently we lack the means to communicate what is happening. And there are new challenges. Hopefully we'll learn from the past or create new ideas of how to do this, how to guarantee the autonomy of the park.

An interesting idea is what has happened in the West, the creation of social centers that provide social services. This is a huge project. It takes lots of money and infrastructure and expertise. But if we can take this on and make it run autonomously and keep it open to the people it's going to be good. It's going to be really good.

The House of Maria Kallas

"The biggest expectations lie ahead of us and we find ourselves in the joyous position of seeking ways to drift along with them."

At 8a.m., March 19th, dozens of comrades occupied a building on the corner of Patision Ave and Skaramaga Street, the former house of Maria Kallas, right between the Athens Polytechnic and the Economics University in Athens. Work inside started immediately. A soundsystem was quickly set up and the subversive "Carmen," sang by Kallas, echoed across Patision Ave. There are many people in the building, the number increasing by the hour. You can come to the beautiful building and gaze at the sea from its rooftop.

The new Patision Commune is here. Strong, sober and uncrushable.

Carrying on…

We are some people who met on the streets and in the occupations during the events of December's revolt—events that derive from historical, class, social, and dispositional causes and of course, from the assassination of Alexis by the cop Korkoneas. December was a peak moment, a spark in the powder keg, upon which the peaceful social consensus is based, an accelerating factor leading to an unprecedented social explosion. An explosion that shattered the suffocating normality of our lives. The feast of December blew apart individualization and the sealed-off private sphere in our lives. A joyous, collective, and wild "we" poured out on the streets. It attacked democracy and its guards; abstaining from any demand or petition, it self-organized everyday life within occupied buildings. It articulated the sharpest critique against the monologue of the commodity, destroying and looting its temples, redistributing social wealth, halting consumption in the very center of the city. It disproved the ambitions of the leftist wanna-be intermediaries, letting them stammer sociological crap on the TV. It canceled out the convulsive muddle of the journalists, making it clear that whoever wanted to understand what was going on only needed to get out of their homes. It abolished, even if temporarily, gendered and spectacular roles. Thousands of people acted as one body, during events where what mattered was what was happening, not who was doing it.

And on the other hand: the State, the bosses, and those with a strong interest in everything staying the same. From the moment they managed to regroup they were anything but spectators. They sought a return to normality by using all means at their disposal. From riot police and paramilitary thugs to the sociologists and sensitive artists. From talk of extremists, gangs, saboteurs, Greek-haters, all the way to the peaceful citizens' claim to the right to celebrate their Christmas. From the hypocritical criticism of the adults to their kids, to the arrest of 265 rebels and the incarceration of sixty-five. They did whatever they could do, in other words, for December to turn into a "sad bracket" where in the end the extremists were punished and those who followed were admonished.

Carrying on,

The meaning of December grows increasingly important. Conditions remain polarized and confrontational on both sides. Only within the context of December's upheaval can one understand events like the acid attack against syndicalist K. Kuneva; the attempted massacre, by hand-grenade, at the migrants' space as well as the proclamations for the restructuring of the legal and military arsenal of the State, the most recent attempt to awaken reactionary social forces.

At the same time, widened social groupings are constantly developing actions, practices, and a voice, using December's events as a clear starting and reference point. From the railway stations to the centers of bureaucratic syndicalism, from workplaces to the hospital receptions, from parks and neighborhoods to the spectacle's temples, self-organized incentives that are diffused, socialized, and enriched emerge as tools, methods, and ways of reshaping reality and attacking the capitalist relations and the democratic condition. These elements constitute a wider process of radicalization that seems to have time, continuity, and qualitative depth.

Carrying on,

To the extent that we constitute a product and a component of these conditions, we decided to reclaim the abandoned building of 61 Patision Avenue and Skaramaga Street, with the aim of grounding our intentions and desires; in order to turn it into a base for the life that we want. To turn it into an open social space where in a self-organized, comradely, and collective way we will comprise a part of the conspiracy for the destruction of this world. Against all forms of hierarchy and authority, against all political and corporative intermediation, against all spectacle-given roles and gendered divisions. And in this attempt of ours we are looking for accomplices…

The revolt is already everywhere.
Solidarity to Konstantina Kuneva.
Immediate release of December's arrestees.

287

The Assassination of Prisoner Katerina Goulioni

According to IMC Athens, Katerina Goulioni, militant prisoners' rights activist, has died in police custody this morning, Wednesday March 18th. Katerina was one of the most active prisoners in defence of prisoners' rights and was often put in isolation.

Katerina was being transferred from the women's prison at Thiva, where she was active in exposing bad conditions and organizing against mistreatment and rape of prisoners, to a prison on the island of Crete. Evidently she was on the same boat to Crete as the fascist prisoner "Periandros." Periandros had previously attacked the anarchist prisoner Yiannis Dimitrakis; Yiannis is in the hospital but is doing well. Afterwards, Periandros was attacked by other prisoners in his own cell, possibly in retaliation, as Yiannis has much support on the inside.

In the boat from Pireaus to Crete, the guards forced Katerina to sit alone, fifteen seats behind the other prisoners, hands tied behind her back. At 6a.m. in the morning Katerina was found dead; according to testimonies by other prisoners, she was badly beaten in the face.

The coroner refuses to give out any information before the official report, though police already claimed Goulioni died of a heart attack. Prisoners at Thiva, approximately 100 km northwest of Athens, quickly began a hunger strike.

Update: On Sunday the 22nd it was reported that the women had set one wing of the prison on fire. Meanwhile prisoners in the Hania prison on Crete also revolted and occupied the prison, and 200 people in Korydallos prison staged a solidarity protest. Simultaneously, a radio station close to Hania was occupied so solidarity messages from and for the prisoners could be broadcast:

> We the prisoners of the juridical prison of Hania, today on the 21st of March 2009 and in reaction to the horrific living conditions, refused to enter our cells in order to demand the immediate de-congestion of the prison. As a solution to this problem, we seek the immediate transfer of the majority of us to other prisons in the country. We ask, in other words, what should be a given. What no one should be denied even for a single moment: humane living conditions. Dignity!
>
> How could we not act, when 157 of us are piled up in a prison, a former Turkish command post, built to house 70, when 57 of us are forced to live in a room designed for 20, when to use a toilet we must book an appointment the day before, when we join up two beds so that three of us can sleep on them, when we have no hot water and shiver, when we shout and nobody listens, when the State hides away from society an untold truth!
>
> Yet again the State becomes an accessory to murder when facing the fact of an unavoidable revolt!
>
> The threats issued against the revolt and the judicial condemnations directed against all of us who participate in it, as insurgents, criminals, do not scare us. The State will always meet with our opposition! Its terrorism shall not pass!
>
> We voted unanimously and with enthusiasm that:

We will continue our struggle until we get a hearing with a representative of the Ministry of Justice, in order for our demands to be met.

—Prisoners of the Juridical Prison of Hania

Conversation on a park bench with a random young person in Thessaloniki

"Excuse me, milas agglika?"

"Nai, ligo. A little."

"Do you know what time it is?"

She shows me her watch. "How do you say... quarter past nine?"

"Yeah, that's right. Thanks. So are you a student here?"

"Yes."

"What do you study?"

"Economics."

"What do you think about the student occupations."

"It's okay, but I think it's hard to study here. It's a lot of work."

She didn't seem to have understood the question, so I went in for some small talk. "Do you like Thessaloniki?"

"Yes, it's a great city."

"Are you from here?"

"No, I'm from Crete. Do you know where is Crete?"

"Yup. What's it like?"

"Very nice. I'm from Hania. It's a big city, not so big, but it's alright. There are four big cities on Crete, Iraklion is the biggest. I think it's the 3rd or 4th biggest of all Greece."

"My name's Alex, what's yours?"

"Ionna. Nice to meet you."

289

"Nice to meet you too. So…" Small talk was harder than it looks. I plunged back in to the topic of politics. "So, were you in the student movement two years ago? You know, the occupations, the *katalipsi* in 2006?"

"Ah no, I was in high school then."

"So what do you think about what happened in December?"

"It was awful!"

"What was awful about it?"

"The police shouldn't have the right to take someone's life. It's very, very bad."

"That's funny, in my country someone would say it's awful and they would be talking about burning the banks—they would have forgotten about the boy getting killed."

"That's terrible."

"Yeah, really. So I bet you smashed like a hundred banks."

"Ha ha! No, but I went to the protests!"

"I like how everywhere there's graffiti here for the prisoners."

She looks to where I point out the slogan written for Polikarpos Giorgiadis, from November 17th, on the wall across from us.

"Yes," she says with a little laugh I can't quite decipher.

"So do the anarchists here have much support? I mean from normal people?"

"Mmmm, I don't know. I think yes among the young people and not so much from other people."

"I went to the *katalipsi* at the university yesterday. They had a talk about Konstantina Kuneva and the workers, that was very interesting."

"Ah yes?"

"Do you know about that case?"

"A little."

"So… are there any good parties on the university this weekend?"

…

Now there's no going back

Sakis and Dina: Two older members of Antiauthoritarian Current in Thessaloniki (speaking from their own point of view and not as spokespersons)

Yes, there was an occupation of the Theater School in December but this action wasn't done by Alpha Kappa. Many of us participated in it, but as individuals. There were also many students. This was an occupation by everybody. We also participated in the protests. In the protests Alpha Kappa usually goes as a tight bloc. We fight with the police but we don't run around and scatter. We stay close, sometimes we link arms, and this way we don't get arrested.

Since December, Greece is totally different, and the anarchist movement here is totally different. Now there's no going back. It's as though in one month things moved forward five years. Greek society moved forward. We saw the anger that everyone feels about the economic system, their jobs, the crisis. For 150 years it's been the same, the politicians just take the money and do whatever they want, but now, for the first time, the Greek people have shown their anger. If I were a fifteen-year-old in December it would affect me for the rest of my life and even when I was thirty whenever I saw a cop or

some other authority figure I would remember what kind of person this really is.

The anarchists didn't expect the riots in December because we know the Greek people and they're not such active members of society. But we saw that there is hope, especially in the young people, and this frightens the politicians. They didn't expect twenty-five cities to be burned at the same time. They were already afraid of the anarchist and left movement, but they never expected this.

The European politicians are very afraid. With the economic crisis, the European politicians believe that there will be many Decembers, in all of Europe. They want to stop this but they don't know how. I believe there will be many more Decembers. I think for many people the crisis is bad, for example I'm in danger of losing my job, but I want the crisis to continue, I want it to become ten times worse, because I think it will bring more Decembers.

After December Alpha Kappa understood that we are at a point where we have to set our sights higher. So now we are moving out of this social center and we are moving to a much larger building in the center, a rented building we will share with other groups, with other Left collectives and individuals. We have decided to do this because it is time to be open to society and be a part of society rather than being like the old closed anarchist groups all dressed in black.

There is also a new house that is squatted, right on Nikis Avenue, right on the sea front, a huge building, and there are other new social centers that are beginning as well. The government, I think, is very afraid. This high judge said that it's time to put an end to these new occupations, and he even named our new house which has only been squatted one month. And he named Yfanet and Terra Incognita and Delta and the others. He said the anarchists now have seven spaces in Thessaloniki, we have to stop them or they'll take over the whole city! So they are looking for legal ways to evict us. I think they will try to start with the squatted buildings because they can pretend it's a matter of legality, they can say it's because those places are illegal, but their real reason is to attack the movement.

But I don't think they will do it. I think they are bluffing. They know we would defend these places. The State knows we could start the war again, easy.

So, now you see we are putting all our things in boxes, getting ready to move to the new social center. This place was a good one, there were always lots of people coming in here and we had lots of events. But it's time to move to a bigger place, and cooperate with other groups. It's time to talk with the people so they understand our analysis, and the words we use, so they understand what we mean by internationalism, our critique of money, our critique of the State, not to make them anarchists but to make them active in society and make them believe that things can change.

We decided to occupy the university rectorate

Kostas: A student in the computer science department involved in the occupation of the administrative building at the Aristoteleous University of Thessaloniki

After the attack on Konstantiva Kuneva we started building a movement. Many students united and started printing papers or sticking up posters all over the university. This university contracts with the same company that employed Kuneva for its own cleaning staff and other staff. We demanded that the administration end its contract with that company and hire on all the staff as permanent, contracted workers—essentially a de-privatization. After one month of action, in March, we decided to occupy the rectorate and establish a center for our struggle. The student unions of three schools decided to participate in the occupation: geology, biology, and electrical engineering.

The staff have held four assemblies. In the first week they decided to initiate a partial strike, working four hours less per day. We organized a march along with the syndicate and five hundred people came out in the center of Thessaloniki. On Monday (March 30th) there is another staff assembly and maybe they'll decide to go on strike. There's also a protest march in Athens they may participate in.

So there is a direct link between this occupation and December. Many students participated in December. At least twenty schools out of about thirty were occupied by their student unions all through December, and there were occupations of the theater school, the workers' center, and the high schools. In the first week the directors tried to close the universities so the students couldn't gather and hold assemblies but despite this decision and despite the police throwing tear gas onto the campus, many students came and occupied their schools. There were also many marches. The largest march included approximately 12,000 people.

In the student occupations the extreme Left and the anarchists started to win over the assemblies. There are many Left organizations and anarchist organizations in the university, but they are all united. Personally, I'm part of a small political party, the Communist Party of Greece (Marxist-Leninist).[1] In my opinion the extreme Left groups and the anarchists have been the only powers in December and in the student movement. The leftist political parties that are in Parliament are not a part of this movement at all. They did not participate in the movement and they are not welcome in it.

This unity and this tradition of student assemblies goes back to the student occupation movement of 2006–2007.

This very important movement created a culture of struggle. Before then there were only one or two assemblies per year, with no more than fifty students. In the 2006–2007 school year there were fifteen to twenty assemblies with at least 400 students participating. The education reform passed in 2007 was forced through with great violence. The law changed how asylum works in the universities. Before, the police could come in only if the students agreed, but now the director of the university can call the police onto the campus without approval from the students. So technically it's easy now for the police to enter the campus—but not in reality because they're afraid of how the students will respond.

Our director is threatening to call in the police to end this occupation, but we will see what happens this week. We have decided to defend the occupation no matter what.

The next steps for the movement in Greece is to address the financial crisis: the basic salary, how many hours you work, the pensions. Everything related to work, because the people in Greece cannot afford basic things. Also some of the immigrants live in very poor conditions. In December there were many immigrants participating. And of course we have no intention to stop fighting against the university privatization law, to force them to repeal the law. In all sectors of society now, there is a tendency to participate in the struggles. In January even the farmers started building a movement. I think you will hear again from the Greek movement.

293

---

1   This is a small extra-parliamentary party, not to be confused with KKE, the Communist Party of Greece that has seats in Parliament.

December is a result of social and political processes going back many years, Part II

Alkis: An anarchist, squatter, publisher, and worker

(*Continued from Chapter 1, this interview expresses the continuity from before December to afterwards*) ...As the events of December showed, those who lost contact with society's most radical and militant expressions were not the anarchists, but those who were flirting with the ideas and structures of authority, claiming a role for themselves as representatives of the social subjects and mediators of social conflicts.

Through a long-lasting process of struggle, which I briefly described before, anarchists and antiauthoritarians gained a lot of ground in the consciousness of the people, something that was not evident to everybody until December. Some believe that the State lost a lot of social ground during the days of December. More accurately the State had lost a lot of ground before the events of December, over a long period of time. This was revealed during the revolt, with the participation of crowds of people in actions that were considered, up to that moment, exclusive to small groups of anarchists.

December of 2008 has a profound historical, political, and social background that is connected to the history of struggles over the last thirty years, and to the presence and participation of anarchists inside those struggles. The anarchists' participation that is characterized by the praxis of social revolt without mediators and without illusions for a change inside the existing system, proposing self-organization against any kind of hierarchical organization, proposing counter-violence against State violence, and solidarity against individualization and the artificial divisions created by power.

Here we could talk about dynamic practices of struggle: the clashes with the police and the occupations of buildings (universities, schools, town halls and many others)—both were appropriated by crowds of people in December. The same happened with self-organization through open, anti-hierarchical assemblies that were created during the days of December and afterwards. Those practices were avoided and downgraded by the Left and the result is that the events surpassed them.

However, even though December is a result of social and political processes going back many years, and it does have similarities and analogies with previous events, it still surpasses them and expresses new situations, needs and desires, creating new potentials. Unlike past events, this time they weren't limited or localized in a specific time and space. They were diffused to numerous cities all over the country and took many different forms, more or less violent but always antagonistic to the State, based each time on the inspi-

294

ration and imagination, the inventiveness of the people who participated.

Furthermore, it is a process that, because of its diffusion and its multiform character, doesn't seem to have an endpoint; rather it seems to continue and renew itself, taking new forms and bearing the promise of new social explosions in spite of the current decline in violent events. Previously events mainly concerned Greek youth but in December what spread all across the country included people of many other nationalities, including migrants and refugees.

Dynamic methods of struggle and processes of self-organization were adopted by many people, without representatives and without putting forward demands. December not only continues a culture of political violence, it is also laying down a new tradition of self-organization as an important social urge, to organize from below. These processes of self-organization don't respond to murderous police violence as their only objective but to all expressions of Authority: from the way we live, the way we work, produce, consume, to issues of health, the environment, everything. Every aspect of authority is a front of struggle for the people who self-organize and fight from below, not always violently but almost always antagonistically to the State.

The revolt also justified certain positions inside the anti-authoritarian movement and disproved others. For example, the notion that everything is under control, that manipulation and control of people is so strong today that revolts are not possible, or that society is dead, that it cannot produce anything healthy and that we anarchists are alone against the State, was disproved. December showed that social revolt is possible.

The subjects of the revolt are another important issue surrounding December. There has been a lot of talk about who rebelled and there has been a major effort by the media and representatives of the political system to determine the subjects of the revolt in order to write the history themselves. They allege that it was a revolt of youth, specifically Greek youth, and especially high school students, based on the fact that part of the revolt was mobilizations of high school students, who, on many occasions, went as far as to demonstrate at police stations and assault them. But this is a very limited and falsified presentation of the revolt. The political system and the media want to conceal the wider social, multinational, and class character of the revolt. It was not only the students who were in the streets! And, in any case, most of the youth who came into the streets did not come down as students, but as insurgents against the world of domination, state violence, authority, and exploitation. The media and politicians want to hide what was evident to everyone who was in the streets: that in those streets there were the poor, the salaried workers, the unemployed, those we call excluded. And a large number of them were immigrants, those who are the cheapest labor force and main victims of labor exploitation, police violence, and state repression.

295

Consequently, the subject that each analyst presents as playing a central role in the revolt indicates his or her political purposes and reflects their subjective perception of the revolt, as well as their future objectives. For example, when they talk about Greek youth, especially about high school students, it is in order to separate the "good" rebels, considering them easier to manipulate, from the "bad," uncontrollable rebels. However the majority of the people who were in the streets basically belonged to the latter category, they were uncontrollable, oppressed people.

Today we are facing two things. One is the repressive moves by the State through the judicial system and the police—such as arrests, imprisonment, people being held hostage through prosecutions, increased public surveillance, the penalization of wearing masks and of insulting the police verbally, the targeting of squats, of self-managed spaces, and generally of the self-organized structures of the movement. On the other hand we have the ideological attack launched by the State in order to divide the rebels of December into "good" students, aiming to incorporate them into the system, and the "bad ones," who cannot or do not want to be incorporated and thus must be isolated and attacked and repressed.

We should also point out that while repression is expressed directly by the state mechanisms, the ideological war is being expressed by them and by other auxiliary mechanisms, such as the parties of the institutional Left. While the judiciary and the police repression are immediately visible and understood as something that comes from outside, the ideological war is more insidious and is generated within the movement itself, since it is expressed not only by those who are hostile to the movement but also by people who appear as friends of the movement and who are selectively projecting those characteristics of the revolt which they like, which means those characteristics they think they can absorb and utilize. And at the same time they slander those characteristics and subjects of the revolt that they don't consider agreeable, naming them non-political, anti-social, or even criminal.

This ideological war aims to incorporate, to terrorize those who are not incorporated, and to isolate those who support the revolt.

The crisis of the system, which is a crisis of its social legitimation, radically limits the possibilities of incorporation for a large portion of the people who react and resist. To clarify, this means that more and more people lose their trust in the institutions or the proponents of the system. This is why, even if they manage to incorporate some, they can't really confine and intercept the influence of the radical ideas.

The ones that we have to be wary of, because of their erosive and undermining presence, are exactly the ones who have one foot in the old world and the other foot with us, talking about a new world. These double-faced enemies of the revolt are the worst, worse than police and judges.

We have to make clear that we're referring specifically to those who play a certain role, not even always an important one, inside the institutions, and not generally to people—workers, neighbors, youth—with whom we meet. As for the latter, people who are being acculturated and educated by the system to have faith in the institutions, it was much easier to communicate with them in the first days of the revolt, because the material conditions and the tension of the events was such that everyone was moving from their old positions to new ones.

Today, as time goes by, our political and personal ability to keep these contacts is being tested. And so is our patience when acting together with people different from us, recognizing that we have a lot more to learn about how to keep contact with all these people whom we met in the streets in December. And the most important way that we meet face-to-face, beyond the usual propaganda material, the texts and flyers, is in the self-organized assemblies. From our side, we encourage the creation of such assemblies, we participate and intervene in them. And it is there also that we're faced with the ideological war I talked about before. But apart from that, there are the prejudices; both the prejudice of other people regarding us, and our prejudice towards people who do not have a clear rejection of the existing system, either out of naivete, out of fear or just because they are accustomed to it.

But we are on the right path. The relations that have been developed between anarchists, antiauthoritarians, and other parts of society constitute a whirlwind and the outcome is unpredictable. For sure it is something positive, as we don't allow

normality and alienation to re-establish themselves. Because in contradiction to the swirl of the revolt where everything is possible and we can hope for the best, normality is a situation where almost everything is predictable and most of the time the result is negative.

Things are unpredictable, not only concerning the relation between anarchists and antiauthoritarians with other people, but within the movement as well. And, mostly, things are unpredictable in terms of the relation between the anarchists, society, and the State. The anarchist/antiauthoritarian social movement produces many initiatives and acts of resistance against the State, some more dynamic and others less so, some more social and others less so. That is to say that there is not any central organ or single nucleus, but a variety of larger and smaller initiatives of struggle from below, some of which are coordinated while others are not. In every case, what should be avoided, in my opinion, is to be socially isolated, to be isolated among us, in the movement, and to be left alone to carry out a confrontation with the State.

We understand that a number of things that are done in Greece, were they done in the US or in Italy, for example, some of us would be dead and many more would be in prison for a lot of years. This balance of power that exists today—the fact that there is such activity and that we can talk about these things—has been thirty years in the making. But our lives and our freedom are always imperilled and targeted by the state mechanisms. After December the State wants to change this balance of power, and it could reverse it. Just as when Alexis Grigoropoulos was murdered and the desire for revolt came from within the people, there could be another moment where, based on a different event, an explosion of state repression could occur; and anarchists, as well as other fighters, could be exposed to tremendous dangers.

The history of the movement in the US, in Europe, and in the world teaches us both what we can do and what we can be faced with. Having a deeper knowledge of what we are and what we want to do, but also of what the State is and what it wants to do with us—to make us disappear—what we should make sure of is not to isolate ourselves from society, but also not to be divided within the movement, so that as a whole we won't be left alone against the State, nor that every individual comrade will be left alone against the State. But it is also important not to restrain our impetus or compromise our inner desires, to act and make things happen, to use our courage and even our craziness.

We haven't said anything so far about the role of spontaneity in the events of December. Spontaneity has always played a role in the anarchist initiatives and did again in December. But there was also the spontaneity of the social groups that participated in the revolt, the spontaneity of the masses. According to Castoriadis, *Spontaneity is the excess of the "result" over the "causes."* There were spontaneous forces that were expressed in December, forces that were hidden inside the masses of the people and that were not predictable

before. And these forces still inherent in society, much more in a society that is on its knees, much more in a society divided into classes, suffocating by the violence of the system, by poverty, despair, fear. For people living in such a society, two possibilities remain: either the passive acceptance of the existing reality, which the State wants to present as the only option; or insurrection, which even when it is not visible as a possibility or choice doesn't mean that it doesn't exist and that it won't burst forth.

And there is one more point: in today's conditions of domination by the State and capitalism in the West, the explosion of revolts is not so rare, including metropolitan riots, mostly by groups of youth and usually triggered by incidents of police violence. We have the events in the French suburbs, or the black revolt in L.A. in '92. And as a different case, we could also mention the Albanian revolt in '97, even though it has many distinct characteristics. But what happened here in December, in comparison with other big insurrectionary events, was that political and social subjects met and interacted. Anarchists met with social subjects ready to revolt.

In this context, revolt becomes much more dangerous for authority; when it is not just an outburst of social rage by a specific oppressed social group, but the fertile meeting of the dynamics of various social groups who direct together their violence against the source of all the exploitation and oppression.

Revolts happen and cannot be avoided. Authority knows that, so, it prefers to suppress each one social group alone and not let revolts take on clear political characteristics, not let them have a total criticism against the existing order. The presence and participation of the anarchists in December gave such wider political characteristics; and to a large extent a subversive criticism of the system as a whole was developed.

And that was right, and it is right for every comrade or group of comrades, wherever they are in the world, to attempt and to realize the meeting with social groups that suffer from the tyranny of the State and capitalism and have the desire to fight back, so that the unavoidable revolts become more widespread and not restricted.

If only we imagine what could happen with the meeting between political subjects who are consciously intending the subversion of the existing order, with all those social subjects who suffocate from the State and capitalism and have reasons to revolt. Only imagining this is enough to understand. And this is what happened to a large degree in Greece in December.

April 2009

You could see the hatred in their eyes

One sunny Friday I donned a suit and went with a friend, similarly attired, into Kolonaki, central Athens' most elite neighborhood, whose luxury shops and expensive cars were the target of substantial popular violence in December and of a well planned anarchist attack executed in early March. We went into a few shops looking for interviews. My friend introduced me as a British reporter and himself as my official translator. I put on my best posh accent to ask about the "disturbances." The best part of it was that my friend had been to this shop in December—with a mask and a sledgehammer. It was all we could do to keep from cracking up during the interview.

Kazana Poli: Manager of the posh clothing store Rococo, in the heart of Kolonaki.

299

My store was vandalized two times, in December and also at the beginning of March. They destroyed the windows completely, and also caused some damages inside the store. It was very bad. In March the troublemakers met in Exarchia, just a few blocks from here, to put their masks on and prepare for their rampage. So lots of people saw them and the police were called in advance. But the police came really late. I don't think they did their job well. They just came to write up all the damages but that's not enough.

Business definitely went down in December and after the attack in March. People in Athens were afraid to come downtown and go shopping. And we here in the shop have been afraid too. Every time I hear a loud noise I think the troublemakers have returned. I'll hear a loud noise and my mind will immediately go back to those moments. And also all the protests they're still holding are keeping the shoppers away.

You can't really be sure if the attacks are related to the episode with the students, in December. Of course there's no real connection. As a businesswoman I think it's quite strange that Kolonaki has been hit twice. I find that quite suspicious. Because as a result people are leaving the city center and going to do their shopping in the big malls in the suburbs. So this vandalism is benefiting major interests like Latsis [a Greek billionaire] and the other people who own the malls. As a merchant, that's my perspective.

But you have to understand that of course I support peaceful protests. If you want to protest something you should go out into the street and do it peacefully. This is how you show your support for an issue. You don't go around breaking things. I was also sad after the killing of that boy but in my view the troublemakers who damaged the shops were bad people. You could see the hatred in their eyes. They were very provocative, the way they would look you right in the eyes as they were smashing the windows. It was just mean. This proves they had nothing to do with the students, who went out into the streets with very just demands. It should be peaceful.

Giorgos Voutsis-Vogiatzis

"With violence as a structural part, the system organizes ignorance and fortifies itself against its deniers. Violence is everywhere. It is in the peitharxika,[1] in the penalties and in the isolation cells. In the city plan and in the war. In the news and in the commercials. In the murderous police and in the environmental looting. In the video games and in the juvenile correctional institutions.
"How much, Mister President, does your democracy say that the life of a robber costs, and how much the life of a cop? How much does the life of a prisoner cost in your modern Greek democracy and how much the life of a prison manager? How much does the life of a reputable judge cost and how much the life of the poor, demonized immigrant? Obviously the value of a human life gets a different meaning when the deceased is a defender of the ruling class. But the bullets cost the same."

—**Giorgos Voutsis-Vogiatzis**

The trial against Giorgos Voutsis-Voutgiatzis, concerning a bank robbery in 2006, started Wednesday the 1st of April in the court of Athens. The charges against him were armed robbery and possession of explosives (a hand grenade was found on him during the arrest). About one hundred people gathered outside the building in solidarity, though only fifteen of them were allowed inside by the cops, which caused some small

---

1   A system of judicial punishment for misbehavior and disobedience committed within the prisons, used to control prisoners throughout the duration of their sentence.

300

disturbances from time to time on the stairs to the entrance. A jury (which in Greece advises the court's verdict, but is not decisive) that was composed of only employees of the bank that was robbed was presented first, and witnesses heard all the testimony during the first day. The defense witnesses were family members, friends, and comrades. They spoke openly about the economic crisis, the social conditions and working conditions, syndicalism of the base. Many also explained how the State and the banks are stealing from us, in order to justify the robbery.

Giorgos stood by his action, which he called a symbolic attack against the banking system. He said he hadn't yet thought about what he would do with the money, that the money wasn't the point. The judge tried to force him to reveal who his accomplice was and he refused, saying it was an insult to his integrity. He criticized the reign of drugs and snitch culture in the prisons and said it was a lie to claim they played any rehabilitative role. And he apologized to the bank workers for manifesting authority over them for thirty-five seconds, which he felt bad about even though it was a negation of the authority that rules every moment of our lives. He ended with a quote from Kazantzakis, and when he was finished everyone in the courtroom applauded.

On Thursday, the 2nd of April, the sentences were delivered. For the robbery, seven years of imprisonment, and one year for possession of explosives, resulting in a total of eight years. Considering the fact that Giorgos had already spent eighteen months in pre-trial detention, and worked inside (one day of work equals two days in prison), a substantial amount of time was deducted from the final sentence. Since prisoners in the Greek system must only serve out 3/5 of their sentence, Giorgos only has to spend another six months in prison. He will be transferred to Korydallos prison in Athens, and freed in September.

During the first day of trial, the nerves and emotions over the prosecution of a comrade were interrupted with joy when it was discovered that two prisoners on trial in the building next door managed to escape. Most of the overwhelming amount of undercover, riot, and prison police were so intensely focused on the growing group of anarchists outside building 13, that two freedom loving birds were able to spread their wings and fly the coop.

We Are Winning

A.G. Schwarz

Another battle is coming. Energized by the fires of December, the movement is claiming more and more ground. They won the fights in the streets, and they still haven't been defeated. Every week they're claiming new buildings to turn into social centers, transforming their new parks into undeniable realities, and pushing the State back. The students in Thessaloniki are demanding that the university de-privatize the cleaning staff and give all the precarious workers permanent contracts. Kuneva's syndicate in Athens is demanding the same for the trams and the trains.

The university director in Thessaloniki has threatened to call in the police. The mayor of Athens has denied the existence of the new park in Exarchia, saying: "I don't see a park there, I see a parking lot." But both of these malakas know that if they touch either occupation, it'll be a war all over again, and we will probably win. But eventually they'll have to act, because like smart guerrillas, we refuse to go on the defensive. We don't mistake these new occupations, these little victories, as ends in themselves. As precious as each one is they are only steps on the road to revolution. We will and we must risk losing them in order to go further because in the war against the State there is no peace or stalemate, and to stop and circle the wagons means to be destroyed. In other words if we do not go further, if we only try to protect what little we've won, we will certainly lose it. So each new liberated space is being developed for the long-term even as it is used as a staging point for the next attack.

We don't disregard these liberated spaces as pawns in a struggle; on the contrary we treasure them. You step into the park in Exarchia and you see the handmade playground and all the new trees and it is obvious that it is a work of love. And if it weren't, so many hundreds of people of all ages wouldn't come here to hang out, and they wouldn't defend it tooth and nail when it's threatened. But we won't settle for this park, or just for its physical existence, giving control of it over to the mayor like he wants. We'll use it as a staging ground for meetings and protests, another bubble of social asylum in the war against the police, and maybe we'll decide one day to convert the bordering streets into pedestrian zones, ripping up all the asphalt. Soon they'll have to strike back. A government cannot continue to issue hollow threats without losing all its legitimacy and inviting more rebellion.

Thursday the 2nd of April was a day of general strike. In the protest march there was a lot of talk about Kuneva. And right next to the march route a group of anarchists entered the office of the company that employed Kuneva and smashed it all up, from the computers to the filing cabinets to the hardwood furniture to the framed art hanging on the walls. These private contractors rent out hyper-exploited immigrant workers, pocketing the greater part of the labor costs budgeted by the government. But that Thursday was payback. The new Delta Force sped to the scene of the crime but they were too late. All the anarchists had disappeared into the crowd, having caused thousands of euros of damage while hanging a banner off the office balcony to the delight of the crowds below. Later in the day, Kuneva's syndicate occupied the offices of the city trains, demanding the private company be dismissed so that all the cleaners could be hired on a permanent contract. Outside, a crowd of anarchists, Alpha Kappa, and some leftists gathered in support, ensuring that the police could not come to save the bosses.

Before long, a cheer went up and the crowd began to clap and talk excitedly. The train company had caved in to the demands, essentially reversing the supposedly unstoppable tide of neoliberal privatizations and austerity measures. The syndicate promised that if their agreement was not honored, they would be back. History was being changed. Outside, the person next to me smiled and proclaimed, "We're winning!"

I remember on the streets of Seattle and Prague, anarchists spray painted that same sentence on the walls, and later, watching it in some documentary, all the hardened activists smirked a little, cynical. But the possibility has returned. In fact it had never left. It's not going to be over tomorrow, but we can win. And it depends largely on having the confidence to change history.

I feel very lucky to be living in these times

Iulia: A participant in the queer and anarchist movements

The situation was boiling before December, all the scandals, the apathy of the bourgeoisie, people wanting to create a change but not knowing how. Then the groups that thought they were the specialists, like the leftists and the anarchists, they lost their place in the hierarchy because immigrants and students and people with no political identity were out in the streets. These specialists were supposed to be leading the struggle but they had lost their status. They had to make alliances with other people who were out on the streets. This opened those groups up. They had to think about their role. It also had a fragmenting effect and opened the gender relationships. A bit of light came in, although I wouldn't say it's wide open. It helped that women had the opportunity to fight in the streets.

A queer movement is developing in Greece, slowly, but we're trying. I was really surprised, during Carnival there was a queer party at Villa Amalias, which is normally very closed, a ghetto, exclusively punk.

I don't want to criticize, I'm just making observations, because things are getting much better, things are happening. But I can see why and how people can be included or how they can be excluded. There are a lot of girls who participate in the violence and that's very positive; and there are a lot of girls in the assemblies. I think there is an equilibrium. But women lack visibility. I would say the biggest problem is that the smaller issues are not discussed, like sexuality, even labor, or gender relations, or art. The good thing with December is that this started to open up. It seems like we're getting closer.

The thinking hasn't changed much. For example there is lots of solidarity with Kuneva but we don't talk about why these women from Bulgaria are in this position. We just denounce precarious work and that's that. But still, because of the attack on Kuneva there are openings. It's just that I'm impatient and I want things to get done. I don't want to criticize because things are getting done slowly, but I want to caution that it needs to go beyond simple solidarity. The anarchists, we take up a cause and it becomes ours because we show better solidarity than anyone else. What we need to do is analyze it, take it to pieces and ask why these women are in such a precarious position, who are they, and I think that's the way to make the movement open to more people, by opening up to their experiences.

The topic of gender relations can work in a fractal way. From the situation with Kuneva there is the potential for things to move off in multiple directions and all the different themes can be discussed instead of being overshadowed by this solidarity umbrella. That's my vision, that it branches off in multiple directions. I wish the movement would talk about the whores. No one talks about them now. In December you had a free zone in Solomou in Exarchia, it was like a liberated zone, yet you still had whores from Nigeria working there. What the fuck? They're still there now and nobody talks about it. How can you intervene in such a situation? There must be a way. It's the same with the drug addicts.

The groups focusing on gender relations are minor and without much visibility. And many anarchists look down on them, as though the issue is not so important. And typically they don't make connections between the struggles. But you can see a change. Connections are starting to be made. I'm optimistic.

Maybe this thing with the parks is quite a feminine project. I'm not fond of using these terms, *feminine, masculine,* because this is a trap, a dualism. But this focus on the parks and the public space has the potential to change the gender relations, because they are self-organized and come from within the movement. In those spaces gender relations can take on different forms because it's not a combat situation with barricades and no time to try out new things, just—*I'll do the first aid and you do the stones.* It is crucial that it's happening in a public space, that it's not closed. And I have a very good feeling about what's going to happen at the new squat on Patision.

Because Greek society is very patriarchal, when we say that things are going to change, the first thing you imagine is that things are going to become more feminine, because that's what's missing, that's the energy that has been suppressed.

But I have a problem with the terminology because it can become a trap, masculine and feminine, using the terms they impose. But then if you don't speak about it I don't think you can change it.

Anyway, I want things to change but I don't want the attacks to stop. I enjoyed the Kolonaki action when I saw it on TV. There's some people making this very awful argument, saying that after these attacks there are more cops on the streets. And they blame the actions for the repression. But the repression is everywhere, in the jobs and the everyday lives. You can't say the repression starts after you go smash a window, it just becomes obvious. They don't understand that repression is everywhere but some people have the courage to play with their own body and risk themselves to reveal this repression.

You also need the battles. They're not necessary for their logic, they're necessary for their passion, and that's the first thing you have to do, you react to this gloom, and it helps you start to organize. There's a paradox that I haven't sorted out. If you favor violence then you personally have to throw stones. You can't just sit on your couch. When the insurrection was happening I had to be there in the streets. Whether I'm going to be up front throwing stones, that's up to me and my courage and my abilities.

The movement still needs to open up more, to leave behind this bourgeois normality, but after December it is getting better. I feel very lucky to be living in these times.

The Political Parties After December

On the 8th of April, the newspaper *Eleftherotipia* published poll results, showing the strength of political parties in 2009, compared with 2004. PASOK, the Socialists, climbed from 34% to 38%. ND, the conservatives, in power since 2004, fell from 43.1% to 33.1%. KKE, the Communists, fell from 9.5% to 8.7%. SYRIZA, the coordination of the far Left, rose from 4.2% to 7.5%. LAOS, the fascist party, rose from 4.1% to 7.9%. The Green Party did not exist in 2004, but in 2009 polled at 4.8%.

Between the two major political parties, ND and PASOK, it was clear that the scandals and the crisis of legitimacy provoked by December would necessitate a house-cleaning, so these two parties were essentially changing places. It speaks volumes that the KKE, the former representative of the resistance to the dictatorship, who unequivocally condemned December's insurrection in its entirety, lost support, while the "pink" or "Euro" communists of SYRIZA, who played with the events of December, gained significantly. It remains to be seen whether they will be able to continue to manipulate the insurrection and recruit its less radical participants. As for the fascists, it is to be expected that when popular revolt threatens authority, the elite will encourage populist fascism, but just because it's predictable doesn't make it any less of a threat.

During the European Parliament elections the media and political analysts were scrambling around trying to explain away the extraordinary situation that over 50% of the Greek citizens had refused to vote, a social phenomenon directly related to the insurrection of December.

Claim of responsibility for an arson attack

Many older dogmas and ideological schemes have collapsed or are gradually collapsing in the face of dilemmas such as career vs. family, entertainment vs. moral temperance, and more extreme and vulgar individualism against the promotion of "the social good." Advanced capitalism penetrates everything. It sells opportunities for social and economic advancement in the form of investment shares. (And whoever fails bears personal responsibility for their poor investment.) It sells mass entertainment, sells the idea that in reality you should only care for yourself: to focus on doing your job well to get a promotion, to acquire a new car, new apartment, new furnishings, new routine. In your free time you seek entertainment spending hours of your life in shopping malls, cafés, clubs, cinemas, theaters, whether in the high culture or some alternative. We are encouraged to seek self-improvement, because you are never good enough according to advertising in hair parlors, beauty salons, gyms, diet centers...

The organization of this lifestyle requires the assurance that nothing will penetrate your personal space, that nothing will disturb your bliss, that there will be no obstacles in your way. Yet in this society coexist the disinherited and excluded, who don't have access to this lifestyle, not out of choice, but social conditions. Expecting not so much the possibility of mere survival, but the wish of living "like everyone else" produces violence, theft, burglary, robberies, kidnappings, often with bloody endings. Other groups of marginalized youth ignore the orders of the legal system and vandalize their environment without a specific reason, just because they want to defuse a rage that they cannot define, but express everywhere.

Schools occupations, the battles in the stadiums, neighborhood gang clashes to control the drug traffic, all of these are dangerous to the status quo. This is where the role of security comes in: "justice" that sends to hell whomever is cast out by the system, the police that offer order, the various police units and their frequent patrols and presence in the metropolis and throughout the country. But as the police may not be ubiquitous, their measures escalate. More cameras appear on the streets, and methods of surveillance become more evolved. As the outcasts become more evolved, so too the systems of security. Scientists work feverishly in universities and other institutions to develop smart solutions using the cutting edge of technology with public or private grants. Individual vendors specialize and can now offer alarms, access control systems, security shutters, electronic locks, motion sensors, all types of cameras, microphones, bugs, etc.

A whole industry has developed, with demand from the general public, because those who do not take special measures have a lot to lose. So many petit bourgeoisie establish small companies of this type and try to earn a few crumbs from the enterprise. A common culture of snitching is also developing, and for every dark spot not watched by a camera there is a vigilant eye watching from behind the shutters. For every delay in the police intervention, there is an indignant citizen who is eager to be a vigilante. But in this same society there are those who refuse, who defy these structures, institutions, and ethical and cultural values, promises, and hopes. Restless agitators who organize and attack the existing in order to eliminate it. Some who arm their desires for action. Some who will never rest until they see the ruins of this world.

There can be no oasis of freedom in this space and time. Everybody owes it to themselves, if they have any dignity, to fight, to test the limits of endurance, and take part in the revolutionary struggle for a world without authoritarian institutions and property, that will not exclude anyone, and therefore will not need the machinery of control and surveillance, and will not be run by the vampires in suits and uniforms, but will be organized by the collective synthesis of our free individual desires in ways that only the experience of the struggle can achieve.

That's why we decided to hit three shops that sell surveillance systems and services, one on Tuesday at dawn in Gizi and two simultaneously on Wednesday morning in Kalithea. Not only has it proven that the great number of cameras in front of these shops cannot protect them but we also humiliated the frequent police patrols that go around like sheriffs in groups of twenty in the city center. Our goal is to spread chaos and insecurity on the enemy's territory, which is where every large or small property mediates human relations, constructing exclusions in every little corner of this rotten world. There is no security system or police patrol that will reverse our intentions, nor those of all the other comrades who are fighting for revolution. Let all the shopping malls fill up with cops, let the security guards get all the work they can, let the shops sell us more security systems, and let the bourgeoisie look under their beds before they go to sleep and they will still awake in the night terrified.

P.S. We salute all the comrades who alone or in organized groups are trying to transmit the virus of the revolutionary violence. We respond to the invitation for a new urban guerrilla whose dimensions are already exploding even across the smallest cities in the countryside.

—Conspiracy for the Promotion of Insecurity
April 15, 2009

The prisoners of December

N. & Mi: Anarchists from Exarchia who participate in, among other things, the movement of solidarity with the prisoners

Apostolis Kiriakopoulos, one of the prisoners of December, is currently in Korydallos. He was arrested in the first days of the insurrection, outside the Polytechnic, and he is in prison awaiting trial. They filed a motion to release him but it was rejected. He is accused of being a very dangerous person who could commit the same actions if released. The judge made clear in his statement that these kind of people have to be eliminated.

Talking about the prisoners of December, we have to mention that there are an unknown number of immigrants who were arrested, and the police never provided any names or lists of them. They say that there were about 300 people arrested in December, and of these seventy were kept in pre-trial detention. Among these are immigrants about whom there is no information, and we only have contact with a few of them. The basic accusations are for rioting and looting. Gradually these cases are going to trial, and some of the detainees have been released. To sort through the chaos the movement created a single blog that includes all the info we have been able to gather, and this helps coordinate the solidarity.

One important group of prisoners were the nineteen high school students arrested for rioting in Larissa. The local judge charged them under the anti-terrorist law. Four of them, as of April, have been locked up for months and were only released recently. Because of the fact that they applied the anti-terrorist law there was massive participation in the solidarity movement in Larissa, especially on the part of other high school students.

Elias Nikolaou was arrested on the 13th of January, 2009, near the scene of an arson attack on a municipal police car. He is currently in the Amfissa prison. Elias is one of the prisoners who was indicted for arson last year and he had been on the run. In November of 2007, the police arrested Vaggelis Botzazis in Thessaloniki. They convicted him for many different arson attacks, on the French car company Renault (in solidarity with the anti-terror arrests in France), a bank, one attack against the building of the electricity company, but they didn't have any proof connecting him to these other actions. Nonetheless the police announced that they had arrested a highly active gang. They said Vaggelis was operating together with three other people, one of whom was Elias.

When the police started to search for the three comrades they went underground. After one year, Vaggelis was released from prison for lack of evidence, and in the meantime he had been active on the inside. One month later the three comrades appeared at a police station and presented themselves. They said there was no proof at all connecting them to these incidents, so there was a meeting with the authorities and they decided not to give them pre-trial detention and just let them await trial on conditional liberty.

In November they let Nikolaou go free and in January they arrested him for burning the cop car. He doesn't speak about this action because he doesn't admit to doing it. In his letters he has explained that he is imprisoned for being an anarchist and this makes him a target for the police. And he will stay in prison at least one year until his trial.

We have to mention that throughout December many incidents also took place inside the prisons in reaction to the murder of Alexis. However, major revolts did not take place, because the prisoners were physically exhausted from their hunger strike and the struggle that lasted all through November. Still, to express their solidarity with the insurrection many prisoners refused to eat during those days.

Letter from Anarchist A. Kiriakopoulos from Korydallos prison

Five months after the explosive events of December and the mass arrests and prosecutions that took place, six of us remain captive in the claws of the State.

Recently, the so-called "justice state" and its servants decided to extend my pre-trial detention, stating that what should come first is the extermination of my person and of my "criminal" activity, for the protection of society. According to their characterization, I am a reckless and fanatical person. To sum it up they characterized me as an enemy of society. But the enemies of society are all those who after the cold-blooded murder of comrade Alexis Grigoropoulos tried to repress the social phenomenon of the violent insurrection in December with the reckless and mass use of tear gas—to the extent that it constituted torture—the beating of protesters, and their swift imprisonment.

It is known for years now that the cops, especially when dealing with anarchist demos, unleash chemical warfare with the slightest pretext so they can torture people. Despite the vicious repression of December's insurrectionary violence, it continues to persist and is proof that the fire that was lit cannot be extinguished. After all, Alexis's murder was the cause and at the same time the pretext for the outbreak of social rage.

As always, the mass media assumed their role, as the low-life journalists' propaganda reached vile limits. After the state murder of Alexis, they reported widespread destruction in the whole of Greece and claimed the police made no arrests. The the fact that all of us imprisoned for the insurrection face the same charges is no coincidence. The line from the State was exactly the same for nearly all of us.

Inside prison, time is the worst enemy. Especially when you are in custody awaiting trial. There is a continuous uncertainty as you never know exactly when you are going to be released. This is a situation that definitely wears you down psychologically. This is also an effect of being locked up against your will with four people for fourteen hours a day in a nine-square-meter cell designed to fit only one person. It is especially felt when relationships of camaraderie or even of understanding are as rare as they are on the other side of the prison bars. Though of course there are always those who choose to stand in dignity and struggle.

Incarceration is an everyday psychological warfare enforced upon you by the system when you are in prison. On top of this you also have the screws usually treating prisoners who take part in struggles (hunger strikes, refusal of prison food, demanding their printed material free of censorship) in a derogatory and sly way. One typical example is the last time prisoners were refusing food as a protest for the murder of Alexis, the warden of the wing came in together with other screws and threatened the prisoners taking part in the protest with disciplinary prison transfers.

Generally, when you are not subjugated to their correctional system they try to create a climate of fear. Anyway, prison is like a large melting pot of souls. If you are a coward it will mince you up and make you even more of a coward but if you are tough it will make you even tougher and colder as a person. The cell makes the prisoner suffocate. Outside in the prison yard there is the illusion of freedom...

Still through all of this nothing has ended, the struggle continues.

Those who are right are the rebels not the snitches and those who bow down

—(A popular Greek anarchist chant)

What the Cops Told Us

Brief reflection on a conversation between an anarchist and a progressive student with many anarchist friends, one night in the occupied park...

We had been talking about the revolt, the tactics of the State, how to win the revolution, what were the weaknesses in the anarchist space, what was going well. Like any other night in Exarchia. At nights the whole neighborhood was one giant multicentric meeting, a hive of the buzzing bees of the revolution, talking, arguing, theorizing, planning, laughing, socializing, making the networks stronger. At one point I mentioned the Kolonaki attacks, to name a method of keeping the struggle fresh in people's minds, to show that the anarchists were capable of acting outside of Exarchia too, even in the richest neighborhoods.

And she says: "But the Kolonaki attacks were done by police."

"What? What are you talking about? I mean the time in March when thirty koukoulofori smashed all the luxury shops."

"Yes, that was police."

"No, it wasn't."

"It was. Some cops admitted this to my friend. They said, yeah, we did that."

"I assure you, it was not the police."

"How do you know?"

"I know."

"How?"

"...We know the people who did it."

"But I don't believe it, why would the police say they were the ones behind it?"

"To create divisions and discredit the people taking more aggressive actions, obviously."

"But this friend isn't political at all, it makes no sense for them to tell lies to some uninvolved student."

"But look how quickly that rumor comes to the anarchist space, and the people at its periphery."

It's the same game as always. Everyone should choose their own level of involvement but everyone needs to support the attacks. They can make criticisms—internal criticisms—but the support has to be there. If we're afraid to show that these attacks give us joy, to claim them, not as our own acts but as a part of our struggle, people will sense the marginality of these actions, and the uncertain ones will latch on to any rumor that the attacks were really a provocation by the State meant to discredit the struggle, and they themselves become the unknowing discrediters. Everyone loves a conspiracy that leaves them as victims in a moral play and not protagonists who have to take bold actions in murky situations. How sad, to think of all the brave combatants written down in history as police provocateurs thanks to the people doing the actual police work of discrediting the foremost attacks of the struggle, which sometimes have poor aim, but always are necessary.

Specialized Guerrilla, Diffuse Guerrilla

In the last days of December, a new aspect of the continuing insurrection began to appear more frequently: urban guerrilla groups expanding their presence and activity. Some of these groups existed long before December and came from the extreme Left, following the tradition of 17 November and ELA. But after December, new groups appeared and began carrying out bold attacks, and the communiques they inevitably released were often laden with an antiauthoritarian analysis. Clandestine anarchist groups carrying out nighttime fire bombings against police vehicles or government buildings had been active for years, but the new manifestations of this tactic after December were calling for urban guerrilla warfare as a decisive strategic course.

This development was the subject of strong, and anonymous, debate. There are multiple conflicting opinions. Some people feel that escalating to guerrilla attacks is going too far too fast, that most people will not be able to make that tactical leap or even understand it, and the anarchists will be isolated and vulnerable to heavy repression that the authorities will justify on the basis of those guerrilla activities. The suggestion was even published that the shooting attacks against the police were acts of provocation orchestrated by the State itself. This sounds too much like the habitual response that fearfully denounces any attack considered too extreme as the work of a government conspiracy: the assumption is that people within the struggle are always victims, always defensive, they never take the initiative to attack and they never make a mistake and go too far. Although the theory itself seems invalid, it does reflect that many people considered the guerrilla attacks to be illegitimate or dangerous for the struggle as a whole.

A more nuanced critique is that Greek society has historical references for specialized Left guerrilla groups, such as 17 November, which enjoyed a good deal of success and popular support, but there is little tradition in Greece of the anarchist model of diffuse guerrilla groups—non-vanguardist groups that intend to encourage a diffusion or spreading of their tactics and that exist as amorphous or flexible entities rather than professional guerrilla organizations. Lacking this set of historical references and traditions, the argument goes, the new strategy will not be successful at getting a broader portion of the population to engage in guerrilla actions. Some years back, 17 November itself made a criticism of an antiauthoritarian group attempting to utilize guerrilla tactics against a broader array of targets. 17 November had a populist analysis and they tended to attack targets that the vast majority of the population hated, such as CIA agents or the US Embassy. It is also worth noting that their greater specialization allowed them to touch targets that would be too difficult for less professional groups to even approach. In their critique, they said that choosing more commonplace targets, which the antiauthoritarians did to accompany their deeper

313

analysis, would generate fear rather than appreciation in the society because people would not know why the target was attacked. In this way, the diffuse guerrillas are more demanding of the people, both because they require a deeper critique of capitalism and the State in order to be understood, and because their strategy requires that more and more people make similar attacks.

A third critique aims at clandestinity itself. The argument is that a strategy of clandestine guerrilla warfare is inherently specializing and spectacular. In other words, it takes such a high degree of specialization and expertise that the vast majority of a society cannot and will not participate, contrary to an insurrection in which everyone can participate in their own way, as long as they can go out on the streets. Given the numerical inferiority of the participants, hence the scarcity of the actions, combined with their higher level of preparation and impact, the guerilla actions are by nature spectacular. Their primary audience, whether intended or not, is virtual reality. The major way an urban riot communicates itself, at least within the city in which it takes place, is to be seen directly. Clandestine attacks, however, are witnessed primarily through the lens of the media, as people rarely happen to be around to see them occur. Hence, people become spectators of the struggle rather than its protagonists, as when they are in the streets, participating in public illegal actions.

As the leading edge of the struggle gets further away from people's lived realities, they are transformed even more permanently into spectators; meanwhile the State and the media themselves spectacularize the attacks and make the attacks the symbol for the entire struggle. Popular participation in the decreasingly significant public struggle decreases, and eventually the State can simply turn off the struggle by directing the media to stop publicizing attacks, thus erasing what had become in the popular consciousness the leading edge and primary manifestation of the struggle. Thus decapitated, what remains of the struggle can be bullied and bribed into collaboration with the institutional Left. According to proponents of this critique, that is what happened in Germany and Italy in the '70s and '80s.

The guerrilla strategy also finds many proponents. Some say that attacks should not be denounced, and denouncing attacks carried out by other comrades in the struggle is doing the divisive work of the State. Furthermore, the guerrilla attacks are just another manifestation of the rage of the people, and a larger portion of society can participate in them if they are legitimized and supported by all the comrades. After all, for an insurrection to grow to a revolution it will have to win an armed conflict with the State and it cannot do this if it is unarmed.

Others counter the argument that a guerrilla strategy spectacularizes the struggle or leads to an unintentional vanguard, pointing out that before December, the anarchists were the only ones firebombing the police and attacking banks, and one could have accused them of being vanguardists, except that their tactics were generalized, adopted by society, and taken out of their control, which is exactly what they wanted. Currently, guerrilla attacks are the most extreme and violent manifestation of the struggle but in a certain moment they could become generalized. During the civil war in Greece, a huge portion of the population supported and participated in the clandestine struggle, and revolution at one point or another entails civil war.

Some anarchists who favor the guerrilla strategy believe that non-vanguardist guerrilla groups need nonetheless to have a strong structure and a certain professionalism in order to prevent immature or unprepared people from taking up the guns or doing something reckless that could not be justified. The idea is that if one escalates to tactics that could easily cause the loss of life, they also need to escalate their level of organization and preparedness to be sure that no one is killed needlessly or accidentally. There is also the fact that carelessness leads to people getting caught needlessly, which gives the State the appearance of more power and efficiency than it actually possesses, and discourages others from participating in these attacks.

Below is one of the few criticisms of the guerrilla strategy to be openly published within the Greek antiauthoritarian movement, authored by the autonomist group TPTG. Else-where in the book, we have published communiques released by guerrilla groups after specific attacks.

EXTRACT FROM "THE REBELLIOUS PASSAGE OF A PROLETARIAN MINORITY THROUGH A BRIEF PERIOD OF TIME" BY TPTG

The spectacular separation of armed "struggle."

The need to mediate proletarian anger politically, even if it is to mediate it with an armed mediation, was not something that stemmed from the struggle itself but it was something that was being imposed on the struggle from the outside and afterwards. In the beginning, there were two attacks by the so-called "armed vanguard," one on the 23rd of December after the peak of the rebellion and one on the 5th of January, when the resurgence of the rebellion was at stake. From a proletarian point of view, even if these attacks were not organized by the state itself, the fact that after a month all of us became spectators of those "exemplary acts," that had not at all been part of our collective practice, was a defeat in itself. The "armed vanguard" avoids admitting not only that they were not the first ones to target the police but also that no "armed vanguard," anywhere, has forced the police from the streets, or frightened individual cops from carrying their official identities with them for a few days. They can't admit that they were surpassed by the movement. Claiming that there is "a need to upgrade" violence, the so-called "armed vanguard" essentially tries to downgrade the socially and geographically diffused proletarian violence and violation of the law; the

315

latter are the true opponents of the "armed vanguard" within the movement and as long as such practices go on no interventionism of "upgrading" things can find a fertile soil. It is on that basis that the armed struggle allies with the State: both are challenged by the proletarian subversive activity, the continuation of which constitutes a threat to the existence of both of them.

The proletarian subversive activity in the rebellion gained a temporary but not so superficial victory: an insubordination that weakened the security-surveillance state for a month and proved that we can change the power relations. This became possible since the rebels targeted the social relations in which they are forced to live, something that no "armed vanguard" has ever managed to do.

Considering the range and the intensity of all the December events, the state repressive apparatus proved practically weak. Since they had to deal with a delegitimization of the institutions of control and not just bullets and grenades, the infamous zero tolerance became a simple tolerance towards the rebels' activities. The state counter-attack could actually become successful in January only by making use of the "armed vanguard" operations: first, on an ideological level, by equating the state murder with the wounding of a riot police cop, thus relegitimizing the police and the security-surveillance state in general. Secondly, on an operational level intensifying its repression. They even exploited the place of the attack (Exarchia), presenting the rebellion as a spectacular vendetta between cops and "anarchists," as a grotesque and banal performance staged in a political ghetto.

As the rebellion was dying away, there was a notable proliferation of attacks against banks and state buildings by several groups, which cannot be placed in the same category with the "armed vanguard" "deeds," since most of them do not claim to be ahead of the actual movement (although they do not necessarily lack a voluntaristic, arrogant posture).

However, the return of the "armed vanguard" proper with the execution of an anti-terrorist-squad cop in early June, when even the memory of the rebellion had weakened, has given militarism and the escalation of pure violence a pretext to present themselves as an attractive alternative to a (small?) part of those who participated in the rebellion, if we are to judge by the political tolerance of the antiauthoritarian milieu towards this action. The limited class composition of the rebellion, its restricted extension beyond the level of the delegitimization of the security-surveillance state and the gradual weakening of several communal projects in the center and the neighborhoods—mostly in Athens—led to the flourishing of a separated kind of blind violence as a dangerous caricature of "struggle," or rather a substitute. As certain important subjects of the rebellion were gradually leaving the stage (the high school students, the university students, the immigrants), its social content got weaker and weaker and political identities became again strengthened as was the norm before. The "armed vanguard" violence is just one of these political identities, even in its naïve and nihilistic form, appearing in an era of a generalized crisis of reproduction where the State and capital are unable to offer any social democratic type of "remedies" to heal the wounds of the rebellion. It's not important for us now to doubt about the real identity of these hit men with the ridiculous but revealing name "Revolutionary Sect"; what causes us some concern is the political tolerance of some quarters toward them, given the fact that it's the first time that in a Greek "armed vanguard's" text there's not one grain of even the good old Leninist "for the people" ideology but instead an antisocial, nihilistic bloodlust. The crisis of neoliberalism, as a certain phase of capitalist accumulation and legitimization, seems to lead to a deeper crisis (even to serious signs of social decomposition) and not to any signs of revival of reformism. Even the recent electoral failure of the governing party combined with the high percentage of election abstention (the highest ever in an excessively politicized country like Greece), which was an indirect result of the legitimization crisis that the rebellion expressed and deepened, have not led to any concessions on the part of the State. With all its own limits, the rebellion made the limits of capitalist integration even more visible than before. The slogan "communism or capitalist civilization" seems more timely than ever.

A Hot Summer...

On July 25, at five in the morning, unknown persons placed a firebomb at the gate of the squatted social center, Fabrika Yfanet. People standing guard at the squat quickly put out the fire. In a suspiciously short amount of time, multiple police vehicles arrived at the scene and began provoking the squatters. Later two riot police squads parked nearby.

Four days earlier, several assailants with molotov cocktails attacked the station of Radio Revolt, a pirate radio station broadcasting from an occupied space in Thessaloniki's Aristotelious University. The attack was also thwarted thanks to the resistance of people guarding the station, and damages were minimal.

In Athens, the summer was stained with the appearance of fascists, walking openly in the streets in areas where they had never been seen before, forming groups to patrol their neighborhoods. Police conducted massive raids to clear the undocumented immigrants out of Omonia, sweeping them off the streets where they had once thronged in the thousands, and the fascists held a march in the same neighborhood, protected by police from the anarchists trying to attack them. In Patras the police destroy a major refugee camp, full of people waiting as they try to get on a boat for other parts of Europe and the greater chances of survival they offer. As the police raids mounted, immigrants in Athens protested and rioted for several days, and the anarchists organized a protest in solidarity with them, attracting more than 4,000 people. In the neighborhood of Aghios Panteleimonos, the fascists took over a park with a playground where immigrants and their children had been hanging out, and they forced the local police station to lock the park. In their attempt to segregate the park, they viciously beat up a father in front of his child for violating the boycott.

In August, in the midst of all these clashes and contradictions, the struggle takes a recess. The heat drives everyone out to the islands, and the cities close down for the month. The squatted social centers put up posters inviting nazis and police to get acquainted with their security teams, which are staying throughout the summer to defend these spaces. The fascists decline to take them up on the offer. But the temperature goes up even more as forest fires are set just north of Athens to illegally clear land for real estate development. Even in the midst of a political crisis of legitimacy and popular rebellion, the capitalists are so greedy that they cannot refrain from rocking the boat for just a few months.

At the end of the month the Greek anarchists and antiauthoritarians continue a recent tradition of making a summer camp at Acheloos, a river in eastern Greece that is being diverted for hydroelectric dams and commercial cotton irrigation in a construction megaproject that is destroying one of the Greek mainland's most important wilderness areas.

On August 25, in Belgrade, Serbia, two molotov cocktails are thrown at the Greek Embassy in solidarity with the Greek prisoner Thodoros Iliopoulos, on hunger strike at the time. On September 4th, five anarchists, Tadej Kurep, Ivan Vulović, Sanja Dojkić, Ratibor Trivunac, and Nikola Mitrovic, are arrested and threatened with international terrorism charges. A sixth person goes on the run.

Early on the 4th of September, police spark a small riot in Exarchia when they pursue two people spraying graffiti into the anarchist stronghold. Residents run to stop police from making the arrests, and the cops pull their guns on the crowd, which reacts aggressively. Delta Force arrives on motorbike in several groups, cutting off streets and arresting five people, kicking them savagely with their jackboots. Subsequently, riot police provocatively attack the liberated park on Navarinou, just above the spot where Alexis was murdered. The arrested are charged with throwing molotovs, even though none had been thrown that night. One of the arrested is seriously injured, suffering a ruptured lung. Three cops are also injured, and two cop cars damaged. The next night, a riot police position nearby is attacked with real molotovs, and residents set up burning barricades to hinder the entrance of police reinforcements. Charges against the five arrested in the park are later dropped.

On September 5, during the International Expo in Thessaloniki, PEKOP, the cleaners' union to which Konstantina

Kuneva belongs, leads a protest of thousands of workers. PEKOP declares:

> In the dark days that they are preparing for us, let's get ready, let's organize and let's hit back without delay with a warm autumn and a hot winter. We do not forget December! We do not forget the bullets that killed Alexis, nor the acid that burned K. Kuneva, PEKOP's general secretary! We live social war everyday here. And Konstantina is the flag of our social struggle [...]
>
> We shall not be the tail of the bureaucrats who constantly team up with the bosses and the State, allotting like "parties of power" the privileges of class collaboration, having the audacity to speak in our name, in the name of the working class, stabbing our struggles in the back. Nor will we give ground to those who constantly want to control us, to transform our struggles to votes, and when December comes they cross to the other side of the river... The workers must march and struggle against the bosses without false mediators and good-willers of this or that bureaucracy. The emancipation of the working class is the work of the working class itself!

Along the march protesters destroy several CCTV surveillance cameras and launch flares at the police. Police respond with tear gas, and after the march attempt to arrest a dozen members of Alpha Kappa, meanwhile gassing an Alpha Kappa social center. A large crowd of protesters comes and unarrests the AK members.

Conversation with the Owner of a Small Hotel, on the Train from Athens to Patras

"So what do you think about what happened in December?"

"What do you mean?"

"You know, all the protests, the riots. Do you think it will happen again?"

"You know what, here in Greece we have the conservatives, the Socialists, the Communists, and all they want is power. So if the conservatives are in power, the others will do things to create disruptions so they can call an election and try to take over the government. The conservatives were in power, it looked like the Socialists would be in the next government, so the Communists wanted to make some problems in the streets."

"But it wasn't the Communists in the streets, not the Communist Party. They were trying to stop the occupations and the riots."

"It's always like this in Greece. One political party is in power and the other ones want to be in power, so they create problems. You'll see, in another few years they'll create some other scandal or outrage so they can call elections and change who is in power. That's all they care about."

"Maybe that's why some people want to get rid of all the politicians and all the political parties."

319

"Yes, but their purpose is to organize the country, someone has to do that."

"People can do that themselves."

"You think so? But what about defending the country? Who will do that? We have Albania, Macedonia, Bulgaria, all of them think part of Greece is theirs. And then there is Turkey, just waiting to invade us the minute we are weak. What do we do about that? Get rid of the politicians, and then you'll be without a house, my friend."

"I mean all the politicians, all the governments, in Turkey too."

"You think they'll get rid of the government in Turkey?"

"I know people there who are trying to. And besides, the other Turkish people believe the same lie told by their politicians, that they need the government to protect them against Greece, or the Kurds."

"Ha! Greece is just nine million. How many is Turkey? They're a lion afraid of a cat."

"There's nothing unusual in that. Israel is afraid of Palestine. America is afraid of Al Qaida. The world is full of lions afraid of cats. It's a very useful lie."

"Ha, this is true. The world is full of lions afraid of cats. The Palestinians are very dangerous, with their rocks, and Osama, hiding in a cave somewhere, is very dangerous to a country with nuclear weapons. Ha! Anyways, the politicians won't be able to make people happy. How can they solve the economic problems? They can't! It's a problem of the economy. Greece doesn't produce anything. We don't make any cars. We just have tourism. How can politicians make the crisis go away, or create jobs? They can't. The only thing they can do is crack down on the immigrants who are taking the jobs of Greek people."

"The immigrants aren't taking anyone's jobs. The bosses are choosing to give those jobs to people they can exploit more, and relying on the politicians to blame the immigrants instead of the bosses."

"True, this is true. But anyways that's all they can do, get rid of the immigrants. What else can the politicians do? Nothing. A politician can't create jobs if the capital is not there. But how can they bring capital? They already let the big companies get away without paying taxes. Me, I own one small hotel and I have to pay all the taxes, but if I owned twenty hotels I wouldn't have to pay anything. The real problem is that Greece doesn't produce anything. If we made cars I bet we'd be happier."

"They produce cars in my country and the people aren't happy."

"No? Hmm. Well, we do make the best oil. Olive oil I mean. I make my own oil, I never buy any, I have my own trees. The very best oil comes from Peleponesus, next best from upstairs, the north I mean. But we don't produce our own brand. Italy buys our oil, mixes it with lower quality stuff to make it more, and sells it with an Italian stamp. It's terrible!"

"That's too bad."

"Ah, look out the window there, you see those trees, all black? There were big fires here. The government says it's from people dropping their cigarettes. I tell you what. Go into the forest, take a pack of cigarettes, light every one, and drop them in an area of five square meters. It won't start a single fire. Not unless you add gasoline. People lit those fires. All the sudden, fires started in 200 places around Greece on the same day. That doesn't happen by accident. It's people who burn down the forests so they can build there..."

Maybe it's gotten worse

Yiannis: An anarchist from Patras

I think we had seven arrests here in Patras in December. The heaviest case, and one which we are still trying to arrange support, is with an old man who was arrested with a backpack full of molotovs. But he's a little bit crazy. We're hoping that will help in his defense and get him a reduced sentence.

Patras is a conservative city because of its history. It has always been very industrial, and the people here only think of themselves. Of course this is a problem everywhere, but it is especially bad here. So after December nothing changed. Maybe it got worse. The government destroyed the major immigrant camp here, they bulldozed all the buildings after the fire. I think most of the immigrants went to Athens, or were arrested, though there are still many here trying to get on a boat for Italy. In the summer we tried to set up a social center but it failed. I don't know what to do. There are a few new people involved here, but not many. And the fascists are active, with the help of the police. It's a difficult situation we face.

The Media Try to Kill Memory

A.G. Schwarz

After the massive riots of December ended and the insurrection continued in new forms, the media adapted their counterinsurgency strategy to the new circumstances. In January and February, mention of the revolt disappeared almost entirely from the media. There were a couple important exceptions to this pattern. A few of the more visible and shocking attacks carried out by anticapitalists in those months were given sensational coverage completely divorced from the ongoing struggle that manifested in continuing protests, occupations, counterinformation, and so forth—all of which had disappeared from the media. These now "senseless" attacks were portrayed as the work of the same disconnected and nihilistic hooligans who ruined the legitimate student movement with too much violence in December. The second exception appeared primarily in the Sunday magazines, which ran photo-filled retrospectives on December that sympathized with the high school students, sanitized their participation in December, forgave their youthful excess, and patted them on the back for their social consciousness. Because photography is assumed to be a presentation of reality more objective than the written word, all the images in these pieces succeeded in the Orwellian exercise of making many of the participants of December themselves believe what was inarguably a lie: that the students limited themselves to protests, occupations, assemblies, and a little fighting on the barricades, but they were not responsible for the smashings, the burnings, the attacks on police. The show of sympathy and the ostensible acknowledgment of their story made this lie much easier for the youth to digest. Thus, in a poll released at the time, the vast majority of the youth expressed the belief that the media coverage in December was completely false and irrelevant, yet a majority also believed that it was outsiders operating with unknown motives who were responsible for smashing the shops. The youth distrusted the media, but they were still influenced by them.

In March, the Greek media tacked into a new wind. They could no longer deny that the revolt was continuing without losing their monopoly on the social narrative, so they gave major, fear-mongering coverage to the continuing attacks. They started with and focused on the daytime anarchist attack on Kolonaki, as though the breaking of a few windows was equivalent to the sacking of Rome (and as though the barbarians weren't perhaps a bit better than the Romans). They also gave coverage to the continuing occupations, particularly in Thessaloniki, where the students had taken over Aristotelous University in solidarity with the struggle of the cleaning workers. They mixed up an alleged increase in crime with the occupation itself, suggesting university asylum functioned as a safe haven for antisocial crime and should thus be abolished.

It seems clear that the anarchists themselves were an intended target of the media coverage, which sought not only to build popular confidence in a police solution but to threaten the anarchists. Building off the frightful Kolonaki spectacle, the newspapers filled the front pages with articles on new police measures every day for several weeks in March. Shop owners called for greater protection to prevent more attacks like the one in Kolonaki! Police specialists from Scotland Yard are coming to advise the Greek police! The government is considering abolishing university asylum! The director of the university in Thessaloniki may call in the police to end the occupation! The government will pass a new law outlawing masks and hoods in demonstrations, and criminalizing the insulting of police officers! A high judge is looking into ways to evict the squats! The police will create Delta Force, a rapid response unit to be deployed around the city in teams on motorcycles, for the express purpose of arresting the criminals responsible for these attacks! On April 5th the Athens newspaper *To Vima* reported that the police had about twenty anarchists suspected of participating in the attacks under surveillance, and they expected to make arrests soon. The arrests did not materialize, and in fact over the next months anarchists demonstrated the capability to carry out attacks against the very directors of the police and intelligence apparatus and get away with it. These articles were not a reflection of reality,

rather they were part of the police counterattack to restore order and show force.

The media also continued their work of distinguishing the good parts of the revolt from the bad parts. For example in April, a large and sympathetic article with color photographs appeared in a major Athens newspaper featuring Nosotros, the social center of the left anarchist group Alpha Kappa. It portrayed the space as a cultural center that hosted artistic events and provided social services, showing that even anarchists can be embraced by the system if they learn to restrict themselves to acting in certain ways. It's beyond me to say whether Alpha Kappa self-censored their combative aspects or whether this was entirely the initiative of the media, but either way the result is the same. The same also happened with many sympathetic articles about the new occupied park in Exarchia.

In May, the media turned their focus on the immigrants with a vengeance. During the December coverage, they had separated out the immigrants as the elements responsible for the looting. In the following months, under the guise of humanitarian analysis, they looked at the crisis of immigrant living conditions in Greece in a way that could only substantiate the fascist portrayal of the immigrants as dirty and disgusting. And of course they interviewed shop owners who, with the pragmatic voice of mass murderers, insisted that the immigrants stole things and scared away shoppers; that the cities needed to be "cleaned up." In May and June, the media prepared the summer's pogrom.

323

It needs to be explained first that the European Union recently enacted a new anti-immigrant law declaring that immigrants without visas had to acquire papers in the first EU country where they arrived. In other words, they could not go on to Belgium or Sweden or any of the dominant member states with a higher standard of living and more social welfare, and if they did they would be sent back to the country of entry, if not deported altogether. As Greece is one of the main entry points, the country as a whole was turned into a giant border prison, and it was responsible for making it as difficult as possible for immigrants to acquire papers. So, for example, the only place where asylum could be requested in the entire country was in Athens, and authorities did all they could to obstruct immigrants travelling from the islands or Turkish border towns to the capital. And the immigrants who did arrive had to wait forever just for a simple interview, after which they were usually denied even the paper that said they had requested asylum and their case was being considered. Practically nobody actually got asylum.

In Athens, there were tens of thousands of immigrants waiting around for their chance to get papers. This visible concentration of immigrants was successfully exploited by fascists, and in May the media announced an "immigration crisis." Naturally, only a policing solution was proposed. In May and June, the government sharply increased the number of immigrant concentration camps around the country. These were fenced-in compounds where immigrants were herded together en masse and locked up against their will. They called them "Welcome Centers" with much the same sense of euphemism as when the Nazis called extermination camps "concentration camps." Amid all the hysteria, the fascist party LAOS gained a relatively high number of seats in the European Parliament elections in June. And in July and August the police carried out pogroms against the two major immigrant districts, in Athens and in Patras, destroying settlements and shipping immigrants off to the concentration camps or deporting them. In central Athens alone, thousands were arrested. And where once parts of Omonia had been bustling immigrant neighborhoods with thousands of people from dozens of different countries on the streets, in public, at all hours of the day, now they were "cleaned up," just as the shop owners had wanted. It was eery, trying to find those streets again, and only seeing pleasant avenues with tourists strolling hand in hand, browsing postcards outside gift shops, with nothing to disturb their comfort.

In September, all the media coverage was focused on the upcoming elections, psychologically preparing the illusion that the government was going to clean house so that when the Socialists came into power, they would start with as much legitimacy as possible. December had successfully challenged the legitimacy of the State itself, and now the media had to do a bait and switch, centering specific controversies in specific political parties, so that the losers of December would be Nea Demokratia and not the government as a whole.

It is necessary to go back and look at the relationship between the media and LAOS over the last years in Greece. Though on not quite as large a scale, it seems that LAOS has mimicked the media machine used by Berlusconi of Italy to engineer the society, undermine radical movements, and set the stage for the return of a fascist party as an important political force. Even before LAOS formed from dissident members of Nea Demokratia, they had been consolidating control over several media outlets, so that now the fascists directly own or control three major television stations in Greece. They also have several influential tabloid newspapers that focus on voyeuristic and moralistic celebrity news in the guise of social problems.

In a sort of FOX News effect, as they brought more right wing commentators and sources into the news programs, the other news channels were pushed rightwards as well. Perhaps even more important than the obvious effects on news coverage, has been the role of talk shows, soap operas, entertainment programs, and telemarketing, just like in the Italian phenomenon. The fascist television stations pioneered telemarketing in Greece, providing themselves with potent funding and flooding the airwaves with infomercials for books, videos, and other products relating to beauty (in this manifestation a very racialized notion reified by blond and brunette models with lilly-white skin), nationalistic Greek history and mythology, hunting, weaponry, and paramilitary gear, xenophobia, and the protection of a homogenous and Orthodox Greek culture, Jewish conspiracy theories, and more.

After December, the celebrity talk shows openly promoted fascist and racist ideas and brought personalities from the far Right into the celebrity market. For example the wedding of a LAOS parliament member was turned into a celebrity event through multiple days of news coverage. Hundreds of people were brought to the wedding itself, making it a spectacular and popular happening. It was a clear attempt at social engineering designed to turn Greek society into a receptive mass every bit as fashion-obsessed, consumeristic, selfish, tolerant of policing and surveillance and unsupportive of social movements as Italian society has become, a society in which people hide behind designer sunglasses, chase after Aryan standards of beauty, despise anything poor, ugly, or foreign, understand politics as a popularity contest, and care more about the lives of celebrities than about the lives of other people in their community.

325

All the people went back to their private lives

Alexander, Thodoris, Vlasis, & Kostas: Two students and two graduates from Exarchia High School

V: The strongest influence for ending the riots was the terror created by the mass media. As the State was facing attacks against police stations all over Greece, from school to school, the mass media organized a propaganda campaign obliging parents to get their kids off the streets and lock them in the houses.

A: I think that the Christmas holidays were a big factor.

December made me understand that there were people looking for a revolution, outside of the public view, and that such a revolution is possible. But still it's not that close. Things aren't different now. People just realized how close we are to something like this happening again. And maybe the politicians are being more careful. But I can't imagine Greece changing. I think it will always be a democracy.

T: Few things changed. What happened is that we gathered and then we split again. In my opinion each person acts individualistically and takes care of himself. First and foremost they want to have a good life, they're worried about how they'll survive.

From the time I came to Greece from Albania when I was three years old until now, nothing has changed. During December we felt that something could change but then we realized that all the people went back to their private lives and nothing really changed. Me, I cannot explain my thoughts so clearly, but I hope that this new generation will achieve a social change. It's possible, we will try. In all the days before December I would never have imagined this kind of change. And this keeps me here to dream and participate in the social struggle.

V: A first step toward general social change could be the elimination of religion, that keeps the people trapped in moral codes that prevent a liberated way of thinking and acting and awakening. And also another limitation that entraps us is all this history of national dogmatism, going back ages. But for me, the biggest threat to all society is the existence of the police. Unfortunately I cannot imagine how a world without police could function. But at the same time I won't trap myself in this and not criticize them, especially when there are murders.

One thing that has been very important for young people and students were the DIY bands that they created. Hip-hop, punk, trance, all kinds of music. They could express their thoughts in public, be creative, organize solidarity concerts to help the prisoners of the social struggles. This was going on before December but it's continuing even stronger now, especially with the solidarity concerts.

K: After December the State did not change. In a way you could say that things became even harder, especially for the immigrants. The riot police beat people much more after December and it became harder to go out on the streets and express your ideas. The only thing that changed is in the society, in the people, for many of them it was an awakening that opened their eyes from many years of deep sleep and now they can see the injustices more clearly. Now... what do you expect me to say to you? That we dream of the revolution? Of course we do. If we didn't we wouldn't be in the streets every day talking with people and fighting...

The Passage to Revolution

Transgressio Legis

The text below is an attempt at evaluating the insurrectionary events of December and placing the priority of the passage to revolution in its proper place. Continuously highlighting this issue is one of the key elements of our political discourse and our actions on the practical level. The death of a fifteen-year-old child at the hands of the modernized security forces of democracy was the beginning of a series of situations, the likes of which have never existed before in this country. The social unrest and the destabilization of the government reached impressive levels, but in our eyes something was missing: the passage from revolt to revolution. An organized offensive using all available means against the State, the police, and all the executive officers of the government, as well as against its supporters and functionaries, and of course against every social class that demonstrates a coherent purpose and activity to obstruct the greater revolutionary goals.

The revolt of December crushed all the practical utopian positions that believed such situations could not occur in modern societies. A perfect, stable utopia that could only be impugned by direct action and the creative desire for destruction. The political and social status quo, which is endorsed by some of the ideologues of the movement, is the main issue that must be resolved for revolution to be achieved. The lack of will and action to promote revolutionary ideas will always bring us in conflict on political and practical levels, and our own choices will be the best response in the face of pathetic behaviors.

The passage to revolution, therefore, can only take place through the immediacy of the attacks, which inevitably will sometimes take on an acute and antisocial nature. We should admit that the concept of "antisocial" does not bother us in the least. In fact, we don't tolerate any such characterization, recognizing that it has been adopted as a negative value by those comrades who have endorsed normality. Why should an extremely realistic opinion recently elaborated within an insurgent urban movement be classified as antisocial? Why should we tolerate social groups that only offer us the denial of the reality of our desires? Why shouldn't we target these groups? The rejection of these attacks is the denial of the reality of the revolutionary civil war.

"He who accepts the class struggle cannot deny civil wars, which in any class society represent the continuity and growth—physiological and in some cases inevitable—of the class struggle. To deny the civil wars or to forget about them would mean to stoop to an extreme opportunism."

—Military Program of the Proletarian Revolution (1905)

Whoever, therefore, insists on believing religiously in the greatness of their ideology will always be our enemy no matter what side they come from. Many people throughout history have believed that the revolt is a beautiful, romantic fairy tale. But now that modern society has suffered this blow, do all these supposed intellectuals and ideologues of the movement revise their views in order to understand the war we are in? Shouldn't they take a clear position on this war, and set aside their stereotypes? Even the mechanisms of government have understood the situation. When Markogiannakis complained on TV about the need for a social consensus around law enforcement and for an anti-terrorism policy, it inevitably divided the community into two rival camps: the petty bourgeoisie and the rebels, those of us who hope to become revolutionary subjects. Anyone who is not among the insurgents is submitting to the social consensus of the system.

We must break with this miserable view of laboring away gradually for an ideal society. The uprising of December has laid strong foundations and on these we must build our own world. The only reliable basis for this transition is for the insurgents to drop their inhibitions and annihilate the existing social system and all its values.

"It must always be assumed that all the appropriate conditions to launch the revolution are already in place. The outbreak of rebellion can make them appear."

—Guerrilla Warfare: Military Texts (Ernesto Che Guevara)

Procrastination must be overcome at all costs. At this point we should emphasize the need to escalate from the conventional battlefield to higher forms of struggle. Of course, the conflicts we encounter along the way are the best teachers for the creation of revolutionary subjects, but an obsession with fixed forms of struggle often leads the insurgents to ultimately lose sight of the revolutionary cause.

The confrontational events of December brought many people into the street battles, with their main target being the expression of accumulated anger after the murder of a fifteen-year-old child, helping them reach an initial level of understanding that the uniformed government assassins, who had once seemed untouchable, could be injured, bloodied, and even killed.

The lack of fear in those moments, the new consciousness, led to great successes in the December revolt, helping along some rebellious subjects as they began the passage to revolution. What was missing from the rebellious crowd was the organizational ability and experience in more targeted and direct attacks, with better results, a shortfall which we believe will be overcome in the next revolt.

The revolt of December was the greatest response to the enthusiasts of the capitalist utopia. The brutality of the conflict was so great that the State avoided a military-style operation, which would have catalyzed the arming of the rebellious crowd, and then we would all now be experiencing the beauty of the revolution. For many, the revolution still remains an unknown path they dare not tread. Those, however, who have decided to cross that line already know the desire to strike a lethal blow to all those who want to impose government, while giving life to more affirmation and action for a different reality. The only thing we wish for is pain for all those in power. Plenty of pain and hatred. And not for a moment will we think of retreating. The fear is for them. The fear, hatred, and the ashes we will leave behind us.

The Unanimity of the Fearful

On 2 September, one bomb was detonated at the Athens Stock Exchange and another at the building of the Ministry of Thrace and Macedonia in Thessaloniki. The "Conspiracy of the Cells of Fire" claimed responsibility, releasing the following communique.

Throughout history, leaders of totalitarian regimes have aimed for social cohesion. Through this cohesion the mass-human is produced—more flexible, more disciplined, and more conservative toward the prevalent social behaviors. It is the contemporary class of these socially integrated citizens who then discover their common identity and crouch around the common interest, common aspirations, and desires. All the loneliness of the western world meets for a moment in the snapshot of consumerist frenzy.

In Greece during the '80s social cohesion was inspired by the dream of "change" and invested in the owner-mania of house-building. Multi-storey flats in Athens and Thessaloniki were built one after another in order to accommodate the absence of life emerging as family ownership: property. Everyone was seeking their own property as recognition of their social value. "Neo-Greek" required property-owner status.

In the '90s came new appliances, mortgaged joy, and the second car. The neo-Greek bourgeoisie were parading their uselessness in a new environment of technological comfort and digital pleasure, promised by Greek capitalism. Loans for new living room couches and electrical appliances became routine.

And so the bourgeoisie acquired all the characteristics of a class. They have common desires, common aspirations, a common language and no consciousness. Yet they also have something else, something that in times of crisis becomes the strongest negotiation strategy for its administrators: they have common fears. Fear of loss of all these material "ideals" acquired with so much compromise, tolerance, and humiliation. The peaceful bourgeoisie is capable of killing someone, should they threaten their property. Because in this very property they have invested everything they are.

In illusions all hopes for a future that will never come are placed; daily humiliations are soothed, stressed micro-egos get to rest. Leaders invest in the politics of crisis and fear once the social cohesion of the common dream collapses, as a natural malfunction of the capitalist machine.

First of all, the notion of a crisis as constantly bombarded upon us through the media is in itself a military order, an order dictating social alert. The social fear parading in front of the unknown of the crisis has its own, very distinct smell. It is the smell of the cowardliness of all that the bourgeoisie have accepted, all the desires they never discovered, all the humiliations they never reacted to, all the roles they played in front of the empty stage of their bourgeois fantasizing. Social fear also has its own expression—it is vengeful, stingy, and conservative.

Social cohesion is reclaimed by fear. From the religious crisis of some "god" to the national crises, even their breathe is tuned in, military style. The entire zombified society dances along the rhythms of the crisis, incapable of even realizing what has happened.

These artificial alerts act as military exercises against social polarization. The times they are tested are chosen very carefully. Because they are not limited to one state, especially the economic crisis, they acquire different versions between them, so as to act more efficiently.

For example, the current economic crisis in the USA as a response of the conservative "white" Republicans to the established Democrats and the restructuring in the health system serve different purposes to the crisis in Greece after the revolt of December. And also, the crisis with the outbreak of the new flu also comes to serve other purposes.

The politics of crisis prove to be a rather successful technique because except for the "wise ones" (political authority, journalists, analysts, "experts" of all sorts) who propagate it, there is also a stupid audience of the faithful (society) ready to accept it and take orders.

In Greece, after all, the technique of crisis is a typical. Often after social tension and clashes, or ruptures caused by the enemy within, such crises of national unanimity make their appearance.

1991 was the year of the mass school occupations and the assassination of teacher Nikos Temponeras while the next year saw the crisis with Skopje and the Macedonian demonstrations. 1995 was the year of the largest mass arrest—500 people in the Athens Polytechnic—while 1996 saw the Imia crisis.[1] 2008 saw the revolt of December and 2009 was the year of the migrant crisis, pogroms, concentration camps, Turkish airspace violations and revelations of the execution of missing Greek-Cypriots by Turkish-Cypriots. This does not mean to say that events were "produced" in order to disorient the zombified public opinion. Imia did not happen to cover the Polytechnic arrests, nor was the supposed migrant issue highlighted to cover for December. Plus the fact that the economy is damaged and collapsing is a reality. The technique of the crisis is simply the director-like ability to highlight certain scenes at the right moment, so to direct the viewer's gaze.

Air-space violations and incidents with Greek rocks have happened many times, and yet in the case of Imia they were particularly promoted. (Undocumented) migrants have been living in the centre of Athens for years, and yet it was now that they had to be "revealed." Illnesses and epidemics exist or are created constantly, yet once their period of usefulness is over

331

_____

1   Skirmishes between the Greek and Turkish armies over a small rock in the middle of the sea.

they disappear without anyone knowing their ending, like in the cases of the Mad Cow Disease and the Asian flu.

The economy is constantly in the red, this has to be emphasized. Tables of statistics have no importance whatsoever, nor do the facts produced by financial authorities or financial analyses. What needs to be understood by the revolutionary force and the new urban guerilla tendency is the social value of the financial crisis, the social value of fear—we need to proceed to our counter-analyses and to launch an attack on all fronts.

Economy is not a mere math equation, it is a factory for the production of relationships. The coming elections are the visible exit from the crisis. They are the diffusion of the amassed social fear and its replacement by the hope for reconstruction of the bourgeois dream. We know that even sad people, who carry the title of citizen as a badge of honor, think of elections as outdated—and yet they are the only thing they have. After all, as we said, illusions and idiocy are nearly totally unbeatable, but not without their weaknesses.

Because we, like other comrades of the new urban guerilla tendency, do not participate in fixed games, nor do we participate in the official fiestas (demonstrations), in called-for marches—such as those against the International Expo in Thessaloniki, we choose our own time to act.

And so at dawn on Wednesday, September 2, we placed a self-made explosive device consisting of two time bombs and 8 kilos of explosives in the back entrance of the Ministry of Macedonia-Thrace. In order to avoid injuries we notified one TV station and the police.

The selection of that particular target was a challenge due to the police protection of the particular location. The policemen by the entrance, the riot police unit in the courtyard, the police blocks on the adjacent Ayiou Dimitriou St., the patrols around the building were all a good opportunity for us to send them run panicking.

Each time that we explain the operational part of a plan we do so not in order to brag of our flawlessness and bravery, that would be nonsense. Whatever we do, we do because we feel it, and it fills us with meaning. These references to some operational details take place as an invitation to new comrades in order to share with them our belief that responsibility, good organizing, trustworthiness, comradely feelings, and decisiveness can attack that which until yesterday seemed unapproachable.

After all, the consecutive attacks that took place in our city during the summer by different groups prove that the new urban guerilla tendency is already under way, and prepares its own charge. Broken doors, smashed shop fronts, smoke from the torched buildings, the chaos of sabotage, it's a unforeseeable network of communication. It is a way to tell our losses, our contradictions, our desires, ignoring the registries of authority and laughing at its established rules. No respect to the authorities of this city and its obedient citizens.

We shall return…

December Revisited

How much were the limits of the insurrection imposed from outside, by the power of the State?

The government trapped in scandals, economical crisis, and inner conflicts is unable to learn from all the ways it was beaten. An Elite that tries to behave like nothing happened can do nothing but forget and place the insurrection in an oblivion.

During the insurrection in the countryside, the towns and small cities, the external influences were much stronger than in Athens and Thessaloniki. For example, in Patras and in Larisa, both big cities that experienced riots that the police were unable to control for days, small but well organized groups of neo-nazis together with riot police were searching for the young people, street by street, and following groups of high school students from the riots to their houses, frightening them and their parents as well.

In small cities and towns, undercover policemen were going from shop to shop to spread false rumors and to inform the owners that wild anarchists were on their way from the big cities to come destroy their shops in the same way the television was portraying an exaggerated destruction of small shops in Athens. So when young people, anarchists, and leftists came out onto the streets of their small town with no intention to smash anything but banks, police stations, and government buildings, the shop owners treated them like vandals rather than their own children. However in most small towns during the insurrection the people generally had an attitude that these were "our own children," and the youth and comrades accomplished unbelievable actions on a local scale.

The influence of conservativism was also much stronger in some right wing towns. Conservatism, the power that keeps our life "as it was," our mind "as we know it," and our activities "as we've always done them," was the strongest factor for sustaining normality before, during, and after the riots all over the country.

Many people opposed the insurrection and they had the power to express their disapproval much more openly and effectively in the countryside. In some of the towns the majority of the locals were obviously against the "tendencies" of the anarchists and the leftists. In these towns it was very difficult for the small number of isolated participants to sustain an insurrectionary enthusiasm for many days, even though in such places actions still took place day after day for weeks, proving that the passion for freedom doesn't fear any authoritarian conservative majority.

The power of the State existed mainly in radio interviews, TV programing, and riot police in the streets. The work of the State was to offer excuses and reinforce the conservative defenses of this society, to sustain normality even in the middle of chaos, and to express with certainty that nothing will change; also to suppress the total chaos without having another dead body on the streets. It was crucial that they do it without filling up the stadiums with thousands of detainees, in order not to create images of dictatorship within the spectacle of social life.

The work of the mass media, as part of the regime, was to offer simplistic excuses for the "children's revolt," to not alienate their parents, to avoid speaking seriously about the specific reasons behind many targets of smashing and burning, to feed the worst fears of the conservative majority and to portray the anarchists as irrelevant to the phenomenon. In this way they were building the separation between the good children and the bad anarchists, immigrants, radicals, extremists—criminals

How much did the limits come from the participants themselves?

In big cities and especially in Athens and Thessaloniki, physical exhaustion had a strong influence after all those days of tear gas, running around the city center, hours of assemblies and all kinds of direct actions, creating and sustaining street barricades and liberated zones, smashing, burning, and fighting the riot police, the undercover police, and the neonazis over vast areas of the city…day after day and through the nights. The boys and girls sleeping inside the occupied universities for many days showed heroic physical strength.

When the schools reopened the students had to go back to class. Three weeks after the start of the revolt the university students started to think it was possible to lose credit for the whole academic year if the occupation of the universities continued after Christmas. After three weeks the students took to the streets less and less. Satisfied by the amazing personal experience of revolt and revenge against the State, they were tired from the street fighting. And they were pushed by their parents to return to normality. The students and youth who were not politically organized began to lose the feeling of togetherness of the first weeks, and started again to express skepticism towards the attitude, decisions, initiatives, and political analysis of the anarchists. Many continued to participate in different actions but they began to keep a distance from the central occupations and riots.

And the workers had their jobs waiting for them. Most of the participants had to work all day and then they participated in the actions in the afternoons and evenings, also expressing an amazing physical strength. The worst moment of the assembly for the occupation of the General Confederation of Greek Workers was when the insurgent workers started to speak out against spending a long time forming a deeper analysis because they had to go to sleep so they could work the next morning. Work was a limitation before, during, and after the insurrection.

After the third day the immigrants, many of whom lacked papers, faced a very strong backlash from the police and in public opinion. Police continued searching for them for months and in the following summer they arrested thousands of so-called illegal immigrants.

In the network of assemblies and conversations there began to reappear many different questions, debates, and the endless disagreements that characterize the Greek radical space. Many of these took the form of hostile dichotomies and enmities, like leftists vs. insurrectionists, antiauthoritarians vs. anarchists, artists vs. anti-artists, independent media journalists vs. anti-media activists, direct action vs. political messaging, naïves vs. extremists, hooliganism vs. antistatism, antistatism vs. criminality, anarcho-communism vs. post-anarchy, junkies vs. serious political revolutionaries, looting vs. burning, and so on. Many people felt this and made conscious efforts to combat it. But by the third week, many of the debates had become long and tedious distractions to the disappointment we felt when we saw that the whole society would not rise up, as many people hoped it would in the early days.

A major defeat came early, when the syndicalist hierarchy decided to cancel the nationwide general strike scheduled for December 10th. This strike had been announced long before the death of Alexis, but they cancelled it to avoid generalizing the insurrection. The historical meeting with the working class failed to happen once more. Never trust the workers. The "working class" followed their leaders, their political parties, their own syndicalist institutions, unions and organizations, their own idols and ghosts. The workers, the farmers, the petit-bourgeoisie did everything in its power to help the regime survive and bring everything back to normal.

So you see, normality was also hiding inside of us, not only around us.

The submission of the majority to the status-quo and the habitual repetitive behavior of work and consumption kept millions of people off the streets. The inability of the insurrection to explain politically the reasons for the actions and to expand this understanding on a scale that could address the problems of common people was a failure that kept the entire society from exploding, from taking up the revolt and continuing it with their own decisions and actions.

For sure, people were not ready for social change, not even for a general confrontation with their own realities. The death of Alexis fell like a thunderclap on their pathetic situation but most of them were unable to understand what caused their own children, their own friends, their own neighbors, to revolt. The society could feel it, they could express empathy, but they were not ready to translate it into a political confrontation with the regime.

In an insurrectionary way of thinking we can say that now, after the insurrection, the consciousness of millions of people has stepped forward and this is the main achievement of the revolt. The insurrection opens horizons. Many things that will happen in the future could never have happened before December.

All the thousands of people who participated offered an invitation to the others, the silent majority. When this silence fills your ears, echoing off the streets of a crowded city that wants to come back to normality after four weeks of endless riots and all kinds of actions, an inner voice forces you to pack up all the inspiration and experience you have won for yourself, to go back to your collective and continue the struggle from there.

Even with most of the markets destroyed the society generated a strange need to reproduce a pseudo-celebratory Christmas. Even though all the walls of the city were painted with the slogan "Christmas Postponed, We Have Insurrection" and the smoke of the tear gas and the smell of burned banks and the ashes of luxury shops still hung in the air, and the death of Alexis filled everyone's thoughts, Christmas happened on December 25 just like every other year. The fucking mayor announced during New Year's Eve from Syntagma Square, next to the brand new Christmas tree, this one protected by riot police, that we are all one, that we are all the same, and we are happy! Thousands of poor immigrants were clapping their hands below the stage, though they hardly understood a word. The three central occupations in Athens (Polytechnic, Nomiki, ASOEE) dissolved one or two days before Christmas.

And you walk in the city center with your friends, four o'clock on New Year's morning, and there are no riots anymore, and you want to smash everything around you and start again from the beginning. And an inner instinct says to you that there is still a lot of work to do before this world will explode… And the insurrection continues traveling in space and time, but still you feel that something is missing, and there are a lot of things we have to take care of.

In what ways were the limits of the insurrection determined by factors in place before it started, such as the infrastructure of antiauthoritarian groups and projects and the culture of resistance in Greece?

For many decades the uncompromising fight of anarchists against the State and capitalism has found its chief expression in the confrontation with all the various bureaus and branches of police across the planet, as can be seen by the local police sections of Prague, Seattle, Genoa, Thessaloniki, Maastricht, Nice, Rostock, Berlin, Copenhagen, Paris, Cancun, Santiago, Buenos Aires, San Francisco, Mexico City, Hamburg, St. Paul, Turin, Johannesburg, Miami, Seoul, and many other places. Of course, as the State is not a castle, the police are not the major protector of the State. Social apathy, habit, acceptance of status, and fear of change are perhaps even stronger protectors of the State than the army, and the comrades in Greece know this well. But, during the "Days for Alexis," the police were the primary target of the attack. The reasons were obvious this time even to the conservatives. The struggle was righteous even for the reformists. The anarchist common-sense for once met with the social common-sense. Unfortunately, common-sense is a great obstacle to wisdom.

The target of the struggle itself, the police, was the greatest limitation to the expanding of the insurrection to a general social insurrection. For most of the common people the police brutality was the target of this struggle and the anarchists, used to fighting against the police for ages, fought hardest alongside the people who wanted to express their rage against police brutality, together with them, sometimes even following them.

But generally they were unable to take the majority of the people with them in a total negation of the roots of the regime and against the real causes of this and all the other murders carried out by the State and capitalism. Most of the people were not ready yet to travel to the roots of their slavery. The society was not ready to face its own failures in the clear light of insurrection.

And the people in the struggle did not expand the dialogue as necessary, to encompass all sides of everyday life. Of the hundreds of communiqués released, only a few could really offer an inspiring political explanation and a solid organizational solution. The affinity groups and the initiatives had the capability to offer high-quality analysis of the conditions and a hard critique of the regime, but they hadn't enough experience to spread enthusiasm for a social victory, visions of a world that could appear from the ashes of the old world,

practical escape routes the dead-ends of a neoliberalism in serious crisis, images from the future we are dreaming of, applicable plans for continuing the struggle once everything is already smashed and burned.

So when the rage started to fade there were no solid answers as to what should come next. Not even in our craziest dreams had any of us come so far. We walked for days and days like shadows inside our own struggles, wondering, through the smoke of the tear gas, about each next step.

Who has the proper answers, who can even narrate this story, who can offer solutions and answers about the way to general social insurrection? No one wanted to oblige the society to go further and the anarchists always dislike this role. Four weeks after the assassination of Alexis everyone knew that this is not a revolution and so nobody gave specific answers for what we had to do in order to go further. What could we do to keep the riots from ending? Is the never ending riot the way to social insurrection?

Most people that participated in the insurrection say that it didn't end. We find great truth in this, as thousands of us participate and stay active in many projects, struggles, and assemblies that were created after December in all the cities and towns. For most people Alexis is still alive. In today's struggles you can find him smiling behind actions, demonstrations, creative plans, and destructive visions

What conflicts have developed after the uprising between groups that participated in it together? Are there bonds and connections

that were possible to maintain during the uprising that have broken down since then?

During the insurrection many old friends lost each other forever and people or groups that hated each other for decades worked in projects and actions together. Many old groups transformed into something completely different and many new affinity groups have been created. As most of the Greek anarchists don't like each other, and deep differences separate groups and people, no one can speak definitively about what is happening and nobody clearly understands what is prepared and by whom. This total fragmentation is very useful during periods of "social peace" as it produces a vast variety of opinions, analysis, and initiatives. The police cannot infiltrate the movement, since such a thing does not exist. Hundreds upon hundreds of groups, people who've known each other for many years and share total trust and empathy, they meet, appearing as if from nowhere and return to nowhere.

In a way, all this fragmentation created the strange situation where all these people, who knew each other for years but would never talk to each other, were suddenly speaking, spending time together, and fighting side by side. December produced strong feelings of solidarity and common struggle.

In the first months of 2009, huge assemblies, mostly accommodated in the university amphitheaters late in the afternoon, were taking place nearly every day. Sometimes people from one assembly started to participate in the one taking place before it, as they waited for it to finish and for the next one to start. Some of them, for example the Assembly for Solidarity with Immigrants, for Solidarity with December's Prisoners, the Fight for Worker Konstantina Kuneva, the Assembly of the School and University Students, the Assembly of Insurgent Doctors and Nurses, of Insurgent Artists, the Assembly of Unknown Artists, the Assembly of The Ones Here and Now and For All of Us, the Assembly of Workers and Unemployed, the Exarchia Neighborhood Initiative Committee, and many other Committees in different neighborhoods, as well as assemblies happening in other cities all over the country, were gathering from 100 to 400 active people every week. And to all these general insurrectionary assemblies of course we have to add all the separate meetings of collectives and groups that were participating in these general assemblies.

Throughout these months there was a poster on the walls of Athens with a wildly naïve dadaist monster saying: "Obedience Ended! Life is Magical!" and for most of us this magical life was to jump from assembly to assembly preparing unbelievable things and putting them in practice with all those people. Those assemblies brought to life all different kinds of actions and projects and visions and crazy dreams you had from when you were fifteen years old or from last week's late night talk with some friends or some secret plan you had with your lover and now was coming true.

Most of the initiatives and the assemblies of artists, romantics, non-ideological people, and creative activists shrank, lost the enthusiasm of the first week and became smaller and more solid creative groups. Various reasons forced people from these assemblies to go back to their individual creativity but many of these groups are still dedicated to their projects.

Week after week, and as people were coming closer and closer, the old conflicts, the differences, the diverse political standpoints and the different needs, expectations, strategies, and methods started to appear again. This brought back to the surface the old separations and the old debates. It proved that the differences were not just ephemeral misunderstandings or personal distrust but were based in deep analysis and long-term differences of practice and ways of thinking.

The interesting thing was that even though most of these general assemblies split or started to attract fewer people and to have less power and less influence, new ways of organizing appeared. After some months of meetings the whole political space took new directions. The general assemblies were not useful anymore as new coalitions, new friendships, and new contacts appeared. Different squats, social centers, and initiatives started to form after the end of the general assemblies. People and groups that met during the insurrection and the period of open creativity and massive open meetings after December now had experience with each other, they knew if they agreed or disagreed, they knew what were the directions and strategies of each group and so new projects, plans, and solid decisions took place. In this way the anarchists and other insurrectionists and radical activists avoided conflicts.

The melting pot of general assemblies broke into much more effective meetings, laboratories of creative chaos, squats, and direct actions.

How effective has government repression been in weakening the movements that started the uprising? What have been the most effective ways to resist this repression?

A basic characteristic of the Greek anarchist space is that through the influence of insurrectionary practices it refuses to see itself as a homogenous "movement" and especially as a movement of "resistance" or "direct action." The idea of direct attack is much more influential. The momentum of the attack is controlled by the groups and the initiatives and not by any collective, central decision-making process.

Of course, in periods of social mobilization like the demonstrations against the privatization of education or of health and public insurance or in big events like the European Union Summit or the G8 there is coordination and communication between the groups. But even under these circumstances the initiative for the direct attack is taken by the groups and individuals. This makes the things very complicated for the State and also for the people. No one can decide what will happen, no one knows what actually transpired until it has already happened.

The anarchist space has the ability to appear very powerful and disappear completely from the stage of confrontation, for short periods of recovery. These short periods without riots hypnotize the State and make the government believe it has

339

other more important things to care about. In these periods of calm, the eye of authority is not focused on the anarchists. Meanwhile the arson groups commit unstoppable attacks against all kinds of targets. During these periods hundreds of assemblies, events, public talks, film shows, free festivals, parties, lectures, workshops, and public non-confrontational demonstrations assure the visibility of the anarchists, autonomists, and anarcho-libertarians. All these political and cultural processes are also responsible for the never ending attraction of new people, the replacement of burnt-out people with fresh ones in the frontline of the riots and the preparation for a new circle of intense confrontation.

It is like a wave. When it's up you can see it in the news, on TV, in the streets, everywhere. When it's down, you don't see it but you feel it. You meet with the wave because it is coming to you and moving unstoppably through the initiatives of thousands of different people.

What are some of the ways that people have had to "recover" from the uprising? Legal troubles? Emotional trauma? Exhaustion?

There was not any emotional trauma from December. The use of molotov cocktails heals the crowds' panic and fear and takes back control of the streets from police. Molotovs used as a defensive tool can keep the riot police away long enough for everyone to run away safely and recover from the tear gas or avoid arrest. When molotovs are used as offensive weapons together with hundreds of stones from broken pavement they give courage to the crowds and spread a feeling of massive power and the belief that they can accomplish amazing things.

As a slogan from December put it: "Action replaces Tears."

Many people participated in the solidarity movement for the sixty-five that were arrested and who stayed in custody for two to eight months. Now all of them are free. The solidarity movement that took over the streets with massive demonstrations and counter-information, that held massive fundraising concerts and organized movement lawyers has made clear to Greek anarchists that in the years to come solidarity must be one of the main methodologies of any movement that wants to participate in a serious confrontation with the regime.

There was no need for "recovering" after December. We also have to clarify that there was no end to the insurrection and especially no ending caused by legal troubles, emotional troubles, exhaustion, or repression. Rather, the anarchist space, in an instinctual and intelligent way, chose to disappear from the central highways and put into practice many other low-tension initiatives that enrich the struggle. This wise, self-preserving urban guerilla strategy also finds its expressions in the appearance of many different projects that started after December and now help the "movement" to deepen its roots in the society and in the local communities.

How has the government used the uprising strategically to strengthen its position, since December? Could this have been avoided?

The government didn't find ways to use the insurrection to strengthen its position. It was difficult to do such a thing as the insurrection was spread among all social classes and backgrounds. Only the immigrants were brought into a worse position as they faced a backlash and the police pogrom against those without papers, that occurred in June. The solidarity shown toward immigrants was strong but unable to protect them. A lot of effort is going into bringing the immigrants closer to the anarchist space but this task is not easy at all. The immigrants have their own limitations, their own interests, their own fears and wishes. Many of them they have a very difficult life and very different cultural and political or non-political backgrounds.

In what ways has the uprising put anarchists in a stronger position? In what ways has it used up energy without putting anarchists in a stronger position? Are there any ways it has put anarchists in a weaker position?

The anarchist movement in Greece underwent a lot of methodological changes over the last years in its efforts to come closer to society, to hear the problems of the people, to avoid an anti-social attitude without falling into reformism, and to try to find ways to participate in and radicalize the social movements of our times. All these efforts bore fruit during December.

The social centers that opened in all major cities of Greece during the last years, rented or squatted, offered the best preparation for the creation of strong, active circles of fighters and assemblies able to produce and spread analysis and propaganda everywhere.

Anarchist participation in the social struggles of the students and workers during the last years was also very important, and it utilized two main strategies, changing according to the circumstances:

1) Separate, visible anarchist blocs, with flags, banners, posters, and pamphlets.

2) Radical direct action, smashings, attacks on the police with molotovs, sticks, and stones.

In this way the Black Bloc spread throughout the whole body of these mass demonstrations, even if only a minority were participating. The adoption of these two strategies by all anarchists according to the tension of the social struggle and the available momentum produced a common ground for different comrades and eliminated inner conflicts. And the anarchist participation empowered those social struggles, gained respect from other political organizations, produced common ground with many different social subjects and attracted many new people to anarchy.

The defense of Exarchia and other areas like it in Greece as autonomous public zones, including street corners and an everyday presence in "our own" cafés and bars, offered a constant meeting point that empowered the relations, the connections, and the coordination of actions. The creation of anarchists squats, social centers, occupied rooms in universities, concerts, events, film showings, and assemblies offered a sustainable ground for the cultivation of anarchist ideas and practices.

All these conditions are much more powerful now after December and it doesn't seem that there is any way to put ourselves in a weaker position. As long as we maintain the ability to listen to the heart and understand the mind of the society, the State cannot defeat the anarchists.

Are you working with new people since December? More people?

Many young people who participated in the riots continue to avoid any political participation, so you will see many new people in the free festivals, DIY concerts, underground rave parties, and even the demonstrations, but not in the assemblies or discussions; however the youth in general seem to be much more critical towards mainstream TV culture than they were before December. On the other hand there is a whole new generation of young anarchists, especially in the countryside, who have become politically active. But the greatest achievement of December is that thousands of people who were anarchists before December but did nothing more than hang around in Exarchia or go to some demonstrations have now become active, they have found confidence in themselves, and they are organizing different projects, writing pamphlets, taking part in the struggle.

Are the arguments and disagreements different? For example when you disagree with someone, does it end the same way now as before December, or is there more possibility, more learning, more solidarity?

This unfortunately has a lot to do with personal relations and local ways of analysis. For sure, it is different from city to city. As an example, the classical conflict between the different sections of Alpha Kappa and the Black Bloc differs completely from city to city. In some areas the people are old friends who hate each other, in other places they organize demonstrations together, in other cities they don't even say hello. In some cities the punks like the Black Bloc and in other cities they punch each other in the squares. In some cities the anarcho-junkies hate the Black Bloc, in other cities they show respect. In some cities the anarcho-hooligans fight with the Black Bloc, in other cities they fight with Antiauthoritarian Current.

The classical technique for solving theoretical and practical differences in the Greek anarchist space continues to be the trading of punches between two crowds, in the middle of the square or during a party in the university or some day after two people have had a fight. These continue to happen same as always. There are always people in every group who try to avoid this method, but it is still a common practice. Generally speaking, December gave all kinds of groups an excuse to explain the spirit and the meanings of the insurrection in their own way. Everybody finds the absolute verification of their own beliefs and conclusions within the spirit of the insurrection. In the long run this fact might cause bigger disagreements than before. For the time being, many people try to create bridges and keep the personal communication open between different people and theoretical streams.

Are there any weaknesses the movement is refusing to look at?

Yes, obviously there are many weaknesses because if they didn't exist we would have completed the "revolution." But do we have the time to think about our weaknesses, to reconcile our conflicts, renegotiate our beliefs and rearrange our strategies? Unfortunately after the self-validation of December the egoism of many comrades only got stronger, so it's more difficult to look at the weaknesses.

On the other hand, a great difference between the Greek movement and the US movement, for example, is that we don't spend so much time analyzing our defeats, we don't speak on public radio, in magazines, newspapers, or books about our problems. We don't overemphasize our inabilities and of course we don't write books or pamphlets or posts on the internet about our inner conflicts and our different opinions on a specific subject. In a way, this is much better. The weaknesses of the movement are not written in books or on the internet, you face them on the street, behind the barricades, outside of the assemblies, or you speak about them on a street corner, late at night, drunk, face to face with your friends and comrades.

Where do you think the movement will be one year from now?

It will be in many different new squats and in the old ones. In new social centers and in the same old squares, the old cafés and new bars created by friends and comrades, a place to feel safe, where you can speak about everything. It will be in taverns getting drunk together, building courage for late night attacks against riot police squads around the city. It will be hunting the neo-nazis from street to street in order to fuck them. Where do you think the movement will be?

It will be in a war against apathy, stupidity, and defeatism. It will be in arson attacks against all kinds of State and capitalist targets. It will be in free festivals and crazy all night parties, it will be drunk and happy having sex or finding a new boyfriend. It will be in the smile of a young boy behind his mask and in the hands of a girl throwing stones at the policemen. It will be all around the country, in the posters on the walls, the communiqués, the books, the hundreds of new blogs talking about new actions. It will be in the graffiti everywhere, an "a" in a circle, or the squat symbol, or the symbol of chaos, the symbol of entropy, the symbol of void or just your tag, your name that means Fuck The Police… It will be in the heart of thousands of new people all around the world and it will be here still, on the same spot where the State assassinated Alexis, defending it from the rank smell of the policemen.

Has the movement gotten more or less arrogant since December?

In the Greek language "arrogant" means the person who believes that he is more important than he is, or the person who underestimates those around him. In this way, yes, many people from the movement became more arrogant towards the State and the police. But many people try to keep themselves in mental balance with dark jokes.

"Arrogant" in Greek also means a specific stance of a warrior's body, to not feel fear and to stand still and proud while defending your point, to have the power to defend your turf and expand into the territory around you. Arrogant means to have the inner power to start fights with enemies who are much stronger than you. In this way, yes, the movement became much more arrogant.

Can you describe contact you have with people who were previously outside of your circle? What new communication and connections do you have?

Never speak in public about your communications and your connections, especially with people you don't know or with people you don't trust 100%. This is the best form of communication with people previously outside of your circle. Of course, during this year of insurrection all of us gained some great new friends and comrades from a vast cultural background and from different economic classes.

What is something that anarchists are doing now that they never did before?

Trying to connect between two powers through the activity of the same people. As you Destroy, you also Create, smashing and burning while making living, functional alternatives. This is an end to the separation between violence and non-violence forever: the violent becomes the non-violent and the non-violent becomes a monster that can confront all kinds of power. There is no morality of non-violence anymore in Greece, even the non-violent activists agree with this. There are no non-violent anarchists, and even the sensitive, naïve romantics are ready to confront the tear gas, build barricades, and fight the police.

As one poster proclaimed from walls all over Athens just before the elections, "Sometimes the most violent thing is to do nothing. Don't vote!"

Violence and Non-Violence are not identities or morals. The same people who fight against the police have the experience and the knowledge to create a park, make non-confrontational political and social demos, write a book, sing a song, play with children in the playground. The same people who make art happenings and dance in front of the police with the drums and the puppets will fight back with molotovs and stones along with the Black Bloc when the police come closer, and they will help their comrades to escape. The same people whom you will meet behind the barricades are the people who will organize a grocery shop with organic vegetables and fruits from the anarchist farms, and all of them participated and will participate again together in the insurrection.

The way that non-violent practices blend into an insurrectionary context is happening here for the first time and it is one of the most extraordinary things to arise after December. The methodology with which the same people express both of these identities in an open and all inclusive experiment produces an explosive new social reality. It destroys the separation between insurrectionism and the creation of alternatives in an effort to avoid the transformation of insurrection into a new separate identity or lifestyle and at the same time to keep the social struggles from falling into reformism. The one strategy can overpass and solve the limitations of the other in a complementary and not an antagonistic manner.

How will anarchists overcome the power of the media?

…and how we will overcome nationalism, conservatism, cynicism, apathy, and the influence of the heavily controlled public or private mass education?

Possibly we will overcome the power of the media only through the building of a strong underground anarchist culture, that will include thousands of dedicated "amateur intellectuals" in the same way that it now includes thousands of amateur DJs or punk band members. We will overcome the power of the media through the free distribution of all kinds of cultural products, books, cds, dvds, hand to hand and face to face. If we count, for example, that many hundreds of these things were published this year in Greece—each at between 1000 and 4000 copies and distributed for free all over the country—you can imagine that whole libraries could be filled with underground cultural products of theory, creativity, and propaganda if thousands of people put this approach into practice through personal and collective efforts.

When we transform information and culture into a gift our culture and information gains the highest possible authenticity and respect from the common people. Through the organization of meeting points, events, and film showings we can transform information into a collective power. We have to entice people out of their prison cells of mainstream stupidity and into a culture without spectators or spectacles. And we can expand the mistrust of the people towards the corporate media through widespread anti-media campaigns, and through the total refusal to collaborate with the mass media in any way. This is a long-term strategy that in the meantime will cause people to rely on the Internet for information when something really important is happening.

We have to create our own myths, our own information, our own incredible actions and to cover them by ourselves. The people are not stupid. Society knows that TV news is full of lies and the younger generation doesn't watch TV news anyway.

But are we capable of really breaking the status of the big media corporations with our creativity? Are we capable of producing such interesting theory, such fascinating films, and such great stories? Are we ready to live great adventures that will spread in seconds all over the planet? Are we capable of finding ways to explain our visions to adults, even though we are adults ourselves? Are we ready to capture the focus of this society and offer an exit from here and some obvious, clear reason to break down the doors that keeps us locked inside?

What new tools and strategies do people have since December?

The most important characteristics are:

1) Consistency: efforts to offer answers and direct responses to all the moves of the State and to keep the fight alive with actions and events that take place almost every day. Also, there are conscious efforts to avoid suicidal or sacrificial moves that will cause arrests or hard defeats. The riots and the clashes with the police are well organized, well equipped, and they occur at the place and time when they'll have the greatest possibility of causing the most damage without paying a high price or putting people in serious danger. With these victories the struggle attracts new people.

2) Political Work: based on direct connection with the problems of the society and not on ideological abstractions. The efforts to listen to the society, keep in contact with the worries and fears of the people, give answers where it seems that there are no answers, and attack the causes of the problems, not just the results. The ability of the movement to play a serious role in the political world of the country depends on the creation of deep roots in the social struggles and the ability to inject anarchist ideas and practices into the hearts of common people and young radicals. This happens through the personal cultivation of critical minds and the collective creation of open, all-inclusive, public confrontation with all forms of authority.

3) Cultural Work: the meetings, the assemblies, the squares, the parks, and the public life tend to include people who have the courage to fight and the capability to think and create. For the first time in many years anarchists now are ready to achieve high visibility in this society and attract new people not only through their destructive power but also through the defense of public spaces (like the parks), and the creation of political spaces (like the squats and the social centers). Also important is the collective culture that allows all individuals to benefit from the communes without losing their personalities within them, as happens in the Left tradition of organizing.

4) Constant Spreading of Counter-Information: the importance of typography, (not digital printing but 70cm x 50cm offset printing!) for printing thousands of copies of large posters and sticking them everywhere is vital. As all different groups produce many different posters, a whole spectrum of theory appears on the walls of the city. You don't need to read anarchist books anymore. The theory is on the walls! Of course it is also very important to use offset machines for thousands of copies of communiqués and books that you hand out for free in your city. These practices go together with the unstoppable use of spray paint to write political slogans on every wall, signed with the circle-A, and to remove any neo-nazi graffiti. Also comrades go frequently to the central square of their city with a small electric generator and small sound system to play their music and read off their communiques, and to pass out pamphlets. With this method of counter-information they attract the focus of the people to specific social struggles, they raise solidarity and have endless dialogues with passersby.

Some important struggles and strategies, as examples:

• The neighborhood assemblies, organized with invitation posters from door to door, offer answers to local problems and connects them with general social problems.

• The occupied parks offer a direct connection between ecological problems and everyday urban life and produce new liberated public spaces where different kinds of people can meet and co-exist (or try to co-exist).

• The different new squats enable all different styles of anarchist thinking to achieve visibility.

• The new social centers offer workshops, free lessons, free food, cheap alcohol, free books, lectures, film shows, DJ sets, concerts, and open social meeting points for all kinds of people. They connect the political activists with common people and young students

• The small urban guerilla arson groups continue fighting. Formed by people who know and trust each other 100% they continue to upgrade their weekly attacks against capitalist and state targets. The huge catalog of arson attacks create a map of institutions, corporations, banks, and offices that society has to eliminate from social life for the people to be free and equal. In this way, the arsonists offer the society a signal that elevates mistrust of these specific targets and encourages suspicion regarding the exploitive function of these targets.

• The active anarchist student groups don't allow the bourgeoisie to control the university. These groups communicate day by day with each other and with all other students. They turn the university into a public space that can accommodate tons of public events every week, organized by comrades from other political and cultural collectives as well. Of course leftist organizations and cultural groups also participate in the struggle to defend university asylum and the struggle for keeping the universities open to the public overnight.

• The defense of public autonomous zones like parks and urban hills, universities as well as urban areas, street corners, squares, and meeting points like Exarchia and other similar points in the rest of Greece from police, mafia, drug dealers, neo-nazis and capitalist investors brings the people together. These meetings in public space produce an explosive mixture of all kinds of people from all kinds of backgrounds who get used to facing the policeman, the mafia, the drug dealer, the neo-nazi and the investor as an enemy. The day to day meetings in the public space empower the groups and the companies of friends to be ready and capable of fighting against the enemies at a moment's notice and to imagine that this area is something completely different from the surrounding territory.

• The empowerment of the imagination, intelligence, and critical mind is the best strategy.

• The solidarity movements encourage the people to continue fighting and take care, as much as possible, of the prisoners of this war.

• The open public solidarity for all prisoners, criminal and political prisoners equally, expresses the total negation towards prison institutions, reveals the real causes of criminality in this society and brings the anarchist prisoners closer with all other prisoners, gaining respect and support for them inside the prison.

• The fight for Kostantina Kuneva and all other workers sends a direct message to the bosses that when they hit one of us they have to confront all of us. Also, it proves that the collective struggle can reveal subject matters and attract the focus of all society.

• All direct syndicalist struggles self-organized from the base prepare in the consciousness of the people, year after year, a deep-rooted, radical strategy that intervenes in the sphere of work.

• Indymedia works like a strategic center for the organization of the struggles and as a digital public space where all the announcements, debates, and invitations can gain attention. In a way, all comrades start their day reading the indymedia calendar to decide what social action or assembly they will participate in.

• The creation of pirate communal radio stations and digital radio stations in universities and social centers sends the message of resistance on the radio waves and creates cultural and political communities around them.

• The critical mass parades, the street parades, the free party movement, the illegal rave parties, the squat events, the DIY concerts, the socially aware hip-hop, punk, indie rock, drum 'n bass, techno & trance scenes attract thousands of young people to temporarily liberated public zones. They offer an existential contact with the underground cultures and the radical movements. The gatherings of the underground cultures, when they are connected in solidarity with the anarchist political space, offer an experiential introduction to the political and social awareness that cannot be replicated in books.

• The demonstrations in malls and luxury areas or in the metro stations transfer the message of insurrection to privatized public spaces at the center of capitalistic illusions.

• The occupation of the National Opera Hall and interruption of the commercial shows created an example of a meeting point between the sphere of the arts and philosophy and the insurrectionary practices and ideas.

• The occupation of the building of the General Confederation of Greek Workers created a public, visible negation of the role of syndicalist leadership in the failures of workers' struggles over the last 100 years.

• The occupation of the offices of the newspaper editors by insurrectionary journalists and comrades active in the creation of underground media produced a lively meeting point for direct criticism to appear against the role of mass media in the building of social apathy.

• The occupation of the National Television Station studio by young artists and activists trashed the speech of the prime minister, expanded mistrust of the mass media, and sent the message onto the screen of every house in Greece: "Switch Off Your TV, Come Into The Streets."

• Occupations of government buildings and municipalities all over the country sent a message to society of a different understanding of public institutions and constituted victorious fights in different causes and struggles.

• The anti-nazi struggle sends the message that there is no mercy for the enemies of freedom.

• The anti-nazi demonstrations in solidarity with the immigrants made obvious to all immigrants that we are standing on their side (but not without criticism of their own limitations).

• Videos and media work uploaded to the Internet and used by mainstream TV channels proved that the police are working with neo-nazis against the immigrants and the social movements. Also they proved to everybody that the neo-nazis are a tool, the long hand of the State against any kind of social resistance.

• Independent amateur videos, like the video of the assassination of Alexis or moments of police brutality, played a very important role in the building of a new kind of public opinion.

• The creation of hundreds of blogs by all kinds of initiatives offered a digital space for the direct expression of the reasons and the theory of each struggle and attracted thousands of readers and participants. The blogs broke the authority and monopoly of mainstream mass media forever.

• The unstoppable writing, printing, and hand to hand free distribution of hundreds of different publications, pamphlets, books, cds, dvds and the creation and display of thousands of posters in all cities bring the analysis to a level capable of covering many different subjects and reaching nearly every part of society. Also, they express the anarchist way of thinking directly to the other people of our times, and not through abstract theories and ideological labyrinths.

We have seen immigrants closed in concentration camps, we saw normality taking revenge expressed in laws as threats, we saw conservatism be the guardian and the protector of the worst side of humanity, we saw greed and exploitation destroying our most beautiful dreams together with the forests, beaches, parks, squares, and hospitals. We saw apathy imprison our lives in fortress-like cities of commerce and mass stupidity...

Maybe now we are closer to the point of no return. To reach this point perhaps we all should have resigned from our jobs last year in December... Perhaps the unemployed had to replace the uncertainty of "personal failure" with the pride of an insurgent collective risk. Maybe the students had to leave school for at least a year of holidays, rediscovering the meaning of public education. Then, the creation of thousands of new websites, blogs, free movies, books, dvds, and pamphlets could undermine the dominance of the mass media. Free

349

underground festivals can destroy the "mass entertainment industry" and occupied universities can offer free accommodation, food, counter-information and meaningful entertainment for thousands of people every evening.

We have to live collectively again, redefining contemporary political philosophy and revolutionary art. Perhaps the creative teams of friends, the affinity groups, the occupied parks, the squats and the social centers can become points for bringing alive all those dreams we lost in the selfishness of our small, insignificant, individual illusions. We may have to fight against many fears, traps, deeply rooted lies, psychological complexes, and insecurities. And then we will link our daily lives with the most magical secret desires to transform the streets of Metropolis in precious moments of freedom and happiness.

The insurrection never ends.

The insurrection will never end.

Maybe we need to start thinking about how the world we would like to live in looks like. We must use moments and images of our present life that we want to expand and activate in all their significance. We don't need any science-fiction plan for our future. We have everything here and now. We have to liberate it all from the State and the market and share it.

Revolution is when the society takes life in its hands and everything that now is merchandise again becomes a gift. Revolution is One Thousand Insurrections, nothing more, nothing less. Insurrections open paths, liberate space and time, reprogram Daily Life, change the relations, invent new words, break hierarchies, smash taboos and fears and limitations, achieving the highest possible public participation in projects and infrastructure that give us the chance to expand ourselves and share our abilities without limits. Insurrections are a never ending fight, a constant struggle between desperation and self-restraint, apathy and action, fear and decisiveness, needs and passions, obligations and desires, obstacles and break-outs. Is it even possible to imagine such a thing? The experience of the insurrection showed us that those wild dreams we were too embarrassed to admit can actually become reality.

—Void Network [Theory, Utopia, Empathy, Ephemeral Arts]

What Greece Means (to me) for Anarchism

A.G. Schwarz

Approximately two years before the insurrection flared up in Greece in December, some anarchists of the Platformist persuasion embarrassingly identified Greece as a country of low social struggle, to back up their mechanistic theory that the insurrectionist strain of anarchism only arises during lows, i.e. it is a product of weakness. After December, other anarchists who were convinced that workers were the only legitimate revolutionary subject either minimized the importance of the revolt because the working class *as such* did not participate, or they skewed and entirely misunderstood the events by emphasizing news of the protests by base unions and the blockades by farmers, as though the irresponsible adventurism of molotov cocktails and firebombs was a phenomenon that existed somehow *outside* the events.

On the other hand, insurrectionary anarchists surviving in the most alienated of countries seemed to subsist entirely on a diet of digital imagery and poorly translated poetic communiqués, snapshots infused with the smell of burning shops but completely separated from their social context, as though these anarchists somehow hungered even more than the media to kill the revolt by spectacularizing it. And while most Greek anarchists I know tend to share the insurrectionary critique of the Left, or more accurately, they simply take it as self-evident, many Western insurrectionists would be shocked to hear the widespread opinion that "insurrectionary anarchism [referring to the Italian school] has had very little influence here." Which does not contradict the fact that illegalist and individualist tendencies were passionately adopted by many segments of the anarchist space in the '90s; however this has manifested as an entirely different phenomenon from the many blogs and papers in English that regurgitate "notes from the global civil war," little news clippings of violent actions from here and there completely stripped of their social context and thus of their political content. I understand the need, in a pacified setting, to glorify the very act of violent resistance itself, but I'm afraid these comrades are digging themselves into a hole every bit as deep as the one constituted by the idealization of a class that sixty years ago willingly adopted all the characteristics of its enemy and dissolved itself.

What happened in Greece arose out of a specific culture and history of struggle. It is not an ideological tool to be used for any faction nor a blueprint to be transported to another country or context. It would be a shame for anarchists to convert the Greek rebellion into a dogmatic plank or to ignore it because it does not confirm a preconceived ideology. And as much as I would like to, it would be wrong of me to use Greece as a tool to urge greater cooperation and solidarity between different antiauthoritarian currents, because all the infighting, the sharp criticisms regarding important questions, are a part of the history of this insurrection, and the rebellion itself was claimed to confirm or contradict people's idea of revolution.

The truth is that all these contradicting currents made up the revolt, and a key characteristic of the revolt that the State and media worked so hard to deny is that at times, in the streets, the many people who were supposed to be different and separate became indistinguishable. But without denying any of the elements that participated, we can and should look at the role they each played, what made them stronger, and what made them weaker.

We are storytellers, not historians. Our job is to relate these happenings to you, not to separate, to objectify, to engrave these living stories and rob them of any connection to the present moment. Just as the solidarity actions in other countries lent more fire to the ongoing insurrection in Greece, the exhilarating smell of smoke rose from Athens and spread around the world. I cannot see it as disconnected that it was also a hot winter in Sofia, Malmö, Oakland, and Guadelupe, nor that anarchists around the world stepped up the struggle after seeing what was going on in Greece.

Several months after December, I was at a small protest in one of those northern social democratic countries where such things as riots aren't meant to happen anymore. But when the police attacked, even though there were only a hundred people in the demo, they rioted, and when the police broke up the riot, they dispersed throughout the city to take revenge by setting afire symbols of wealth, property, and authority. The only similarity between their situation and Greece was that in both places people had the confidence to fight back. And that is an element that no material conditions and no historical process can give you. It may be easier to come by in some cultures than in others but it is entirely yours to claim or disown.

Confidence played a major role in the Greek anarchist practice in all the years before December. Anarchists had enough confidence in their ideas to communicate them with society, and enough confidence that their struggle was right that they continued attacking the State and boldly upholding an ethic of solidarity with all the oppressed and no compromise with authority, even when they were the only ones doing so.

And in this way they won presence in their society, and everyone, even if they disagreed, knew who the anarchists were—the ones who fought against all authority, who stood alongside the most marginalized members of society, the ones who self-organized, and the ones who never acted like politicians. This social connection was perhaps the greatest foundation of the insurrection. Many anarchists insisted on seeing society as distinct from the State. They participated in all the social struggles, offering a different analysis than the political parties and refusing to sugarcoat or hide their radical ideas, even when this made communication more difficult in the short-term. And whenever there was a social problem or important event or tragedy, they would meet and take the initiative to respond, so that the government did not have a monopoly on discourse while managing the problem. The anarchists created examples of uncompromising struggles, and trusted that when people were ready they would choose to adopt these examples as their own.

There are also many antisocial elements within the anarchist space, and these play an important role as well, because even though society is our most crucial ally, there are plenty of reasons to hate it in its current form, and many people want to drop out from it or stand outside of it. While most Greek anarchists I know look just like any other Greeks—they do not differentiate themselves *as anarchists* in their mode of dress—there are also the anarchist punks and hippies and junkies and metalheads and goths. In other words, anarchism is not a subculture, but it is present in nearly all the subcultures, and in the mainstream culture as well. Anarchism needs to be there for those who hate society for what it is not and those who love it for what it could be.

An antisocial edge has also helped those parts of the anarchist space carry out unpopular and shocking actions without flinching. Society is often conservative, and under capitalism all its members are tied in to their own oppression. Anarchists often have to clash with the reigning order, and this clash creates inconveniences for all those who depend on that order to get them through their miserable lives. Social anarchists who are excessively populist will be unable to do this.

Although the Greek anarchists argue and fight with one another, there is another side to this, harder to see from the outside. They also have a habit of ignoring those they disagree with, and this makes sense, because they do not have enough in common to work together, and no need to try and change one another. They are other people, doing their own thing, and this difference does not entail a contradiction because anarchists don't go marching to the same drummer.

Many anarchists, primarily in Protestant countries, set themselves the primary activity of perfecting and purifying the anarchist space, and they go about massacring ideological opponents, petty enemies, and perpetrators of bad manners with all the righteousness of Crusaders. The personal is political; however it is precisely because there is no clear line between inside the movement and outside the movement that we should not try to erect such a line by attacking the flaws of our selves and our allies with more enthusiasm than we attack the State.

What the rebellion in Greece showed once again is that people do not need vanguards or political parties, that self-organization, direct action, and self-defense are second-nature to everyone. The people who express their rage or illuminate the targets of the struggle with fiery actions far more extreme than what the majority might consent to are not acting as a vanguard because in a given moment, all the exploited and dissatisfied members of society might take up these tactics and go even further than yesterday's extremists.

But in this moment, the anarchists still have a crucial role to play, and we must be confident enough to play it. We have to learn how to communicate and cooperate with society at a higher level, once we meet in the street. We have to keep the institutional Left from recuperating the struggle without creating divisions by judging people in the street by the color of the flag they carry. We have to point out new and more difficult targets as our power to attack increases, otherwise the revolt will exhaust itself smashing banks and police stations without ever becoming a revolution against capitalism and the State. We have to contradict and ultimately silence the media as they try to fabricate hollow explanations for the insurrection and generate fear. We must have the faith in our imaginations to suggest long-term answers to the problems of society and start creating those answers as though we might actually win.

Part of the task of communication with society involves identifying traditions and symbols in a particular society that foster the ideas we want to communicate. One can't simply take the Greek practice and put it to use in Great Britain. Every society has its archetypes of justified violence and heroic defiance, but what exactly those are differs from one society to the next. In a country like Great Britain, that prides itself on the centuries-long stability and longevity of its government, or one like the Netherlands that touts its political culture of dialogue and compromise, this is a difficult task. In the US there is a deep and lively tradition of hatred for the government, but it is mostly found outside the Left. In Germany, on the contrary, there is a diverse tradition of defiance coming from within the Left, but it runs up against the popular demand for public order.

One of the most powerful specific strategies of counter-insurgency used by the State, which the anarchists will have to overcome in Greece and anywhere else we rise up, is racism. The natives and the immigrants, the whites and the blacks, is one of the most effective divisions to hamstring society, because there are real cultural differences and thanks to imperialism there is a history of antagonism as well. People from both sides of the line will have to meet and learn to work together to communicate with others, so as not to be separated from society and cast as a scapegoat for the social problems, or to be validated as part of national community and placed unwittingly alongside one's mortal enemies.

I am afraid that if the Greek insurrection does not continue to grow stronger, if it is defeated, the crucial moment will have been its failure to extend *effective* solidarity to the immigrants when the State and the fascists carried out their major operation of ethnic cleansing in the summer. And this failure was probably not due to a lack of response in the moment it occurred—although many anarchists did pass up the opportunity to participate in the immigrant riots—but due to the fact that they had not prepared enough in advance, had not identified this as a key strategic weakness and worked to improve their connection with the immigrants, had not done more to counteract the racism that was being instilled from above by spreading their anti-racist analysis throughout society, and had not made more personal contacts so that when the protests and riots started, they could be instantly notified about what was happening like they were with the death of Alexis. Without these close contacts, the strong and immediate mobilization that occurred after Alexis' death could simply not occur in solidarity with the immigrants, and in fact most Athens anarchists found out about the immigrant riots in June through the media or because they saw the fires by chance. Even though they had met intimately in the streets and occupations in December, they had not held on to these contacts so that when the immigrants had an emergency, they could call their friends the anarchists.

It must also be said that the immigrants were not passive victims, and on the whole they chose the search for a better quality of life rather than the struggle for a better reality. In accepting the reality of capitalism and only trying to improve their position within it, the majority of immigrants have also accepted the whims, machinations, and violence of capitalism that will always be directed against them, no matter what part of the world they live in or how much money they make.

The second major shortfall, in my opinion, is the disillusionment felt by many youth after the rush of December ended and the many blackmails of capitalism returned to dominate their lives. People who already had a deep anarchist understanding and an experience in the struggle were theoretically and emotionally equipped to deal with the low. They knew that reaction and repression litter the road to revolution and they could take strength from December without expecting the fight to be over in just a month. But the apolitical people, most of them very young, had never imagined an insurrection before, and it changed their lives, but after it ended the depression was profound because their already hopeless lives became even more miserable after seeing that another world was possible and having it slip between their fingers and retreat to an unimaginable distance. The experienced anarchists could have preserved some of the enthusiasm of December by sharing their long-term understanding of the struggle with the new generation and making more efforts to invite the newcomers into the autonomous spaces where the flames of insurrection burn a little brighter.

Most of my Greek comrades disagree with this point, and they clearly understand the situation better. They point out that this ecstatic wave of revolt and then the subsequent disillusionment was something they all went through, with the student movements of each generation, in '91, '99, and so forth. The intensity of the struggle showed them what was possible, and the doldrums that followed taught them that the struggle was long and hard. And while I agree that learning to survive profound disappointment is essential to being a revolutionary, I think that more young people would hold on to the courage to hope if they weren't so alone, if more experienced radicals took them under their wings and actively invited them to participate in existing initiatives and structures, precisely to break out of this timeless cycle of resistance and repression; to seize on the delirious momentum of the revolt and help the new generation see that things don't have to go back to normal

355

if they don't let them. After all, after December many Greek anarchists concluded that what was lacking was not popular consciousness but more opportunities for new people to get involved, for the anarchists and the other people to continue meeting like they met in the streets.

The necessity to overcome the isolation which the State ceaselessly works to impose requires a Herculean journey to communicate with society and all its potentially rebellious parts. This communication can take myriad forms, from flyers, to protests, to exemplary and violent attacks. All the different types of antiauthoritarians can make their contribution. The revolt in Greece, that continues today, has been built by students, immigrants, theorists, fighters, terrorists, dropouts, activists, kids, grandparents, artists, ascetics, journalists, small store owners, academics, feminists, machos, drunkards, straight-edgers, soldiers, and union organizers. The revolt has been attacked by politicians, fascists, cops, left wing party activists, journalists, the media, small store owners, academics, capitalists, bureaucrats, the military, and labor unions.

Though all the participation in the revolt should be valued, not all is equal. By analyzing the attempts to recuperate the revolt and turn it into a harmless thing, we can understand the meaning of the specific elements. SYRIZA, the only political party to participate in the street protests in December, was called on to denounce its actions just before the elections. Predictably, they said that the students were justified in their cause. What they denounced was the violence. They blamed 150 extremists for exploiting December and turning it into something subversive.

In the Left's history of December, the revolt was only about anger over a police shooting, and the desperation of youth whose future was threatened by an economic crisis. The history of the struggle and the depth of its negation are censored. Its refusal to make demands is willfully misinterpreted as a lack of political analysis. The violence was its ugly side, but it also had a positive side, praised by many parts of the far Left, especially SYRIZA. These include the creation of parks, the peaceful protests, actions and occupations by artists, even the foundation of new social centers. This politically correct version of December attempts to erase the centrality of the Polytechnic occupation and everything it symbolizes: the continuation of the civil war despite the transition to democracy, uncompromising rebellion against the entire system, constant struggle against the police and the total destruction of corporate stores, the mixing of youth and adults, immigrants and Greeks, anarchists and non-political people. If there were good insurgents and bad insurgents, those described by this symbol, whether they were at the Polytechnic or anywhere else, were undeniably the bad insurgents, and that is precisely why for me they constitute the most important element of the revolt, because they are the only element the State finds indigestible.

The artistic actions, the parties, the occupation of the National Opera, the social centers, the peaceful protests: these elements should not be censored or derided as the weak and reformist side of the insurrection, because they represent the widening of the struggle to the point that it could include anyone who chose to come out on the streets. But it is the uncompromising and violent elements that give the softer elements their meaning, their ability to constitute an attack on the system. Dividing the one from the other is precisely what the State has tried to do in order to defeat the continuing insurrection.

The insurrection is the meeting of society at the barricades assembled from the smashed remains of everything that isolates us. For me it is a vital concept in the anarchist vision of revolution, and it is something that we must prepare the ground for and fertilize at every moment, even and especially when it seems like the wrong moment. Just as the anarchists of Spain would never have been able to resist Franco's coup and create space for a revolution if the *pistoleros* had not "irresponsibly" embarked on a course of armed struggle a decade earlier, I think the anarchists in Greece facilitated a social insurrection when they wed their uncompromising and illegal approaches with recognition of the importance of communicating with society, in the years before December 2008. The ability to be antisocial allowed them to adopt a course Greek society was not ready for, and the need to be social brought them back to the people who would eventually rise up, because the insurrection is a function of society and not of a political movement, as important as those movements may be in the development of necessary social characteristics.

The anarchist participation in those movements, because it was both critical and enthusiastic, won a greater visibility for anarchists and their ideas. Simultaneously, the fact that the anarchists had never succeeded in consolidating as a single movement seems to have helped them immensely to diversify and spread and include a greater portion of society. And in December, the lack of a single program and the diversity of strategies made the task of police repression impossible.

What the rebellion in Greece shows, as do the rebellions in Kabylia, Oaxaca, and China, is that although insurrection becomes second nature to everyone and vanguards can only get in the way, the insurrection does not spontaneously provide the people with what they need in order to go from insurrection to revolution. We still have to find the answers to certain questions, and those of us who never go back to normality, those of us who keep dreaming of freedom, need to suggest and deploy these answers when the moment comes. Once we've burned everything, how do we reveal and attack the social relationships that underpin capitalism and the State? What structures and infrastructure can we target that will weaken the counterinsurgency without putting society in a passive disaster mode, waiting to be rescued? How do we help other people believe in another world they would be willing to fight for, and to spread visions of stateless, communal societies that begin now? How do we escalate to revolutionary civil war—that is to say a two-sided war rather than the one-sided war waged against us permanently—without losing social support and participation?

These questions were not answered in Greece, and that is why their insurrection is still an insurrection and not a revolution. Spontaneity is a crucial element without which the insurrection would not exist, but spontaneity is not a God that will deliver us from Egypt if we walk through this desert for long enough. The anarchists, doing what they always do, miss strategic opportunities that have previously not been possible. The apolitical people, exercising secret desires, will have their spirits crushed when a temporary return of order prevents them from being the selves they only just discovered, and with the help of this demoralization the temporary return of order will win the appearance of being permanent.

But order is never permanent. Although we may never achieve the world we want, the very dynamics of control and rebellion ensure that we will never lose and the State will never win. Either we will destroy it, or we will continue fighting against it and troubling its pathological dreams forever. Nature itself is chaotic, making total control impossible. We may not have ultimate defeats and they may not have ultimate victories, but there are steps forward and steps backward. It remains to be seen whether Greek society holds onto the ground it won in December, but it is certain that the anarchists in Greece strengthened themselves for the battles to come. Learning from their experiences, the rest of us can, too.

358

Nothing Changed, Everything is the Different

Tasos Sagris from Void Network

It's Autumn 2009, the middle of September, in the daytime.

I walk in the streets of Athens from Monastiraki, the flea market, down from Acropolis, up to Exarchia, through the luxury market area, past Parliament, the business district, the offices, government buildings, bars, cinemas, and hotels.

Downtown Athens.

I pass through buildings that burned down completely during the December riots, huge multi-floor corner buildings, still smelling of fire and rage: silent monuments of an outcry, remains of a thunderbolt that came from the sky and hit the city like a wild nightmare. The city breathes hard work, blackmail, exhaustion, obligation, exploitation, and cheap amusements. Museums, galleries, stadiums, and clubs inhale the fears, misery, and rage and turn them into a fake smile.

Merry Crisis and a Happy New Fear

—Graffiti remaining on the wall from last Christmas

NOTHING CHANGED

This ancient city continued her way to normality, with all her fears and her cheap excuses, walking through this century like a slave girl in a parade, like a chained animal in a global circus, like you and I squandering our last and only lifetimes in a luxury mall or near the pool, drinking an expensive cocktail with our last euros, pretending to be the heroes of a Hollywood movie.

So many cars burned, but the streets are still full of them, going everywhere like empty private countries moving in the city's veins and feeding the crisis. More than 500 shops were turned into debris and ashes, but in this city the market still works like an amusement park in the middle of a vast cemetery. The banks of all the major cities in Greece were smashed and burned, but people are still struggling with their clocks and their suspensions to pay back huge loans and high taxes. The workers' strike was successful, but human beings still spend their lives in offices, keeping a mechanism that leads life on earth towards extinction in good working order. All the universities were squatted for a month, but the students are still taking exams and dreaming of good careers, good money, and two weeks of crazy holidays somewhere away from here.

Nothing changed: the clock of this world rings us out of sleep at 6:30 in the morning here same as anywhere else. We have to run to survive, we have to obey to stay out of prison, we have to forget our dreams to stay employed, we have to buy our lives from the supermarket and pay for the water we drink and the air we breathe and the place we put our bed to sleep.

Nothing changed… The government announces elections and the Parliament is voting on our future; the politicians speak on TV every afternoon and plan our opinions; the policemen put immigrants without papers into concentration camps and small paramilitary groups of Nazis go around kicking Arabs and Balkan people out of the squares. People go around in the streets like ghosts without lives of their own, and kids spend their time in front of computer screens in dismal internet shops and petit-bourgeois apartments.

The same moves, the same decisions, the same confusion, the same doubts, the same wishes, the same answers, the same payments, the same walks, the same bars, the same clothes and shoes and makeup, the same songs and films and television programs, the same apologies, the same timetables. The production goes on and consumption consumes our days; the shops sell dreams that turn every night into individualized fears and collective social apathy.

Society sleeps in the night of oblivion. People try to find a way to live, or else to leave, to get away from here. Paradise still waits after death, somewhere beyond our lifetimes. Nothing has changed.

Alexis is still lying dead on that pedestrian street corner in Exarchia.

Nothing Changed,
but

…everything is Different.

To express our rage with words or gestures is useless, ridiculous or dangerous, mindless or false common sense. Only the cold-blooded animals are poisonous.

EVERYTHING IS DIFFERENT…

More than 100,000 people took part in the insurrection of December 2008 and many more were influenced by those days. They wait in the veins of this society, ready to explode at any moment. Perhaps they can't force the body of society in a specific direction, but when 100,000 cells explode in the veins of the social body, the body collapses on its knees, like the Greek state during December 2008. The bureaucrats of the State know this, and the Business Administration does too.

There are thousands of young girls and boys walking the streets of this country who, just a few months ago, encircled the police stations of their neighborhoods and threw stones at them, burned the local banks, and refused to go to school or work for weeks.

There are hundreds of workers who forced out the syndicalists who ruled the General Workers Union and assembled in their offices. There are hundreds of thousands of unemployed people who hate the system, and lazy kids who hate working, and millions of dissatisfied producers and consumers of a life that offers nothing.

All these lonely people discovered their dignity during the insurrection, experiencing their personal and collective power to explode as the cities and villages caught fire and their horizons opened up beyond the white fog of teargas. Those horizons remained open night after night, and still stay open so long as the memory of the insurrection is a wound in your body and in the body of society.

Through our open wounds, we are observing the horizons of our future. We are an image from the future.

There are thousands and thousands of people who don't trust any government and hate the banks and the corporations. The insurrection helped millions of people across the world to stop, to see their lives with the clarity of a flashback, shifting their way of thinking for a moment and observing this world naked. The fairytale revealed its ugliest face and the beautiful smiles of the journalists and politicians froze, unable to continue the narration that keeps the populace in deep sleep.

We stay awake in the deep night of social apathy. Around us millions of people continue sleeping, but the dreams are turning into nightmares that make them sweat as their hearts race and they weep silent teardrops that might wake them at any moment.

There are millions of people who don't trust any official ideology or academic authority or any political leadership, who don't vote for any legal organization, who mistrust rich philanthropists. The people of our times don't believe in any universal truth or any specific lifestyle, any way of life or spiritual value system, any political agenda. They don't read serious political or philosophical books or the announcements of the activists or even the free press except when they are in the metro for fifteen minutes. They don't hear the right wing president when he speaks, or the speeches of the Communist Party; they want to go to a party, get drunk, find a boyfriend, go to the back of the garden and make love in the moonlight.

NOTHING CHANGED, BUT EVERYTHING IS DIFFERENT

Hundreds of squatted social centers and radical student groups function in the universities, the schools and in the streets of all Europe. Social initiatives, affinity groups, groups of friends, political gangs, and underground meeting points in the streets and in squatted buildings bring the heat of their action into the soft belly of the regime.

Arson attacks, riots, demonstrations, free festivals and distribution of analysis and propaganda are organized every week, day after day, by common people. These actions send signals to the society that there are targets, institutions to mistrust, places to avoid, ways that have to change, places and relations of enslavement, places and relations of emancipation, points of no return.

Nobody trusts the government. Everyone knows that capitalism is destroying the planet, turning life into commodities, humanity into a destructive mechanism, suppressing creativity, love, fantasy, turning basic needs into a constant problem, offering none of the happiness promised to the ex-Soviet Bloc countries.

Neo-Liberalism is dying. Everything is different.

We are here in the highways and in the squares, out in the streets, downtown in Exarchia and in the city center, still hanging around on the corner where Alexis liked to meet his friends. A whole new generation of people is around—you make so many new friends during an insurrection: so many new comrades to decide their own future and offer their new directions.

Everything is different. Week after week there are wild demonstrations for Freedom of Public Space from the State, Freedom of Immigrants from Borders, Freedom of All Prisoners from the causes of Imprisonment, Freedom for All Workers from their imprisoned lives. These demonstrations are traveling on the body of the city searching for the wild riots of the future, preparing with their chants the spirit of active negation, the fire of radical change, the hope for a general social uprising.

People are beginning to reflect again on what general social revolt will look like. It will look like December 2008, and we are here and waiting.

Now we are here and waiting: for society to digest the smoke of the burned luxuries, to express openly its distrust of state institutions and make directions and decisions that will appear on the social horizon for the first time. Hundreds upon hundreds of small pamphlets of radical analysis are distributed week after week by amateur intellectuals preparing the end of the classical Western way of thinking. Thousands

361

of posters hang in the streets of each neighborhood, by the local squats and social centers, sending a signal to the petit-bourgeoisie that the days of obedience, work, consumerism, and individualism are coming to an end. Thousands of short films and paragraphs of critical thought utilize the internet to transmit the real stories of our lives, the real news of our actions, to connect the moments in order to produce the myths and dreams of coming insurrections.

The "important" people of this world try to persuade us that all these are not important. Anyway, they say, all these underground books and pamphlets are published by non-existent publishers, the short videos on the internet are just childish games for kids and naïve romantics, the radical blogs are not efficient, the squats are places for criminal activity, and the youth cultures are the commodities of the near future. Anyway, they say, nothing changed: the television doesn't speak about "all these" anymore except when a "terrorist" action occurs, the demonstrations are just some small riots around Exarchia. All that happened in December was a childish revolt over the accidental death of a child, which a few isolated anarchists took advantage of to express their nihilism, they say.

AT THE SAME TIME... "IT'S MIDNIGHT IN EUROPE."

There is a feeling of the end of an era all across Europe and amazing phenomenons of stupidity are happening in the heads of postmodern thinkers as postmodernism dies.

Nobody controls the spirit of the age, nobody can offer solid analysis about what is happening around us, no one can predict what this world will look like in fifty years. The young boys and girls smile silently behind their black masks near the barricades, imagining a world with no obligations.

Everything is different. Maybe the elites, the rich, the famous and "important" people act like nothing changed, but nothing is normal anymore and no one has the authority to speak in the name of the people. The people express more mistrust towards the regime than ever, and perhaps they are ready to speak for themselves in such a way that no sociologist or journalist will be capable of understanding their language.

In the night, everywhere, the people speak about the general failure; in the bottom of their hearts, they know that everything has to change, that many things have to burn to ashes for humanity to continue its way in space and time.

I walk around in Exarchia. I pass through the squatted self-organized park, where old people from the neighborhood stay in the shade of trees and speak with young girls about last night's police attack on the area. A few meters away, at the place Alexis was shot, there is a marble monument with flowers and posters all around the walls, and a lit candle.... It's early in the afternoon; some boys and girls stand around talking. People from a new squat give me a 32-page pamphlet analyzing everyday racism on a molecular social scale; on the other side of the pedestrian street, I see two people from an underground post-rock band that I know from free festivals talking with people from a DIY drum 'n bass collective.

No one will propagate a new way of life with words alone, there are no theories that can describe our passions. Maybe we are the ones who will take back life in our hands from capitalism and aristocracy. Maybe we will be shot in the streets of our cities, like Alexis. There is no plan, or even a specific goal, or a single achievement we are fighting for. There are no futuristic visions of paradise inside the heads of the people, not even a wish to be in such a place, except perhaps for short-term expensive holidays. We fight to survive, to maintain our dignity, humanity, and critical thinking from one day to the next; we fight off the businessmen, politicians, armies, and kings of this world as they attempt to steal our future and turn it into coins—day after day after day. We are the survivors of humanity in a war with our most pathetic selves .

We are lost in the darkness of a world in which we are strangers, foreigners, customers, guests, separate individuals, or we are just slaves that share some small personal salary to survive. We are survivors in the desert. When we meet, we meet in void, in void we live, the void we share. When we decide to attack, our attack is like a thunder that comes from outer space and breaks the night of social apathy. We are waiting, waiting for the proper moment....

Nothing will stay like it was.

We Are an Image from The Future.

1–2. The self-organized park in Exarchia, fifty meters from where Alexis was murdered. Thousands parrticipated in the creation of the park and the reclamation of public space.

3. Squat in Exarchia. Occupied by the Assembly of the Polymorphic Anarchist Movement.

4. The State tried and failed to shut older squats like Villa Amalias that has been around for over twenty years.

5. Patision 61 Squat is the former residence of Maria Kallas. It was occupied after December as an extension of the Assembly of the Athens School of Economics.

6. Nosotros Free Social Space, started five years ago by Void Network and Antiauthoritarian Current in Exarchia.

7

9

10

8

11

12

13

7. Neighborhood assemblies and celebrations, playgrounds, and the self-organization of public space is viewed as a direct attack against the State and capitalism, sowing seeds of freedom and equality.

8. Theater in the park.

9. Proper use of public space, Exarchia.

10. Community garden.

11. Scene from one of the free lessons / workshops for immigrants and students organized after December.

12–13. Scenes from the racist pogrom of 2009. Police rounded up 3,000 immigrants without papers into concentration camps.

We are an Image from the Future

14

16

18

15

17

19

14–15. Assemblies of leftists and anarchists organized large demonstrations and actions across Greece as an answer to the State's counter-insurrection efforts, the corporate media's coverage, and the paramilitary violence condoned by police.

16. More than 10,000 people attended the 14th Annual Anti-Racist Festival featuring concerts, public talks, and great food from most ethnic groups in Greece.

17. The 5th Annual Pride Parade in Athens drew over 7,000 people, including many leftists and anarchists.

18. Scene from the 19th Annual Indie Free Festival against police presence in Exarchia, 8,000 attend.

19. Bfest: A four-day-long event that consists of an international anarchist conference, concerts, and raves. 30,000 people attend.

20

22

23

21

24

25

20. Nazis and police collaborating against their common enemies—leftists, anarchists, and immigrants.

21–23. Hundreds of arson attacks and attacks on government buildings, luxury shops, and corporate headquarters were carried out in the year following December, 2008.

24. The Stock Exchange after an attack by the group Revolutionary Struggle.

25. Outside the American Embassy, 60,000 demonstrators participate in the 39th anniversary of the 1973 Polytechnic revolt on November 17, 2009. Anarchists populated three blocks, in a group totaling 10,000.

Glossary

anarchist space—anarhikos horos, the anarchist space, is the most common way to refer to what we in the English-speaking world would call the anarchist movement or anarchist struggle. The distinction acknowledges that there is no single body or direction chosen by the anarchists. Rather, they occupy a non-homogenous part of the political terrain, just as they spread out spatially within their cities, with the anarcho-junkies hanging out in that square, the nihilists hanging out on this corner, the libertarians hanging out in that bar, the hippies hanging out in that park, the Situationists hanging out in that squat, the classical anarcho-communists in that café and the insurrectionists in this one. They meet and communicate without coming to agreement, or they keep their distance from one another, but if the police ever invade their turf, they band together to fight back.

anarchists, autonomists, and libertarians (oh my!)—Many, but not all, Greek antiauthoritarians use these terms in the following way. Anarchists are those who identify themselves with the specific anarchist tradition, going back to (but by no means limited to) Bakunin), even though the major influences probably come from the events of May '68, as well as other more recent manifestations of new and old theories and struggles. The autonomists are not necessarily dissident Marxists as they are in other countries, but perhaps dissident anarchists who favor a materialist analysis. The libertarians focus on the idea of freedom, philosophically and culturally. All of these currents are grouped together as antiauthoritarians, although sometimes the term "antiauthoritarian" is used in contrast to "anarchist," to refer to those antiauthoritarians who do not specifically identify themselves as anarchists. These are all crass and clumsy generalizations, but hopefully they can help the foreign reader untangle all the varied terms.

AK—Alpha Kappa, or Antiauthoritarian Current (most commonly mistranslated as Antiauthoritarian Movement) an anarchist organization with sections in several cities, that often works with the extra-parliamentary Left.

ASOEE—The University of Economics and Business in Athens, located on Patision Ave. about a ten minute walk north of the Polytechnic and Exarchia.

asylum—In recognition of the important role the students played in overthrowing the dictatorship and the heavy repression that was visited upon them, an important legal principle of the new democratic government, written into the constitution, was that any university campus was considered a place of asylum, and the police could not enter there. Due to Plan Bolonya, the neoliberal restructuring of higher education being forced on all the member states of the European Union, the Greek government must abolish the asylum. In 2007, the Greek government voted to limit asylum, so that police could enter a campus at the invitation of the university president. In practice, asylum still exists thanks to the proximity of the university administrators to the everyday force of the social movements created by the students, who would take any breach of the asylum as a declaration of war and respond accordingly.

base union—A common term used by Greek antiauthoritarians to denote a grassroots workers union that acts as a vehicle for the coordination of information, action, and protest by workers, as distinct from the institutional labor unions that act as permanent governing bodies for the workers, and collaborate with the political parties and the General Confederation of Workers.

Delta Force—The name given, apparently without any sense of irony, to the new special police force created in Athens in March. They travel in groups from six to fifty, riding two to a motorbike. They are intended to serve as a rapid response team to carry out arrests against anarchists. The Force recruits the most fascist, brutal, and hooliganistic elements of all the different police sections.

Eleftheros Typos—"Free Press." Unfortunately, this is both the name of the anarchist publisher founded in 1976, and the major right wing newspaper later bought by the elite family that was also the driving force behind the Athens Olympics. Neither of these are to be confused with Eleftherotipia, the third largest newspaper in Greece, and staunchly leftist, known for publishing the communiques of 17 November and even running articles sympathetic to the anarchists or the autonomy of Exarchia.

gas canister bomb—a small homemade bomb frequently used in attacks claimed by small anarchist groups, this bomb basically entails a group of exploding camping gas canister. The damage produced is mostly symbolic, and is unlikely to produce injuries.

General Confederation of Greek Workers—The GSEE, an organization that brings together all the major labor unions, and has its central offices in Athens on Patision Ave., between Polytechnic and ASOEE. It is alternatively translated as the General Confederation of Labour of Greece.

general strike—In Greece, nationwide general strikes organized by the GSEE typically occur every several months, lasting for a single day and serving above all as a protest and a platform to demonstrate the clout of the major unions and the political parties that have retained them.

Golden Dawn—A long-standing and formerly illegal neonazi organization that has gained some popularity in Greece over the last years. The government allowed them to participate in the 2009 national elections, in which they gathered 17,000 votes throughout Greece.

Ermou—A posh shopping street leading down from Syntagma Square.

Exarchia—A countercultural and rebellious neighborhood of central Athens that has long been a stronghold of the anarchists. At different times over the last decades, the neighborhood has been either a relatively autonomous zone in terms of a lack of police presence or it has been under armed police occupation. (A common alternative spelling, which adheres to the characters used in the Greek alphabet rather than to the pronunciation, is "Exarheia.")

KKE—The Communist Party of Greece, and the last real Communist Party of all Europe, still defending Stalinism as a beneficial period in Russian society and spreading conservative ideas "to the masses." They were once a major force in controlling the workers' struggles, but now hold only a small number of seats in Parliament. Incidentally, Communist refers to Party members or the Party collectively, whereas communist refers to the people who identify with that political position and tradition without necessarily being Party members. In fact, before and during the civil war, many communists were killed by the Communists.

Kolonaki—A wealthy neighborhood of central Athens, full of luxury boutiques and expensive apartments, just a few minutes walk from Exarchia, in one direction, or Syntagma, in the other.

Konstantina Kuneva—A Bulgarian migrant who led a base union of precarious cleaning workers, and was attacked for her organizing activity on 23 December. "Kouneva," a frequent alternative spelling, is a transliteration of her name rendered in Greek.

koukoulofori—"Hooded ones," the term used by the Greek media and State to dismissively describe the anarchists without giving them a political content. The singular is koukouloforos. A creative alternative translation that gives a good sense of the connotation of the word is "masketeer." The earlier terms were "provocateurs" and then "known unknowns."

LAOS—An extreme right political party with growing visibility in Greece, with a Le Pen-style fascism based on a popularistic

369

xenophobia and emphasis on religion and family.

Le Pen—An influential French politician and former member of the Foreign Legion, Jean-Marie Le Pen has been instrumental in developing the new European cryptofascism on the rise since the '80s. His antisemitism, homophobia, racism, xenophobia, and connections to right wing paramilitary groups hide behind a populist and nationalist conservatism.

Maria Kallas—A famous Greek opera singer, who was said to live in the large building on Patision Avenue, Athens, occupied by anarchists in March 2009.

MAT—The hated Greek riot police. These "Sections of Direct Order" were created by PASOK in the early '80s to confront the violence of the early Greek Black Bloc and the wildcat strikes of those times.

metapolitefsi—The period of political transition during the '70s, from the dictatorship to the democratic government.

ND—Nea Demokratia or New Democracy, the conservative political party in power at the time of the December insurrections and the following months. During those times it had been particularly scandal-wracked and governed with a majority of only one representative in Parliament.

Nomiki—The Law University, located on the other side of Akadimias Ave. from Exarchia, relatively close to Kolonaki and Syntagma.

Omonia—A major square in central Athens, close to the Polytechnic and about a fifteen minute walk from Syntagma. The neighborhood on one side of Omonia has become well known as an immigrant ghetto.

Panepistimio—The area of the University Rectorate, halfway between Omonia and Syntagma, next to Nomiki, and just below Exarchia.

This is a common starting point for demonstrations, which typically march to Omonia and turn around to go to Syntagma, one street farther down from Panepistimio.

PAOK—a football hooligan club with a strong presence throughout Greece, and distinct antifascist and antiauthoritarian tendencies. Together with AEK from Athens, Asteras Exarchion (the amateur team of Exarchia) and some other football teams in the countryside they galvanize many hundreds of anarchists and antifascist Greek hooligans (whose participation in the riots of Genoa achieved international visibility). In contrast to other European countries Greek anarchists and antifascists refuse to abandon the football stadiums and offer them to neo-nazis following the false analysis that "the hooligans are not serious political fighters."

PASOK—The Socialist Party of Greece, one of the two largest political parties, with a social democratic line similar to SPD in Germany.

Polytechnic—The Polytechnic University of Athens, located in the center of the city on Patision Avenue close to Omonia, and alongside Exarchia, and a place of great symbolic importance for its central role in the major riots and insurrections from November 1973 to December 2008.

Popular Revolutionary Struggle—(ELA) A large anarcho-autonomist armed group active in the '70s, '80s, and '90s. Some of their members were arrested in the early '00s. Unlike their more famous contemporaries, 17 November, they carried out no assassinations.

Revolutionary Struggle—An extreme Left armed struggle group that appeared in 2003. Their most spectacular action was a 2007 rocket attack against the US Embassy.

Sect of Revolutionaries—An antiauthoritarian armed group that became active after December.

17 November—A leftist urban guerrilla group responsible for a number of political assassinations and other attacks, active in the '70s, '80s, and '90s. Their name is a reference to a major date in the insurrection against the dictatorship in 1973. Several of their members were arrested in the early '00s.

Stournari—The street that runs alongside the Polytechnic, going towards Exarchia Square. There are many major computer stores on this street that were completely burned in December.

Syntagma—The square that stands before the Greek Parliament, the destination for many protest marches, and a site of many major street battles.

SYRIZA—A small party of the European Social Forum that unites many leftist organizations, also known as the pink communists or Euro communists, and the only parliamentary party to participate in the December protests, alongside many tiny Marxist-Leninist, Trotskyist, and Maoist parties. They were all denounced by the KKE for aiding the protestors, and denounced by the protestors for trying to manipulate and represent the struggle. Their bid to capitalize on the youth demographic in the European Parliament elections in June failed wonderfully, as few people who participated in the insurrection went to the polls and SYRIZA received few votes.

Photo Credits

December 6 and 7, 2009. Over 100,000 people demonstrate and riot on the anniversary of Alexis's murder and the first days of the insurrection. Nothing is over… Everything continues.

We saw the future… and it comes in flames.

Support AK Press!

AK Press is one of the world's largest and most productive anarchist publishing houses. We're entirely worker-run and democratically managed. We operate without a corporate structure—no boss, no managers, no bullshit. We publish close to twenty books every year, and distribute thousands of other titles published by other like-minded independent presses from around the globe.

The Friends of AK program is a way that you can directly contribute to the continued existence of AK Press, and ensure that we're able to keep publishing great books just like this one! Friends pay a minimum of $25 per month, for a minimum three month period, into our publishing account. In return, Friends automatically receive (for the duration of their membership), as they appear, one free copy of every new AK Press title. They're also entitled to a 20% discount on everything featured in the AK Press Distribution catalog and on the website, on any and every order. You or your organization can even sponsor an entire book if you should so choose!

There's great stuff in the works—so sign up now to become a Friend of AK Press, and let the presses roll!

Won't you be our friend? Email friendsofak@akpress.org for more info, or visit the Friends of AK Press website: http://www.akpress.org/programs/friendsofak